LLE...

2 · 0...

ASTROLOGICAL

POCKET PLANNER

Daily Ephemeris & Aspectarian
2023–2025

Cover design by Shannon McKuhen
Edited by Hanna Grimson

A special thanks to Beth Koch Rosato for astrological proofreading.

Astrological calculations compiled and programmed by Rique Pottenger, based on
the earlier work of Neil F. Michelsen. Reuse is prohibited.

Published by
LLEWELLYN WORLDWIDE LTD.
2143 Wooddale Drive
Woodbury, MN 55125-2989
www.llewellyn.com

Printed in China
Typography property of Llewellyn Worldwide Ltd.
Llewellyn is a registered trademark of Llewellyn Worldwide Ltd.

Table of Contents

Mercury Retrograde 2024

	DATE	ET	PT			DATE	ET	PT
Mercury Retrograde	12/12/23		11:09 pm	—	Mercury Direct	1/1	**10:08 pm**	7:08 pm
Mercury Retrograde	12/13/23	**2:09 am**		—	Mercury Direct	1/1	**10:08 pm**	7:08 pm
Mercury Retrograde	4/1	**6:14 pm**	3:14 pm	—	Mercury Direct	4/25	**8:54 am**	5:54 am
Mercury Retrograde	8/4		9:56 pm	—	Mercury Direct	8/28	**5:14 pm**	2:14 pm
Mercury Retrograde	8/5	**12:56 am**		—	Mercury Direct	8/28	**5:14 pm**	2:14 pm
Mercury Retrograde	11/25	**9:42 pm**	6:42 pm	—	Mercury Direct	12/15	**3:56 pm**	12:56 pm

Moon Void-of-Course 2024

Times are listed in Eastern time in this table only. All other information in the *Pocket Planner* is listed in both Eastern time and Pacific time. Refer to "Time Zone Conversions" on page 8 for changing to other time zones. Note: All times are corrected for Daylight Saving Time.

Last Aspect		Moon Enters New Sign			Last Aspect		Moon Enters New Sign			Last Aspect		Moon Enters New Sign		
Date	Time	Date	Sign	Time	Date	Time	Date	Sign	Time	Date	Time	Date	Sign	Time
JANUARY					**FEBRUARY**					**MARCH**				
2	6:36 pm	2	♎	7:47 pm	1	4:03 am	1	♏	3:37 pm	2	2:47 am	2	♐	8:56 am
5	6:41 am	5	♏	7:39 am	3	10:24 am	4	♐	1:28 am	4	10:41 am	4	♑	4:15 pm
7	3:22 pm	7	♐	4:08 pm	6	12:06 am	6	♑	7:08 am	6	2:35 pm	6	♒	7:38 pm
9	1:24 pm	9	♑	8:33 pm	8	2:52 am	8	♒	8:59 am	8	1:56 pm	8	♓	8:03 pm
11	9:33 pm	11	♒	10:01 pm	9	5:59 pm	10	♓	8:42 am	10	3:45 pm	10	♈	8:19 pm
13	4:59 am	13	♓	10:29 pm	12	7:32 am	12	♈	8:26 am	12	7:08 am	12	♉	8:28 pm
15	11:33 pm	15	♈	11:49 pm	14	5:21 am	14	♉	10:02 am	14	6:29 pm	14	♊	11:16 pm
18	3:03 am	18	♉	3:12 am	16	10:01 am	16	♊	2:39 pm	17	12:43 am	17	♋	5:40 am
20	8:57 am	20	♊	8:58 am	18	10:21 pm	18	♋	10:25 pm	19	2:52 pm	19	♌	3:33 pm
22	3:40 pm	22	♋	4:51 pm	21	1:38 am	21	♌	8:40 am	22	2:34 am	22	♍	3:42 am
24	5:58 pm	25	♌	2:37 am	22	11:18 pm	23	♍	8:38 pm	24	11:49 am	24	♎	4:37 pm
26	4:19 pm	27	♍	2:11 pm	26	2:35 am	26	♎	9:29 am	26	7:09 pm	27	♏	5:03 am
29	6:20 pm	30	♎	3:04 am	27	1:22 pm	28	♏	10:09 pm	29	11:40 am	29	♐	3:52 pm
										31	8:16 pm	4/1	♑	12:05 am

Moon Void-of-Course 2024 (cont.)

APRIL

Last Aspect		Moon Enters New Sign		
Date	Time	Date	Sign	Time
3/31	8:16 pm	1	♑	12:05 am
3	1:40 am	3	♒	5:08 am
5	1:40 am	5	♓	7:13 am
7	4:27 am	7	♈	7:25 am
8	10:39 pm	9	♉	7:23 am
11	6:04 am	11	♊	8:59 am
13	10:46 am	13	♋	1:45 pm
15	7:22 pm	15	♌	10:24 pm
18	8:02 am	18	♍	10:10 am
20	8:20 pm	20	♎	11:08 pm
22	7:24 pm	23	♏	11:20 am
25	7:17 pm	25	♐	9:37 pm
28	3:31 am	28	♑	5:37 am
30	11:19 am	30	♒	11:20 am

MAY

Last Aspect		Moon Enters New Sign		
Date	Time	Date	Sign	Time
2	5:28 am	2	♓	2:52 pm
4	3:06 pm	4	♈	4:41 pm
6	1:57 am	6	♉	5:42 pm
8	5:55 pm	8	♊	7:20 pm
10	9:49 pm	10	♋	11:13 pm
13	5:13 am	13	♌	6:36 am
15	12:41 pm	15	♍	5:33 pm
18	5:09 am	18	♎	6:23 am
19	11:48 am	20	♏	6:34 pm
23	3:28 am	23	♐	4:24 am
25	10:47 am	25	♑	11:36 am
27	4:02 pm	27	♒	4:45 pm
29	10:20 am	29	♓	8:33 pm
31	10:55 pm	31	♈	11:28 pm

JUNE

Last Aspect		Moon Enters New Sign		
Date	Time	Date	Sign	Time
2	6:04 pm	3	♉	1:55 am
5	4:09 am	5	♊	4:36 am
7	8:16 am	7	♋	8:41 am
9	3:05 pm	9	♌	3:29 pm
11	3:16 pm	12	♍	1:39 am
14	1:54 pm	14	♎	2:12 pm
17	2:05 am	17	♏	2:38 am
19	12:19 pm	19	♐	12:32 pm
21	6:58 pm	21	♑	7:08 pm
23	11:05 pm	23	♒	11:14 pm
25	6:30 pm	26	♓	2:08 am
28	4:45 am	28	♈	4:52 am
30	12:56 am	30	♉	8:00 am

JULY

Last Aspect		Moon Enters New Sign		
Date	Time	Date	Sign	Time
2	11:43 am	2	♊	11:50 am
4	4:44 pm	4	♋	4:51 pm
6	11:47 pm	6	♌	11:56 pm
9	2:04 am	9	♍	9:48 am
11	9:55 pm	11	♎	10:06 pm
13	6:49 pm	14	♏	10:53 am
16	9:10 pm	16	♐	9:25 pm
19	3:58 am	19	♑	4:14 am
21	7:26 am	21	♒	7:43 am
23	5:58 am	23	♓	9:23 am
25	10:31 am	25	♈	10:52 am
26	6:14 pm	27	♉	1:23 pm
29	4:59 pm	29	♊	5:28 pm
31	10:46 pm	31	♋	11:19 pm

AUGUST

Last Aspect		Moon Enters New Sign		
Date	Time	Date	Sign	Time
3	6:31 am	3	♌	7:10 am
5	11:16 am	5	♍	5:17 pm
8	4:40 am	8	♎	5:31 am
9	5:45 pm	10	♏	6:34 pm
13	5:01 am	13	♐	6:01 am
15	12:52 pm	15	♑	1:51 pm
17	4:43 pm	17	♒	5:45 pm
19	2:26 pm	19	♓	6:52 pm
21	5:54 pm	21	♈	7:02 pm
23	8:44 am	23	♉	8:00 pm
25	9:40 pm	25	♊	11:04 pm
28	3:14 am	28	♋	4:47 am
30	11:24 am	30	♌	1:09 pm

SEPTEMBER

Last Aspect		Moon Enters New Sign		
Date	Time	Date	Sign	Time
1	8:25 pm	1	♍	11:48 pm
4	12:06 pm	4	♎	12:12 pm
7	1:08 am	7	♏	1:18 am
9	1:11 pm	9	♐	1:26 pm
11	8:21 pm	11	♑	10:38 pm
14	3:35 am	14	♒	3:53 am
16	1:04 am	16	♓	5:39 am
18	5:02 am	18	♈	5:24 am
20	4:39 am	20	♉	5:03 am
22	6:14 am	22	♊	6:24 am
24	7:59 am	24	♋	10:50 am
26	6:12 pm	26	♌	6:47 pm
28	11:36 pm	29	♍	5:42 am

OCTOBER

Last Aspect		Moon Enters New Sign		
Date	Time	Date	Sign	Time
1	5:39 pm	1	♎	6:20 pm
4	6:40 am	4	♏	7:22 am
6	6:52 pm	6	♐	7:34 pm
9	1:54 am	9	♑	5:38 am
11	11:53 am	11	♒	12:31 pm
13	10:11 am	13	♓	3:55 pm
15	4:00 pm	15	♈	4:34 pm
17	3:26 pm	17	♉	4:00 pm
19	3:33 pm	19	♊	4:07 pm
21	5:00 pm	21	♋	6:50 pm
24	12:47 am	24	♌	1:24 am
26	4:04 am	26	♍	11:47 am
28	11:54 pm	29	♎	12:30 am
31	12:57 pm	31	♏	1:29 pm

NOVEMBER

Last Aspect		Moon Enters New Sign		
Date	Time	Date	Sign	Time
3	12:51 am	3	♐	1:19 am
5	5:23 am	5	♑	10:17 am
7	5:38 pm	7	♒	5:58 pm
9	7:23 pm	9	♓	11:00 pm
12	1:13 am	12	♈	1:26 am
14	1:50 am	14	♉	1:59 am
16	2:03 am	16	♊	2:09 am
17	11:09 pm	18	♋	3:50 am
20	6:20 am	20	♌	8:51 am
22	8:15 am	22	♍	6:01 pm
25	12:35 am	25	♎	6:20 am
27	4:14 am	27	♏	7:21 pm
30	1:19 am	30	♐	6:53 am

DECEMBER

Last Aspect		Moon Enters New Sign		
Date	Time	Date	Sign	Time
2	10:47 am	2	♑	4:09 pm
4	6:34 pm	4	♒	11:21 pm
6	7:01 pm	6	♓	4:49 am
9	3:45 am	9	♈	8:38 am
10	5:13 pm	11	♉	10:55 am
13	7:39 am	13	♊	12:11 pm
15	9:32 am	15	♋	2:21 pm
17	1:33 pm	17	♌	6:39 pm
20	12:19 am	20	♍	2:37 am
22	8:27 am	22	♎	2:08 pm
24	5:44 am	25	♏	3:06 am
27	9:24 am	27	♐	2:46 pm
29	6:34 pm	29	♑	11:37 pm

How to Use the *Pocket Planner*

by Leslie Nielsen

This handy guide contains information that can be most valuable to you as you plan your daily activities. As you read through the first few pages, you can start to get a feel for how well organized this guide is.

Read the Symbol Key on the next page, which is rather like astrological shorthand. The characteristics of the planets can give you direction in planning your strategies. Much like traffic signs that signal "go," "stop," or even "caution," you can determine for yourself the most propitious time to get things done.

You'll find tables that show the dates when Mercury is retrograde (℞) or direct (D). Because Mercury deals with the exchange of information, a retrograde Mercury makes miscommunication more noticeable.

There's also a section dedicated to the times when the Moon is void-of-course (V/C). These are generally poor times to conduct business because activities begun during these times usually end badly or fail to get started. If you make an appointment during a void-of-course, you might save yourself a lot of aggravation by confirming the time and date later. The Moon is only void-of-course for 7 percent of the time when business is usually conducted during a normal workday (that is, 8:00 am to 5:00 pm). Sometimes, by waiting a matter of minutes or a few hours until the Moon has left the void-of-course phase, you have a much better chance to make action move more smoothly. Moon voids can also be used successfully to do routine activities or inner work, such as dream therapy or personal contemplation.

You'll find Moon phases, as well as each of the Moon's entries into a new sign. Times are expressed in Eastern time (in bold type) and Pacific time (in regular type). The New Moon time is generally best for beginning new activities, as the Moon is increasing in light and can offer the element of growth to our endeavors. When the Moon is Full, its illumination is greatest and we can see the results of our efforts. When it moves from the Full stage back to the New stage, it can best be used to reflect on our projects. If necessary, we can make corrections at the New Moon.

The section of "Planetary Stations" on page 9 will give you the times when the planets are changing signs or direction, thereby affording us opportunities for new starts.

The ephemeris in the back of your *Pocket Planner* can be very helpful to you. As you start to work with the ephemeris, you may notice that not all planets seem to be comfortable in every sign. Think of the planets as actors and the signs as the costumes they wear. Sometimes, costumes just itch. If you find this to be so for a certain time period, you may choose to delay your plans for a time or be more creative with the energies at hand.

As you turn to the daily pages, you'll find information about the Moon's sign, phase, and the time it changes phase. You'll find icons indicating the best days to plant and fish. Also, you will find times and dates when the planets and asteroids change signs and go either retrograde or direct, major holidays, a three-month calendar, and room to record your appointments.

This guide is a powerful tool. Make the most of it!

Symbol Key

Planets:	☉ Sun	⚳ Ceres	♄ Saturn
	☽ Moon	⚴ Pallas	⚷ Chiron
	☿ Mercury	⚵ Juno	♅ Uranus
	♀ Venus	⚶ Vesta	♆ Neptune
	♂ Mars	♃ Jupiter	♇ Pluto
Signs:	♈ Aries	♌ Leo	♐ Sagittarius
	♉ Taurus	♍ Virgo	♑ Capricorn
	♊ Gemini	♎ Libra	♒ Aquarius
	♋ Cancer	♏ Scorpio	♓ Pisces
Aspects:	☌ Conjunction (0°)	⊻ Semisextile (30°)	⚹ Sextile (60°)
	□ Square (90°)	△ Trine (120°)	
	⚻ Quincunx (150°)	☍ Opposition (180°)	
Motion:	℞ Retrograde	D Direct	

Best Days for Planting: ✿   Best Days for Fishing: 🐟

World Map of Time Zones

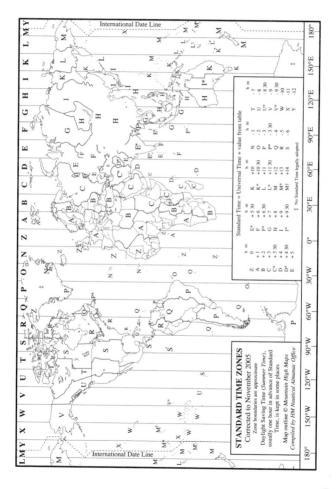

International Date Line

Standard Time = Universal Time + value from table

	h m
Z	0
A	+1
B	+2
C	+3
C*	+3 30
D	+4
D*	+4 30
E	+5

	h m
E*	+5 30
F	+6
F*	+6 30
G	+7
H	+8
I	+9
I*	+9 30

	h m
K	+10
K*	+10 30
L	+11
L*	+11 30
M	+12
M*	+13
M†	+14

	h m
N	-1
O	-2
P	-3
P*	-3 30
Q	-4
R	-5
S	-6

	h m
T	-7
U	-8
U*	-8 30
V	-9
V*	-9 30
W	-10
X	-11
Y	-12

‡ No Standard Time legally adopted

STANDARD TIME ZONES
Corrected to November 2005
Zone boundaries are approximate
Daylight Saving Time (*Summer Time*),
usually one hour in advance of Standard
Time, is kept in some places
Map outline © Mountain High Maps
Compiled by HM Nautical Almanac Office

International Date Line

7

Time Zone Conversions

World Time Zones
Compared to Eastern Standard Time

( ) From Map
(S) CST/Subtract 1 hour
(R) EST
(Q) Add 1 hour
(P) Add 2 hours
(O) Add 3 hours
(N) Add 4 hours
(Z) Add 5 hours
(T) MST/Subtract 2 hours
(U) PST/Subtract 3 hours
(V) Subtract 4 hours
(W) Subtract 5 hours
(X) Subtract 6 hours

(Y) Subtract 7 hours
(A) Add 6 hours
(B) Add 7 hours
(C) Add 8 hours
(D) Add 9 hours
(E) Add 10 hours
(F) Add 11 hours
(G) Add 12 hours
(H) Add 13 hours
(I) Add 14 hours
(K) Add 15 hours
(L) Add 16 hours
(M) Add 17 hours

(C*) Add 8.5 hours
(D*) Add 9.5 hours
(E*) Add 10.5 hours
(F*) Add 11.5 hours
(I*) Add 14.5 hours
(K*) Add 15.5 hours
(L*) Add 16.5 hours
(M*) Add 18 hours
(P*) Add 2.5 hours
(U*) Subtract 3.5 hours
(V*) Subtract 4.5 hours

World Map of Time Zones is supplied by HM Nautical Almanac Office © Center for the Central Laboratory of the Research Councils. Note: This is not an official map. Countries change their time zones as they wish.

Planetary Stations for 2024

	JAN	FEB	MAR	APR	MAY	JUN	JUL	AUG	SEP	OCT	NOV	DEC
☿	℞			4/1–4/25				8/5–8/28			11/25–12/15	
♀												
♂												12/6–2/23/25
♃											10/9–2/4/25	
♄									6/29–11/15			
♅										9/1–1/30/25		
♆									7/2–12/7			
♇							5/2–10/11					
⚷										7/26–12/29		
☊	8/28/23–1/27											
⚴							5/15–8/26					
⚵					3/29–7/9							
⚶		1/12–4/21										
⚳	11/2/23–2/8											

9

1 Monday

3rd ♍
☿ D   **10:08 pm**   7:08 pm

Kwanzaa ends • New Year's Day

2 Tuesday

3rd ♍
☽ v/c   **6:36 pm**   3:36 pm
☽ enters ♎   **7:47 pm**   4:47 pm

3 Wednesday

3rd ♎
4th Quarter **10:30 pm**   7:30 pm

4 Thursday

4th ♎
♂ enters ♑   **9:58 am**   6:58 am

Eastern time in bold type
Pacific time in medium type

5 Friday

4th ♎︎
☽ v/c   **6:41 am** 3:41 am
☽ enters ♏︎ **7:39 am** 4:39 am

6 Saturday

4th ♏︎

7 Sunday

4th ♏︎
☽ v/c   **3:22 pm** 12:22 pm
☽ enters ♐︎ **4:08 pm** 1:08 pm

December 2023						
S	M	T	W	T	F	S
					1	2
3	4	5	6	7	8	9
10	11	12	13	14	15	16
17	18	19	20	21	22	23
24	25	26	27	28	29	30
31						

January 2024						
S	M	T	W	T	F	S
	1	2	3	4	5	6
7	8	9	10	11	12	13
14	15	16	17	18	19	20
21	22	23	24	25	26	27
28	29	30	31			

February 2024						
S	M	T	W	T	F	S
				1	2	3
4	5	6	7	8	9	10
11	12	13	14	15	16	17
18	19	20	21	22	23	24
25	26	27	28	29		

8 Monday
4th ♐

9 Tuesday
4th ♐
☽ v/c   **1:24 pm** 10:24 am
☽ enters ♑   **8:33 pm** 5:33 pm

10 Wednesday
4th ♑

11 Thursday
4th ♑
New Moon   **6:57 am** 3:57 am
☽ v/c   **9:33 pm** 6:33 pm
☽ enters ≈   **10:01 pm** 7:01 pm

12 Friday

1st ♒
⚨ ℞   **11:55 pm**   8:55 pm

13 Saturday

1st ♒
☽ v/c   **4:59 am**   1:59 am
☿ enters ♑   **9:49 pm**   6:49 pm
☽ enters ♓ **10:29 pm**   7:29 pm

14 Sunday

1st ♓

December 2023						
S	M	T	W	T	F	S
					1	2
3	4	5	6	7	8	9
10	11	12	13	14	15	16
17	18	19	20	21	22	23
24	25	26	27	28	29	30
31						

January 2024						
S	M	T	W	T	F	S
	1	2	3	4	5	6
7	8	9	10	11	12	13
14	15	16	17	18	19	20
21	22	23	24	25	26	27
28	29	30	31			

February 2024						
S	M	T	W	T	F	S
				1	2	3
4	5	6	7	8	9	10
11	12	13	14	15	16	17
18	19	20	21	22	23	24
25	26	27	28	29		

Eastern time in bold type
Pacific time in medium type

15 Monday

1st ♓
☽ v/c **11:33 pm** 8:33 pm
☽ enters ♈ **11:49 pm** 8:49 pm

Martin Luther King Jr. Day

16 Tuesday

1st ♈

17 Wednesday

1st ♈
2nd Quarter **10:53 pm** 7:53 pm

18 Thursday

2nd ♈
☽ v/c **3:03 am** 12:03 am
☽ enters ♉ **3:12 am** 12:12 am

Eastern time in bold type
Pacific time in medium type

19 Friday
2nd ♉

20 Saturday
2nd ♉
☽ v/c	**8:57 am**	5:57 am
☽ enters ♊	**8:58 am**	5:58 am
☉ enters ♒	**9:07 am**	6:07 am
☿ enters ♒	**7:50 pm**	4:50 pm

Sun enters Aquarius

21 Sunday
2nd ♊

December 2023							January 2024							February 2024						
S	M	T	W	T	F	S	S	M	T	W	T	F	S	S	M	T	W	T	F	S
					1	2		1	2	3	4	5	6					1	2	3
3	4	5	6	7	8	9	7	8	9	10	11	12	13	4	5	6	7	8	9	10
10	11	12	13	14	15	16	14	15	16	17	18	19	20	11	12	13	14	15	16	17
17	18	19	20	21	22	23	21	22	23	24	25	26	27	18	19	20	21	22	23	24
24	25	26	27	28	29	30	28	29	30	31				25	26	27	28	29		
31																				

22 Monday

2nd ♊
☽ v/c   **3:40 pm** 12:40 pm
☽ enters ♋   **4:51 pm** 1:51 pm

23 Tuesday

2nd ♋
♀ enters ♑ **3:50 am** 12:50 am

24 Wednesday

2nd ♋
☽ v/c   **5:58 pm** 2:58 pm
☽ enters ♌   11:37 pm

25 Thursday

2nd ♋
☽ enters ♌ **2:37 am**
Full Moon **12:54 pm** 9:54 am

26 Friday
3rd ♌
☽ v/c   **4:19 pm**   1:19 pm
♅ D   11:35 pm

27 Saturday
3rd ♌
♅ D   **2:35 am**
☽ enters ♍   **2:11 pm**   11:11 am

28 Sunday
3rd ♍

December 2023								January 2024								February 2024						
S	M	T	W	T	F	S		S	M	T	W	T	F	S		S	M	T	W	T	F	S
					1	2			1	2	3	4	5	6						1	2	3
3	4	5	6	7	8	9		7	8	9	10	11	12	13		4	5	6	7	8	9	10
10	11	12	13	14	15	16		14	15	16	17	18	19	20		11	12	13	14	15	16	17
17	18	19	20	21	22	23		21	22	23	24	25	26	27		18	19	20	21	22	23	24
24	25	26	27	28	29	30		28	29	30	31					25	26	27	28	29		
31																						

Eastern time in bold type
Pacific time in medium type

29 Monday
3rd ♍
☽ v/c   **6:20 pm**   3:20 pm

30 Tuesday
3rd ♍
☽ enters ♎   **3:04 am** 12:04 am

31 Wednesday
3rd ♎

1 Thursday
3rd ♎
☽ v/c   **4:03 am**   1:03 am
☽ enters ♏   **3:37 pm** 12:37 pm

Eastern time in bold type
Pacific time in medium type

2 Friday
3rd ♏
4th Quarter **6:18 pm** 3:18 pm

Imbolc • Groundhog Day

3 Saturday
4th ♏
☽ v/c **10:24 pm** 7:24 pm
☽ enters ♐ 10:28 pm

4 Sunday
4th ♏
☽ enters ♐ **1:28 am**
☿ enters ♒ 9:10 pm

January 2024						
S	M	T	W	T	F	S
	1	2	3	4	5	6
7	8	9	10	11	12	13
14	15	16	17	18	19	20
21	22	23	24	25	26	27
28	29	30	31			

February 2024						
S	M	T	W	T	F	S
				1	2	3
4	5	6	7	8	9	10
11	12	13	14	15	16	17
18	19	20	21	22	23	24
25	26	27	28	29		

March 2024						
S	M	T	W	T	F	S
					1	2
3	4	5	6	7	8	9
10	11	12	13	14	15	16
17	18	19	20	21	22	23
24	25	26	27	28	29	30
31						

5 Monday

4th ♐
☿ enters ≈ **12:10 am**
☽ v/c   9:06 pm

6 Tuesday

4th ♐
☽ v/c   **12:06 am**
♀ enters ♐ **3:09 am** 12:09 am
☽ enters ♑ **7:08 am** 4:08 am

7 Wednesday

4th ♑
♃ enters ♑ **6:11 am** 3:11 am
☽ v/c   11:52 pm

8 Thursday

4th ♑
☽ v/c   **2:52 am**
⛢ D   **4:41 am** 1:41 am
☽ enters ≈ **8:59 am** 5:59 am

9 Friday
4th ≈
| ☽ v/c | **5:59 pm** | 2:59 pm |
| New Moon | **5:59 pm** | 2:59 pm |

10 Saturday
1st ≈
☽ enters ♓   **8:42 am**   5:42 am

Lunar New Year (Dragon)

11 Sunday
1st ♓

January 2024								February 2024								March 2024					
S	M	T	W	T	F	S		S	M	T	W	T	F	S		S	M	T	W	T	F	S
	1	2	3	4	5	6						1	2	3							1	2
7	8	9	10	11	12	13		4	5	6	7	8	9	10		3	4	5	6	7	8	9
14	15	16	17	18	19	20		11	12	13	14	15	16	17		10	11	12	13	14	15	16
21	22	23	24	25	26	27		18	19	20	21	22	23	24		17	18	19	20	21	22	23
28	29	30	31					25	26	27	28	29				24	25	26	27	28	29	30
																31						

12 Monday
1st ♓
☽ v/c   **7:32 am**   4:32 am
☽ enters ♈ **8:26 am**   5:26 am
♂ enters ♒   10:05 pm

13 Tuesday
1st ♈
♂ enters ♒ **1:05 am**

Mardi Gras (Fat Tuesday)

14 Wednesday

1st ♈
☽ v/c   **5:21 am**   2:21 am
☽ enters ♉ **10:02 am**   7:02 am

Valentine's Day • Ash Wednesday

15 Thursday

1st ♉

16 Friday

1st ♉
☽ v/c	**10:01 am**	7:01 am
2nd Quarter	**10:01 am**	7:01 am
♀ enters ♒	**11:05 am**	8:05 am
☽ enters ♊	**2:39 pm**	11:39 am

17 Saturday

2nd ♊

18 Sunday

2nd ♊
☽ v/c	**10:21 pm**	7:21 pm
☽ enters ♋	**10:25 pm**	7:25 pm
☉ enters ♓	**11:13 pm**	8:13 pm

Sun enters Pisces

January 2024							February 2024							March 2024						
S	M	T	W	T	F	S	S	M	T	W	T	F	S	S	M	T	W	T	F	S
	1	2	3	4	5	6					1	2	3						1	2
7	8	9	10	11	12	13	4	5	6	7	8	9	10	3	4	5	6	7	8	9
14	15	16	17	18	19	20	11	12	13	14	15	16	17	10	11	12	13	14	15	16
21	22	23	24	25	26	27	18	19	20	21	22	23	24	17	18	19	20	21	22	23
28	29	30	31				25	26	27	28	29			24	25	26	27	28	29	30
														31						

19 Monday

2nd ♋

Presidents' Day

20 Tuesday

2nd ♋
☽ v/c   10:38 pm

21 Wednesday

2nd ♋
☽ v/c   **1:38 am**
☽ enters ♌   **8:40 am**   5:40 am

22 Thursday

2nd ♌
☽ v/c   **11:18 pm**   8:18 pm
☿ enters ♓   11:29 pm

23 Friday

2nd ♌
☿ enters ♓ **2:29 am**
☽ enters ♍ **8:38 pm** 5:38 pm

24 Saturday

2nd ♍
Full Moon **7:30 am** 4:30 am

25 Sunday

3rd ♍
☽ v/c 11:35 pm

January 2024						
S	M	T	W	T	F	S
	1	2	3	4	5	6
7	8	9	10	11	12	13
14	15	16	17	18	19	20
21	22	23	24	25	26	27
28	29	30	31			

February 2024						
S	M	T	W	T	F	S
				1	2	3
4	5	6	7	8	9	10
11	12	13	14	15	16	17
18	19	20	21	22	23	24
25	26	27	28	29		

March 2024						
S	M	T	W	T	F	S
					1	2
3	4	5	6	7	8	9
10	11	12	13	14	15	16
17	18	19	20	21	22	23
24	25	26	27	28	29	30
31						

Eastern time in bold type
Pacific time in medium type

26 Monday
3rd ♍
☽ v/c   **2:35 am**
☽ enters ♎   **9:29 am**   6:29 am

27 Tuesday
3rd ♎
☽ v/c   **1:22 pm** 10:22 am

28 Wednesday
3rd ♎
☽ enters ♏   **10:09 pm**   7:09 pm

29 Thursday
3rd ♏

Leap Day

1 Friday
3rd ♏
☽ v/c   11:47 pm

2 Saturday
3rd ♏
☽ v/c   **2:47 am**
☽ enters ♐   **8:56 am**   5:56 am

3 Sunday
3rd ♐
4th Quarter **10:23 am** 7:23 am

February 2024						
S	M	T	W	T	F	S
				1	2	3
4	5	6	7	8	9	10
11	12	13	14	15	16	17
18	19	20	21	22	23	24
25	26	27	28	29		

March 2024						
S	M	T	W	T	F	S
					1	2
3	4	5	6	7	8	9
10	11	12	13	14	15	16
17	18	19	20	21	22	23
24	25	26	27	28	29	30
31						

April 2024						
S	M	T	W	T	F	S
	1	2	3	4	5	6
7	8	9	10	11	12	13
14	15	16	17	18	19	20
21	22	23	24	25	26	27
28	29	30				

Eastern time in bold type
Pacific time in medium type

4 Monday

4th ♐
☽ v/c	**10:41 am**	7:41 am
☽ enters ♑	**4:15 pm**	1:15 pm

5 Tuesday

4th ♑

6 Wednesday

4th ♑
☽ v/c	**2:35 pm**	11:35 am
☽ enters ≈	**7:38 pm**	4:38 pm

7 Thursday

4th ≈

8 Friday

4th ≈
☽ v/c   **1:56 pm** 10:56 am
☽ enters ♓   **8:03 pm** 5:03 pm

9 Saturday

4th ♓
☿ enters ♈ **11:03 pm** 8:03 pm

10 Sunday

4th ♓
New Moon   **5:00 am** 1:00 am
☽ v/c   **3:45 pm** 12:45 pm
☽ enters ♈ **8:19 pm** 5:19 pm

Ramadan begins at sundown • Daylight Saving Time begins at 2 am

February 2024						
S	M	T	W	T	F	S
				1	2	3
4	5	6	7	8	9	10
11	12	13	14	15	16	17
18	19	20	21	22	23	24
25	26	27	28	29		

March 2024						
S	M	T	W	T	F	S
					1	2
3	4	5	6	7	8	9
10	11	12	13	14	15	16
17	18	19	20	21	22	23
24	25	26	27	28	29	30
31						

April 2024						
S	M	T	W	T	F	S
	1	2	3	4	5	6
7	8	9	10	11	12	13
14	15	16	17	18	19	20
21	22	23	24	25	26	27
28	29	30				

Eastern time in bold type
Pacific time in medium type

11 Monday

1st ♈
♀ enters ♓   **5:50 pm**   2:50 pm

12 Tuesday

1st ♈
☽ v/c   **7:08 am**   4:08 am
☽ enters ♉   **8:28 pm**   5:28 pm

13 Wednesday

1st ♉

14 Thursday

1st ♉
☽ v/c   **6:29 pm**   3:29 pm
☽ enters ♊   **11:16 pm**   8:16 pm

Eastern time in bold type
Pacific time in medium type

15 Friday
1st ♊

16 Saturday
1st ♊
2nd Quarter   9:11 pm
☽ v/c   9:43 pm

17 Sunday
1st ♊
2nd Quarter **12:11 am**
☽ v/c   **12:43 am**
☽ enters ♋   **5:40 am**   2:40 am

St. Patrick's Day

| February 2024 |
S	M	T	W	T	F	S
				1	2	3
4	5	6	7	8	9	10
11	12	13	14	15	16	17
18	19	20	21	22	23	24
25	26	27	28	29		

| March 2024 |
S	M	T	W	T	F	S
					1	2
3	4	5	6	7	8	9
10	11	12	13	14	15	16
17	18	19	20	21	22	23
24	25	26	27	28	29	30
31						

| April 2024 |
S	M	T	W	T	F	S
	1	2	3	4	5	6
7	8	9	10	11	12	13
14	15	16	17	18	19	20
21	22	23	24	25	26	27
28	29	30				

Eastern time in bold type
Pacific time in medium type

18 Monday
2nd ♋

19 Tuesday
2nd ♋
☽ v/c   **2:52 pm** 11:52 am
☽ enters ♌   **3:33 pm** 12:33 pm
☉ enters ♈ **11:06 pm**   8:06 pm

International Astrology Day
Sun enters Aries • Ostara • Spring Equinox • 11:06 pm EDT/8:06 pm PDT

20 Wednesday
2nd ♌

21 Thursday
2nd ♌
☽ v/c   11:34 pm

22 Friday

2nd ♌

☽ v/c	**2:34 am**	
☽ enters ♍	**3:42 am**	12:42 am
♂ enters ♓	**7:47 pm**	4:47 pm

23 Saturday

2nd ♍

Purim begins at sundown

24 Sunday

2nd ♍

| ☽ v/c | **11:49 am** | 8:49 am |
| ☽ enters ♎ | **4:37 pm** | 1:37 pm |

Palm Sunday

February 2024								March 2024								April 2024						
S	M	T	W	T	F	S		S	M	T	W	T	F	S		S	M	T	W	T	F	S
				1	2	3							1	2			1	2	3	4	5	6
4	5	6	7	8	9	10		3	4	5	6	7	8	9		7	8	9	10	11	12	13
11	12	13	14	15	16	17		10	11	12	13	14	15	16		14	15	16	17	18	19	20
18	19	20	21	22	23	24		17	18	19	20	21	22	23		21	22	23	24	25	26	27
25	26	27	28	29				24	25	26	27	28	29	30		28	29	30				
								31														

25 Monday

2nd ♎
Full Moon   **3:00 am** 12:00 am

Lunar Eclipse 5° ♎ 07'

26 Tuesday

3rd ♎
☽ v/c   **7:09 pm** 4:09 pm

27 Wednesday

3rd ♎
☽ enters ♏   **5:03 am** 2:03 am

28 Thursday

3rd ♏

Eastern time in bold type
Pacific time in medium type

29 Friday

3rd ♏

☿ ℞	**9:17 am**	6:17 am
☽ v/c	**11:40 am**	8:40 am
☽ enters ♐	**3:52 pm**	12:52 pm

Good Friday

30 Saturday

3rd ♐

31 Sunday

3rd ♐

☿ enters ♋	**7:02 am**	4:02 am
☽ v/c	**8:16 pm**	5:16 pm
☽ enters ♑		9:05 pm

Easter

February 2024								March 2024								April 2024					
S	M	T	W	T	F	S		S	M	T	W	T	F	S		S	M	T	W	T	F	S
				1	2	3							1	2			1	2	3	4	5	6
4	5	6	7	8	9	10		3	4	5	6	7	8	9		7	8	9	10	11	12	13
11	12	13	14	15	16	17		10	11	12	13	14	15	16		14	15	16	17	18	19	20
18	19	20	21	22	23	24		17	18	19	20	21	22	23		21	22	23	24	25	26	27
25	26	27	28	29				24	25	26	27	28	29	30		28	29	30				
								31														

1 Monday

3rd ♐
☽ enters ♑ **12:05 am**
☿ R̄ **6:14 pm** 3:14 pm
4th Quarter **11:15 pm** 8:15 pm

April Fools' Day (All Fools' Day—Pagan) • Mercury retrograde until 4/25

2 Tuesday

4th ♑
☽ v/c 10:40 pm

3 Wednesday

4th ♑
☽ v/c **1:40 am**
☽ enters ♒ **5:08 am** 2:08 am

4 Thursday

4th ♒
♀ enters ♈ 9:00 pm
☽ v/c 10:40 pm

5 Friday

4th ≈
♀ enters ♈ **12:00 am**
☽ v/c   **1:40 am**
☽ enters ♓   **7:13 am**   4:13 am

6 Saturday

4th ♓

7 Sunday

4th ♓
☽ v/c   **4:27 am**   1:27 am
☽ enters ♈   **7:25 am**   4:25 am

	March 2024							April 2024							May 2024					
S	M	T	W	T	F	S	S	M	T	W	T	F	S	S	M	T	W	T	F	S
					1	2		1	2	3	4	5	6				1	2	3	4
3	4	5	6	7	8	9	7	8	9	10	11	12	13	5	6	7	8	9	10	11
10	11	12	13	14	15	16	14	15	16	17	18	19	20	12	13	14	15	16	17	18
17	18	19	20	21	22	23	21	22	23	24	25	26	27	19	20	21	22	23	24	25
24	25	26	27	28	29	30	28	29	30					26	27	28	29	30	31	
31																				

8 Monday

4th ♈

| New Moon | **2:21 pm** | 11:21 am |
| D v/c | **10:39 pm** | 7:39 pm |

Solar Eclipse 19° ♈ 24'

9 Tuesday

1st ♈

| D enters ♉ | **7:23 am** | 4:23 am |

Ramadan ends

10 Wednesday

1st ♉

11 Thursday

1st ♉

| D v/c | **6:04 am** | 3:04 am |
| D enters ♊ | **8:59 am** | 5:59 am |

Eastern time in bold type
Pacific time in medium type

12 Friday
1st ♊

13 Saturday
1st ♊
☽ v/c **10:46 am** 7:46 am
☽ enters ♋ **1:45 pm** 10:45 am

14 Sunday
1st ♋

March 2024						
S	M	T	W	T	F	S
					1	2
3	4	5	6	7	8	9
10	11	12	13	14	15	16
17	18	19	20	21	22	23
24	25	26	27	28	29	30
31						

April 2024						
S	M	T	W	T	F	S
	1	2	3	4	5	6
7	8	9	10	11	12	13
14	15	16	17	18	19	20
21	22	23	24	25	26	27
28	29	30				

May 2024						
S	M	T	W	T	F	S
			1	2	3	4
5	6	7	8	9	10	11
12	13	14	15	16	17	18
19	20	21	22	23	24	25
26	27	28	29	30	31	

Eastern time in bold type
Pacific time in medium type

15 Monday

1st ♋
2nd Quarter **3:13 pm** 12:13 pm
☽ v/c **7:22 pm** 4:22 pm
☽ enters ♌ **10:24 pm** 7:24 pm

16 Tuesday

2nd ♌

17 Wednesday

2nd ♌

18 Thursday

2nd ♌
☽ v/c **8:02 am** 5:02 am
☽ enters ♍ **10:10 am** 7:10 am

19 Friday
2nd ♏
☉ enters ♉ **10:00 am** 7:00 am

Sun enters Taurus

20 Saturday
2nd ♏
☽ v/c **8:20 pm** 5:20 pm
☽ enters ♎ **11:08 pm** 8:08 pm

21 Sunday
2nd ♎
♇ D **10:58 pm** 7:58 pm

March 2024						
S	M	T	W	T	F	S
					1	2
3	4	5	6	7	8	9
10	11	12	13	14	15	16
17	18	19	20	21	22	23
24	25	26	27	28	29	30
31						

April 2024						
S	M	T	W	T	F	S
	1	2	3	4	5	6
7	8	9	10	11	12	13
14	15	16	17	18	19	20
21	22	23	24	25	26	27
28	29	30				

May 2024						
S	M	T	W	T	F	S
			1	2	3	4
5	6	7	8	9	10	11
12	13	14	15	16	17	18
19	20	21	22	23	24	25
26	27	28	29	30	31	

Eastern time in bold type
Pacific time in medium type

22 Monday

2nd ♎
☽ v/c   **7:24 pm**   4:24 pm

Passover begins at sundown • Earth Day

23 Tuesday

2nd ♎
☽ enters ♏ **11:20 am**   8:20 am
Full Moon   **7:49 pm**   4:49 pm

24 Wednesday

3rd ♏

25 Thursday

3rd ♏
☿ D   **8:54 am**   5:54 am
☽ v/c   **7:17 pm**   4:17 pm
☽ enters ♐ **9:37 pm**   6:37 pm

Eastern time in bold type
Pacific time in medium type

26 Friday
3rd ✗

27 Saturday
3rd ✗

28 Sunday
3rd ✗
☽ v/c   **3:31 am** 12:31 am
☽ enters ♑   **5:37 am** 2:37 am

March 2024						
S	M	T	W	T	F	S
					1	2
3	4	5	6	7	8	9
10	11	12	13	14	15	16
17	18	19	20	21	22	23
24	25	26	27	28	29	30
31						

April 2024						
S	M	T	W	T	F	S
	1	2	3	4	5	6
7	8	9	10	11	12	13
14	15	16	17	18	19	20
21	22	23	24	25	26	27
28	29	30				

May 2024						
S	M	T	W	T	F	S
			1	2	3	4
5	6	7	8	9	10	11
12	13	14	15	16	17	18
19	20	21	22	23	24	25
26	27	28	29	30	31	

Eastern time in bold type
Pacific time in medium type

29 Monday

3rd ♐
♀ enters ♉   **7:31 am**   4:31 am

30 Tuesday

3rd ♐
☽ v/c   **11:19 am**   8:19 am
☽ enters ≈   **11:20 am**   8:20 am
♂ enters ♈   **11:33 am**   8:33 am

Passover ends

1 Wednesday

3rd ≈
4th Quarter   **7:27 am**   4:27 am

Beltane

2 Thursday

4th ≈
☽ v/c   **5:28 am**   2:28 am
☿ ℞   **1:46 pm** 10:46 am
☽ enters ♓   **2:52 pm** 11:52 am

Eastern time in bold type
Pacific time in medium type

3 Friday
4th ♓

Orthodox Good Friday

4 Saturday
4th ♓
☽ v/c   **3:06 pm** 12:06 pm
☽ enters ♈   **4:41 pm** 1:41 pm

5 Sunday
4th ♈
☽ v/c   10:57 pm

Orthodox Easter • Cinco de Mayo

April 2024						
S	M	T	W	T	F	S
	1	2	3	4	5	6
7	8	9	10	11	12	13
14	15	16	17	18	19	20
21	22	23	24	25	26	27
28	29	30				

May 2024						
S	M	T	W	T	F	S
			1	2	3	4
5	6	7	8	9	10	11
12	13	14	15	16	17	18
19	20	21	22	23	24	25
26	27	28	29	30	31	

June 2024						
S	M	T	W	T	F	S
						1
2	3	4	5	6	7	8
9	10	11	12	13	14	15
16	17	18	19	20	21	22
23	24	25	26	27	28	29
30						

6 Monday
4th ♈
☽ v/c   **1:57 am**
☽ enters ♉   **5:42 pm** 2:42 pm

7 Tuesday
4th ♉
New Moon **11:22 pm** 8:22 pm

8 Wednesday
1st ♉
☽ v/c   **5:55 pm** 2:55 pm
☽ enters ♊   **7:20 pm** 4:20 pm

9 Thursday
1st ♊

10 Friday
1st ♊
| ☽ v/c | **9:49 pm** | 6:49 pm |
| ☽ enters ♋ | **11:13 pm** | 8:13 pm |

11 Saturday
1st ♋

12 Sunday
1st ♋

Mother's Day

April 2024						
S	M	T	W	T	F	S
	1	2	3	4	5	6
7	8	9	10	11	12	13
14	15	16	17	18	19	20
21	22	23	24	25	26	27
28	29	30				

May 2024						
S	M	T	W	T	F	S
			1	2	3	4
5	6	7	8	9	10	11
12	13	14	15	16	17	18
19	20	21	22	23	24	25
26	27	28	29	30	31	

June 2024						
S	M	T	W	T	F	S
						1
2	3	4	5	6	7	8
9	10	11	12	13	14	15
16	17	18	19	20	21	22
23	24	25	26	27	28	29
30						

Eastern time in bold type
Pacific time in medium type

13 Monday

1st ♋
☽ v/c **5:13 am** 2:13 am
☽ enters ♌ **6:36 am** 3:36 am

14 Tuesday

1st ♌
♃ R **10:34 pm**

15 Wednesday

1st ♌
♃ R **1:34 am**
2nd Quarter **7:48 am** 4:48 am
☽ v/c **12:41 pm** 9:41 am
☿ enters ♉ **1:05 pm** 10:05 am
☽ enters ♍ **5:33 pm** 2:33 pm

16 Thursday

2nd ♍
♀ enters ♏ **1:23 pm** 10:23 am

17 Friday
2nd ♍

18 Saturday
2nd ♍
☽ v/c **5:09 am** 2:09 am
☽ enters ♎ **6:23 am** 3:23 am

19 Sunday
2nd ♎
☽ v/c **11:48 am** 8:48 am

April 2024						
S	M	T	W	T	F	S
	1	2	3	4	5	6
7	8	9	10	11	12	13
14	15	16	17	18	19	20
21	22	23	24	25	26	27
28	29	30				

May 2024						
S	M	T	W	T	F	S
			1	2	3	4
5	6	7	8	9	10	11
12	13	14	15	16	17	18
19	20	21	22	23	24	25
26	27	28	29	30	31	

June 2024						
S	M	T	W	T	F	S
						1
2	3	4	5	6	7	8
9	10	11	12	13	14	15
16	17	18	19	20	21	22
23	24	25	26	27	28	29
30						

Eastern time in bold type
Pacific time in medium type

20 Monday

2nd ♎︎
☉ enters ♊︎ **8:59 am** 5:59 am
☽ enters ♏︎ **6:34 pm** 3:34 pm

Sun enters Gemini

21 Tuesday

2nd ♏︎

22 Wednesday

2nd ♏︎

23 Thursday

2nd ♏︎
☽ v/c **3:28 am** 12:28 am
☽ enters ♐︎ **4:24 am** 1:24 am
Full Moon **9:53 am** 6:53 am
♀ enters ♊︎ **4:30 pm** 1:30 pm

24 Friday
3rd ✗

25 Saturday
3rd ✗

☽ v/c	**10:47 am**	7:47 am
☽ enters ♑	**11:36 am**	8:36 am
♃ enters ♊	**7:15 pm**	4:15 pm

26 Sunday
3rd ♑

April 2024							May 2024							June 2024						
S	M	T	W	T	F	S	S	M	T	W	T	F	S	S	M	T	W	T	F	S
	1	2	3	4	5	6				1	2	3	4							1
7	8	9	10	11	12	13	5	6	7	8	9	10	11	2	3	4	5	6	7	8
14	15	16	17	18	19	20	12	13	14	15	16	17	18	9	10	11	12	13	14	15
21	22	23	24	25	26	27	19	20	21	22	23	24	25	16	17	18	19	20	21	22
28	29	30					26	27	28	29	30	31		23	24	25	26	27	28	29
														30						

Eastern time in bold type
Pacific time in medium type

27 Monday

3rd ♑
℟ v/c   **4:02 pm**   1:02 pm
℟ enters ♒   **4:45 pm**   1:45 pm

Memorial Day

28 Tuesday

3rd ♒

29 Wednesday

3rd ♒
℟ v/c   **10:20 am**   7:20 am
℟ enters ♓   **8:33 pm**   5:33 pm

30 Thursday

3rd ♓
4th Quarter   **1:13 pm**   10:13 am

Eastern time in bold type
Pacific time in medium type

31 Friday
4th ♓

| ☽ v/c | **10:55 pm** | 7:55 pm |
| ☽ enters ♈ | **11:28 pm** | 8:28 pm |

1 Saturday
4th ♈

2 Sunday
4th ♈

| ☽ v/c | **6:04 pm** | 3:04 pm |
| ☽ enters ♉ | | 10:55 pm |

May 2024						
S	M	T	W	T	F	S
			1	2	3	4
5	6	7	8	9	10	11
12	13	14	15	16	17	18
19	20	21	22	23	24	25
26	27	28	29	30	31	

June 2024						
S	M	T	W	T	F	S
						1
2	3	4	5	6	7	8
9	10	11	12	13	14	15
16	17	18	19	20	21	22
23	24	25	26	27	28	29
30						

July 2024						
S	M	T	W	T	F	S
	1	2	3	4	5	6
7	8	9	10	11	12	13
14	15	16	17	18	19	20
21	22	23	24	25	26	27
28	29	30	31			

Eastern time in bold type
Pacific time in medium type

3 Monday

4th ♈

☽ enters ♉	**1:55 am**	
☿ enters ♊	**3:37 am**	12:37 am

4 Tuesday

4th ♉

5 Wednesday

4th ♉

☽ v/c	**4:09 am**	1:09 am
☽ enters ♊	**4:36 am**	1:36 am

6 Thursday

4th ♊

New Moon	**8:38 am**	5:38 am

7 Friday

1st ♊
☽ v/c   **8:16 am**   5:16 am
☽ enters ♋   **8:41 am**   5:41 am

8 Saturday

1st ♋
♂ enters ♉   9:35 pm

9 Sunday

1st ♋
♂ enters ♉   **12:35 am**
☽ v/c   **3:05 pm**   12:05 pm
☽ enters ♌   **3:29 pm**   12:29 pm

May 2024						
S	M	T	W	T	F	S
			1	2	3	4
5	6	7	8	9	10	11
12	13	14	15	16	17	18
19	20	21	22	23	24	25
26	27	28	29	30	31	

June 2024						
S	M	T	W	T	F	S
						1
2	3	4	5	6	7	8
9	10	11	12	13	14	15
16	17	18	19	20	21	22
23	24	25	26	27	28	29
30						

July 2024						
S	M	T	W	T	F	S
	1	2	3	4	5	6
7	8	9	10	11	12	13
14	15	16	17	18	19	20
21	22	23	24	25	26	27
28	29	30	31			

10 Monday
1st ♌

---

11 Tuesday
1st ♌
☽ v/c   **3:16 pm** 12:16 pm
☽ enters ♍   10:39 pm

Shavuot begins at sundown

---

12 Wednesday
1st ♌
☽ enters ♍ **1:39 am**

---

13 Thursday
1st ♍
2nd Quarter   10:18 pm

Eastern time in bold type
Pacific time in medium type

14 Friday

1st ♍

2nd Quarter	**1:18 am**	
☽ v/c	**1:54 pm**	10:54 am
☽ enters ♎	**2:12 pm**	11:12 am

Flag Day

15 Saturday

2nd ♎

16 Sunday

2nd ♎

☽ v/c	11:05 pm
♀ enters ♋	11:20 pm
☽ enters ♏	11:38 pm

Father's Day

May 2024						
S	M	T	W	T	F	S
			1	2	3	4
5	6	7	8	9	10	11
12	13	14	15	16	17	18
19	20	21	22	23	24	25
26	27	28	29	30	31	

June 2024						
S	M	T	W	T	F	S
						1
2	3	4	5	6	7	8
9	10	11	12	13	14	15
16	17	18	19	20	21	22
23	24	25	26	27	28	29
30						

July 2024						
S	M	T	W	T	F	S
	1	2	3	4	5	6
7	8	9	10	11	12	13
14	15	16	17	18	19	20
21	22	23	24	25	26	27
28	29	30	31			

Eastern time in bold type
Pacific time in medium type

17 Monday

2nd ♎︎
☽ v/c   **2:05 am**
♀ enters ♋︎ **2:20 am**
☽ enters ♏︎ **2:38 am**
☿ enters ♋︎ **5:07 am**   2:07 am

18 Tuesday

2nd ♏︎

19 Wednesday

2nd ♏︎
☽ v/c   **12:19 pm**   9:19 am
☽ enters ♐︎ **12:32 pm**   9:32 am
⚸ enters ♌︎ **6:11 pm**   3:11 pm

Juneteenth

20 Thursday

2nd ♐︎
☉ enters ♋︎ **4:51 pm**   1:51 pm

Sun enters Cancer • Litha • Summer Solstice • 4:51 pm EDT/1:51 pm PDT

Eastern time in bold type
Pacific time in medium type

21 Friday

2nd ♐

☽ v/c	**6:58 pm**	3:58 pm
☽ enters ♑	**7:08 pm**	4:08 pm
Full Moon	**9:08 pm**	6:08 pm

22 Saturday

3rd ♑

23 Sunday

3rd ♑

☽ v/c	**11:05 pm**	8:05 pm
☽ enters ♒	**11:14 pm**	8:14 pm

May 2024						
S	M	T	W	T	F	S
			1	2	3	4
5	6	7	8	9	10	11
12	13	14	15	16	17	18
19	20	21	22	23	24	25
26	27	28	29	30	31	

June 2024						
S	M	T	W	T	F	S
						1
2	3	4	5	6	7	8
9	10	11	12	13	14	15
16	17	18	19	20	21	22
23	24	25	26	27	28	29
30						

July 2024						
S	M	T	W	T	F	S
	1	2	3	4	5	6
7	8	9	10	11	12	13
14	15	16	17	18	19	20
21	22	23	24	25	26	27
28	29	30	31			

Eastern time in bold type
Pacific time in medium type

24 Monday
3rd ≈

25 Tuesday
3rd ≈
☽ v/c   **6:30 pm**   3:30 pm
☽ enters ♓   11:08 pm

26 Wednesday
3rd ≈
☽ enters ♓   **2:08 am**

27 Thursday
3rd ♓

Eastern time in bold type
Pacific time in medium type

28 Friday

3rd ♓

☽ v/c	**4:45 am**	1:45 am
☽ enters ♈	**4:52 am**	1:52 am
4th Quarter	**5:53 pm**	2:53 pm

29 Saturday

4th ♈

| ♄ ℞ | **3:07 pm** | 12:07 pm |
| ☽ v/c | | 9:56 pm |

30 Sunday

4th ♈

| ☽ v/c | **12:56 am** | |
| ☽ enters ♉ | **8:00 am** | 5:00 am |

May 2024	June 2024	July 2024
S M T W T F S	S M T W T F S	S M T W T F S
1 2 3 4	1	1 2 3 4 5 6
5 6 7 8 9 10 11	2 3 4 5 6 7 8	7 8 9 10 11 12 13
12 13 14 15 16 17 18	9 10 11 12 13 14 15	14 15 16 17 18 19 20
19 20 21 22 23 24 25	16 17 18 19 20 21 22	21 22 23 24 25 26 27
26 27 28 29 30 31	23 24 25 26 27 28 29	28 29 30 31
	30	

Eastern time in bold type
Pacific time in medium type

1 Monday

4th ♉

2 Tuesday

4th ♉

♆ R⟋	**6:40 am**	3:40 am
☿ enters ♌	**8:50 am**	5:50 am
☽ v/c	**11:43 am**	8:43 am
☽ enters ♊	**11:50 am**	8:50 am

3 Wednesday

4th ♊

4 Thursday

4th ♊

☽ v/c	**4:44 pm**	1:44 pm
☽ enters ♋	**4:51 pm**	1:51 pm

Independence Day

Eastern time in bold type
Pacific time in medium type

5 Friday
4th ♋
New Moon   **6:57 pm**   3:57 pm

6 Saturday
1st ♋

☽ v/c   **11:47 pm**   8:47 pm
☽ enters ♌   **11:56 pm**   8:56 pm

7 Sunday
1st ♌

Islamic New Year begins at sundown

June 2024						
S	M	T	W	T	F	S
						1
2	3	4	5	6	7	8
9	10	11	12	13	14	15
16	17	18	19	20	21	22
23	24	25	26	27	28	29
30						

July 2024						
S	M	T	W	T	F	S
	1	2	3	4	5	6
7	8	9	10	11	12	13
14	15	16	17	18	19	20
21	22	23	24	25	26	27
28	29	30	31			

August 2024						
S	M	T	W	T	F	S
				1	2	3
4	5	6	7	8	9	10
11	12	13	14	15	16	17
18	19	20	21	22	23	24
25	26	27	28	29	30	31

Eastern time in bold type
Pacific time in medium type

8 Monday

1st ♌
☽ v/c   11:04 pm

9 Tuesday

1st ♌
☽ v/c   **2:04 am**
☽ enters ♍   **9:48 am**   6:48 am
♀ D   **10:46 pm**   7:46 pm

10 Wednesday

1st ♍

11 Thursday

1st ♍
♀ enters ♌   **12:19 pm**   9:19 am
☽ v/c   **9:55 pm**   6:55 pm
☽ enters ♎   **10:06 pm**   7:06 pm

12 Friday
1st ♎

13 Saturday

1st ♎
| ☽ v/c | **6:49 pm** | 3:49 pm |
| 2nd Quarter | **6:49 pm** | 3:49 pm |

14 Sunday

2nd ♎
☽ enters ♏, **10:53 am** 7:53 am

June 2024						
S	M	T	W	T	F	S
						1
2	3	4	5	6	7	8
9	10	11	12	13	14	15
16	17	18	19	20	21	22
23	24	25	26	27	28	29
30						

July 2024						
S	M	T	W	T	F	S
	1	2	3	4	5	6
7	8	9	10	11	12	13
14	15	16	17	18	19	20
21	22	23	24	25	26	27
28	29	30	31			

August 2024						
S	M	T	W	T	F	S
				1	2	3
4	5	6	7	8	9	10
11	12	13	14	15	16	17
18	19	20	21	22	23	24
25	26	27	28	29	30	31

Eastern time in bold type
Pacific time in medium type

15 Monday
2nd ♏

16 Tuesday
2nd ♏
☽ v/c   **9:10 pm**   6:10 pm
☽ enters ♐   **9:25 pm**   6:25 pm

17 Wednesday
2nd ♐

18 Thursday
2nd ♐

Eastern time in bold type
Pacific time in medium type

19 Friday
2nd ♐
☽ v/c   **3:58 am** 12:58 am
☽ enters ♑   **4:14 am** 1:14 am

20 Saturday
2nd ♑
♂ enters ♊   **4:43 pm** 1:43 pm

21 Sunday
2nd ♑
Full Moon   **6:17 am** 3:17 am
☽ v/c   **7:26 am** 4:26 am
☽ enters ♒   **7:43 am** 4:43 am

June 2024						
S	M	T	W	T	F	S
						1
2	3	4	5	6	7	8
9	10	11	12	13	14	15
16	17	18	19	20	21	22
23	24	25	26	27	28	29
30						

July 2024						
S	M	T	W	T	F	S
	1	2	3	4	5	6
7	8	9	10	11	12	13
14	15	16	17	18	19	20
21	22	23	24	25	26	27
28	29	30	31			

August 2024						
S	M	T	W	T	F	S
				1	2	3
4	5	6	7	8	9	10
11	12	13	14	15	16	17
18	19	20	21	22	23	24
25	26	27	28	29	30	31

Eastern time in bold type
Pacific time in medium type

22 Monday

3rd ≈
☉ enters ♌ **3:44 am** 12:44 am

Sun enters Leo

23 Tuesday

3rd ≈
☽ v/c **5:58 am** 2:58 am
☽ enters ♓ **9:23 am** 6:23 am

24 Wednesday

3rd ♓

25 Thursday

3rd ♓
☽ v/c **10:31 am** 7:31 am
☽ enters ♈ **10:52 am** 7:52 am
☿ enters ♍ **6:42 pm** 3:42 pm

Eastern time in bold type
Pacific time in medium type

26 Friday
3rd ♈
☿ ℞   **9:59 am** 6:59 am
☽ v/c   **6:14 pm** 3:14 pm

27 Saturday
3rd ♈
☽ enters ♉ **1:23 pm** 10:23 am
4th Quarter **10:52 pm** 7:52 pm

28 Sunday
4th ♉

June 2024						
S	M	T	W	T	F	S
						1
2	3	4	5	6	7	8
9	10	11	12	13	14	15
16	17	18	19	20	21	22
23	24	25	26	27	28	29
30						

July 2024						
S	M	T	W	T	F	S
	1	2	3	4	5	6
7	8	9	10	11	12	13
14	15	16	17	18	19	20
21	22	23	24	25	26	27
28	29	30	31			

August 2024						
S	M	T	W	T	F	S
				1	2	3
4	5	6	7	8	9	10
11	12	13	14	15	16	17
18	19	20	21	22	23	24
25	26	27	28	29	30	31

Eastern time in bold type
Pacific time in medium type

29 Monday

4th ♉
☽ v/c   **4:59 pm**   1:59 pm
☽ enters ♊   **5:28 pm**   2:28 pm

30 Tuesday

4th ♊

31 Wednesday

4th ♊
☽ v/c   **10:46 pm**   7:46 pm
☽ enters ♋   **11:19 pm**   8:19 pm

1 Thursday

4th ♋

Lammas

2 Friday
4th ♋

3 Saturday
4th ♋
☽ v/c   **6:31 am**   3:31 am
☽ enters ♌   **7:10 am**   4:10 am

4 Sunday
4th ♌
New Moon   **7:13 am**   4:13 am
♀ enters ♍   **10:23 pm** 7:23 pm
☿ ℞   9:56 pm

Mercury retrograde until 8/28 (PDT)

July 2024						
S	M	T	W	T	F	S
	1	2	3	4	5	6
7	8	9	10	11	12	13
14	15	16	17	18	19	20
21	22	23	24	25	26	27
28	29	30	31			

August 2024						
S	M	T	W	T	F	S
				1	2	3
4	5	6	7	8	9	10
11	12	13	14	15	16	17
18	19	20	21	22	23	24
25	26	27	28	29	30	31

September 2024						
S	M	T	W	T	F	S
1	2	3	4	5	6	7
8	9	10	11	12	13	14
15	16	17	18	19	20	21
22	23	24	25	26	27	28
29	30					

5 Monday

1st ♌
☿ ℞   **12:56 am**
☽ v/c   **11:16 am**   8:16 am
☽ enters ♍   **5:17 pm**   2:17 pm

Mercury retrograde until 8/28 (EDT)

6 Tuesday

1st ♍

7 Wednesday

1st ♍

8 Thursday

1st ♍
☽ v/c   **4:40 am**   1:40 am
☽ enters ♎   **5:31 am**   2:31 am

Eastern time in bold type
Pacific time in medium type

9 Friday
1st ♎︎
☿ enters ♎︎ **12:35 pm** 9:35 am
☽ v/c   **5:45 pm** 2:45 pm

10 Saturday
1st ♎︎
☽ enters ♏︎ **6:34 pm** 3:34 pm

11 Sunday
1st ♏︎

July 2024						
S	M	T	W	T	F	S
	1	2	3	4	5	6
7	8	9	10	11	12	13
14	15	16	17	18	19	20
21	22	23	24	25	26	27
28	29	30	31			

August 2024						
S	M	T	W	T	F	S
				1	2	3
4	5	6	7	8	9	10
11	12	13	14	15	16	17
18	19	20	21	22	23	24
25	26	27	28	29	30	31

September 2024						
S	M	T	W	T	F	S
1	2	3	4	5	6	7
8	9	10	11	12	13	14
15	16	17	18	19	20	21
22	23	24	25	26	27	28
29	30					

12 Monday

1st ♏
2nd Quarter **11:19 am** 8:19 am

13 Tuesday
2nd ♏
☽ v/c   **5:01 am** 2:01 am
☽ enters ♐ **6:01 am** 3:01 am

14 Wednesday
2nd ♐
☿ enters ♌ **8:16 pm** 5:16 pm

15 Thursday
2nd ♐
☽ v/c   **12:52 pm** 9:52 am
☽ enters ♑ **1:51 pm** 10:51 am

Eastern time in bold type
Pacific time in medium type

16 Friday
2nd ♑

17 Saturday
2nd ♑
☽ v/c   **4:43 pm**   1:43 pm
☽ enters ♒   **5:45 pm**   2:45 pm

18 Sunday
2nd ♒

July 2024						
S	M	T	W	T	F	S
	1	2	3	4	5	6
7	8	9	10	11	12	13
14	15	16	17	18	19	20
21	22	23	24	25	26	27
28	29	30	31			

August 2024						
S	M	T	W	T	F	S
				1	2	3
4	5	6	7	8	9	10
11	12	13	14	15	16	17
18	19	20	21	22	23	24
25	26	27	28	29	30	31

September 2024						
S	M	T	W	T	F	S
1	2	3	4	5	6	7
8	9	10	11	12	13	14
15	16	17	18	19	20	21
22	23	24	25	26	27	28
29	30					

19 Monday

2nd ♒
☽ v/c	**2:26 pm**	11:26 am
Full Moon	**2:26 pm**	11:26 am
☽ enters ♓	**6:52 pm**	3:52 pm

20 Tuesday

3rd ♓

21 Wednesday

3rd ♓
☽ v/c	**5:54 pm**	2:54 pm
☽ enters ♈	**7:02 pm**	4:02 pm

22 Thursday

3rd ♈
☉ enters ♍	**10:55 am**	7:55 am

Sun enters Virgo

Eastern time in bold type
Pacific time in medium type

23 Friday
3rd ♈
☽ v/c **8:44 am** 5:44 am
☽ enters ♉ **8:00 pm** 5:00 pm

24 Saturday
3rd ♉
⚷ enters ♍ **7:38 pm** 4:38 pm

25 Sunday
3rd ♉
☽ v/c **9:40 pm** 6:40 pm
☽ enters ♊ **11:04 pm** 8:04 pm

July 2024						
S	M	T	W	T	F	S
	1	2	3	4	5	6
7	8	9	10	11	12	13
14	15	16	17	18	19	20
21	22	23	24	25	26	27
28	29	30	31			

August 2024						
S	M	T	W	T	F	S
				1	2	3
4	5	6	7	8	9	10
11	12	13	14	15	16	17
18	19	20	21	22	23	24
25	26	27	28	29	30	31

September 2024						
S	M	T	W	T	F	S
1	2	3	4	5	6	7
8	9	10	11	12	13	14
15	16	17	18	19	20	21
22	23	24	25	26	27	28
29	30					

Eastern time in bold type
Pacific time in medium type

Llewellyn's 2024 Pocket Planner and Ephemeris

26 Monday
3rd ♊
♀ D **3:37 am** 12:37 am
4th Quarter **5:26 am** 2:26 am

27 Tuesday
4th ♊

28 Wednesday
4th ♊
☽ v/c **3:14 am** 12:14 am
☽ enters ♋ **4:47 am** 1:47 am
☿ D **5:14 pm** 2:14 pm

29 Thursday
4th ♋
♀ enters ♎ **9:23 am** 6:23 am

30 Friday

4th ♋
| ☽ v/c | **11:24 am** | 8:24 am |
| ☽ enters ♌ | **1:09 pm** | 10:09 am |

31 Saturday

4th ♌

1 Sunday

4th ♌
♅ ℞	**11:18 am**	8:18 am
♀ enters ♑	**8:10 pm**	5:10 pm
☽ v/c	**8:25 pm**	5:25 pm
☽ enters ♍	**11:48 pm**	8:48 pm

August 2024						
S	M	T	W	T	F	S
				1	2	3
4	5	6	7	8	9	10
11	12	13	14	15	16	17
18	19	20	21	22	23	24
25	26	27	28	29	30	31

September 2024						
S	M	T	W	T	F	S
1	2	3	4	5	6	7
8	9	10	11	12	13	14
15	16	17	18	19	20	21
22	23	24	25	26	27	28
29	30					

October 2024						
S	M	T	W	T	F	S
		1	2	3	4	5
6	7	8	9	10	11	12
13	14	15	16	17	18	19
20	21	22	23	24	25	26
27	28	29	30	31		

2 Monday
4th ♍
New Moon　**9:56 pm**　6:56 pm

Labor Day

3 Tuesday
1st ♍

4 Wednesday
1st ♍
☽ v/c　　**12:06 pm**　9:06 am
☽ enters ♎ **12:12 pm**　9:12 am
♂ enters ♋ **3:46 pm** 12:46 pm

5 Thursday
1st ♎

6 Friday

1st ♎︎
☽ v/c   10:08 pm
☽ enters ♏︎   10:18 pm

7 Saturday

1st ♎︎
☽ v/c   **1:08 am**
☽ enters ♏︎   **1:18 am**

8 Sunday

1st ♏︎
♀ enters ♐︎   **6:29 am**   3:29 am
☿ enters ♍︎   11:50 pm

August 2024						
S	M	T	W	T	F	S
				1	2	3
4	5	6	7	8	9	10
11	12	13	14	15	16	17
18	19	20	21	22	23	24
25	26	27	28	29	30	31

September 2024						
S	M	T	W	T	F	S
1	2	3	4	5	6	7
8	9	10	11	12	13	14
15	16	17	18	19	20	21
22	23	24	25	26	27	28
29	30					

October 2024						
S	M	T	W	T	F	S
		1	2	3	4	5
6	7	8	9	10	11	12
13	14	15	16	17	18	19
20	21	22	23	24	25	26
27	28	29	30	31		

Eastern time in bold type
Pacific time in medium type

9 Monday

1st ♏
☿ enters ♍ **2:50 am**
☽ v/c   **1:11 pm** 10:11 am
☽ enters ♐ **1:26 pm** 10:26 am

10 Tuesday

1st ♐
2nd Quarter   11:06 pm

11 Wednesday

1st ♐
2nd Quarter **2:06 am**
☽ v/c   **8:21 pm** 5:21 pm
☽ enters ♑ **10:38 pm** 7:38 pm

12 Thursday

2nd ♑

13 Friday
2nd ♑

14 Saturday
2nd ♑
☽ v/c   **3:35 am** 12:35 am
☽ enters ♒   **3:53 am** 12:53 am

15 Sunday
2nd ♒
☽ v/c   10:04 pm

August 2024						
S	M	T	W	T	F	S
				1	2	3
4	5	6	7	8	9	10
11	12	13	14	15	16	17
18	19	20	21	22	23	24
25	26	27	28	29	30	31

September 2024						
S	M	T	W	T	F	S
1	2	3	4	5	6	7
8	9	10	11	12	13	14
15	16	17	18	19	20	21
22	23	24	25	26	27	28
29	30					

October 2024						
S	M	T	W	T	F	S
		1	2	3	4	5
6	7	8	9	10	11	12
13	14	15	16	17	18	19
20	21	22	23	24	25	26
27	28	29	30	31		

Eastern time in bold type
Pacific time in medium type

16 Monday

2nd ≈
☽ v/c   **1:04 am**
☽ enters ♓ **5:39 am** 2:39 am

17 Tuesday

2nd ♓
Full Moon **10:34 pm** 7:34 pm

Lunar Eclipse 25° ♓ 41'

18 Wednesday

3rd ♓
☽ v/c   **5:02 am** 2:02 am
☽ enters ♈ **5:24 am** 2:24 am

19 Thursday

3rd ♈

Eastern time in bold type
Pacific time in medium type

20 Friday

3rd ♈
☽ v/c   **4:39 am**   1:39 am
☽ enters ♉   **5:03 am**   2:03 am

21 Saturday

3rd ♉

UN International Day of Peace

22 Sunday

3rd ♉
☽ v/c   **6:14 am**   3:14 am
☽ enters ♊   **6:24 am**   3:24 am
☉ enters ♎ **8:44 am**   5:44 am
♀ enters ♏ **10:36 pm** 7:36 pm

Sun enters Libra • Mabon • Fall Equinox • 8:44 am EDT/ 5:44 am PDT

August 2024						
S	M	T	W	T	F	S
				1	2	3
4	5	6	7	8	9	10
11	12	13	14	15	16	17
18	19	20	21	22	23	24
25	26	27	28	29	30	31

September 2024						
S	M	T	W	T	F	S
1	2	3	4	5	6	7
8	9	10	11	12	13	14
15	16	17	18	19	20	21
22	23	24	25	26	27	28
29	30					

October 2024						
S	M	T	W	T	F	S
		1	2	3	4	5
6	7	8	9	10	11	12
13	14	15	16	17	18	19
20	21	22	23	24	25	26
27	28	29	30	31		

Eastern time in bold type
Pacific time in medium type

23 Monday
3rd ♊

24 Tuesday

3rd ♊
☽ v/c	**7:59 am**	4:59 am
☽ enters ♋	**10:50 am**	7:50 am
4th Quarter	**2:50 pm**	11:50 am

25 Wednesday

4th ♋

26 Thursday

4th ♋
☿ enters ♎	**4:09 am**	1:09 am
☽ v/c	**6:12 pm**	3:12 pm
☽ enters ♌	**6:47 pm**	3:47 pm

27 Friday

4th ♌

28 Saturday

4th ♌
☽ v/c   **11:36 pm**   8:36 pm

29 Sunday

4th ♌
☽ enters ♍   **5:42 am**   2:42 am

August 2024						
S	M	T	W	T	F	S
				1	2	3
4	5	6	7	8	9	10
11	12	13	14	15	16	17
18	19	20	21	22	23	24
25	26	27	28	29	30	31

September 2024						
S	M	T	W	T	F	S
1	2	3	4	5	6	7
8	9	10	11	12	13	14
15	16	17	18	19	20	21
22	23	24	25	26	27	28
29	30					

October 2024						
S	M	T	W	T	F	S
		1	2	3	4	5
6	7	8	9	10	11	12
13	14	15	16	17	18	19
20	21	22	23	24	25	26
27	28	29	30	31		

30 Monday
4th ♍

1 Tuesday
4th ♍
| ☽ v/c | **5:39 pm** | 2:39 pm |
| ☽ enters ♎ | **6:20 pm** | 3:20 pm |

2 Wednesday
4th ♎
New Moon **2:49 pm** 11:49 am

Rosh Hashanah begins at sundown • Solar Eclipse 10° ♎ 04'

3 Thursday
1st ♎

4 Friday

1st ♎︎
D v/c **6:40 am** 3:40 am
D enters ♏︎ **7:22 am** 4:22 am

5 Saturday

1st ♏︎

6 Sunday

1st ♏︎
D v/c **6:52 pm** 3:52 pm
D enters ♐︎ **7:34 pm** 4:34 pm

September 2024						
S	M	T	W	T	F	S
1	2	3	4	5	6	7
8	9	10	11	12	13	14
15	16	17	18	19	20	21
22	23	24	25	26	27	28
29	30					

October 2024						
S	M	T	W	T	F	S
		1	2	3	4	5
6	7	8	9	10	11	12
13	14	15	16	17	18	19
20	21	22	23	24	25	26
27	28	29	30	31		

November 2024						
S	M	T	W	T	F	S
					1	2
3	4	5	6	7	8	9
10	11	12	13	14	15	16
17	18	19	20	21	22	23
24	25	26	27	28	29	30

7 Monday
1st ✗

8 Tuesday
1st ✗
☽ v/c   10:54 pm

9 Wednesday
1st ✗
☽ v/c   **1:54 am**
♃ Rx   **3:05 am** 12:05 am
☽ enters ♑ **5:38 am** 2:38 am

10 Thursday

1st ♑
2nd Quarter **2:55 pm** 11:55 am

11 Friday

2nd ♑

☽ v/c	**11:53 am**	8:53 am
☽ enters ♒	**12:31 pm**	9:31 am
☿ D	**8:34 pm**	5:34 pm

Yom Kippur begins at sundown

12 Saturday

2nd ♒

13 Sunday

2nd ♒

☽ v/c	**10:11 am**	7:11 am
☿ enters ♏	**3:23 pm**	12:23 pm
☽ enters ♓	**3:55 pm**	12:55 pm

September 2024						
S	M	T	W	T	F	S
1	2	3	4	5	6	7
8	9	10	11	12	13	14
15	16	17	18	19	20	21
22	23	24	25	26	27	28
29	30					

October 2024						
S	M	T	W	T	F	S
		1	2	3	4	5
6	7	8	9	10	11	12
13	14	15	16	17	18	19
20	21	22	23	24	25	26
27	28	29	30	31		

November 2024						
S	M	T	W	T	F	S
					1	2
3	4	5	6	7	8	9
10	11	12	13	14	15	16
17	18	19	20	21	22	23
24	25	26	27	28	29	30

14 Monday
2nd ♓

Indigenous Peoples' Day

15 Tuesday
2nd ♓
| ☽ v/c | **4:00 pm** | 1:00 pm |
| ☽ enters ♈ | **4:34 pm** | 1:34 pm |

16 Wednesday
2nd ♈

Sukkot begins at sundown

17 Thursday
2nd ♈
Full Moon	**7:26 am**	4:26 am
☽ v/c	**3:26 pm**	12:26 pm
♀ enters ♐	**3:28 pm**	12:28 pm
☽ enters ♉	**4:00 pm**	1:00 pm

18 Friday
3rd ♉

19 Saturday
3rd ♉
☽ v/c   **3:33 pm** 12:33 pm
☽ enters ♊   **4:07 pm** 1:07 pm

20 Sunday
3rd ♊

September 2024						
S	M	T	W	T	F	S
1	2	3	4	5	6	7
8	9	10	11	12	13	14
15	16	17	18	19	20	21
22	23	24	25	26	27	28
29	30					

October 2024						
S	M	T	W	T	F	S
		1	2	3	4	5
6	7	8	9	10	11	12
13	14	15	16	17	18	19
20	21	22	23	24	25	26
27	28	29	30	31		

November 2024						
S	M	T	W	T	F	S
					1	2
3	4	5	6	7	8	9
10	11	12	13	14	15	16
17	18	19	20	21	22	23
24	25	26	27	28	29	30

21 Monday
3rd ♊
☽ v/c **5:00 pm** 2:00 pm
☽ enters ♋ **6:50 pm** 3:50 pm

22 Tuesday
3rd ♋
☉ enters ♏ **6:15 pm** 3:15 pm

Sun enters Scorpio

23 Wednesday
3rd ♋
☽ v/c 9:47 pm
☽ enters ♌ 10:24 pm

Sukkot ends

24 Thursday
3rd ♋
☽ v/c **12:47 am**
☽ enters ♌ **1:24 am**
4th Quarter **4:03 am** 1:03 am

Eastern time in bold type
Pacific time in medium type

25 Friday
4th ♌

26 Saturday
4th ♌
☽ v/c **4:04 am** 1:04 am
☽ enters ♍ **11:47 am** 8:47 am
⚷ enters ♎ 11:35 pm

27 Sunday
4th ♍
⚷ enters ♎ **2:35 am**

September 2024						
S	M	T	W	T	F	S
1	2	3	4	5	6	7
8	9	10	11	12	13	14
15	16	17	18	19	20	21
22	23	24	25	26	27	28
29	30					

October 2024						
S	M	T	W	T	F	S
		1	2	3	4	5
6	7	8	9	10	11	12
13	14	15	16	17	18	19
20	21	22	23	24	25	26
27	28	29	30	31		

November 2024						
S	M	T	W	T	F	S
					1	2
3	4	5	6	7	8	9
10	11	12	13	14	15	16
17	18	19	20	21	22	23
24	25	26	27	28	29	30

Eastern time in bold type
Pacific time in medium type

28 Monday
4th ♍
| ☽ v/c | **11:54 pm** | 8:54 pm |
| ☽ enters ♎ | | 9:30 pm |

29 Tuesday
4th ♍
| ☽ enters ♎ | **12:30 am** |

30 Wednesday
4th ♎

31 Thursday
4th ♎
| ☽ v/c | **12:57 pm** | 9:57 am |
| ☽ enters ♏ | **1:29 pm** | 10:29 am |

Halloween • Samhain

Eastern time in bold type
Pacific time in medium type

1 Friday
4th ♏
New Moon   **8:47 am**   5:47 am

All Saints' Day

2 Saturday
1st ♏
☿ enters ♐   **3:18 pm**   12:18 pm
☽ v/c   9:51 pm
☽ enters ♐   10:19 pm

3 Sunday
1st ♏
☽ v/c   **12:51 am**
☽ enters ♐   **1:19 am**
♀ enters ♏   **3:35 am**   1:35 am
♂ enters ♌   **11:10 pm**   8:10 pm

Daylight Saving Time ends at 2 am

October 2024						
S	M	T	W	T	F	S
		1	2	3	4	5
6	7	8	9	10	11	12
13	14	15	16	17	18	19
20	21	22	23	24	25	26
27	28	29	30	31		

November 2024						
S	M	T	W	T	F	S
					1	2
3	4	5	6	7	8	9
10	11	12	13	14	15	16
17	18	19	20	21	22	23
24	25	26	27	28	29	30

December 2024						
S	M	T	W	T	F	S
1	2	3	4	5	6	7
8	9	10	11	12	13	14
15	16	17	18	19	20	21
22	23	24	25	26	27	28
29	30	31				

4 Monday
1st ✗

5 Tuesday
1st ✗
☽ v/c   **5:23 am**   2:23 am
☽ enters ♑ **10:17 am** 7:17 am

Election Day (general)

6 Wednesday
1st ♑

7 Thursday
1st ♑
☽ v/c   **5:38 pm**   2:38 pm
☽ enters ≈   **5:58 pm**   2:58 pm

Eastern time in bold type
Pacific time in medium type

8 Friday
1st ≈
2nd Quarter   9:55 pm

9 Saturday

1st ≈
2nd Quarter **12:55 am**
☽ v/c   **7:23 pm**   4:23 pm
☽ enters ♓   **11:00 pm**   8:00 pm

10 Sunday
2nd ♓

October 2024							November 2024							December 2024						
S	M	T	W	T	F	S	S	M	T	W	T	F	S	S	M	T	W	T	F	S
		1	2	3	4	5						1	2	1	2	3	4	5	6	7
6	7	8	9	10	11	12	3	4	5	6	7	8	9	8	9	10	11	12	13	14
13	14	15	16	17	18	19	10	11	12	13	14	15	16	15	16	17	18	19	20	21
20	21	22	23	24	25	26	17	18	19	20	21	22	23	22	23	24	25	26	27	28
27	28	29	30	31			24	25	26	27	28	29	30	29	30	31				

11 Monday

2nd ♓
♀ enters ♑ **1:26 pm** 10:26 am
☽ v/c 10:13 pm
☽ enters ♈ 10:26 pm

Veterans Day

12 Tuesday

2nd ♓
☽ v/c **1:13 am**
☽ enters ♈ **1:26 am**

13 Wednesday

2nd ♈
☽ v/c 10:50 pm
☽ enters ♉ 10:59 pm

14 Thursday

2nd ♈
☽ v/c **1:50 am**
☽ enters ♉ **1:59 am**

Eastern time in bold type
Pacific time in medium type

15 Friday

2nd ♉

♄ D	**9:20 am**	6:20 am
Full Moon	**4:28 pm**	1:28 pm
☽ v/c		11:03 pm
☽ enters ♊		11:09 pm

16 Saturday

3rd ♉

☽ v/c	**2:03 am**	
☽ enters ♊	**2:09 am**	

17 Sunday

3rd ♊

☽ v/c	**11:09 pm**	8:09 pm

	October 2024					
S	M	T	W	T	F	S
		1	2	3	4	5
6	7	8	9	10	11	12
13	14	15	16	17	18	19
20	21	22	23	24	25	26
27	28	29	30	31		

	November 2024					
S	M	T	W	T	F	S
					1	2
3	4	5	6	7	8	9
10	11	12	13	14	15	16
17	18	19	20	21	22	23
24	25	26	27	28	29	30

	December 2024					
S	M	T	W	T	F	S
1	2	3	4	5	6	7
8	9	10	11	12	13	14
15	16	17	18	19	20	21
22	23	24	25	26	27	28
29	30	31				

18 Monday
3rd ♊
☽ enters ♋ **3:50 am** 12:50 am

19 Tuesday
3rd ♋
♀ enters ♒ **3:29 pm** 12:29 pm

20 Wednesday
3rd ♋
☽ v/c **6:20 am** 3:20 am
☽ enters ♌ **8:51 am** 5:51 am

21 Thursday
3rd ♌
☉ enters ♐ **2:56 pm** 11:56 am

Sun enters Sagittarius

Eastern time in bold type
Pacific time in medium type

22 Friday
3rd ♌
☽ v/c	**8:15 am**	5:15 am
☽ enters ♍	**6:01 pm**	3:01 pm
4th Quarter	**8:28 pm**	5:28 pm

23 Saturday
4th ♍

24 Sunday
4th ♍
☽ v/c   9:35 pm

October 2024						
S	M	T	W	T	F	S
		1	2	3	4	5
6	7	8	9	10	11	12
13	14	15	16	17	18	19
20	21	22	23	24	25	26
27	28	29	30	31		

November 2024						
S	M	T	W	T	F	S
					1	2
3	4	5	6	7	8	9
10	11	12	13	14	15	16
17	18	19	20	21	22	23
24	25	26	27	28	29	30

December 2024						
S	M	T	W	T	F	S
1	2	3	4	5	6	7
8	9	10	11	12	13	14
15	16	17	18	19	20	21
22	23	24	25	26	27	28
29	30	31				

Eastern time in bold type
Pacific time in medium type

25 Monday

4th ♍
)) v/c   **12:35 am**
)) enters ♎   **6:20 am**   3:20 am
☿ R̟   **9:42 pm**   6:42 pm

Mercury retrograde until 12/15

26 Tuesday

4th ♎

27 Wednesday

4th ♎
)) v/c   **4:14 am**   1:14 am
)) enters ♏   **7:21 pm**   4:21 pm

28 Thursday

4th ♏

Thanksgiving Day

Eastern time in bold type
Pacific time in medium type

29 Friday
4th ♏
☽ v/c   10:19 pm

30 Saturday
4th ♏
☽ v/c   **1:19 am**
☽ enters ♐   **6:53 am**   3:53 am
♀ enters ♑   **5:37 pm**   2:37 pm
New Moon   10:21 pm

1 Sunday
4th ♐
New Moon   **1:21 am**

November 2024						
S	M	T	W	T	F	S
					1	2
3	4	5	6	7	8	9
10	11	12	13	14	15	16
17	18	19	20	21	22	23
24	25	26	27	28	29	30

December 2024						
S	M	T	W	T	F	S
1	2	3	4	5	6	7
8	9	10	11	12	13	14
15	16	17	18	19	20	21
22	23	24	25	26	27	28
29	30	31				

January 2025						
S	M	T	W	T	F	S
			1	2	3	4
5	6	7	8	9	10	11
12	13	14	15	16	17	18
19	20	21	22	23	24	25
26	27	28	29	30	31	

Eastern time in bold type
Pacific time in medium type

2 Monday

1st ♐
☽ v/c   **10:47 am**   7:47 am
☽ enters ♑   **4:09 pm**   1:09 pm

3 Tuesday

1st ♑

4 Wednesday

1st ♑
☽ v/c   **6:34 pm**   3:34 pm
☽ enters ≈   **11:21 pm**   8:21 pm

5 Thursday

1st ≈

6 Friday

1st ≈
σ ℞   **6:33 pm** 3:33 pm
☽ v/c   **7:01 pm** 4:01 pm
♀ enters ≈   10:13 pm

7 Saturday

1st ≈
♀ enters ≈   **1:13 am**
♄ enters ≈   **4:16 am** 1:16 am
☽ enters ♓   **4:49 am** 1:49 am
♆ D   **6:43 pm** 3:43 pm

8 Sunday

1st ♓
2nd Quarter **10:27 am** 7:27 am

November 2024						
S	M	T	W	T	F	S
					1	2
3	4	5	6	7	8	9
10	11	12	13	14	15	16
17	18	19	20	21	22	23
24	25	26	27	28	29	30

December 2024						
S	M	T	W	T	F	S
1	2	3	4	5	6	7
8	9	10	11	12	13	14
15	16	17	18	19	20	21
22	23	24	25	26	27	28
29	30	31				

January 2025						
S	M	T	W	T	F	S
			1	2	3	4
5	6	7	8	9	10	11
12	13	14	15	16	17	18
19	20	21	22	23	24	25
26	27	28	29	30	31	

Eastern time in bold type
Pacific time in medium type

9 Monday

2nd ♓
☽ v/c   **3:45 am** 12:45 am
☽ enters ♈   **8:38 am**   5:38 am

10 Tuesday

2nd ♈
☽ v/c   **5:13 pm**   2:13 pm

11 Wednesday

2nd ♈
☽ enters ♉   **10:55 am**   7:55 am

12 Thursday

2nd ♉

13 Friday

2nd ♉
》 v/c   **7:39 am**   4:39 am
》 enters ♊ **12:22 pm** 9:22 am

14 Saturday

2nd ♊

15 Sunday

2nd ♊
Full Moon   **4:02 am**   1:02 am
》 v/c   **9:32 am**   6:32 am
》 enters ♋ **2:21 pm** 11:21 am
☿ D   **3:56 pm** 12:56 pm

November 2024						
S	M	T	W	T	F	S
					1	2
3	4	5	6	7	8	9
10	11	12	13	14	15	16
17	18	19	20	21	22	23
24	25	26	27	28	29	30

December 2024						
S	M	T	W	T	F	S
1	2	3	4	5	6	7
8	9	10	11	12	13	14
15	16	17	18	19	20	21
22	23	24	25	26	27	28
29	30	31				

January 2025						
S	M	T	W	T	F	S
			1	2	3	4
5	6	7	8	9	10	11
12	13	14	15	16	17	18
19	20	21	22	23	24	25
26	27	28	29	30	31	

Eastern time in bold type
Pacific time in medium type

16 Monday
3rd ♋

17 Tuesday
3rd ♋
☽ v/c   **1:33 pm** 10:33 am
☽ enters ♌ **6:39 pm** 3:39 pm

18 Wednesday
3rd ♌

19 Thursday
3rd ♌
☽ v/c   9:19 pm
☽ enters ♍   11:37 pm

20 Friday
3rd ♌
☽ v/c   **12:19 am**
☽ enters ♍   **2:37 am**

21 Saturday
3rd ♍
☉ enters ♑   **4:21 am**   1:21 am

Sun enters Capricorn • Yule • Winter Solstice • 4:21 am EST/1:21 am PST

22 Sunday
3rd ♍
☽ v/c   **8:27 am**   5:27 am
☽ enters ♎   **2:08 pm**   11:08 am
4th Quarter   **5:18 pm**   2:18 pm

November 2024						
S	M	T	W	T	F	S
					1	2
3	4	5	6	7	8	9
10	11	12	13	14	15	16
17	18	19	20	21	22	23
24	25	26	27	28	29	30

December 2024						
S	M	T	W	T	F	S
1	2	3	4	5	6	7
8	9	10	11	12	13	14
15	16	17	18	19	20	21
22	23	24	25	26	27	28
29	30	31				

January 2025						
S	M	T	W	T	F	S
			1	2	3	4
5	6	7	8	9	10	11
12	13	14	15	16	17	18
19	20	21	22	23	24	25
26	27	28	29	30	31	

Eastern time in bold type
Pacific time in medium type

23 Monday
4th ♎

24 Tuesday
4th ♎
☽ v/c   **5:44 am** 2:44 am

Christmas Eve

25 Wednesday
4th ♎
☽ enters ♏ **3:06 am** 12:06 am

Christmas Day • Hanukkah begins at sundown

26 Thursday
4th ♏

Kwanzaa begins

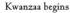

Eastern time in bold type
Pacific time in medium type

27 Friday
4th ♏
D v/c   **9:24 am**   6:24 am
D enters ♐   **2:46 pm**   11:46 am

28 Saturday
4th ♐

29 Sunday
4th ♐
Ⓨ D   **4:13 pm**   1:13 pm
D v/c   **6:34 pm**   3:34 pm
D enters ♑   **11:37 pm**   8:37 pm

November 2024						
S	M	T	W	T	F	S
					1	2
3	4	5	6	7	8	9
10	11	12	13	14	15	16
17	18	19	20	21	22	23
24	25	26	27	28	29	30

December 2024						
S	M	T	W	T	F	S
1	2	3	4	5	6	7
8	9	10	11	12	13	14
15	16	17	18	19	20	21
22	23	24	25	26	27	28
29	30	31				

January 2025						
S	M	T	W	T	F	S
			1	2	3	4
5	6	7	8	9	10	11
12	13	14	15	16	17	18
19	20	21	22	23	24	25
26	27	28	29	30	31	

Eastern time in bold type
Pacific time in medium type

30 Monday

4th V
New Moon   **5:27 pm**   2:27 pm

31 Tuesday

1st V
$\mathbb{D}$ v/c   10:02 pm

New Year's Eve

1 Wednesday

1st V
$\mathbb{D}$ v/c   **1:02 am**
$\mathbb{D}$ enters $\approx$ **5:50 am**   2:50 am

Kwanzaa ends • New Year's Day

2 Thursday

1st $\approx$
Ψ enters M, **6:15 pm**   3:15 pm
$\mathcal{Q}$ enters $\mathcal{H}$ **10:24 pm**   7:24 pm
$\mathbb{D}$ v/c   **11:13 pm**   8:13 pm

Hanukkah ends

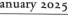

3 Friday
1st ♒
☽ enters ♓ **10:21 am** 7:21 am

4 Saturday
1st ♓

5 Sunday
1st ♓
☽ v/c   **9:30 am** 6:30 am
☽ enters ♈ **2:01 pm** 11:01 am

December 2024						
S	M	T	W	T	F	S
1	2	3	4	5	6	7
8	9	10	11	12	13	14
15	16	17	18	19	20	21
22	23	24	25	26	27	28
29	30	31				

January 2025						
S	M	T	W	T	F	S
			1	2	3	4
5	6	7	8	9	10	11
12	13	14	15	16	17	18
19	20	21	22	23	24	25
26	27	28	29	30	31	

February 2025						
S	M	T	W	T	F	S
						1
2	3	4	5	6	7	8
9	10	11	12	13	14	15
16	17	18	19	20	21	22
23	24	25	26	27	28	

Eastern time in bold type
Pacific time in medium type

The Year 2024

January

S	M	T	W	T	F	S
	1	2	3	4	5	6
7	8	9	10	11	12	13
14	15	16	17	18	19	20
21	22	23	24	25	26	27
28	29	30	31			

February

S	M	T	W	T	F	S
				1	2	3
4	5	6	7	8	9	10
11	12	13	14	15	16	17
18	19	20	21	22	23	24
25	26	27	28	29		

March

S	M	T	W	T	F	S
					1	2
3	4	5	6	7	8	9
10	11	12	13	14	15	16
17	18	19	20	21	22	23
24	25	26	27	28	29	30
31						

April

S	M	T	W	T	F	S
	1	2	3	4	5	6
7	8	9	10	11	12	13
14	15	16	17	18	19	20
21	22	23	24	25	26	27
28	29	30				

May

S	M	T	W	T	F	S
			1	2	3	4
5	6	7	8	9	10	11
12	13	14	15	16	17	18
19	20	21	22	23	24	25
26	27	28	29	30	31	

June

S	M	T	W	T	F	S
						1
2	3	4	5	6	7	8
9	10	11	12	13	14	15
16	17	18	19	20	21	22
23	24	25	26	27	28	29
30						

July

S	M	T	W	T	F	S
	1	2	3	4	5	6
7	8	9	10	11	12	13
14	15	16	17	18	19	20
21	22	23	24	25	26	27
28	29	30	31			

August

S	M	T	W	T	F	S
				1	2	3
4	5	6	7	8	9	10
11	12	13	14	15	16	17
18	19	20	21	22	23	24
25	26	27	28	29	30	31

September

S	M	T	W	T	F	S
1	2	3	4	5	6	7
8	9	10	11	12	13	14
15	16	17	18	19	20	21
22	23	24	25	26	27	28
29	30					

October

S	M	T	W	T	F	S
		1	2	3	4	5
6	7	8	9	10	11	12
13	14	15	16	17	18	19
20	21	22	23	24	25	26
27	28	29	30	31		

November

S	M	T	W	T	F	S
					1	2
3	4	5	6	7	8	9
10	11	12	13	14	15	16
17	18	19	20	21	22	23
24	25	26	27	28	29	30

December

S	M	T	W	T	F	S
1	2	3	4	5	6	7
8	9	10	11	12	13	14
15	16	17	18	19	20	21
22	23	24	25	26	27	28
29	30	31				

The Year 2025

January
S	M	T	W	T	F	S
			1	2	3	4
5	6	7	8	9	10	11
12	13	14	15	16	17	18
19	20	21	22	23	24	25
26	27	28	29	30	31	

February
S	M	T	W	T	F	S
						1
2	3	4	5	6	7	8
9	10	11	12	13	14	15
16	17	18	19	20	21	22
23	24	25	26	27	28	

March
S	M	T	W	T	F	S
						1
2	3	4	5	6	7	8
9	10	11	12	13	14	15
16	17	18	19	20	21	22
23	24	25	26	27	28	29
30	31					

April
S	M	T	W	T	F	S
		1	2	3	4	5
6	7	8	9	10	11	12
13	14	15	16	17	18	19
20	21	22	23	24	25	26
27	28	29	30			

May
S	M	T	W	T	F	S
				1	2	3
4	5	6	7	8	9	10
11	12	13	14	15	16	17
18	19	20	21	22	23	24
25	26	27	28	29	30	31

June
S	M	T	W	T	F	S
1	2	3	4	5	6	7
8	9	10	11	12	13	14
15	16	17	18	19	20	21
22	23	24	25	26	27	28
29	30					

July
S	M	T	W	T	F	S
		1	2	3	4	5
6	7	8	9	10	11	12
13	14	15	16	17	18	19
20	21	22	23	24	25	26
27	28	29	30	31		

August
S	M	T	W	T	F	S
					1	2
3	4	5	6	7	8	9
10	11	12	13	14	15	16
17	18	19	20	21	22	23
24	25	26	27	28	29	30
31						

September
S	M	T	W	T	F	S
	1	2	3	4	5	6
7	8	9	10	11	12	13
14	15	16	17	18	19	20
21	22	23	24	25	26	27
28	29	30				

October
S	M	T	W	T	F	S
			1	2	3	4
5	6	7	8	9	10	11
12	13	14	15	16	17	18
19	20	21	22	23	24	25
26	27	28	29	30	31	

November
S	M	T	W	T	F	S
						1
2	3	4	5	6	7	8
9	10	11	12	13	14	15
16	17	18	19	20	21	22
23	24	25	26	27	28	29
30						

December
S	M	T	W	T	F	S
	1	2	3	4	5	6
7	8	9	10	11	12	13
14	15	16	17	18	19	20
21	22	23	24	25	26	27
28	29	30	31			

JANUARY 2023

Last Aspect / Ingress / Last Aspect / Ingress (top tables)

☽ Last Aspect		☽ Ingress		
day	ET / hr:mn / PT	asp.	sign day	ET / hr:mn / PT
2	5:16 pm 2:16 pm	△♀	♊ 2	9:44 am 6:44 am
4	7:08 pm 4:08 pm	□♀	⊗ 5	6:15 am
5	5:23 pm 2:23 pm	△♄	♍ 7	9:40 pm 6:40 pm
9	8:52 pm 5:52 pm	△♂	♎ 10	10:15 am 7:15 am
12	6:06 pm 3:06 pm	□♀	♏ 12	9:56 pm 6:56 pm
15	3:40 am 12:40 am	✶♀	♐ 15	7:08 am 4:08 am
17	9:27 am 6:27 am	□♄	♑ 17 12:33 pm 9:33 am
19	5:09 pm 2:09 pm	△♀	⌛ 19	2:11 pm 11:11 am
21 10:52 pm 7:52 pm	△♀	≈ 21	1:29 pm 10:29 am
23	5:19 am 2:19 am	□♀	♓ 23 12:36 pm 9:36 am

☽ Last Aspect		☽ Ingress		
day	ET / hr:mn / PT	asp.	sign day	ET / hr:mn / PT
25 11:12 am 8:12 am	✶♄	♈ 25	1:48 pm 10:48 am
27	4:01 pm 1:01 pm	△♀	♉ 27	6:42 pm 3:42 pm
	9:52 pm	□♀	♊ 30	1:01 am 12:35 am
30 12:52 am		♊ 30	3:35 am 12:35 am

☽ Phases & Eclipses

	day	ET / hr:mn / PT
Full Moon	6	6:08 pm 3:08 pm
4th Quarter	14	9:10 pm 6:10 pm
New Moon	21	3:53 pm 12:53 pm
2nd Quarter	28 10:19 am 7:19 am

Planet Ingress

	day	ET / hr:mn / PT
♀ ≈	2	9:09 pm 6:09 pm
♀ ♈	12	10:30 pm
✶✶✶♓	18	1:30 am
♀ ♓	20	3:30 am 12:30 am
☉ ≈	26	9:33 pm 6:33 pm

Planetary Motion

	day	ET / hr:mn / PT
♂ D	12	3:56 pm 12:56 pm
♅ D	22	8:12 am 5:12 am
♇ D	22	5:59 pm 2:59 pm

---

1 SUNDAY
☽ ✶ ♄ 12:25 am
☉ □ ♇ 5:09 am 2:09 am
☽ □ ♀ 8:42 am 5:42 am
☽ △ ♀ 4:52 pm 1:52 pm

2 MONDAY
☽ ✶ ♀ 1:44 am
☽ △ ♀ 7:15 am 4:15 am
☽ ✶ ♄ 7:53 am 4:53 am
☽ ☌ ♀ 10:59 am 7:59 am
☽ △ ♄ 9:48 am 6:48 am

3 TUESDAY
☽ 12:37 am
☽ ✶ ♀ 2:47 am 11:47 pm
9:30 am

4 WEDNESDAY
☽ 12:30 am
☽ △ ♀ 3:30 am 12:30 am
☽ ☌ ♀ 4:08 am 1:08 am
☽ ✶ ♄ 2:10 am 11:10 am
☽ □ ♀ 6:54 pm 3:54 pm
☽ ✶ ♀ 7:08 pm 4:08 pm

5 THURSDAY
☽ ✶ ♀ 4:50 am 1:50 am
☽ □ ♀ 11:43 am 8:43 am

6 FRIDAY
☽ ☌ ♀ 2:08 am
☽ ✶ ♄ 3:30 am 12:30 am
☽ △ ♀ 6:08 am 3:08 am
☽ ✶ ♀ 8:36 am 5:36 am

7 SATURDAY
☽ △ ♄ 7:30 am 4:30 am
☽ ✶ ♀ 7:42 am 4:42 am
☽ □ ♀ 7:57 am 4:57 am
☽ △ ♀ 5:23 pm 11:00 pm

8 SUNDAY
☽ □ ♀ 2:00 am
☽ ✶ ♀ 11:52 am 8:52 am
☽ △ ♄ 2:19 pm 11:19 am
☽ ✶ ♀ 6:23 pm 3:23 pm

9 MONDAY
☽ △ ♀ 3:05 am 12:05 am
☽ □ ♄ 4:02 am 1:02 am
☽ ✶ ♀ 10:22 am 7:22 am
☽ △ ♀ 12:26 pm 9:26 am
☽ ☌ ♀ 8:52 pm 5:52 pm

10 TUESDAY
☽ 12:50 am 9:50 am
☽ ✶ ♀ 4:16 pm 1:16 pm
11:56 pm

11 WEDNESDAY
☽ ✶ ♀ 2:36 am
☽ □ ♀ 5:58 am 4:25 am
☽ △ ♀ 4:17 pm 6:58 am
☽ △ ♀ 10:02 pm 1:17 pm
7:02 pm

12 THURSDAY
☽ ☌ ♀ 6:06 am 3:08 am
☽ ✶ ♄ 6:21 am 5:21 am
☽ △ ♀ 3:25 am 6:25 am
☽ □ ♀ 6:06 pm 3:06 pm

13 FRIDAY
☽ □ ♀ 3:34 am 12:34 am
☽ ✶ ♄ 4:11 am 6:11 am
☽ △ ♀ 1:46 pm 10:46 am
☽ ✶ ♀ 4:55 pm 1:55 pm
9:58 pm
11:54 pm

14 SATURDAY
☽ 12:58 am 12:05 pm
☽ ✶ ♀ 1:47 pm 1:02 am
☽ △ ♀ 2:54 am 7:22 am
☽ △ ♀ 6:22 pm 9:26 am
7:47 pm 5:52 pm

15 SUNDAY
☽ □ ♀ 8:22 am 5:22 pm
☽ □ ♀ 9:10 am 6:10 pm

16 MONDAY
☽ ✶ ♀ 3:40 am 12:40 am
☽ ✶ ♀ 1:07 pm 10:07 am
☽ △ ♀ 10:08 pm 7:08 pm
10:47 pm

17 TUESDAY
☽ ☌ ♀ 10:17 am 7:17 am
☽ ✶ ♄ 2:09 pm 11:09 am
9:48 pm
10:42 am
11:27 pm

18 WEDNESDAY
☽ 12:48 am
☽ ✶ ♀ 7:36 am 4:36 am
☽ □ ♀ 9:27 am 6:27 am
☽ □ ♀ 6:41 pm 3:41 pm
11:39 pm

19 THURSDAY
☽ △ ♀ 3:17 am 12:17 am
☽ ✶ ♀ 5:09 am 2:09 am
☽ □ ♀ 11:24 am 10:13 am
☽ △ ♀ 1:13 pm 8:29 am
☽ ✶ ♀ 8:29 pm 5:29 pm

20 FRIDAY
☽ △ ♀ 3:30 am 12:30 am
☽ ✶ ♀ 3:42 am 12:42 am
☽ ☌ ♀ 1:55 pm 10:55 am
☽ □ ♀ 8:06 pm 5:06 pm
11:10 pm

21 SATURDAY
☽ ✶ ♀ 2:10 am
☽ △ ♀ 3:01 am 12:01 am
☽ □ ♀ 10:52 am 7:52 am
☽ □ ♀ 12:43 pm 9:43 am
☽ ✶ ♀ 8:09 pm 12:53 pm
5:09 pm

22 SUNDAY
☽ △ ♀ 3:02 am 12:02 am
☽ ✶ ♀ 3:36 am 12:36 am
☽ □ ♀ 12:49 pm 9:49 am
☽ △ ♀ 5:13 pm 2:13 pm
11:03 pm

23 MONDAY
☽ △ ♀ 2:03 am
☽ ✶ ♀ 5:19 am 2:19 am
6:44 am
7:05 pm

24 TUESDAY
☽ ✶ ♀ 10:02 am 7:02 am
☽ ☌ ♀ 6:30 am 3:30 am
☽ ✶ ♀ 7:59 pm 4:59 pm
9:33 pm 11:56 pm

25 WEDNESDAY
☽ ☌ ♀ 2:56 am 1:59 am
☽ ✶ ♀ 4:59 am 9:43 am
☽ ✶ ♀ 12:43 pm 5:30 pm
8:30 pm 11:42 pm

26 THURSDAY
☽ ☌ ♀ 2:42 am 2:30 am
☽ ✶ ♄ 5:30 am 7:45 am
☽ □ ♀ 10:45 am 8:12 am
☽ ✶ ♀ 3:59 pm 12:59 pm
☽ ✶ ♀ 11:59 pm 8:59 pm

27 FRIDAY
☽ ✶ ♀ 5:40 am 2:40 am
☽ △ ♀ 10:08 am 7:08 am
☽ ✶ ♀ 3:38 pm 12:38 pm

28 SATURDAY
☽ ✶ ♀ 6:50 am 3:50 am
☽ △ ♀ 10:13 am 7:13 am
☽ ✶ ♀ 4:01 pm 1:01 pm
☽ ☌ ♀ 8:56 pm 5:56 pm

29 SUNDAY
☽ ✶ ♀ 3:02 am
☽ □ ♀ 7:03 am 3:45 am
☽ △ ♀ 8:45 am 6:16 am
☽ ✶ ♀ 9:16 am 9:52 am

30 MONDAY
☽ ☌ ♀ 12:52 am 9:24 am
☽ □ ♀ 12:24 am 5:45 am
☽ △ ♀ 3:01 am 6:16 pm
☽ ✶ ♀ 11:27 am 9:52 pm

31 TUESDAY
☽ △ ♀ 1:24 am
☽ □ ♀ 9:06 am 6:06 am
☽ △ ♀ 12:27 pm 9:27 am
☽ ✶ ♀ 6:14 pm 3:14 pm
11:21 pm

Eastern time in bold type
Pacific time in medium type

JANUARY 2023

DATE	SID.TIME	SUN	MOON	NODE	MERCURY	VENUS	MARS	JUPITER	SATURN	URANUS	NEPTUNE	PLUTO	CERES	PALLAS	JUNO	VESTA	CHIRON
1 Su	6 41 33	10♑17 02	3♑39	11♉45℞	23♑42℞	27♑23	9♊04℞	1♈12	22≈25	15♉09℞	22♓52	27♑39	3♎09	20♋49℞	24♊34	14≈01	11♈58
2 M	6 45 30	11 18 11	16 14	11 44	23 06	28 38	8 55	1 19	22 31	15 08	22 53	27 41	3 22	20 30	25 00	14 25	11 59
3 T	6 49 26	12 19 19	28 36	11 44	22 18	29 53	8 47	1 26	22 37	15 07	22 54	27 43	3 34	20 10	25 25	14 48	11 59
4 W	6 53 23	13 20 27	10≈48	11 39	21 20	1≈08	8 39	1 34	22 43	15 06	22 55	27 45	3 46	19 50	25 51	15 12	12 00
5 Th	6 57 19	14 21 35	22 53	11 33	20 13	2 23	8 32	1 42	22 49	15 05	22 56	27 47	3 58	19 30	26 17	15 36	12 00
6 F	7 1 16	15 22 43	4♓52	11 23	18 59	3 39	8 26	1 50	22 56	15 04	22 57	27 49	4 09	19 10	26 43	16 00	12 01
7 Sa	7 5 13	16 23 51	16 47	11 11	17 40	4 54	8 21	1 58	23 02	15 03	22 59	27 51	4 20	18 50	27 10	16 24	12 02
8 Su	7 9 9	17 24 59	28 41	10 58	16 20	6 09	8 17	2 06	23 08	15 02	23 00	27 53	4 31	18 29	27 37	16 48	12 03
9 M	7 13 6	18 26 06	10♈33	10 44	15 00	7 24	8 14	2 14	23 15	15 02	23 01	27 55	4 41	18 09	28 03	17 12	12 04
10 T	7 17 2	19 27 14	22 26	10 32	13 42	8 39	8 11	2 23	23 21	15 01	23 01	27 57	4 51	17 49	28 30	17 37	12 05
11 W	7 20 59	20 28 21	4♉21	10 21	12 31	9 54	8 09	2 32	23 28	15 01	23 03	27 59	5 01	17 29	28 58	18 01	12 06
12 Th	7 24 55	21 29 29	16 21	10 13	11 26	11 09	8 08 D	2 40	23 34	15 00	23 03	28 01	5 10	17 09	29 25	18 26	12 07
13 F	7 28 52	22 30 36	28 30	10 08	10 30	12 24	8 08	2 49	23 41	15 00	23 05	28 03	5 19	16 49	29 53	18 50	12 08
14 Sa	7 32 48	23 31 43	10♊51	10 05	9 42	13 39	8 08	2 58	23 47	14 59	23 06	28 05	5 28	16 29	0♋20	19 15	12 09
15 Su	7 36 45	24 32 50	23 29	10 04 D	9 05	14 54	8 09	3 08	23 54	14 58	23 09	28 07	5 36	16 10	0 48	19 40	12 10
16 M	7 40 42	25 33 57	6♋28	10 05℞	8 37	16 09	8 11	3 17	24 00	14 58	23 10	28 09	5 44	15 51	1 16	20 05	12 11
17 T	7 44 38	26 35 04	19 53	10 04	8 19	17 24	8 14	3 26	24 07	14 57	23 11	28 11	5 52	15 32	1 44	20 29	12 12
18 W	7 48 35	27 36 10	3♌47	9 58	8 09 D	18 39	8 18	3 36	24 14	14 57	23 13	28 12	5 59	15 13	2 13	20 54	12 13
19 Th	7 52 31	28 37 17	18 10	9 51	8 09	19 54	8 22	3 46	24 21	14 57	23 14	28 14	6 06	14 55	2 41	21 20	12 14
20 F	7 56 28	29 38 23	3♍00	9 41	8 17	21 08	8 27	3 56	24 27	14 57	23 16	28 16	6 12	14 38	3 10	21 45	12 15
21 Sa	8 0 24	0≈39 29	18 11	9 30	8 32	22 23	8 32	4 06	24 34	14 57	23 17	28 18	6 18	14 20	3 39	22 10	12 16
22 Su	8 4 21	1 40 34	3♎32	9 18	8 54	23 38	8 39	4 16	24 41	14 56 D	23 19	28 20	6 23	14 04	4 08	22 35	12 20
23 M	8 8 17	2 41 38	18 53	9 07	9 22	24 53	8 46	4 26	24 48	14 56	23 21	28 22	6 29	13 47	4 37	23 01	12 22
24 T	8 12 14	3 42 42	4♏00	8 59	9 56	26 08	8 53	4 36	24 55	14 56	23 23	28 24	6 33	13 32	5 06	23 26	12 23
25 W	8 16 11	4 43 44	18 46	8 53	10 35	27 23	9 02	4 47	25 02	14 57	23 24	28 26	6 38	13 16	5 36	23 52	12 25
26 Th	8 20 7	5 44 46	3♐03	8 51	11 19	28 37	9 10	4 57	25 09	14 57	23 27	28 28	6 42	13 02	6 05	24 17	12 27
27 F	8 24 4	6 45 46	16 51	8 50	12 07	29 52	9 20	5 08	25 16	14 57	23 29	28 30	6 45	12 48	6 35	24 43	12 28
28 Sa	8 28 0	7 46 46	0♑10	8 50	12 58	1♓07	9 30	5 19	25 23	14 57	23 31	28 32	6 48	12 34	7 05	25 08	12 30
29 Su	8 31 57	8 47 44	13 03	8 50	13 54	2 21	9 41	5 30	25 30	14 57	23 32	28 34	6 51	12 22	7 35	25 34	12 32
30 M	8 35 53	9 48 41	25 35	8 49	14 52	3 36	9 52	5 41	25 37	14 57	23 34	28 36	6 53	12 10	8 05	26 00	12 34
31 T	8 39 50	10 49 37	7≈51	8 47	15 53	4 51	10 04	5 52	25 44	14 58	23 36	28 38	6 55	11 58	8 36	26 26	12 36

EPHEMERIS CALCULATED FOR 12 MIDNIGHT GREENWICH MEAN TIME. ALL OTHER DATA AND FACING ASPECTARIAN PAGE IN **EASTERN TIME (BOLD)** AND PACIFIC TIME (REGULAR).

FEBRUARY 2023

⟩ Last Aspect			⟩ Ingress			
day	ET / hr:mn / PT	asp	sign	day	ET / hr:mn / PT	
1	6:58 am 3:58 am	△ ♀	≈	1	3:11 pm 12:11 pm	
3	10:19 pm	♂ ♀	⌂	3	3:48 am 12:48 am	
4	1:19 am	♂ ♀	⌂	3	3:48 am 12:48 am	
6	9:15 am 6:15 am	♂ ♀	♈	6	4:14 am 1:14 am	
8	10:40 pm	△ ♀	♉	8	3:47 am 12:47 am	
9	1:40 am	♂ ♀	♉	8	3:47 am 12:47 am	
11	11:41 am 8:41 am	♂ ♀	♊	11	1:34 am 10:34 am	
13	6:52 am 3:52 am	♂ ♀	♋	13	8:31 am 5:31 am	
15	8:06 am 5:06 am	✶ ♀	♌	15	6:12:00 am	

⟩ Last Aspect			⟩ Ingress			
day	ET / hr:mn / PT	asp	sign	day	ET / hr:mn / PT	
17	1:18 pm 8:18 am	♂ ♀	≈	17		9:35 pm
18			≈	18	12:35 am	
19	9:00 pm 6:00 pm		♈	19	11:56 pm	8:56 pm
21	11:06 pm 8:06 pm		♈	21		9:14 pm
22			Ⴒ	22	12:14 am	
23		11:22 pm	Ⴒ	24	12:29 am	
24	2:22 am		♉	24	3:29 am 12:29 am	
26	9:42 am 6:42 am		♊	26	10:48 am 7:48 am	
28	8:07 pm 5:07 pm		♋	28	9:40 pm 6:40 pm	

Planet Ingress

		day	ET / hr:mn / PT	
♀	≈	11	7:11:47 pm 8:47 pm	
♂	≈	11	6:22 am 3:22 am	
⊙	ℋ	18	5:34 am 2:34 am	
♀	ℋ	20	2:56 am 11:56 pm	

Phases & Eclipses

phase	day	ET / hr:mn / PT
Full Moon	5	1:29 pm 10:29 am
4th Quarter	13	11:01 am 8:01 am
New Moon	19	11:06 pm
New Moon	20	2:06 am
2nd Quarter	27	3:06 am 12:06 am

Planetary Motion

		day	ET / hr:mn / PT
♂	R	3	2:13 pm 11:13 am
♀	D	16	9:26 am 6:26 am

---

1 WEDNESDAY
♀ 2:21 am
♀ 6:58 am 3:58 am
♀ 9:33 am

2 THURSDAY
♀ 3:55 am 12:55 am
♀ 7:15 am 4:15 am
♀ 12:42 pm 9:42 am
♀ 7:12 pm 4:12 pm
♀ 9:27 pm 6:27 pm

3 FRIDAY
♀ 7:09 am 3:09 am
♀ 3:02 pm 12:02 pm
♀ 8:09 pm 5:09 pm
♀ 9:50 pm 6:50 pm

4 SATURDAY
♀ 1:19 am
♀ 5:34 am 2:34 am
♀ 10:29 am

5 SUNDAY
♀ 2:35 am
♀ 2:58 am
♀ 10:08 am 7:08 am
♀ 1:29 pm 10:29 am

6 MONDAY
♀ 2:37 am
♀ 3:44 am 12:44 am
♀ 9:15 am 6:15 am
♀ 1:26 am 10:56 am

7 TUESDAY
♀ 6:51 am 3:51 am
♀ 4:05 pm 1:05 pm
♀ 9:01 pm 6:01 pm
♀ 10:16 pm 7:16 pm

8 WEDNESDAY
♀ 12:29 am
♀ 6:58 am 3:58 am
♀ 9:32 pm 6:32 pm
♀ 9:49 pm 6:49 pm

9 THURSDAY
♀ 1:40 am
♀ 7:02 am 4:02 am

10 FRIDAY
♀ 4:25 am 1:25 am
♀ 9:08 am 6:08 am
♀ 12:16 pm 9:16 am
♀ 3:18 am 12:18 am
♀ 10:39 pm 7:39 pm

11 SATURDAY
♀ 2:54 am
♀ 8:07 am 5:07 am
♀ 11:41 am 8:41 am
♀ 2:27 am 11:27 pm

12 SUNDAY
♀ 2:07 am
♀ 2:28 am
♀ 5:43 am 2:43 am
♀ 6:37 am 3:37 am

13 MONDAY
♀ 3:16 am
♀ 3:49 am
♀ 7:01 am 4:01 am
♀ 8:52 am 5:52 am

14 TUE-DAY
♀ 3:39 am 12:39 am
♀ 11:56 am 8:56 am
♀ 10:26 pm 7:26 pm
♀ 3:59 pm 12:59 pm

15 WEDNESDAY
♀ 7:25 am 4:25 am
♀ 2:06 pm 11:06 am
♀ 5:43 pm 2:43 pm
♀ 7:03 pm 4:03 pm
♀ 10:33 am

16 THURSDAY
♀ 11:48 am 8:48 am
♀ 12:17 pm 9:17 am
♀ 3:11 pm 12:11 pm
♀ 9:12 am
♀ 9:55 am

17 FRIDAY
♀ 12:12 am
♀ 2:28 am
♀ 3:16 am 12:16 am
♀ 8:06 am 5:06 am
♀ 9:13 am 6:13 am
♀ 9:15 am 6:15 am
♀ 10:23 am 7:23 am
♀ 11:18 am 8:18 am
♀ 11:22 pm 8:22 pm

18 SATURDAY
♀ 9:51 am 6:51 am
♀ 11:32 am 8:32 am
♀ 3:51 pm 12:51 pm
♀ 5:35 pm 2:35 pm
♀ 9:42 pm
♀ 10:01 pm

19 SUNDAY
♀ 12:42 am
♀ 1:01 am
♀ 12:05 pm 9:05 am
♀ 2:48 pm 11:48 am
♀ 9:00 pm 6:00 pm

20 MONDAY
♀ 2:06 am
♀ 3:57 am 12:57 am
♀ 7:24 am
♀ 9:20 am
♀ 10:44 am

21 TUESDAY
♀ 12:20 am
♀ 1:44 am
♀ 2:52 pm 11:52 am
♀ 5:22 pm 2:22 pm
♀ 9:35 pm 6:35 pm
♀ 11:06 pm 8:06 pm

22 WEDNESDAY
♀ 4:26 am 1:26 am
♀ 6:07 am 3:07 am
♀ 3:14 pm 12:14 pm
♀ 5:48 pm 2:48 pm
♀ 11:01 pm

23 THURSDAY
♀ 2:01 am
♀ 4:44 am 1:44 am
♀ 6:03 am 3:03 am
♀ 5:34 am 2:34 am
♀ 10:06 am
♀ 11:22 am

24 FRIDAY
♀ 1:06 am
♀ 1:12 pm 10:12 am
♀ 2:02 pm 11:02 am
♀ 11:19 pm 8:19 pm

25 SATURDAY
♀ 7:25 am 4:25 am
♀ 11:51 am 8:51 am
♀ 7:16 pm 4:16 pm
♀ 9:15 pm

26 SUNDAY
♀ 12:15 am
♀ 8:45 am 5:45 am
♀ 9:42 am 6:42 am
♀ 11:11 am 8:11 am

27 MONDAY
♀ 3:06 am 12:06 am
♀ 3:24 am 12:24 am
♀ 9:08 am 6:08 am
♀ 11:03 am 8:03 am
♀ 4:51 pm 1:51 pm
♀ 11:21 pm 8:21 pm

28 TUESDAY
♀ 10:46 am 7:46 am
♀ 2:27 pm 11:27 am
♀ 8:07 pm 5:07 pm
♀ 8:41 pm 5:40 pm

Eastern time in bold type
Pacific time in medium type

FEBRUARY 2023

DATE	SID.TIME	SUN	MOON	NODE	MERCURY	VENUS	MARS	JUPITER	SATURN	URANUS	NEPTUNE	PLUTO	CERES	PALLAS	JUNO	VESTA	CHIRON
1 W	8 43 46	11≈50 31	19♊56	8♉42R	16♑57	6♓05	10♊17	6♈03	25≈51	14♉59	23♓36	28♑36	6♎57	11♋47R	9♈06	26♓52	12♈38
2 Th	8 47 43	12 51 25	1♋54	8 35	18 03	7 20	10 30	6 15	25 58	14 59	23 38	28 42	6 58	11 37	9 37	27 18	12 40
3 F	8 51 40	13 52 17	13 47	8 24	19 12	8 34	10 43	6 26	26 05	15 00	23 40	28 44	6 58R	11 28	10 07	27 44	12 42
4 Sa	8 55 36	14 53 08	25 39	8 11	20 22	9 49	10 57	6 38	26 13	15 00	23 41	28 46	6 58	11 19	10 38	28 10	12 45
5 Su	8 59 33	15 53 58	7♌31	7 56	21 35	11 03	11 12	6 49	26 20	15 01	23 43	28 48	6 58	11 11	11 09	28 36	12 47
6 M	9 3 29	16 54 46	19 25	7 41	22 49	12 18	11 27	7 01	26 27	15 02	23 45	28 49	6 57	11 03	11 40	29 02	12 49
7 T	9 7 26	17 55 34	1♍23	7 27	24 05	13 32	11 43	7 13	26 34	15 02	23 47	28 51	6 56	10 56	12 11	29 28	12 51
8 W	9 11 22	18 56 20	13 25	7 15	25 21	14 46	11 59	7 25	26 41	15 03	23 49	28 53	6 54	10 50	12 42	29 55	12 54
9 Th	9 15 19	19 57 05	25 32	7 06	26 40	16 01	12 15	7 37	26 48	15 04	23 51	28 55	6 52	10 45	13 14	0♈21	12 56
10 F	9 19 15	20 57 49	7♎48	7 00	28 00	17 15	12 32	7 49	26 56	15 05	23 53	28 57	6 50	10 40	13 45	0 47	12 58
11 Sa	9 23 12	21 58 32	20 13	6 56	29 21	18 29	12 49	8 01	27 03	15 06	23 55	28 59	6 47	10 36	14 17	1 14	13 01
12 Su	9 27 9	22 59 14	2♏53	6 55D	0≈43	19 43	13 07	8 13	27 10	15 07	23 57	29 01	6 44	10 33	14 48	1 40	13 03
13 M	9 31 5	23 59 54	15 50	6 55R	2 07	20 58	13 25	8 25	27 17	15 08	23 59	29 02	6 40	10 30	15 20	2 07	13 06
14 T	9 35 2	25 00 34	29 09	6 55	3 32	22 12	13 44	8 38	27 25	15 09	24 01	29 04	6 36	10 28	15 52	2 33	13 08
15 W	9 38 58	26 01 13	12♐51	6 54	4 57	23 26	14 03	8 50	27 32	15 10	24 03	29 06	6 31	10 27	16 24	3 00	13 11
16 Th	9 42 55	27 01 51	26 51	6 51	6 24	24 40	14 22	9 03	27 39	15 12	24 05	29 08	6 26	10 26D	16 56	3 26	13 14
17 F	9 46 51	28 02 27	11♑34	6 45	7 52	25 54	14 42	9 15	27 46	15 13	24 07	29 10	6 20	10 26	17 28	3 53	13 16
18 Sa	9 50 48	29 03 02	26 30	6 37	9 21	27 08	15 02	9 28	27 54	15 14	24 09	29 11	6 14	10 26	18 00	4 20	13 19
19 Su	9 54 45	0♓03 36	11≈39	6 27	10 51	28 22	15 23	9 41	28 01	15 16	24 11	29 13	6 08	10 29	18 33	4 46	13 22
20 M	9 58 41	1 04 09	26 53	6 16	12 22	29 36	15 44	9 54	28 08	15 17	24 14	29 15	6 01	10 29	19 05	5 13	13 24
21 T	10 2 38	2 04 39	11♓59	6 07	13 53	0♈49	16 05	10 07	28 16	15 18	24 16	29 17	5 54	10 32	19 38	5 40	13 27
22 W	10 6 34	3 05 09	26 49	5 59	15 26	2 03	16 27	10 20	28 23	15 20	24 18	29 18	5 46	10 35	20 10	6 07	13 30
23 Th	10 10 31	4 05 36	11♈14	5 54	17 00	3 17	16 49	10 33	28 30	15 21	24 20	29 20	5 38	10 39	20 43	6 34	13 33
24 F	10 14 27	5 06 01	25 11	5 52D	18 35	4 31	17 11	10 46	28 37	15 23	24 22	29 22	5 30	10 43	21 16	7 01	13 36
25 Sa	10 18 24	6 06 25	8♉39	5 51	20 10	5 44	17 33	10 59	28 44	15 25	24 24	29 23	5 21	10 48	21 49	7 27	13 39
26 Su	10 22 20	7 06 47	21 39	5 52	21 47	6 58	17 56	11 12	28 52	15 26	24 27	29 25	5 12	10 53	22 22	7 54	13 42
27 M	10 26 17	8 07 07	4♊17	5 53R	23 24	8 11	18 19	11 25	28 59	15 28	24 29	29 26	5 02	10 59	22 55	8 21	13 45
28 T	10 30 13	9 07 25	16 35	5 52	25 03	9 25	18 43	11 39	29 06	15 30	24 31	29 28	4 53	11 06	23 28	8 48	13 48

EPHEMERIS CALCULATED FOR 12 MIDNIGHT GREENWICH MEAN TIME. ALL OTHER DATA AND FACING ASPECTARIAN PAGE IN **EASTERN TIME (BOLD)** AND PACIFIC TIME (REGULAR).

MARCH 2023

☽ Last Aspect day	ET / hr:mn / PT		asp	☽ Ingress sign	day	ET / hr:mn / PT	
3	9:22 am	6:22 am	☍♇	♌	3	10:16 am	7:16 am
5	10:18 pm	7:18 pm	☍♄	♍	5	10:38 pm	7:38 pm
8	9:07 am	6:07 am	△♇	♎	8	9:44 am	6:44 am
10	6:37 pm	3:37 pm	□♇	♏	10	7:06 pm	4:06 pm
12		11:58 pm	⚹♇	♐	13	3:21 am	12:21 am
13	2:58 am		⚹♇	♐	13	3:21 am	12:21 am
15	4:50 am	1:50 am	△♀	♑	15	8:06 am	5:06 am
17	10:14 am	7:14 am	☌♇	♒	17	10:25 am	7:25 am
19	6:33 am	3:33 am	△♂	♓	19	11:12 am	8:12 am
21	11:58 am	8:58 am	⚹♇	♈	21	12:01 pm	9:01 am
23	1:13 pm	10:13 am	⚹♂	♉	23	2:42 pm	11:42 am
25	12:19 pm	9:19 am	⚹♆	♊	25	8:42 pm	5:42 pm
27	9:39 pm	6:39 pm	□♆	♋	28	6:22 am	3:22 am
30	9:45 am	6:45 am	△♆	♌	30	6:31 pm	3:31 pm

☽ Phases & Eclipses phase	day	ET / hr:mn / PT	
Full Moon	7	7:40 am	4:40 am
4th Quarter	14	10:08 pm	7:08 pm
New Moon	21	1:23 pm	10:23 am
2nd Quarter	28	10:32 pm	7:32 pm

Planet Ingress		day	ET / hr:mn / PT	
☿	♓	2	5:52 pm	2:52 pm
♄	♓	7	8:35 am	5:35 am
⚵	♉	11	11:15 am	8:15 am
♀	♉	16	6:34 pm	3:34 pm
☿	♈	18		9:24 pm
☿	♈	19	12:24 am	
☉	♈	20	5:24 pm	2:24 pm
⚳	♍	22	11:38 pm	8:38 pm
♇	♒	23	8:13 am	5:13 am
♂	♋	25	7:45 am	4:45 am

Planetary Motion	day	ET / hr:mn / PT

1 WEDNESDAY
☽ △ ☉ 8:10 pm 5:10 pm
☽ □ ♀ 9:50 pm 6:50 pm
☽ □ ♃ 10:04 pm 7:04 pm
♀ ☌ ♃ 9:36 pm

2 THURSDAY
♀ ☌ ♃ 12:36 am
☽ ⚹ ♅ 5:03 am 2:03 am
☿ ☌ ♄ 9:34 am 6:34 am
☿ ⚺ ♇ 11:21 am 8:21 am
☽ ⚺ ♂ 1:39 pm 10:39 am
☽ △ ♆ 11:23 pm 8:23 pm
☉ ⚺ ♃ 9:40 pm

3 FRIDAY
☉ ⚺ ♃ 12:40 am
☽ ⚻ ♄ 9:19 am 6:19 am
☽ ☍ ♇ 9:22 am 6:22 am
☽ ⚻ ☿ 1:01 pm 10:01 am
♄ ⚺ ♇ 5:26 pm 2:26 pm

4 SATURDAY
☽ △ ♃ 11:56 am 8:56 am
☽ ⚻ ☉ 2:27 pm 11:27 am
☽ △ ♀ 5:28 pm 2:28 pm
☽ □ ♅ 5:54 pm 2:54 pm
♀ ⚺ ♅ 9:46 pm 6:46 pm

5 SUNDAY
☽ ⚹ ♂ 4:26 am 1:26 am
☽ ⚻ ♆ 12:06 pm 9:06 am
☽ ⚻ ♇ 9:54 pm 6:54 pm
☽ ☍ ♄ 10:18 pm 7:18 pm

6 MONDAY
☉ ⚹ ♅ 8:42 am 5:42 am
☽ ☍ ☿ 11:32 am 8:32 am
☽ ⚻ ♃ 10:00 pm

7 TUESDAY
☽ ⚻ ♃ 1:00 am
☽ △ ♅ 5:51 am 2:51 am
☽ ☍ ☉ 7:40 am 4:40 am
☽ ⚻ ♀ 11:53 am 8:53 am
☽ □ ♂ 6:06 pm 3:06 pm
☽ ☍ ♆ 11:39 pm 8:39 pm

8 WEDNESDAY
☽ △ ♇ 9:07 am 6:07 am
☽ ⚻ ♄ 9:58 am 6:58 am

9 THURSDAY
☽ ⚻ ☿ 8:10 am 5:10 am
☽ ☍ ♃ 12:27 pm 9:27 am
☽ ⚻ ♅ 4:15 pm 1:15 pm
☽ ⚻ ☉ 10:52 pm 7:52 pm

10 FRIDAY
☽ ☍ ♀ 4:07 am 1:07 am
☽ △ ♂ 6:00 am 3:00 am
☽ ⚻ ♆ 9:30 am 6:30 am
☿ ⚺ ♃ 5:04 pm 2:04 pm
☽ □ ♇ 6:37 pm 3:37 pm
☽ △ ♄ 7:51 pm 4:51 pm

11 SATURDAY
♀ ⚹ ♂ 10:35 am 7:05 am
☿ ⚹ ♅ 4:34 pm 1:04 pm
☽ ⚻ ♃ 9:55 pm 6:55 pm
☽ ☍ ♅ 9:43 pm
☽ △ ☿ 11:07 pm

12 SUNDAY
☽ ☍ ♅ 12:43 am
☽ △ ☿ 3:07 am
☽ △ ☉ 12:32 pm 9:32 am
♀ ⚺ ♆ 3:09 pm 12:09 pm
☽ ⚻ ♂ 4:43 pm 1:43 pm
☽ △ ♆ 6:18 pm 3:18 pm
☽ ⚻ ♀ 6:37 pm 3:37 pm
☽ ⚹ ♇ 11:58 pm

13 MONDAY
☽ ⚹ ♇ 2:58 am
☽ □ ♄ 4:34 am 1:34 am

14 TUESDAY
☽ △ ♃ 5:57 am 2:57 am
☽ ⚻ ♅ 7:49 am 4:49 am
☽ □ ☿ 5:38 pm 2:38 pm
♂ □ ♆ 7:39 pm 4:39 pm
☽ □ ☉ 10:08 pm 7:08 pm
☽ □ ♆ 11:38 pm 8:38 pm
☽ ☍ ♂ 11:45 pm 8:45 pm

15 WEDNESDAY
☽ △ ♀ 4:50 am 1:50 am
☽ ⚺ ♇ 7:49 am 4:49 am
☽ ⚹ ♄ 9:41 am 6:41 am
☉ ☌ ♆ 7:39 pm 4:39 pm

16 THURSDAY
☽ □ ♃ 10:17 am 7:17 am
☽ △ ♅ 11:22 am 8:22 am
☿ ☌ ♆ 1:13 pm 10:13 am
☉ □ ♂ 2:10 pm 11:10 am
♀ □ ♇ 3:59 pm 12:59 pm
☿ □ ♂ 9:49 pm
☽ ⚹ ♆ 11:26 pm

17 FRIDAY
☿ □ ♂ 12:49 am
☽ ⚹ ♆ 2:26 am
☽ ⚻ ♂ 4:04 am 1:04 am
☽ ⚹ ☿ 4:28 am 1:28 am
☽ ⚹ ☉ 4:37 am 1:37 am
☉ ☌ ☿ 6:45 am 3:45 am
☽ ☌ ♇ 10:14 am 7:14 am
☽ □ ♀ 11:50 am 8:50 am
☽ ⚺ ♄ 12:20 pm 9:20 am
♀ ⚹ ♄ 6:25 pm 3:25 pm

18 SATURDAY
☽ ⚹ ♃ 12:27 pm 9:27 am
☽ □ ♅ 12:50 pm 9:50 am
☿ ⚹ ♇ 11:24 pm 8:24 pm

19 SUNDAY
☽ ⚺ ♆ 3:30 am 12:30 am
☽ △ ♂ 6:33 am 3:33 am
☽ ⚺ ☉ 9:02 am 6:02 am
☽ ⚺ ♇ 11:05 am 8:05 am
☽ ⚺ ☿ 12:52 pm 9:52 am
☽ ☌ ♄ 1:28 pm 10:28 am
☽ ⚹ ♀ 4:54 pm 1:54 pm
☿ ⚺ ♄ 5:30 pm 2:30 pm
♃ ⚺ ♅ 6:06 pm 3:06 pm

20 MONDAY
☽ ⚹ ♅ 1:34 pm 10:34 am
☽ ⚺ ♃ 1:49 pm 10:49 am
☉ ⚹ ♇ 4:12 pm 1:12 pm

21 TUESDAY
☽ ☌ ♆ 4:20 am 1:20 am
☽ □ ♂ 8:55 am 5:55 am
☽ ⚹ ♇ 11:58 am 8:58 am
☽ ☌ ☉ 1:23 pm 10:23 am
☽ ⚺ ♄ 2:43 pm 11:43 am
☽ ☌ ☿ 9:34 pm 6:34 pm
☽ ⚺ ♀ 10:17 pm 7:17 pm

22 WEDNESDAY
☿ ⚺ ♀ 9:14 am 6:14 am
☉ ⚺ ♄ 11:00 am 8:00 am
☽ ⚺ ♅ 3:19 pm 12:19 pm
☽ ☌ ♃ 4:17 pm 1:17 pm

23 THURSDAY
☽ ⚺ ♆ 6:44 am 3:44 am
☽ ⚹ ♂ 1:13 pm 10:13 am
☽ □ ♇ 2:42 pm 11:42 am
☽ ⚹ ♄ 5:57 pm 2:57 pm
☽ ⚺ ☉ 8:05 pm 5:05 pm

24 FRIDAY
☽ ☌ ♀ 6:31 am 3:31 am
☽ ⚺ ☿ 9:45 am 6:45 am
☽ ☌ ♅ 7:52 pm 4:52 pm
☽ ⚺ ♃ 9:40 pm 6:40 pm

25 SATURDAY
♂ ⚻ ♇ 9:34 am 6:34 am
☽ ⚹ ♆ 12:19 pm 9:19 am
☽ △ ♇ 8:46 pm 5:46 pm
☽ ⚺ ♂ 9:12 pm 6:12 pm
☽ □ ♄ 9:38 pm

26 SUNDAY
☽ □ ♄ 12:38 am
☽ ⚹ ☉ 7:03 am 4:03 am
☽ ⚺ ♀ 7:25 pm 4:25 pm

27 MONDAY
☽ ⚹ ☿ 3:39 am 12:39 am
☽ ⚺ ♅ 4:08 am 1:08 am
☿ ⚺ ♅ 6:45 am 3:45 am
☽ ⚹ ♃ 6:57 am 3:57 am
☽ □ ♆ 9:39 pm 6:39 pm
☿ ☌ ♃ 11:50 pm

28 TUESDAY
☿ ☌ ♃ 2:50 am
☽ ⚻ ♇ 6:32 am 3:32 am
☽ ☌ ♂ 9:19 am 6:19 am
☽ △ ♄ 11:04 am 8:04 am
☽ □ ☉ 10:32 pm 7:32 pm

29 WEDNESDAY
☽ ⚹ ♀ 12:50 pm 9:50 am
☽ ⚹ ♅ 3:40 pm 12:40 pm
☽ □ ♃ 7:35 pm 4:35 pm
☽ □ ☿ 11:30 pm

30 THURSDAY
☽ □ ☿ 2:30 am
☽ △ ♆ 9:45 am 6:45 am
♂ △ ♄ 3:03 pm 12:03 pm
♀ ☌ ♅ 6:26 pm 3:26 pm
☽ ☍ ♇ 6:46 pm 3:46 pm
☽ ⚻ ♄ 11:51 pm 8:51 pm
☽ ⚺ ♂ 9:10 pm

31 FRIDAY
☽ ⚺ ♂ 12:10 am
☽ △ ☉ 4:29 pm 1:29 pm
☿ ⚺ ♆ 10:39 pm

Eastern time in bold type
Pacific time in medium type

MARCH 2023

DATE	SID.TIME	SUN	MOON	NODE	MERCURY	VENUS	MARS	JUPITER	SATURN	URANUS	NEPTUNE	PLUTO	CERES	PALLAS	JUNO	VESTA	CHIRON
1 W	10 34 10	10 ♓ 07 41	28 ♉ 40	5 ♉ 50 R	26 ≈ 43	10 ♓ 38	19 ♊ 07	11 ♈ 52	29 ≈ 13	15 ♉ 32	24 ♓ 33	29 ♑ 30	4 ≈ 42 R	11 ♍ 13	24 ♈ 01	9 ♈ 15	13 ♈ 51
2 Th	10 38 7	11 07 55	10 ♊ 36	5 46	28 23	11 52	19 31	12 06	29 20	15 34	24 35	29 31	4 32	11 20	24 34	9 42	13 54
3 F	10 42 3	12 08 06	22 28	5 39	0 ♓ 05	13 05	19 55	12 19	29 28	15 36	24 38	29 33	4 21	11 29	25 08	10 09	13 57
4 Sa	10 46 0	13 08 16	4 ♋ 19	5 31	1 48	14 18	20 19	12 33	29 35	15 38	24 40	29 34	4 10	11 37	25 41	10 36	14 00
5 Su	10 49 56	14 08 24	16 12	5 21	3 31	15 31	20 44	12 46	29 42	15 40	24 42	29 36	3 59	11 46	26 15	11 03	14 03
6 M	10 53 53	15 08 30	28 11	5 11	5 16	16 44	21 09	13 00	29 49	15 42	24 44	29 37	3 47	11 56	26 48	11 31	14 06
7 T	10 57 49	16 08 34	10 ♌ 19	5 01	7 02	17 58	21 35	13 14	29 56	15 44	24 47	29 39	3 35	12 06	27 22	11 58	14 10
8 W	11 1 46	17 08 36	22 27	4 53	8 49	19 10	22 00	13 27	0 ♓ 03	15 46	24 49	29 40	3 23	12 17	27 56	12 25	14 13
9 Th	11 5 42	18 08 36	4 ♍ 47	4 47	10 37	20 23	22 26	13 41	0 10	15 48	24 51	29 42	3 11	12 28	28 29	12 52	14 16
10 F	11 9 39	19 08 35	17 17	4 43	12 26	21 36	22 52	13 55	0 17	15 50	24 53	29 43	2 58	12 39	29 03	13 19	14 19
11 Sa	11 13 36	20 08 32	29 57	4 42 D	14 17	22 49	23 18	14 09	0 24	15 52	24 56	29 45	2 45	12 51	29 37	13 46	14 23
12 Su	11 17 32	21 08 27	12 ♎ 50	4 42	16 08	24 02	23 45	14 23	0 31	15 55	24 58	29 46	2 32	13 03	0 ♉ 11	14 13	14 26
13 M	11 21 29	22 08 20	25 56	4 43	18 01	25 14	24 11	14 37	0 38	15 57	25 00	29 47	2 19	13 16	0 45	14 41	14 29
14 T	11 25 25	23 08 12	9 ♏ 19	4 44	19 54	26 27	24 38	14 51	0 45	15 59	25 02	29 49	2 06	13 29	1 19	15 08	14 32
15 W	11 29 22	24 08 02	22 59	4 45 R	21 49	27 39	25 05	15 05	0 52	16 02	25 05	29 50	1 52	13 42	1 53	15 35	14 36
16 Th	11 33 18	25 07 50	6 ♐ 59	4 44	23 45	28 52	25 32	15 19	0 59	16 04	25 07	29 51	1 39	13 56	2 27	16 02	14 39
17 F	11 37 15	26 07 37	21 17	4 42	25 42	0 ♉ 04	26 00	15 33	1 06	16 07	25 09	29 52	1 25	14 10	3 02	16 29	14 43
18 Sa	11 41 11	27 07 22	5 ♑ 51	4 38	27 40	1 17	26 27	15 47	1 12	16 09	25 12	29 54	1 11	14 25	3 36	16 57	14 46
19 Su	11 45 8	28 07 06	20 36	4 33	29 38	2 29	26 55	16 01	1 19	16 12	25 14	29 55	0 58	14 40	4 10	17 24	14 49
20 M	11 49 5	29 06 47	5 ♒ 27	4 28	1 ♈ 38	3 41	27 23	16 15	1 26	16 14	25 16	29 56	0 44	14 55	4 45	17 51	14 53
21 T	11 53 1	0 ♈ 06 27	20 14	4 23	3 38	4 53	27 51	16 30	1 33	16 17	25 18	29 57	0 30	15 11	5 19	18 19	14 56
22 W	11 56 58	1 06 04	4 ♓ 49	4 18	5 38	6 05	28 20	16 44	1 39	16 20	25 21	29 58	0 16	15 27	5 53	18 46	15 00
23 Th	12 0 54	2 05 40	19 07	4 16	7 39	7 17	28 48	16 58	1 46	16 22	25 23	29 59	0 02	15 43	6 28	19 13	15 03
24 F	12 4 51	3 05 13	3 ♈ 02	4 15 D	9 40	8 29	29 17	17 12	1 52	16 25	25 25	0 ≈ 01	29 ♑ 48	16 00	7 03	19 40	15 05
25 Sa	12 8 47	4 04 45	16 32	4 16	11 41	9 41	29 46	17 27	1 59	16 28	25 27	0 02	29 34	16 17	7 37	20 08	15 07
26 Su	12 12 44	5 04 14	29 38	4 17	13 41	10 52	0 ♋ 15	17 41	2 05	16 31	25 30	0 03	29 21	16 34	8 12	20 35	15 13
27 M	12 16 40	6 03 41	12 ♉ 20	4 19	15 41	12 04	0 44	17 55	2 12	16 33	25 32	0 04	29 07	16 52	8 46	21 02	15 17
28 T	12 20 37	7 03 06	24 44	4 20	17 40	13 15	1 13	18 10	2 18	16 36	25 34	0 05	28 54	17 09	9 21	21 30	15 20
29 W	12 24 34	8 02 28	6 ♊ 52	4 21 R	19 38	14 27	1 43	18 24	2 25	16 39	25 36	0 06	28 40	17 27	9 56	21 57	15 24
30 Th	12 28 30	9 01 48	18 51	4 20	21 33	15 38	2 12	18 38	2 31	16 42	25 39	0 07	28 27	17 46	10 31	22 24	15 27
31 F	12 32 27	10 01 06	0 ♋ 44	4 19	23 27	16 49	2 42	18 53	2 37	16 45	25 41	0 07	28 14	18 04	11 06	22 52	15 31

EPHEMERIS CALCULATED FOR 12 MIDNIGHT GREENWICH MEAN TIME. ALL OTHER DATA AND FACING ASPECTARIAN PAGE IN **EASTERN TIME (BOLD)** AND PACIFIC TIME (REGULAR).

APRIL 2023

☽ Last Aspect day	ET / hr:mn / PT		asp	☽ Ingress sign	day	ET / hr:mn / PT	
1		11:03 pm	△☿	♍	2	**6:57 am**	3:57 am
2	**2:03 am**		△☿	♍	2	**6:57 am**	3:57 am
4	**9:50 am**	6:50 am	☍♆	♎	4	**5:51 pm**	2:51 pm
6	**8:43 am**	5:43 am	☍♃	♏	6		11:29 pm
6	**8:43 am**	5:43 am	☍♃	♏	7	**2:29 am**	
9	**5:09 am**	2:09 am	☍♀	♐	9	**8:57 am**	5:57 am
11	**6:48 am**	3:48 am	□♆	♑	11	**1:33 pm**	10:33 am
13	**10:14 am**	7:14 am	⚹♆	♒	13	**4:42 pm**	1:42 pm
15	**11:16 am**	8:16 am	⚹⊙	♓	15	**6:57 pm**	3:57 pm
17	**2:57 pm**	11:57 am	☌♆	♈	17	**9:09 pm**	6:09 pm
19		9:13 pm	☌⊙	♉	19		9:30 pm
20	**12:13 am**		☌⊙	♉	20	**12:30 am**	
21	**11:41 pm**	8:41 pm	⚹♆	♊	22	**6:11 am**	3:11 am
24	**8:15 am**	5:15 am	□♆	♋	24	**2:58 pm**	11:58 am
26	**7:41 pm**	4:41 pm	△♆	♌	26		11:30 pm
26	**7:41 pm**	4:41 pm	△♆	♌	27	**2:30 am**	
29	**6:53 am**	3:53 am	△♃	♍	29	**2:59 pm**	11:59 am

☽ Phases & Eclipses phase	day	ET / hr:mn / PT	
Full Moon	5		9:34 pm
Full Moon	6	**12:34 am**	
4th Quarter	13	**5:11 am**	2:11 am
New Moon	19		9:13 pm
New Moon	20	**12:13 am**	
●	20	29° ♈ 50'	
2nd Quarter	27	**5:20 pm**	2:20 pm

Planet Ingress		day	ET / hr:mn / PT	
☿	♉	3	**12:22 pm**	9:22 am
♀	♊	10		9:47 pm
♀	♊	11	**12:47 am**	
⚶	♉	15	**1:01 pm**	10:01 am
⊙	♉	20	**4:14 am**	1:14 am

Planetary Motion		day	ET / hr:mn / PT	
☿	℞	21	**4:35 am**	1:35 am

1 SATURDAY
☿ ⚺ ♆ **1:39 am**
☽ □ ♅ **4:30 am** 1:30 am
☽ □ ♀ **8:06 am** 5:06 am
☽ △ ♃ **9:25 am** 6:25 am
☽ ⚻ ♆ **10:28 pm** 7:28 pm
♀ ⚺ ♃ 9:18 pm
☽ △ ☿ 11:03 pm

2 SUNDAY
♀ ⚺ ♃ **12:18 am**
☽ △ ☿ **2:03 am**
☽ ⚻ ♇ **7:16 am** 4:16 am
☽ ☍ ♄ **12:44 pm** 9:44 am
☽ ⚹ ♂ **3:08 pm** 12:08 pm

3 MONDAY
☽ ⚻ ⊙ **9:49 am** 6:49 am
☿ □ ♇ **2:55 pm** 11:55 am
☽ △ ♅ **4:28 pm** 1:28 pm
☽ ⚻ ♃ **10:12 pm** 7:12 pm
☽ △ ♀ 11:04 pm

4 TUESDAY
☽ △ ♀ **2:04 am**
☽ ☍ ♆ **9:50 am** 6:50 am
☽ △ ♇ **6:13 pm** 3:13 pm
☽ ⚻ ☿ **10:16 pm** 7:16 pm
☽ ⚻ ♄ **11:54 pm** 8:54 pm

5 WEDNESDAY
☽ □ ♂ **4:12 am** 1:12 am
☿ ⚹ ♄ **12:21 pm** 9:21 am
☽ ☍ ⊙ 9:34 pm
☽ ⚻ ♅ 11:21 pm

6 THURSDAY
☽ ☍ ⊙ **12:34 am**
☽ ⚻ ♅ **2:21 am**
☽ ☍ ♃ **8:43 am** 5:43 am
☽ ⚻ ♀ **5:06 pm** 2:06 pm
☽ ⚻ ♆ **6:57 pm** 3:57 pm
⊙ ⚺ ♅ 9:42 pm
☽ □ ♇ 11:54 pm

7 FRIDAY
⊙ ⚺ ♅ **12:42 am**
☽ □ ♇ **2:54 am**
☽ △ ♄ **8:44 am** 5:44 am
☽ ☍ ☿ **1:53 pm** 10:53 am
♀ ⚹ ♆ **1:58 pm** 10:58 am
☽ △ ♂ **2:42 pm** 11:42 am
☿ ⚹ ♂ 11:29 pm

8 SATURDAY
☿ ⚹ ♂ **2:29 am**
☽ ☍ ♅ **9:56 am** 6:56 am
☽ ⚻ ⊙ **12:27 pm** 9:27 am
☽ ⚻ ♃ **4:51 pm** 1:51 pm
☽ △ ♆ 10:50 pm

9 SUNDAY
☽ △ ♆ **1:50 am**
☽ ☍ ♀ **5:09 am** 2:09 am
☽ ⚹ ♇ **9:23 am** 6:23 am
☽ □ ♄ **3:21 pm** 12:21 pm
☽ ⚻ ♂ **10:51 pm** 7:51 pm
☽ ⚻ ☿ 10:23 pm

10 MONDAY
☽ ⚻ ☿ **1:23 am**
☽ ⚻ ♅ **3:29 pm** 12:29 pm
☽ △ ⊙ **9:48 pm** 6:48 pm
☽ △ ♃ **10:55 pm** 7:55 pm

11 TUESDAY
♀ △ ♇ **6:14 am** 3:14 am
☽ □ ♆ **6:48 am** 3:48 am
☽ ⚺ ♇ **2:01 pm** 11:01 am
☽ ⚻ ♀ **2:43 pm** 11:43 am
⊙ ☌ ♃ **6:07 pm** 3:07 pm
☽ ⚹ ♄ **8:08 pm** 5:08 pm

12 WEDNESDAY
☽ ☍ ♂ **5:03 am** 2:03 am
☽ △ ☿ **9:35 am** 6:35 am
☽ △ ♅ **7:24 pm** 4:24 pm

13 THURSDAY
☽ □ ♃ **3:20 am** 12:20 am
☽ □ ⊙ **5:11 am** 2:11 am
☽ ⚹ ♆ **10:14 am** 7:14 am
☽ ☌ ♇ **5:11 pm** 2:11 pm
☽ △ ♀ **10:23 pm** 7:23 pm
☽ ⚺ ♄ **11:28 pm** 8:28 pm

14 FRIDAY
☽ ⚻ ♂ **9:47 am** 6:47 am
♀ □ ♄ **12:38 pm** 9:38 am
☽ □ ☿ **3:16 pm** 12:16 pm
☽ □ ♅ **10:08 pm** 7:08 pm

15 SATURDAY
☽ ⚹ ♃ **6:36 am** 3:36 am
☽ ⚹ ⊙ **11:16 am** 8:16 am
☽ ⚺ ♆ **12:41 pm** 9:41 am
☽ ⚺ ♇ **7:27 pm** 4:27 pm
☽ ☌ ♄ 10:58 pm

16 SUNDAY
☽ ☌ ♄ **1:58 am**
☽ □ ♀ **4:58 am** 1:58 am
⊙ ⚺ ♆ **8:43 am** 5:43 am
☽ △ ♂ **1:49 pm** 10:49 am
☽ ⚹ ☿ **7:24 pm** 4:24 pm
☽ ⚹ ♅ 9:25 pm

17 MONDAY
☽ ⚹ ♅ **12:25 am**
☽ ⚺ ♃ **9:35 am** 6:35 am
☽ ☌ ♆ **2:57 pm** 11:57 am
☽ ⚺ ⊙ **5:06 pm** 2:06 pm
☽ ⚹ ♇ **9:42 pm** 6:42 pm

18 TUESDAY
☽ ⚺ ♄ **4:34 am** 1:34 am
☽ ⚹ ♀ **11:47 am** 8:47 am
☽ □ ♂ **6:16 pm** 3:16 pm
☽ ⚺ ☿ **11:15 pm** 8:15 pm

19 WEDNESDAY
☽ ⚺ ♅ **3:20 am** 12:20 am
☽ ☌ ♃ **1:27 pm** 10:27 am
☽ ⚺ ♆ **6:12 pm** 3:12 pm
☽ ☌ ⊙ 9:13 pmc
☽ □ ♇ 10:04 pm

20 THURSDAY
☽ ☌ ⊙ **12:13 am**
☽ □ ♇ **1:04 am**
☽ ⚹ ♄ **8:30 am** 5:30 am
⊙ □ ♇ **12:27 pm** 9:27 am
☽ ⚺ ♀ **8:29 pm** 5:29 pm
☽ ⚹ ♂ 9:37 pm

21 FRIDAY
☽ ⚹ ♂ **12:37 am**
☽ ☌ ☿ **4:05 am** 1:05 am
☽ ☌ ♅ **8:09 am** 5:09 am
☽ ⚺ ♃ **7:32 pm** 4:32 pm
☽ ⚹ ♆ **11:41 pm** 8:41 pm

22 SATURDAY
☽ △ ♇ **6:49 am** 3:49 am
☽ ⚺ ⊙ **10:14 am** 7:14 am
☽ □ ♄ **3:00 pm** 12:00 pm

23 SUNDAY
☽ ☌ ♀ **8:43 am** 5:43 am
☽ ⚺ ♂ **10:06 am** 7:06 am
☽ ⚺ ☿ **10:54 am** 7:54 am
☽ ⚺ ♅ **3:55 pm** 12:55 pm
☿ ⚹ ♂ **11:19 pm** 8:19 pm

24 MONDAY
☽ ⚹ ♃ **4:49 am** 1:49 am
☿ ⚺ ♀ **5:04 am** 2:04 am
☽ □ ♆ **8:15 am** 5:15 am
♀ ⚺ ♂ **12:50 pm** 9:50 am
☽ ⚻ ♇ **3:40 pm** 12:40 pm
☽ ⚹ ⊙ 9:11 pm
☽ △ ♄ 9:40 pm

25 TUESDAY
☽ ⚹ ⊙ **12:11 am**
☽ △ ♄ **12:40 am**
⊙ ⚹ ♄ **6:48 am** 3:48 am
☽ ⚹ ☿ **7:47 pm** 4:47 pm
☽ ☌ ♂ **11:08 pm** 8:08 pm
☽ ⚺ ♀ 10:00 pm
☽ ⚹ ♅ 11:45 pm

26 WEDNESDAY
☽ ⚺ ♀ **1:00 am**
☽ ⚹ ♅ **2:45 am**
☽ □ ♃ **5:09 pm** 2:09 pm
☽ △ ♆ **7:41 pm** 4:41 pm
♀ ⚺ ♅ **8:35 pm** 5:35 pm

27 THURSDAY
☽ ☍ ♇ **3:13 am** 12:13 am
☽ ⚻ ♄ **12:54 pm** 9:54 am
☽ □ ⊙ **5:20 pm** 2:20 pm

28 FRIDAY
☽ □ ☿ **5:44 am** 2:44 am
☽ ⚺ ♂ **2:22 pm** 11:22 am
☽ □ ♅ **3:26 pm** 12:26 pm
☽ ⚹ ♀ **7:42 pm** 4:42 pm

29 SATURDAY
☽ △ ♃ **6:53 am** 3:53 am
☽ ⚻ ♆ **8:20 am** 5:20 am
☽ ⚻ ♇ **3:43 pm** 12:43 pm
♂ ⚹ ♅ **4:05 pm** 1:05 pm
☽ ☍ ♄ 10:41 pm

30 SUNDAY
☽ ☍ ♄ **1:41 am**
☽ △ ⊙ **10:59 am** 7:59 am
☽ △ ☿ **3:05 pm** 12:05 pm

Eastern time in bold type
Pacific time in medium type

APRIL 2023

DATE	SID.TIME	SUN	MOON	NODE	MERCURY	VENUS	MARS	JUPITER	SATURN	URANUS	NEPTUNE	PLUTO	CERES	PALLAS	JUNO	VESTA	CHIRON
1 Sa	12 36 23	11♈00 21	12♌36	4♉16℞	25♈18	18♉01	3♋12	19♈07	2♓44	16♉48	25♓43	0♒08	28♏01℞	18♋23	11♊41	23♈19	15♈35
2 Su	12 40 20	11 59 34	24 31	4 13	27 06	19 12	3 42	19 22	2 50	16 51	25 45	0 09	27 48	18 42	12 15	23 46	15 38
3 M	12 44 16	12 58 45	6♍14	4 09	28 51	20 22	4 12	19 36	2 56	16 54	25 48	0 10	27 36	19 02	12 50	24 13	15 41
4 T	12 48 13	13 57 54	18 45	4 06	0♉32	21 33	4 42	19 51	3 02	16 57	25 50	0 11	27 24	19 21	13 25	24 41	15 45
5 W	12 52 9	14 57 00	1♎07	4 03	2 09	22 44	5 13	20 05	3 08	17 00	25 52	0 12	27 12	19 41	14 00	25 08	15 49
6 Th	12 56 6	15 56 05	13 42	4 01	3 41	23 55	5 43	20 20	3 14	17 03	25 54	0 12	27 00	20 01	14 35	25 35	15 52
7 F	13 0 2	16 55 07	26 30	4 00D	5 09	25 05	6 14	20 34	3 20	17 06	25 56	0 13	26 48	20 21	15 10	26 03	15 56
8 Sa	13 3 59	17 54 07	9♏32	4 00	6 32	26 16	6 45	20 48	3 26	17 09	25 58	0 14	26 37	20 42	15 45	26 30	15 59
9 Su	13 7 56	18 53 06	22 46	4 01	7 49	27 26	7 16	21 03	3 32	17 12	26 01	0 14	26 26	21 02	16 21	26 57	16 03
10 M	13 11 52	19 52 02	6♐14	4 02	9 01	28 36	7 47	21 17	3 37	17 15	26 03	0 15	26 16	21 23	16 56	27 24	16 06
11 T	13 15 49	20 50 57	19 53	4 03	10 08	29 46	8 18	21 32	3 43	17 19	26 05	0 16	26 05	21 44	17 31	27 52	16 10
12 W	13 19 45	21 49 51	3♑44	4 04	11 08	0♊56	8 49	21 46	3 49	17 22	26 07	0 16	25 55	22 06	18 06	28 19	16 13
13 Th	13 23 42	22 48 42	17 46	4 04℞	12 03	2 06	9 20	22 01	3 54	17 25	26 09	0 17	25 45	22 27	18 41	28 46	16 17
14 F	13 27 38	23 47 32	1≈32	4 04	12 51	3 16	9 52	22 15	4 00	17 28	26 11	0 17	25 36	22 49	19 16	29 13	16 20
15 Sa	13 31 35	24 46 20	16 16	4 04	13 34	4 25	10 23	22 30	4 05	17 32	26 13	0 18	25 27	23 10	19 52	29 41	16 24
16 Su	13 35 32	25 45 07	0♓38	4 03	14 10	5 35	10 55	22 44	4 11	17 35	26 15	0 19	25 18	23 32	20 27	0♉08	16 27
17 M	13 39 28	26 43 51	15 00	4 02	14 40	6 44	11 26	22 59	4 16	17 38	26 17	0 19	25 10	23 54	21 02	0 35	16 31
18 T	13 43 25	27 42 34	29 19	4 01	15 03	7 53	11 58	23 13	4 22	17 41	26 19	0 20	25 02	24 17	21 38	1 02	16 34
19 W	13 47 21	28 41 15	13♈29	4 01	15 21	9 02	12 30	23 28	4 27	17 45	26 21	0 20	24 55	24 39	22 13	1 30	16 38
20 Th	13 51 18	29 39 54	27 25	4 00D	15 32	10 11	13 02	23 42	4 32	17 48	26 23	0 20	24 48	25 02	22 48	1 57	16 41
21 F	13 55 14	0♉38 31	11♉05	4 00	15 37℞	11 20	13 34	23 57	4 37	17 51	26 25	0 21	24 41	25 24	23 24	2 24	16 45
22 Sa	13 59 11	1 37 07	24 26	4 01	15 36	12 29	14 06	24 11	4 42	17 55	26 27	0 21	24 34	25 47	23 59	2 51	16 48
23 Su	14 3 7	2 35 40	7♊27	4 01	15 30	13 37	14 39	24 25	4 47	17 58	26 29	0 21	24 29	26 10	24 34	3 18	16 52
24 M	14 7 4	3 34 12	20 10	4 01℞	15 18	14 46	15 11	24 40	4 52	18 02	26 31	0 21	24 23	26 33	25 10	3 45	16 55
25 T	14 11 0	4 32 41	2♋35	4 01	15 00	15 54	15 43	24 54	4 57	18 05	26 33	0 22	24 18	26 57	25 45	4 12	16 58
26 W	14 14 57	5 31 08	14 46	4 01D	14 39	17 02	16 16	25 08	5 02	18 08	26 35	0 22	24 13	27 20	26 20	4 40	17 02
27 Th	14 18 54	6 29 33	26 46	4 01	14 13	18 10	16 49	25 23	5 06	18 12	26 37	0 22	24 09	27 43	26 56	5 07	17 05
28 F	14 22 50	7 27 56	8♌41	4 01	13 43	19 18	17 21	25 37	5 11	18 15	26 38	0 22	24 05	28 07	27 31	5 34	17 09
29 Sa	14 26 47	8 26 17	20 34	4 01	13 10	20 26	17 54	25 51	5 15	18 19	26 40	0 22	24 02	28 31	28 07	6 01	17 12
30 Su	14 30 43	9 24 36	2♍30	4 01	12 35	21 33	18 27	26 06	5 20	18 22	26 42	0 22	23 56	28 55	28 42	6 28	17 15

EPHEMERIS CALCULATED FOR 12 MIDNIGHT GREENWICH MEAN TIME. ALL OTHER DATA AND FACING ASPECTARIAN PAGE IN **EASTERN TIME (BOLD)** AND PACIFIC TIME (REGULAR).

MAY 2023

☽ Last Aspect day	ET / hr:mn / PT	asp	☽ Ingress sign	day	ET / hr:mn / PT
1	**7:53 pm** 4:53 pm	☍♆	♎	1	11:09 pm
1	**7:53 pm** 4:53 pm	☍♆	♎	2	**2:09 am**
4	**5:17 am** 2:17 am	☍♃	♏	4	**10:32 am** 7:32 am
6	**10:38 am** 7:38 am	△♆	♐	6	**4:04 pm** 1:04 pm
8	**4:28 pm** 1:28 pm	△♃	♑	8	**7:33 pm** 4:33 pm
10	**7:52 pm** 4:52 pm	□♃	♒	10	**10:05 pm** 7:05 pm
12	**11:15 pm** 8:15 pm	✶♃	♓	12	9:39 pm
12	**11:15 pm** 8:15 pm	✶♃	♓	13	**12:39 am**
14	**10:56 pm** 7:56 pm	☌♆	♈	15	**3:56 am** 12:56 am
17	**5:10 am** 2:10 am	□♂	♉	17	**8:28 am** 5:28 am

☽ Last Aspect day	ET / hr:mn / PT	asp	☽ Ingress sign	day	ET / hr:mn / PT
19	**1:51 pm** 10:51 am	✶♂	♊	19	**2:48 pm** 11:48 am
21	**6:12 pm** 3:12 pm	□♆	♋	21	**11:28 pm** 8:28 pm
24	**5:12 am** 2:12 am	△♆	♌	24	**10:35 am** 7:35 am
25	11:38 pm	□♅	♍	26	**11:05 pm** 8:05 pm
26	**2:38 am**	□♅	♍	26	**11:05 pm** 8:05 pm
29	**5:46 am** 2:46 am	☍♆	♎	29	**10:51 am** 7:51 am
31	**10:53 am** 7:53 am	□♀	♏	31	**7:45 pm** 4:45 pm

☽ Phases & Eclipses phase	day	ET / hr:mn / PT
Full Moon	5	**1:34 pm** 10:34 am
●	5	14° ♏ 58'
4th Quarter	12	**10:28 am** 7:28 am
New Moon	19	**11:53 am** 8:53 am
2nd Quarter	27	**11:22 am** 8:22 am

Planet Ingress		day	ET / hr:mn / PT
⚵	♊	1	9:50 pm
⚵	♊	2	**12:50 am**
♀	♌	2	**1:03 pm** 10:03 am
♀	♋	7	**10:25 am** 7:25 am
♃	♉	16	**1:20 pm** 10:20 am
♂	♌	20	**11:31 am** 8:31 am
☉	♊	21	**3:09 am** 12:09 am

Planetary Motion		day	ET / hr:mn / PT
♇	℞	1	**1:09 pm** 10:09 am
⚳	D	6	**3:24 pm** 12:24 pm
☿	D	14	**11:17 pm** 8:17 pm

1 MONDAY
☽△♅ **3:38 am** 12:38 am
☽✶♂ **5:08 am** 2:08 am
☽□♀ **1:31 pm** 10:31 am
☉☌☿ **7:28 pm** 4:28 pm
☽⚻♃ **7:30 pm** 4:30 pm
☽☍♆ **7:53 pm** 4:53 pm
☽△♇ 11:51 pm

2 TUESDAY
☽△♇ **2:51 am**
☽⚻♄ **12:46 pm** 9:46 am
♃⚺♆ **6:03 pm** 3:03 pm
☽⚻☿ **10:26 pm** 7:26 pm
☽⚻☉ 11:09 pm

3 WEDNESDAY
☽⚻☉ **2:09 am**
☽⚻♅ **1:26 pm** 10:26 am
☽□♂ **5:10 pm** 2:10 pm

4 THURSDAY
☽△♀ **3:54 am** 12:54 am
☽⚻♆ **4:43 am** 1:43 am
☽☍♃ **5:17 am** 2:17 am
☽□♇ **11:12 am** 8:12 am
♀□♆ **1:40 pm** 10:40 am
☽△♄ **8:53 pm** 5:53 pm
♀✶♃ 9:03 pm

5 FRIDAY
♀✶♃ **12:03 am**
☽☍☿ **3:15 am** 12:15 am
☽☍☉ **1:34 pm** 10:34 am
☽☍♅ **8:13 pm** 5:13 pm
☽△♂ 10:51 pm

6 SATURDAY
☽△♂ **1:51 am**
☽△♆ **10:38 am** 7:38 am
☽⚻♃ **11:59 am** 8:59 am
☽⚻♀ **2:28 pm** 11:28 am
☽✶♇ **4:41 pm** 1:41 pm
☽□♄ 11:12 pm

7 SUNDAY
☽□♄ **2:12 am**
☽⚻☿ **5:58 am** 2:58 am
♀⚻♇ **6:10 pm** 3:10 pm
☽⚻☉ **9:50 pm** 6:50 pm
☽⚻♅ 9:34 pm

8 MONDAY
☽⚻♅ **12:34 am**
☽⚻♂ **7:55 am** 4:55 am
☽□♆ **2:22 pm** 11:22 am
☽△♃ **4:28 pm** 1:28 pm
☽⚺♇ **8:09 pm** 5:09 pm
☽☍♀ **10:20 pm** 7:20 pm

9 TUESDAY
☽✶♄ **5:39 am** 2:39 am
☽△☿ **7:28 am** 4:28 am
☉☌♅ **3:56 pm** 12:56 pm

10 WEDNESDAY
☽△♅ **3:32 am** 12:32 am
☽△☉ **4:20 am** 1:20 am
☽☍♂ **12:38 pm** 9:38 am
☽✶♆ **5:03 pm** 2:03 pm
☽□♃ **7:52 pm** 4:52 pm
☽☌♇ **10:40 pm** 7:40 pm

11 THURSDAY
☽⚻♀ **5:01 am** 2:01 am
☽⚺♄ **8:20 am** 5:20 am
☽□☿ **8:45 am** 5:45 am

12 FRIDAY
☿✶♄ **4:42 am** 1:42 am
☽□♅ **6:12 am** 3:12 am
☽□☉ **10:28 am** 7:28 am
☽⚻♂ **5:13 pm** 2:13 pm
☽⚺♆ **7:40 pm** 4:40 pm
☿✶♀ **10:44 pm** 7:44 pm
☽✶♃ **11:15 pm** 8:15 pm
☽⚺♇ 10:13 pm
♀△♄ 11:57 pm

13 SATURDAY
☽⚺♇ **1:13 am**
♀△♄ **2:57 am**
☽✶☿ **10:44 am** 7:44 am
☽☌♄ **11:12 am** 8:12 am
☽△♀ **11:51 am** 8:51 am

14 SUNDAY
☽✶♅ **9:22 am** 6:22 am
☽✶☉ **5:17 pm** 2:17 pm
☽△♂ **10:30 pm** 7:30 pm
☽☌♆ **10:56 pm** 7:56 pm

15 MONDAY
☽⚺♃ **3:22 am** 12:22 am
☽✶♇ **4:29 am** 1:29 am
♂△♆ **9:44 am** 6:44 am
☽⚺☿ **2:05 pm** 11:05 am
☽⚺♄ **2:54 pm** 11:54 am
☽□♀ **7:42 pm** 4:42 pm

16 TUESDAY
☽⚺♅ **1:37 pm** 10:37 am
☽⚺☉ 10:30 pm

17 WEDNESDAY
☽⚺☉ **1:30 am**
☽⚺♆ **3:25 am** 12:25 am
☽□♂ **5:10 am** 2:10 am
☽☌♃ **8:47 am** 5:47 am
☽□♇ **9:00 am** 6:00 am
☽☌☿ **7:27 pm** 4:27 pm
☽✶♄ **7:57 pm** 4:57 pm
♃□♇ **9:11 pm** 6:11 pm

18 THURSDAY
☉✶♆ **5:00 am** 2:00 am
☽✶♀ **5:18 am** 2:18 am
☽☌♅ **7:28 pm** 4:28 pm
☿✶♄ 11:40 pm

19 FRIDAY
☿✶♄ **2:40 am**
☽✶♆ **9:39 am** 6:39 am
☽☌☉ **11:53 am** 8:53 am
☽✶♂ **1:51 pm** 10:51 am
☽△♇ **3:20 pm** 12:20 pm
☽⚺♃ **4:06 pm** 1:06 pm
☽□♄ 11:58 pm

20 SATURDAY
☽□♄ **2:58 am**
☽⚺☿ **3:33 am** 12:33 am
☽⚺♀ **5:28 pm** 2:28 pm
♂☍♇ **11:12 pm** 8:12 pm

21 SUNDAY
☽⚺♅ **3:32 am** 12:32 am
☉△♇ **9:58 am** 6:58 am
☽□♆ **6:12 pm** 3:12 pm
☽⚻♇ 9:00 pm
☽⚺☉ 10:11 pm
☽⚺♂ 10:12 pm
☽✶♃ 10:54 pm
☉✶♂ 10:57 pm

22 MONDAY
☽⚻♇ **12:00 am**
☽⚺☉ **1:11 am**
☽⚺♂ **1:12 am**
☽✶♃ **1:54 am**
☉✶♂ **1:57 am**
☽△♄ **12:24 pm** 9:24 am
☉⚺♃ **12:55 pm** 9:55 am
☽✶☿ **3:07 pm** 12:07 pm
♂□♃ 10:13 pm

23 TUESDAY
♂□♃ **1:13 am**
☽☌♀ **8:45 am** 5:45 am
☽✶♅ **2:07 pm** 11:07 am

24 WEDNESDAY
☽△♆ **5:12 am** 2:12 am
☽☍♇ **11:04 am** 8:04 am
☽□♃ **2:13 pm** 11:13 am
☽☌♂ **3:21 pm** 12:21 pm
☽✶☉ **5:31 pm** 2:31 pm
☽⚻♄ 9:09 pm

25 THURSDAY
☽⚻♄ **12:09 am**
☽□☿ **6:11 am** 3:11 am
☽⚺♀ 11:33 pm
☽□♅ 11:38 pm

26 FRIDAY
☽⚺♀ **2:33 am**
☽□♅ **2:38 am**
♀✶♅ **3:37 am** 12:37 am
☽⚻♆ **5:45 pm** 2:45 pm
☽⚻♇ **11:31 pm** 8:31 pm

27 SATURDAY
☽△♃ **3:53 am** 12:53 am
☽⚺♂ **6:57 am** 3:57 am
☽□☉ **11:22 am** 8:22 am
☽☍♄ **12:53 pm** 9:53 am
☽△☿ **11:07 pm** 8:07 pm

28 SUNDAY
☉□♄ **6:46 am** 3:46 am
☽△♅ **3:12 pm** 12:12 pm
☽✶♀ **8:19 pm** 5:19 pm

29 MONDAY
☽☍♆ **5:46 am** 2:46 am
☽△♇ **11:13 am** 8:13 am
☽⚻♃ **4:33 pm** 1:33 pm
☽✶♂ **9:21 pm** 6:21 pm
☽⚻♄ 9:18 pm

30 TUESDAY
☽⚻♄ **12:18 am**
☽△☉ **3:39 am** 12:39 am
☽⚻☿ **2:50 pm** 11:50 am
☽⚻♅ 10:29 pm

31 WEDNESDAY
☽⚻♅ **1:29 am**
☽□♀ **10:53 am** 7:53 am
☽⚻♆ **3:02 pm** 12:02 pm
☽□♇ **8:02 pm** 5:02 pm
☽☍♃ 11:04 pm

Eastern time in bold type
Pacific time in medium type

MAY 2023

DATE	SID.TIME	SUN	MOON	NODE	MERCURY	VENUS	MARS	JUPITER	SATURN	URANUS	NEPTUNE	PLUTO	CERES	PALLAS	JUNO	VESTA	CHIRON
1 M	14 34 40	10♉52 52	14♍34	4♉02	11♉57℞	22♊40	19♋06	26♈20	5♓24	18♉26	26♓44	0♒22℞	23♍56℞	29♋19	29♋17	6♋55	17♈19
2 T	14 38 36	11 21 07	26 49	4 02	11 19	23 48	19 33	26 34	5 29	18 29	26 46	0 22	23 54	29 43	29 53	7 22	17 22
3 W	14 42 33	12 19 19	9≏11	4 03	10 40	24 55	20 06	26 48	5 33	18 32	26 47	0 22	23 52	0♌07	0♌28	7 49	17 25
4 Th	14 46 29	13 17 30	22 06	4 04℞	10 02	26 01	20 39	27 02	5 37	18 36	26 49	0 22	23 50	0 31	1 04	8 16	17 28
5 F	14 50 26	14 15 39	5♏10	4 04	9 24	27 08	21 12	27 17	5 41	18 39	26 51	0 22	23 49D	0 56	1 39	8 43	17 32
6 Sa	14 54 23	15 13 46	18 35	4 03	8 48	28 14	21 45	27 31	5 45	18 43	26 52	0 22	23 49	1 20	2 15	9 09	17 35
7 Su	14 58 19	16 11 52	2♐16	4 03	8 14	29 20	22 19	27 45	5 49	18 46	26 54	0 21	23 49	1 45	2 50	9 36	17 38
8 M	15 2 16	17 09 56	16 10	4 01	7 43	0♋26	22 52	27 59	5 53	18 50	26 56	0 21	23 49	2 09	3 25	10 03	17 41
9 T	15 6 12	18 07 59	0♑16	3 59	7 15	1 32	23 26	28 13	5 57	18 53	26 57	0 21	23 50	2 34	4 01	10 30	17 44
10 W	15 10 9	19 06 00	14 39	3 58	6 50	2 38	23 59	28 27	6 00	18 57	26 59	0 21	23 50	2 59	4 36	10 57	17 48
11 Th	15 14 5	20 04 00	28 45	3 56	6 30	3 43	24 33	28 41	6 04	19 00	27 00	0 21	23 52	3 24	5 12	11 24	17 51
12 F	15 18 2	21 01 58	13≈02	3 55D	6 13	4 48	25 06	28 55	6 07	19 04	27 02	0 20	23 54	3 49	5 47	11 50	17 54
13 Sa	15 21 59	21 59 55	27 15	3 55	6 01	5 53	25 40	29 09	6 11	19 07	27 03	0 20	23 57	4 14	6 22	12 17	17 57
14 Su	15 25 55	22 57 51	11♓23	3 56	5 54	6 58	26 14	29 23	6 14	19 11	27 05	0 20	23 59	4 39	6 58	12 44	18 00
15 M	15 29 52	23 55 46	25 24	3 57	5 51D	8 02	26 48	29 36	6 17	19 14	27 06	0 19	24 02	5 04	7 33	13 10	18 03
16 T	15 33 48	24 53 39	9♈16	3 59	5 52	9 06	27 22	29 50	6 21	19 18	27 08	0 19	24 06	5 30	8 08	13 37	18 06
17 W	15 37 45	25 51 31	22 58	4 00℞	5 59	10 10	27 56	0♉04	6 24	19 21	27 09	0 19	24 10	5 55	8 44	14 04	18 09
18 Th	15 41 41	26 49 22	6♉28	4 00	6 10	11 14	28 30	0 17	6 27	19 25	27 11	0 18	24 14	6 21	9 19	14 30	18 12
19 F	15 45 38	27 47 12	19 45	3 59	6 25	12 17	29 04	0 31	6 30	19 28	27 12	0 18	24 19	6 46	9 54	14 57	18 15
20 Sa	15 49 34	28 45 00	2♊49	3 57	6 45	13 21	29 38	0 45	6 32	19 31	27 13	0 18	24 24	7 12	10 30	15 24	18 17
21 Su	15 53 31	29 42 47	15 38	3 54	7 09	14 24	0♌12	0 58	6 35	19 35	27 14	0 17	24 29	7 37	11 05	15 50	18 20
22 M	15 57 28	0♊40 33	28 12	3 50	7 38	15 26	0 46	1 12	6 38	19 38	27 16	0 16	24 35	8 03	11 40	16 17	18 23
23 T	16 1 24	1 38 17	10♋33	3 45	8 10	16 28	1 21	1 25	6 40	19 42	27 17	0 16	24 41	8 29	12 16	16 43	18 26
24 W	16 5 21	2 35 59	22 42	3 41	8 47	17 31	1 55	1 39	6 43	19 45	27 18	0 15	24 47	8 55	12 51	17 10	18 29
25 Th	16 9 17	3 33 40	4♌02	3 37	9 27	18 32	2 29	1 52	6 45	19 49	27 19	0 14	24 54	9 21	13 26	17 36	18 31
26 F	16 13 14	4 31 20	16 36	3 34	10 11	19 34	3 04	2 05	6 47	19 52	27 21	0 14	25 01	9 47	14 01	18 02	18 34
27 Sa	16 17 10	5 28 57	28 28	3 33D	10 59	20 35	3 38	2 18	6 49	19 55	27 22	0 13	25 09	10 13	14 37	18 29	18 37
28 Su	16 21 7	6 26 34	10♍24	3 32	11 50	21 35	4 13	2 32	6 52	19 59	27 23	0 13	25 16	10 39	15 12	18 55	18 39
29 M	16 25 3	7 24 09	22 27	3 33	12 45	22 36	4 48	2 45	6 53	20 02	27 24	0 12	25 25	11 05	15 47	19 21	18 42
30 T	16 29 0	8 21 42	4≏42	3 35	13 43	23 36	5 22	2 58	6 55	20 05	27 25	0 12	25 33	11 31	16 22	19 47	18 44
31 W	16 32 57	9 19 15	17 15	3 36	14 45	24 35	5 57	3 11	6 57	20 09	27 26	0 10	25 42	11 57	16 57	20 14	18 47

EPHEMERIS CALCULATED FOR 12 MIDNIGHT GREENWICH MEAN TIME. ALL OTHER DATA AND FACING ASPECTARIAN PAGE IN **EASTERN TIME (BOLD)** AND PACIFIC TIME (REGULAR).

JUNE 2023

☽ Last Aspect day	ET / hr:mn / PT		asp	☽ Ingress sign	day	ET / hr:mn / PT	
2	**8:51 pm**	5:51 pm	△♀	♐	2		10:03 pm
2	**8:51 pm**	5:51 pm	△♀	♐	3	**1:03 am**	
4	**11:24 pm**	8:24 pm	□♆	♑	5	**3:31 am**	12:31 am
6		9:40 pm	⚹♆	♒	7	**4:42 am**	1:42 am
7	**12:40 am**		⚹♆	♒	7	**4:42 am**	1:42 am
8		9:24 pm	□☿	♓	9	**6:14 am**	3:14 am
9	**12:24 am**		□☿	♓	9	**6:14 am**	3:14 am
11	**9:20 am**	6:20 am	⚹♇	♈	11	**9:20 am**	6:20 am
13	**2:27 pm**	11:27 am	□♇	♉	13	**2:31 pm**	11:31 am
15	**9:36 pm**	6:36 pm	△♇	♊	15	**9:46 pm**	6:46 pm

☽ Last Aspect day	ET / hr:mn / PT		asp	☽ Ingress sign	day	ET / hr:mn / PT	
17		11:24 pm	□♆	♋	18	**6:58 am**	3:58 am
18	**2:24 am**		□♆	♋	18	**6:58 am**	3:58 am
20	**5:43 pm**	2:43 pm	☍♇	♌	20	**6:04 pm**	3:04 pm
22	**1:01 pm**	10:01 am	□♅	♍	23	**6:35 am**	3:35 am
25	**6:24 pm**	3:24 pm	△♇	♎	25	**6:57 pm**	3:57 pm
28	**4:19 am**	1:19 am	□♇	♏	28	**4:55 am**	1:55 am
30	**10:20 am**	7:20 am	⚹♇	♐	30	**10:59 am**	7:59 am

☽ Phases & Eclipses phase	day	ET / hr:mn / PT	
Full Moon	3	**11:42 pm**	8:42 pm
4th Quarter	10	**3:31 pm**	12:31 pm
New Moon	17		9:37 pm
New Moon	18	**12:37 am**	
2nd Quarter	26	**3:50 am**	12:50 am

Planet Ingress		day	ET / hr:mn / PT	
♀	♌	5	**9:46 am**	6:46 am
♇	♑	11	**5:47 am**	2:47 am
☿	♊	11	**6:27 am**	3:27 am
⚳	♎	21	**7:30 am**	4:30 am
☉	♋	21	**10:58 am**	7:58 am
⚵	♋	22	**7:40 am**	4:40 am
⚶	♊	22	**3:17 pm**	12:17 pm
☿	♋	26	**8:24 pm**	5:24 pm

Planetary Motion		day	ET / hr:mn / PT	
♄	℞	17	**1:27 pm**	10:27 am
♆	℞	30	**5:07 pm**	2:07 pm

1 THURSDAY

☽☍♃	**2:04 am**		
☽□♂	**8:11 am**	5:11 am	
☽△♄	**8:30 am**	5:30 am	
♂⚻♄	**3:31 pm**	12:31 pm	
☽⚻☉	**3:50 pm**	12:50 pm	
☽☍☿		11:53 pm	

2 FRIDAY

☽☍☿	**2:53 am**	
☽☍♅	**8:10 am**	5:10 am
♀△♆	**6:42 pm**	3:42 pm
☽△♆	**8:42 pm**	5:42 pm
☽△♀	**8:51 pm**	5:51 pm
☽⚹♇		10:16 pm

3 SATURDAY

☽⚹♇	**1:16 am**	
☽⚻♃	**7:48 am**	4:48 am
☽□♄	**1:07 pm**	10:07 am
☽△♂	**2:59 pm**	11:59 am
☽☍☉	**11:42 pm**	8:42 pm

4 SUNDAY

☽⚻☿	**11:12 am**	8:12 am
☽⚻♅	**11:35 am**	8:35 am
☿☌♅	**3:49 pm**	12:49 pm
☽□♆	**11:24 pm**	8:24 pm

5 MONDAY

☽⚻♀	**3:05 am**	12:05 am
☽⚺♇	**3:40 am**	12:40 am
☽△♃	**10:44 am**	7:44 am
♀☍♇	**12:05 pm**	9:05 am
☽⚹♄	**3:12 pm**	12:12 pm
☽⚻♂	**7:00 pm**	4:00 pm

6 TUESDAY

☽⚻☉	**4:51 am**	1:51 am
☽△♅	**1:10 pm**	10:10 am
☽△☿	**5:34 pm**	2:34 pm
☽⚹♆		9:40 pm

7 WEDNESDAY

☽⚹♆	**12:40 am**	
☽☌♇	**4:48 am**	1:48 am
☽☍♀	**7:39 am**	4:39 am
☽□♃	**12:35 pm**	9:35 am
☽⚺♄	**4:23 pm**	1:23 pm
☽☍♂	**10:11 pm**	7:11 pm

8 THURSDAY

☽△☉	**9:29 am**	6:29 am
☽□♅	**2:37 pm**	11:37 am
☽□☿		9:24 pm
☽⚺♆		11:10 pm

9 FRIDAY

☽□☿	**12:24 am**	
☽⚺♆	**2:10 am**	
☽⚺♇	**6:17 am**	3:17 am
☽⚻♀	**12:41 pm**	9:41 am
☽⚹♃	**3:02 pm**	12:02 pm
☿⚹♆	**5:14 pm**	2:14 pm
☽☌♄	**6:16 pm**	3:16 pm
☽⚻♂		11:20 pm

Eastern time in bold type
Pacific time in medium type

10 SATURDAY

☽⚻♂	**2:20 am**	
☽□☉	**3:31 pm**	12:31 pm
☽⚹♅	**5:21 pm**	2:21 pm

11 SUNDAY

☽☌♆	**5:09 am**	2:09 am
☿△♇	**6:26 am**	3:26 am
☽⚹♇	**9:20 am**	6:20 am
☽⚹☿	**9:43 am**	6:43 am
♀□♃	**11:40 am**	8:40 am
☽⚺♃	**7:16 pm**	4:16 pm
☉⚺♅	**7:37 pm**	4:37 pm
☽△♀	**7:40 pm**	4:40 pm
☽⚺♄	**9:53 pm**	6:53 pm

12 MONDAY

☽△♂	**8:35 am**	5:35 am
☽⚺♅	**10:04 pm**	7:04 pm
☽⚹☉	**11:59 pm**	8:59 pm

13 TUESDAY

♀⚻♄	**5:59 am**	2:59 am
☽⚺♆	**10:12 am**	7:12 am
☽□♇	**2:27 pm**	11:27 am
☽⚺☿	**10:35 pm**	7:35 pm
☽☌♃		10:40 pm

14 WEDNESDAY

☽☌♃	**1:40 am**	
☽⚹♄	**3:36 am**	12:36 am
☽□♀	**5:08 am**	2:08 am
☽□♂	**5:15 pm**	2:15 pm
☿⚺♃		9:24 pm

15 THURSDAY

☿⚺♃	**12:24 am**	
☽☌♅	**4:55 am**	1:55 am
☽⚺☉	**11:04 am**	8:04 am
☿□♄	**12:09 pm**	9:09 am
☽⚹♆	**5:19 pm**	2:19 pm
☽△♇	**9:36 pm**	6:36 pm

16 FRIDAY

☽⚺♃	**10:12 am**	7:12 am
☽□♄	**11:20 am**	8:20 am
☽☌☿	**3:12 pm**	12:12 pm
☽⚹♀	**4:57 pm**	1:57 pm

17 SATURDAY

☽⚹♂	**4:14 am**	1:14 am
☿⚹♀	**11:29 am**	8:29 am
☽⚺♅	**1:45 pm**	10:45 am
☽☌☉		9:37 pm
☽□♆		11:24 pm

18 SUNDAY

☽☌☉	**12:37 am**	
☽□♆	**2:24 am**	
☽⚻♇	**6:43 am**	3:43 am
☽⚹♃	**8:45 pm**	5:45 pm
☽△♄	**9:00 pm**	6:00 pm
☉□♆	**11:54 pm**	8:54 pm

19 MONDAY

☽⚺♀	**7:02 am**	4:02 am
☽⚺☿	**11:41 am**	8:41 am
♃⚹♄	**11:53 am**	8:53 am
☽⚺♂	**5:28 pm**	2:28 pm
☽⚹♅		9:33 pm

20 TUESDAY

☽⚹♅	**12:33 am**	
☽△♆	**1:24 pm**	10:24 am
☽⚺☉	**4:37 pm**	1:37 pm
☽☍♇	**5:43 pm**	2:43 pm

21 WEDNESDAY

☉⚻♇	**6:20 am**	3:20 am
☽⚻♄	**8:30 am**	5:30 am
☽□♃	**9:15 am**	6:15 am
☿⚹♂	**11:23 am**	8:23 am
☽☌♀	**11:08 pm**	8:08 pm

22 THURSDAY

☽☌♂	**8:41 am**	5:41 am
☽⚹☿	**11:51 am**	8:51 am
☽□♅	**1:01 pm**	10:01 am
☿⚺♅	**6:37 pm**	3:37 pm
☽⚻♆		10:52 pm

23 FRIDAY

☽⚻♆	**1:52 am**	
☽⚻♇	**6:08 am**	3:08 am
☽⚹☉	**10:24 am**	7:24 am
☽☍♄	**9:07 pm**	6:07 pm
☽△♃	**10:53 pm**	7:53 pm

24 SATURDAY

☽⚺♀	**3:59 pm**	12:59 pm
☽⚺♂		9:33 pm
☽△♅		10:53 pm

25 SUNDAY

☽⚺♂	**12:33 am**	
☽△♅	**1:53 am**	
☽□☿	**1:25 pm**	10:25 am
☽☍♆	**2:20 pm**	11:20 am
☽△♇	**6:24 pm**	3:24 pm
☿□♆	**6:36 pm**	3:36 pm

26 MONDAY

☽□☉	**3:50 am**	12:50 am
♂□♅	**5:23 am**	2:23 am
☽⚻♄	**9:04 am**	6:04 am
☽⚻♃	**11:44 am**	8:44 am
☿⚻♇	**5:07 pm**	2:07 pm

27 TUESDAY

☽⚹♀	**6:56 am**	3:56 am
☽⚻♅	**12:58 pm**	9:58 am
☽⚹♂	**2:26 pm**	11:26 am
☽⚻♆		9:35 pm

28 WEDNESDAY

☽⚻♆	**12:35 am**	
☽□♇	**4:19 am**	1:19 am
☽△☿	**11:32 am**	8:32 am
☽△☉	**5:49 pm**	2:49 pm
☽△♄	**6:07 pm**	3:07 pm
☽☍♃	**9:29 pm**	6:29 pm
☉△♄	**9:43 pm**	6:43 pm

29 THURSDAY

☽□♀	**5:32 pm**	2:32 pm
☽☍♅	**8:22 pm**	5:22 pm
☽□♂		9:05 pm
☿△♄		11:24 pm

30 FRIDAY

☽□♂	**12:05 am**	
☿△♄	**2:24 am**	
☽△♆	**6:58 am**	3:58 am
☽⚹♇	**10:20 am**	7:20 am
☽□♄	**11:08 pm**	8:08 pm
☉☌☿		10:06 pm
☽⚻☉		11:48 pm
☽⚻☿		11:58 pm

JUNE 2023

DATE	SID.TIME	SUN	MOON	NODE	MERCURY	VENUS	MARS	JUPITER	SATURN	URANUS	NEPTUNE	PLUTO	CERES	PALLAS	JUNO	VESTA	CHIRON
1 Th	16 36 53	10♊16 45	0♊08	3♉37 Rx	15♉49	25♊35	6♌32	3♉24	6♓59	20♉12	27♓27	0♒09 Rx	25♍51	12♋23	17♊32	20♉40	18♈49
2 F	16 40 50	11 14 15	13 24	3 35	16 57	26 33	7 07	3 37	7 00	20 15	27 28	0 09	26 00	12 50	18 07	21 06	18 52
3 Sa	16 44 46	12 11 44	27 04	3 35	18 08	27 32	7 41	3 49	7 02	20 19	27 29	0 08	26 10	13 16	18 42	21 32	18 54
4 Su	16 48 43	13 09 11	11♐07	3 31	19 21	28 30	8 16	4 02	7 03	20 22	27 30	0 07	26 20	13 42	19 18	21 58	18 57
5 M	16 52 39	14 06 38	25 27	3 26	20 38	29 27	8 51	4 15	7 05	20 25	27 30	0 06	26 30	14 09	19 53	22 24	18 59
6 T	16 56 36	15 04 03	10♑01	3 20	21 58	0♋24	9 26	4 28	7 06	20 28	27 31	0 05	26 41	14 35	20 27	22 50	19 01
7 W	17 0 32	16 01 28	24 41	3 14	23 20	1 21	10 01	4 40	7 07	20 32	27 32	0 04	26 52	15 02	21 02	23 16	19 04
8 Th	17 4 29	16 58 52	9♒22	3 08	24 46	2 17	10 36	4 53	7 08	20 35	27 33	0 03	27 03	15 28	21 37	23 42	19 06
9 F	17 8 26	17 56 16	23 52	3 04	26 14	3 13	11 12	5 05	7 09	20 38	27 33	0 02	27 15	15 55	22 12	24 08	19 08
10 Sa	17 12 22	18 53 38	8♓12	3 02 D	27 45	4 08	11 47	5 17	7 10	20 41	27 34	0 01	27 26	16 22	22 47	24 33	19 10
11 Su	17 16 19	19 51 01	22 17	3 01	29 18	5 02	12 22	5 30	7 10	20 44	27 35	0 00	27 39	16 48	23 22	24 59	19 12
12 M	17 20 15	20 48 22	6♈07	3 02	0♊55	5 56	12 57	5 42	7 11	20 47	27 35	29♑59	27 51	17 15	23 57	25 25	19 14
13 T	17 24 12	21 45 44	19 41	3 03	2 34	6 50	13 33	5 54	7 12	20 51	27 36	29 58	28 03	17 42	24 32	25 51	19 16
14 W	17 28 8	22 43 05	3♉02	3 04 Rx	4 16	7 43	14 08	6 06	7 12	20 54	27 37	29 57	28 16	18 08	25 06	26 16	19 18
15 Th	17 32 5	23 40 25	16 09	3 03	6 01	8 35	14 43	6 18	7 12	20 57	27 37	29 56	28 29	18 35	25 41	26 42	19 20
16 F	17 36 1	24 37 45	29 04	3 00	7 48	9 26	15 19	6 30	7 12	21 00	27 38	29 55	28 43	19 02	26 16	27 07	19 22
17 Sa	17 39 58	25 35 05	11♊47	2 55	9 38	10 17	15 54	6 41	7 13 Rx	21 03	27 38	29 54	28 56	19 29	26 50	27 33	19 24
18 Su	17 43 55	26 32 24	24 20	2 47	11 30	11 08	16 30	6 53	7 13	21 06	27 39	29 53	29 10	19 56	27 25	27 58	19 26
19 M	17 47 51	27 29 42	6♋42	2 38	13 25	11 57	17 05	7 05	7 13	21 09	27 39	29 52	29 24	20 22	28 00	28 24	19 27
20 T	17 51 48	28 27 00	18 54	2 28	15 22	12 46	17 41	7 16	7 12	21 12	27 39	29 51	29 38	20 49	28 34	28 49	19 29
21 W	17 55 44	29 24 17	0♌58	2 18	17 22	13 34	18 17	7 28	7 12	21 15	27 40	29 49	29 53	21 16	29 09	29 14	19 31
22 Th	17 59 41	0♋21 34	12 55	2 08	19 24	14 22	18 53	7 39	7 12	21 18	27 40	29 48	0♎08	21 43	29 43	29 40	19 32
23 F	18 3 37	1 18 50	24 47	2 01	21 27	15 08	19 28	7 50	7 11	21 20	27 40	29 47	0 23	22 10	0♋18	0♊05	19 34
24 Sa	18 7 34	2 16 05	6♍37	1 55	23 33	15 54	20 04	8 02	7 11	21 23	27 40	29 46	0 38	22 37	0 52	0 30	19 35
25 Su	18 11 30	3 13 20	18 31	1 52	25 40	16 39	20 40	8 13	7 10	21 26	27 41	29 45	0 53	23 04	1 26	0 55	19 37
26 M	18 15 27	4 10 34	0♎32	1 51 D	27 48	17 23	21 16	8 24	7 08	21 29	27 41	29 43	1 09	23 31	2 01	1 20	19 38
27 T	18 19 24	5 07 47	12 45	1 51	29 58	18 05	21 52	8 34	7 08	21 32	27 41	29 42	1 25	23 58	2 35	1 45	19 40
28 W	18 23 20	6 05 00	25 08	1 51 Rx	2♋09	18 47	22 28	8 45	7 07	21 35	27 41	29 41	1 41	24 26	3 09	2 10	19 41
29 Th	18 27 17	7 02 13	7♏08	1 51	4 19	19 28	23 04	8 56	7 06	21 37	27 41	29 40	1 57	24 53	3 44	2 35	19 42
30 F	18 31 13	7 59 25	21 27	1 50	6 30	20 08	23 40	9 06	7 05	21 40	27 41 Rx	29 38	2 14	25 20	4 18	3 00	19 43

EPHEMERIS CALCULATED FOR 12 MIDNIGHT GREENWICH MEAN TIME. ALL OTHER DATA AND FACING ASPECTARIAN PAGE IN **EASTERN TIME (BOLD)** AND PACIFIC TIME (REGULAR).

JULY 2023

☽ Last Aspect day	ET / hr:mn / PT		asp	☽ Ingress sign	day	ET / hr:mn / PT	
2	**9:33 am**	6:33 am	□♆	♑	2	**1:20 pm**	10:20 am
4	**12:45 pm**	9:45 am	☌♇	♒	4	**1:30 pm**	10:30 am
6	**9:42 am**	6:42 am	☍♂	♓	6	**1:33 pm**	10:33 am
8	**2:22 pm**	11:22 am	⚹♇	♈	8	**3:19 pm**	12:19 pm
10	**7:11 pm**	4:11 pm	□☿	♉	10	**7:55 pm**	4:55 pm
12		11:11 pm	△♇	♊	13	**3:26 am**	12:26 am
13	**2:11 am**		△♇	♊	13	**3:26 am**	12:26 am
15	**8:35 am**	5:35 am	□♆	♋	15	**1:13 pm**	10:13 am
17	**11:06 pm**	8:06 pm	☍♇	♌	18		9:39 pm
17	**11:06 pm**	8:06 pm	☍♇	♌	18	**12:39 am**	

☽ Last Aspect day	ET / hr:mn / PT		asp	☽ Ingress sign	day	ET / hr:mn / PT	
20	**10:08 am**	7:08 am	☌♀	♍	20	**1:13 pm**	10:13 am
22		9:06 pm	△♇	♎	22		10:54 pm
23	**12:06 am**		△♇	♎	23	**1:54 am**	
25	**11:05 am**	8:05 am	□♇	♏	25	**12:55 pm**	9:55 am
27	**6:36 pm**	3:36 pm	⚹♇	♐	27	**8:24 pm**	5:24 pm
29	**7:51 pm**	4:51 pm	△♀	♑	29	**11:44 pm**	8:44 pm
31	**10:13 pm**	7:13 pm	☌♇	♒	31	**11:58 pm**	8:58 pm

☽ Phases & Eclipses phase	day	ET / hr:mn / PT	
Full Moon	3	**7:39 am**	4:39 am
4th Quarter	9	**9:48 pm**	6:48 pm
New Moon	17	**2:32 pm**	11:32 am
2nd Quarter	25	**6:07 pm**	3:07 pm

Planet Ingress		day	ET / hr:mn / PT	
♀	♍	9		11:55 pm
♀	♍	10	**2:55 am**	
♂	♍	10	**7:40 am**	4:40 am
☿	♌	10		9:11 pm
☿	♌	11	**12:11 am**	
☉	♌	22	**9:50 pm**	6:50 pm
☿	♍	28	**5:31 pm**	2:31 pm

Planetary Motion		day	ET / hr:mn / PT	
♀	℞	22	**9:33 pm**	6:33 pm
⚷	℞	23	**8:42 am**	5:42 am

1 SATURDAY
☉ ☌ ☿ **1:06 am**
☽ ⚻ ☉ **2:48 am**
☽ ⚻ ☿ **2:58 am**
☽ ⚻ ♃ **3:00 am** 12:00 am
☿ ⚹ ♃ **3:10 am** 12:10 am
☉ ⚹ ♃ **6:26 am** 3:26 am
☽ △ ♀ **11:21 pm** 8:21 pm
☽ ⚻ ♅ **11:48 pm** 8:48 pm

2 SUNDAY
☽ △ ♂ **5:19 am** 2:19 am
☽ □ ♆ **9:33 am** 6:33 am
♀ □ ♅ **10:34 am** 7:34 am
☽ ⚺ ♇ **12:39 pm** 9:39 am
☽ ⚹ ♄ 9:43 pm

3 MONDAY
☽ ⚹ ♄ **12:43 am**
☽ △ ♃ **5:02 am** 2:02 am
☽ ☍ ☉ **7:39 am** 4:39 am
☽ ☍ ☿ **12:50 pm** 9:50 am
☽ △ ♅ 9:30 pm
☽ ⚻ ♀ 10:55 pm

4 TUESDAY
☽ △ ♅ **12:30 am**
☽ ⚻ ♀ **1:55 am**
☽ ⚻ ♂ **7:43 am** 4:43 am
☽ ⚹ ♆ **9:49 am** 6:49 am
☽ ☌ ♇ **12:45 pm** 9:45 am
☽ ⚺ ♄ 9:35 pm

Eastern time in bold type
Pacific time in medium type

5 WEDNESDAY
☽ ⚺ ♄ **12:35 am**
☽ □ ♃ **5:28 am** 2:28 am
☽ ⚻ ☉ **10:46 am** 7:46 am
☽ ⚻ ☿ **8:36 pm** 5:36 pm
☽ □ ♅ 9:30 pm

6 THURSDAY
☽ □ ♅ **12:30 am**
☽ ☍ ♀ **3:38 am** 12:38 am
☽ ☍ ♂ **9:42 am** 6:42 am
☽ ⚺ ♆ **9:47 am** 6:47 am
♂ ⚻ ♆ **11:48 am** 8:48 am
☽ ⚺ ♇ **12:43 pm** 9:43 am
☽ ☌ ♄ 9:47 pm
☿ ⚹ ♅ 9:55 pm

7 FRIDAY
☽ ☌ ♄ **12:47 am**
☿ ⚹ ♅ **12:55 am**
☽ ⚹ ♃ **6:28 am** 3:28 am
☽ △ ☉ **2:48 pm** 11:48 am
☽ ⚹ ♅ 10:48 pm

8 SATURDAY
☽ ⚹ ♅ **1:48 am**
☽ △ ☿ **5:56 am** 2:56 am
☽ ⚻ ♀ **6:42 am** 3:42 am
☽ ☌ ♆ **11:22 am** 8:22 am
☿ ⚺ ♀ **12:45 pm** 9:45 am
☽ ⚻ ♂ **1:30 pm** 10:30 am
☽ ⚹ ♇ **2:22 pm** 11:22 am

9 SUNDAY
☽ ⚺ ♄ **3:02 am** 12:02 am
♂ ⚻ ♀ **8:54 am** 5:54 am
☽ ⚺ ♃ **9:44 am** 6:44 am
☿ △ ♆ **7:57 pm** 4:57 pm
☽ □ ☉ **9:48 pm** 6:48 pm

10 MONDAY
☽ ⚺ ♅ **5:45 am** 2:45 am
☽ △ ♀ **12:34 pm** 9:34 am
☽ ⚺ ♆ **3:43 pm** 12:43 pm
☿ ☍ ♇ **4:48 pm** 1:48 pm
☽ □ ♇ **6:50 pm** 3:50 pm
☽ □ ☿ **7:11 pm** 4:11 pm
☽ △ ♂ **8:31 pm** 5:31 pm

11 TUESDAY
☿ ⚺ ♂ **7:36 am** 4:36 am
☽ ⚹ ♄ **8:11 am** 5:11 am
☽ ☌ ♃ **4:04 pm** 1:04 pm

12 WEDNESDAY
☽ ⚹ ☉ **8:30 am** 5:30 am
☽ ☌ ♅ **12:42 pm** 9:42 am
☽ □ ♀ **9:24 pm** 6:24 pm
☽ ⚹ ♆ **10:59 pm** 7:59 pm
☽ △ ♇ 11:11 pm

13 THURSDAY
☽ △ ♇ **2:11 am**
☽ □ ♂ **6:51 am** 3:51 am
☽ ⚹ ☿ **12:40 pm** 9:40 am
☽ □ ♄ **4:06 pm** 1:06 pm
☽ ⚺ ♃ 10:11 pm

14 FRIDAY
☽ ⚺ ♃ **1:11 am**
☿ ⚻ ♄ **11:17 am** 8:17 am
☉ ⚹ ♅ **7:02 pm** 4:02 pm
☽ ⚺ ♅ **10:08 pm** 7:08 pm
☽ ⚺ ☉ **10:23 pm** 7:23 pm

15 SATURDAY
☽ ⚹ ♀ **8:27 am** 5:27 am
☽ □ ♆ **8:35 am** 5:35 am
☽ ⚻ ♇ **11:49 am** 8:49 am
♀ ⚻ ♆ **2:42 pm** 11:42 am
☽ ⚹ ♂ **7:48 pm** 4:48 pm
☽ △ ♄ 11:06 pm

16 SUNDAY
☽ △ ♄ **2:06 am**
☽ ⚺ ☿ **9:08 am** 6:08 am
☽ ⚹ ♃ **12:23 pm** 9:23 am

17 MONDAY
☿ □ ♃ **8:49 am** 5:49 am
☽ ⚹ ♅ **9:21 am** 6:21 am
☽ ☌ ☉ **2:32 pm** 11:32 am
☽ △ ♆ **7:52 pm** 4:52 pm
☽ ⚺ ♀ **8:55 pm** 5:55 pm
☽ ☍ ♇ **11:06 pm** 8:06 pm

18 TUESDAY
☽ ⚺ ♂ **10:37 am** 7:37 am
☽ ⚻ ♄ **1:36 pm** 10:36 am
☽ □ ♃ 10:02 pm

19 WEDNESDAY
☽ □ ♃ **1:02 am**
☽ ☌ ☿ **7:23 am** 4:23 am
☽ □ ♅ **9:51 pm** 6:51 pm

20 THURSDAY
☽ ⚺ ☉ **8:14 am** 5:14 am
☽ ⚻ ♆ **8:19 am** 5:19 am
☉ △ ♆ **9:07 am** 6:07 am
☽ ☌ ♀ **10:08 am** 7:08 am
☽ ⚻ ♇ **11:31 am** 8:31 am
♂ ☍ ♄ **4:39 pm** 1:39 pm
☽ ☍ ♄ 11:03 pm
☽ ☌ ♂ 11:36 pm

21 FRIDAY
☽ ☍ ♄ **2:03 am**
☽ ☌ ♂ **2:36 am**
☉ ⚺ ♀ **9:39 am** 6:39 am
☽ △ ♃ **2:30 pm** 11:30 am
☉ ☍ ♇ **11:53 pm** 8:53 pm

22 SATURDAY
☽ ⚺ ☿ **6:07 am** 3:07 am
☽ △ ♅ **10:48 am** 7:48 am
☽ ☍ ♆ **9:00 pm** 6:00 pm
☽ ⚺ ♀ **11:06 pm** 8:06 pm
☽ △ ♇ 9:06 pm
☽ ⚹ ☉ 11:15 pm

23 SUNDAY
☽ △ ♇ **12:06 am**
☽ ⚹ ☉ **2:15 am**
☽ ⚻ ♄ **2:18 pm** 11:18 am

☿ □ ♅ **5:39 pm** 2:39 pm
☽ ⚺ ♂ **6:22 pm** 3:22 pm

24 MONDAY
☽ ⚻ ♃ **3:24 am** 12:24 am
☽ ⚻ ♅ **10:35 pm** 7:35 pm
☽ ⚹ ☿ 11:39 pm

25 TUESDAY
☽ ⚹ ☿ **2:39 am**
☽ ⚻ ♆ **8:10 am** 5:10 am
☽ ⚹ ♀ **10:00 am** 7:00 am
☽ □ ♇ **11:05 am** 8:05 am
☽ □ ☉ **6:07 pm** 3:07 pm
☽ △ ♄ 9:27 pm

26 WEDNESDAY
☽ △ ♄ **12:27 am**
☽ ⚹ ♂ **7:31 am** 4:31 am
☽ ☍ ♃ **1:38 pm** 10:38 am
☿ ⚻ ♆ 9:00 pm

27 THURSDAY
☿ ⚻ ♆ **12:00 am**
☽ ☍ ♅ **7:10 am** 4:10 am
☿ ☌ ♀ **11:16 am** 8:16 am
☽ △ ♆ **3:56 pm** 12:56 pm
☽ □ ♀ **5:06 pm** 2:06 pm
☽ □ ☿ **5:53 pm** 2:53 pm
☽ ⚹ ♇ **6:36 pm** 3:36 pm
☿ ⚻ ♇ 9:24 pm

28 FRIDAY
☿ ⚻ ♇ **12:24 am**
☽ △ ☉ **5:22 am** 2:22 am

☽ □ ♄ **6:52 am** 3:52 am
☽ □ ♂ **4:09 pm** 1:09 pm
☽ ⚻ ♃ **7:44 pm** 4:44 pm
☉ ⚻ ♄ 10:38 pm

29 SATURDAY
☉ ⚻ ♄ **1:38 am**
☽ ⚻ ♅ **11:35 am** 8:35 am
☽ □ ♆ **7:32 pm** 4:32 pm
☽ △ ♀ **7:51 pm** 4:51 pm
☽ ⚺ ♇ **9:59 pm** 6:59 pm
☽ △ ☿ 11:55 pm

30 SUNDAY
☽ △ ☿ **2:55 am**
☽ ⚹ ♄ **9:15 am** 6:15 am
☽ ⚻ ☉ **11:35 am** 8:35 am
♀ ⚻ ♆ **12:25 pm** 9:25 am
☽ △ ♂ **8:18 pm** 5:18 pm
☽ △ ♃ **9:51 pm** 6:51 pm

31 MONDAY
☽ △ ♅ **12:29 pm** 9:29 am
☽ ⚻ ♀ **7:17 pm** 4:17 pm
☽ ⚹ ♆ **7:55 pm** 4:55 pm
☽ ☌ ♇ **10:13 pm** 7:13 pm

JULY 2023

DATE	SID.TIME	SUN	MOON	NODE	MERCURY	VENUS	MARS	JUPITER	SATURN	URANUS	NEPTUNE	PLUTO	CERES	PALLAS	JUNO	VESTA	CHIRON
1 Sa	18 35 10	8♋56 36	5♐14	1♉46R	8♋41	20♌47	24♌16	9♉17	7♓04R	21♉42	27♓41R	29♑37R	2♌30	25♌47	4♋52	3♊25	19♈45
2 Su	18 39 6	9 53 48	19 28	1 40	10 52	21 24	24 52	9 27	7 03	21 45	27 41	29 36	2 47	26 14	5 26	3 49	19 46
3 M	18 43 3	10 50 59	4♑06	1 31	13 02	22 00	25 28	9 38	7 01	21 47	27 41	29 34	3 04	26 41	6 00	4 14	19 47
4 T	18 47 0	11 48 10	19 01	1 22	15 11	22 36	26 04	9 48	7 00	21 50	27 41	29 33	3 21	27 09	6 34	4 39	19 48
5 W	18 50 56	12 45 21	4≈25	1 12	17 19	23 09	26 41	9 58	6 58	21 52	27 41	29 32	3 39	27 36	7 08	5 03	19 49
6 Th	18 54 53	13 42 32	19 07	1 03	19 26	23 42	27 17	10 08	6 56	21 55	27 41	29 30	3 56	28 03	7 42	5 28	19 50
7 F	18 58 49	14 39 43	3♓58	0 56	21 32	24 13	27 53	10 17	6 55	21 57	27 41	29 29	4 14	28 30	8 16	5 52	19 51
8 Sa	19 2 46	15 36 55	18 32	0 51	23 36	24 42	28 29	10 27	6 53	22 00	27 40	29 28	4 32	28 58	8 49	6 16	19 51
9 Su	19 6 42	16 34 06	2♈45	0 49	25 39	25 11	29 06	10 37	6 51	22 02	27 40	29 26	4 50	29 25	9 23	6 41	19 52
10 M	19 10 39	17 31 18	16 34	0 48D	27 40	25 37	29 42	10 46	6 49	22 04	27 40	29 25	5 08	29 52	9 57	7 05	19 53
11 T	19 14 35	18 28 31	0♉03	0 48R	29 39	26 02	0♍19	10 56	6 46	22 07	27 40	29 23	5 26	0♍19	10 31	7 29	19 54
12 W	19 18 32	19 25 44	13 11	0 47	1♌33	26 25	0 55	11 05	6 44	22 09	27 39	29 22	5 45	0 47	11 04	7 53	19 54
13 Th	19 22 29	20 22 58	26 04	0 46	3 33	26 47	1 32	11 14	6 42	22 11	27 39	29 21	6 04	1 14	11 38	8 17	19 55
14 F	19 26 25	21 20 12	8♊42	0 46	5 26	27 07	2 08	11 23	6 39	22 13	27 39	29 19	6 22	1 41	12 11	8 41	19 55
15 Sa	19 30 22	22 17 26	21 10	0 41	7 18	27 25	2 45	11 32	6 37	22 15	27 38	29 18	6 41	2 09	12 45	9 05	19 56
16 Su	19 34 18	23 14 41	3♋27	0 34	9 08	27 41	3 22	11 40	6 34	22 17	27 38	29 16	7 01	2 36	13 18	9 28	19 56
17 M	19 38 15	24 11 57	15 37	0 24	10 57	27 55	3 58	11 49	6 32	22 19	27 37	29 15	7 20	3 04	13 52	9 52	19 57
18 T	19 42 11	25 09 13	27 40	0 11	12 43	28 07	4 35	11 58	6 29	22 21	27 37	29 14	7 39	3 31	14 25	10 16	19 57
19 W	19 46 8	26 06 29	9♌38	29♈58	14 27	28 18	5 12	12 06	6 26	22 23	27 36	29 12	7 59	3 58	14 58	10 39	19 57
20 Th	19 50 4	27 03 45	21 31	29 44	16 10	28 26	5 49	12 14	6 23	22 25	27 36	29 11	8 19	4 26	15 32	11 03	19 57
21 F	19 54 1	28 01 02	3♍21	29 31	17 51	28 31	6 26	12 22	6 20	22 27	27 35	29 09	8 39	4 53	16 05	11 26	19 57
22 Sa	19 57 58	28 58 19	15 11	29 20	19 31	28 35	7 03	12 30	6 17	22 29	27 35	29 08	8 59	5 21	16 38	11 50	19 58
23 Su	20 1 54	29 55 36	27 04	29 12	21 06	28 36R	7 40	12 38	6 14	22 31	27 34	29 06	9 19	5 48	17 11	12 13	19 58R
24 M	20 5 51	0♌52 54	9♎04	29 07	22 42	28 35	8 17	12 45	6 11	22 33	27 33	29 05	9 39	6 16	17 44	12 36	19 58
25 T	20 9 47	1 50 12	21 15	29 04	24 15	28 32	8 54	12 53	6 08	22 34	27 33	29 04	9 59	6 43	18 17	12 59	19 58
26 W	20 13 44	2 47 31	3♏42	29 03	25 46	28 26	9 31	13 00	6 04	22 36	27 32	29 02	10 20	7 11	18 50	13 22	19 58
27 Th	20 17 40	3 44 49	16 32	29 02	27 13	28 18	10 08	13 07	6 01	22 37	27 31	29 01	10 40	7 38	19 23	13 45	19 58
28 F	20 21 37	4 42 09	29 47	29 01	28 43	28 07	10 45	13 14	5 57	22 39	27 30	28 59	11 01	8 06	19 55	14 08	19 57
29 Sa	20 25 33	5 39 28	13♐31	28 57	0♍09	27 54	11 22	13 21	5 54	22 41	27 29	28 58	11 22	8 33	20 28	14 30	19 57
30 Su	20 29 30	6 36 49	27 44	28 51	1 32	27 39	12 00	13 28	5 50	22 42	27 28	28 56	11 43	9 01	21 01	14 53	19 57
31 M	20 33 27	7 34 10	12♑26	28 42	2 54	27 21	12 37	13 35	5 46	22 44	27 27	28 55	12 04	9 28	21 33	15 15	19 56

EPHEMERIS CALCULATED FOR 12 MIDNIGHT GREENWICH MEAN TIME. ALL OTHER DATA AND FACING ASPECTARIAN PAGE IN **EASTERN TIME (BOLD)** AND PACIFIC TIME (REGULAR).

AUGUST 2023

D Last Aspect / D Ingress

day	ET / hr:mn / PT		sign	day	ET / hr:mn / PT
4	5:15 pm 2:15 pm	8:05 pm	✶ ♀	1	11:05 pm 8:05 pm
4	9:21 pm 6:21 pm	8:19 pm	♈ 1	4	11:19 pm 8:19 pm
6		9:13 pm	♉ 6		11:25 pm
9	12:13 am		♊ 9	2:25 am	6:05 am
9	6:39 am 3:39 am		♋ 11	9:05 am	6:05 am
11	1:27 pm 10:27 am		♌ 11	6:52 pm 3:52 pm	
14	3:46 pm 12:46 pm		♍ 14	6:36 am 3:36 am	
16	5:38 pm 2:38 pm		♎ 16	7:14 pm 4:14 pm	
19	4:51 am 1:51 am		♏ 19	7:53 am 4:53 am	
21	4:31 pm 1:31 pm		♐ 21	7:22 pm 4:22 pm	

day	ET / hr:mn / PT		sign	day	ET / hr:mn / PT
23		10:10 pm	♑ 23	4:07 am 1:07 am	
24	1:10 am		♒ 24	4:07 am 1:07 am	
26	7:56 am 4:56 am		♓ 26	9:05 am 6:05 am	
28	7:49 am 4:49 am		♈ 28	10:32 am 7:32 am	
29	11:04 pm 8:04 pm		♉ 30	9:56 am 6:56 am	

Planet Ingress

	day	ET / hr:mn / PT
♀ ♌	15	3:29 pm 12:29 pm
☉ ♍	23	5:01 am 2:01 am
♂ ♎	27	9:20 am 6:20 am

Phases & Eclipses

phase	day	ET / hr:mn / PT
Full Moon	1	2:32 pm 11:32 am
4th Quarter	8	6:28 am 3:28 am
New Moon	16	5:38 am 2:38 am
2nd Quarter	24	5:57 am 2:57 am
Full Moon	30	9:36 pm 6:36 pm

Planetary Motion

	day	ET / hr:mn / PT
♀ R₍	23	3:59 pm 12:59 pm
♄ R₍	28	10:39 pm 7:39 pm

---

1 TUESDAY
☽ △ ⚷ 7:37 am 4:37 am
☽ △ ♄ 8:54 am 5:54 am
☽ △ ♃ 2:32 pm 11:32 am
☽ ♂ ♃ 4:45 am 1:45 am
☽ □ ♀ 9:38 am 6:38 am
☽ △ ♅ 9:48 am 6:48 am
☽ ✶ ♀ 10:18 pm 7:18 pm

2 WEDNESDAY
☽ ♂ ♄ 11:44 am 8:44 am
☽ △ ♂ 5:15 pm 2:15 pm
☽ □ ☿ 7:00 am 4:00 am
☽ ✶ ♀ 9:16 pm 6:16 pm

3 THURSDAY
☽ ✶ ♆ 7:53 am 4:53 am
☽ □ ♅ 11:03 am 8:03 am
☽ △ ♀ 4:59 am 1:59 am
☽ □ ♂ 9:20 am 6:20 am
☽ ♂ ♀ 10:15 pm 8:15 pm

4 FRIDAY
☽ △ ☿ 11:35 am 8:35 am
☽ □ ♆ 3:49 am 12:49 am
☽ ✶ ♄ 7:00 am 4:00 am
☽ □ ♀ 9:21 am 6:21 am

5 SATURDAY
☽ ✶ ♅ 8:18 am 5:18 am
☽ ♂ ♆ 4:14 am 1:14 am
☽ △ ♄ 9:40 am 6:40 am
☽ ♂ ☿ 2 11:03 pm 8:03 pm

6 SUNDAY
☽ ✶ ♂ 3:03 am 12:03 am
☽ △ ♃ 1:57 pm 10:57 am
☽ □ ♀ 4:35 pm 1:35 pm
☽ ✶ ♀ 8:03 pm 5:03 pm
☽ △ ♀ 9:43 pm 6:43 pm

7 MONDAY
☽ ♂ ♂ 12:13 am
☽ △ ♄ 11:46 am 8:46 am
☽ □ ♀ 10:10 pm

8 TUESDAY
☽ △ ♀ 1:10 am
☽ ✶ ☿ 4:11 am 1:11 am
☽ △ ♅ 6:28 am 3:28 am
☽ □ ♃ 10:46 am 7:46 am
☽ ✶ ♆ 7:50 pm 4:50 pm
☽ ♂ ♀ 8:21 pm 5:21 pm

9 WEDNESDAY
☽ ✶ ♀ 4:00 am 1:00 am
☽ △ ♃ 6:39 am 3:39 am
☽ □ ♂ 7:08 am 4:08 am
☽ ✶ ♄ 6:45 pm 3:45 pm
☽ □ ☿ 8:47 pm 5:47 pm

10 THURSDAY
☽ △ ☿ 12:51 pm 9:51 am
☽ △ ♀ 2:02 pm 11:02 am
☽ ✶ ♀ 7:37 pm 4:37 pm

11 FRIDAY
☽ □ ♆ 1:10☽ pm
☽ ✶ ♀ 11:52 pm

12 SATURDAY
☽ ♂ ♀ 1:37 am
☽ △ ♅ 4:47 am 2:03 am
☽ ✶ ♂ 4:13 pm 10:27 am
☽ △ ♄ 1:13 pm

13 SUNDAY
☽ △ ♆ 1:37 am
☽ ✶ ♀ 5:15 am
☽ □ ♀ 9:06 pm

14 MONDAY
☽ ♂ ♀ 12:57 am
☽ ✶ ♄ 3:56 am 12:46 am
☽ △ ♀ 4:11 pm 1:12 pm
☽ □ ♂ 10:10 pm

15 TUESDAY
☽ ✶ ☿ 1:1 am
☽ ☌ ☉ 12:1 pm
☽ ♂ ♅ 11:19 pm 9:44 am
☽ △ ♆ 8:4 pm 10:04 am
☽ 5:44 pm

16 WEDNESDAY
☽ ✶ ♀ 4:48 am 1:48 am
☽ □ ♀ 5:04 am 2:04 am
☽ □ ♂ 9:53 am 6:53 am
☽ ✶ ♄ 1:26 pm 10:26 am
☽ △ ♀ 4:17 pm 1:17 pm

17 THURSDAY
☽ ♂ ♀ 4:32 pm 1:32 pm

18 FRIDAY
☽ △ ♂ 1:48 am
☽ □ ♄ 6:35 am 3:35 am
☽ ♂ ☿ 1:09 pm 10:09 am
☽ ✶ ♀ 8:51 pm 5:51 pm
☽ △ ♀ 3:19 pm 12:19 pm
☽ ✶ ♆ 11:42 pm 8:42 pm

19 SATURDAY
☽ ♂ ♂ 2:01 pm 11:01 am
☽ △ ♀ 4:51 am 1:51 am
☽ □ ♀ 4:43 pm 1:43 pm

20 SUNDAY
☉ ✶ ♀ 3:40 pm 12:40 pm
☽ △ ♀ 2:19 pm 11:19 am
☽ ✶ ♄ 4:07 pm 1:07 pm

---

21 MONDAY
☽ △ ♅ 2:50 am
☽ ✶ ♀ 12:02 pm 9:02 am
☽ □ ♀ 5:47 am 2:47 am
☽ △ ♃ 2:07 pm 11:07 am
☽ ☌ ♆ 4:19 pm 1:19 pm
☽ ✶ ♀ 4:31 pm 1:31 pm

22 TUESDAY
☽ ♂ ♂ 3:33 am 12:33 am
☽ ✶ ♀ 8:16 am 5:16 am
☽ △ ♄ 4:34 pm 1:34 pm
☽ ✶ ♀ 9:10 pm
☽ □ ☿ 9:48 pm

23 WEDNESDAY
☽ ✶ ♀ 12:10 am
☽ □ ♀ 12:48 am
☽ △ ♅ 1:03 pm 10:03 am
☽ □ ♀ 3:19 pm 12:19 pm
☽ ♂ ♆ 10:33 pm 7:33 pm
☽ △ ♃ 9:09 pm
☽ □ ♀ 10:10 pm

24 THURSDAY
☽ □ ♀ 12:09 am
☽ △ ♀ 5:57 am 1:51 am
☽ ♂ ♄ 6:23 pm 1:43 pm

25 FRIDAY
☽ ✶ ♂ 5:27 am 2:57 am
☽ △ ♀ 7:49 am 4:49 am

26 SATURDAY
☽ □ ♀ 3:49 pm 12:49 pm
☽ ☌ ♀ 9:12 am 6:12 am
☽ ✶ ♄ 3:43 pm

27 SUNDAY
☉ ✶ ♀ 4:28 am 1:28 am
☽ △ ♀ 7:28 am 4:28 am
☽ ✶ ♆ 7:58 am 4:58 am
☽ ♂ ♀ 8:00 pm 5:00 pm
☽ □ ♀ 11:22 am 8:22 am

28 MONDAY
☽ □ ♀ 5:29 am 2:29 am
☽ □ ♀ 7:49 am 4:49 am
☽ △ ♂ 11:39 am 8:39 am
☽ ✶ ♄ 4:29 pm 1:29 pm
☽ ✶ ♀ 7:08 pm 4:08 pm

29 TUESDAY
☽ ☌ ♀ 6:56 am 3:56 am
☽ ♂ ♀ 11:11 am 8:11 am
☽ ✶ ♀ 6:18 pm 3:18 pm
☽ □ ♄ 11:04 pm 8:04 pm

30 WEDNESDAY
☽ △ ♀ 4:56 am 1:56 am
☽ □ ♆ 7:14 am 4:14 am
☽ △ ☿ 1:07 pm 10:07 am

31 THURSDAY
☽ ✶ ♀ 5:33 am 2:33 am
☽ □ ♀ 8:16 am 10:25 am 3:16 am
☽ ☌ ♀ 3:25 pm 12:25 pm
☽ △ ♅ 10:20 pm 7:20 pm

Eastern time in bold type
Pacific time in medium type

AUGUST 2023

DATE	SID.TIME	SUN	MOON	NODE	MERCURY	VENUS	MARS	JUPITER	SATURN	URANUS	NEPTUNE	PLUTO	CERES	PALLAS	JUNO	VESTA	CHIRON
1 T	20 37 23	8Ω31 23	27♍39	28♈31	4♍14	27♌02R	13♍14	13♉47	5♓43R	22♉45	27♓25R	28♑54R	12≏25	9♍56	22♋06	15♊38	19♈56R
2 W	20 41 20	9 28 53	12≈45	28 21	5 31	26 39	13 51	13 47	5 39	22 46	27 25	28 52	12 47	10 23	22 38	16 00	19 55
3 Th	20 45 16	10 26 16	28 02	28 11	6 47	26 15	14 29	13 53	5 35	22 48	27 24	28 51	13 08	10 51	23 11	16 22	19 55
4 F	20 49 13	11 23 40	13♑10	28 04	8 00	25 49	15 06	13 59	5 31	22 49	27 23	28 49	13 30	11 18	23 43	16 45	19 54
5 Sa	20 53 9	12 21 05	27 59	27 59	9 11	25 20	15 44	14 05	5 27	22 50	27 22	28 48	13 51	11 46	24 15	17 07	19 54
6 Su	20 57 6	13 18 31	12♈23	27 56	10 20	24 50	16 21	14 11	5 23	22 51	27 21	28 47	14 13	12 13	24 47	17 29	19 53
7 M	21 1 2	14 15 59	26 21	27 55D	11 26	24 19	16 59	14 16	5 19	22 52	27 20	28 45	14 35	12 41	25 20	17 50	19 52
8 T	21 4 59	15 13 28	9♉52	27 55R	12 30	23 46	17 36	14 21	5 15	22 53	27 19	28 44	14 57	13 08	25 52	18 12	19 52
9 W	21 8 56	16 10 58	23 00	27 55	13 31	23 11	18 14	14 26	5 11	22 54	27 18	28 43	15 19	13 36	26 24	18 34	19 51
10 Th	21 12 52	17 08 29	5Ⅱ47	27 53	14 31	22 36	18 52	14 31	5 07	22 55	27 17	28 41	15 41	14 04	26 56	18 55	19 50
11 F	21 16 49	18 06 02	18 17	27 50	15 25	22 00	19 29	14 36	5 03	22 56	27 15	28 40	16 03	14 31	27 28	19 17	19 49
12 Sa	21 20 45	19 03 36	0♋35	27 44	16 18	21 23	20 07	14 41	4 58	22 57	27 14	28 39	16 25	14 59	27 59	19 39	19 48
13 Su	21 24 42	20 01 12	12 42	27 35	17 08	20 46	20 45	14 45	4 54	22 58	27 13	28 37	16 48	15 26	28 31	19 59	19 47
14 M	21 28 38	20 58 49	24 43	27 24	17 54	20 08	21 23	14 49	4 50	22 59	27 12	28 36	17 10	15 54	29 03	20 20	19 46
15 T	21 32 35	21 56 27	6Ω39	27 12	18 37	19 31	22 01	14 53	4 45	23 00	27 10	28 35	17 33	16 21	29 34	20 41	19 45
16 W	21 36 31	22 54 06	18 32	27 00	19 16	18 54	22 39	14 57	4 41	23 00	27 09	28 33	17 55	16 49	0♌06	21 02	19 44
17 Th	21 40 28	23 51 47	0♍23	26 49	19 51	18 18	23 17	15 01	4 37	23 01	27 08	28 32	18 18	17 17	0 37	21 22	19 42
18 F	21 44 25	24 49 29	12 13	26 39	20 22	17 43	23 55	15 05	4 32	23 01	27 07	28 31	18 41	17 44	1 09	21 43	19 41
19 Sa	21 48 21	25 47 12	24 06	26 32	20 49	17 08	24 33	15 08	4 28	23 02	27 05	28 30	19 04	18 12	1 40	22 03	19 40
20 Su	21 52 18	26 44 56	6≏02	26 27	21 12	16 35	25 11	15 11	4 23	23 02	27 04	28 28	19 27	18 39	2 11	22 24	19 39
21 M	21 56 14	27 42 42	18 06	26 25D	21 29	16 03	25 49	15 14	4 19	23 03	27 02	28 27	19 50	19 07	2 43	22 44	19 37
22 T	22 0 11	28 40 28	0♏39	26 26	21 42	15 33	26 27	15 17	4 14	23 03	27 01	28 26	20 13	19 35	3 14	23 04	19 36
23 W	22 4 7	29 38 16	12 48	26 26	21 49R	15 04	27 05	15 19	4 10	23 03	27 00	28 25	20 36	20 02	3 45	23 24	19 34
24 Th	22 8 4	0♍36 05	25 35	26 27R	21 51	14 38	27 44	15 22	4 05	23 04	26 58	28 24	20 59	20 30	4 16	23 43	19 33
25 F	22 12 0	1 33 55	8♐46	26 26	21 47	14 13	28 22	15 24	4 01	23 04	26 57	28 23	21 23	20 57	4 46	24 03	19 31
26 Sa	22 15 57	2 31 47	22 23	26 25	21 38	13 50	29 00	15 26	3 56	23 04	26 55	28 21	21 46	21 25	5 17	24 22	19 30
27 Su	22 19 54	3 29 40	6♑28	26 21	21 22	13 30	29 39	15 28	3 52	23 04	26 54	28 20	22 09	21 52	5 48	24 42	19 28
28 M	22 23 50	4 27 34	21 00	26 15	21 00	13 12	0≏17	15 29	3 47	23 04	26 52	28 20	22 33	22 20	6 19	25 01	19 26
29 T	22 27 47	5 25 29	5≈56	26 08	20 33	12 56	0 56	15 31	3 43	23 05R	26 51	28 18	22 57	22 48	6 49	25 20	19 24
30 W	22 31 43	6 23 25	21 07	26 01	20 00	12 43	1 34	15 32	3 38	23 05	26 49	28 17	23 20	23 15	7 20	25 39	19 23
31 Th	22 35 40	7 21 23	6♓24	25 54	19 21	12 32	2 13	15 33	3 34	23 04	26 48	28 16	23 44	23 43	7 50	25 57	19 21

EPHEMERIS CALCULATED FOR 12 MIDNIGHT GREENWICH MEAN TIME. ALL OTHER DATA AND FACING ASPECTARIAN PAGE IN **EASTERN TIME (BOLD)** AND PACIFIC TIME (REGULAR).

SEPTEMBER 2023

☽ Last Aspect day	ET / hr:mn / PT	asp	☽ Ingress sign	day	ET / hr:mn / PT
1	**6:36 am** 3:36 am	⚹♇	♈	1	**9:25 am** 6:25 am
3	**7:57 am** 4:57 am	□♇	♉	3	**11:00 am** 8:00 am
5	**12:46 pm** 9:46 am	△♇	♊	5	**4:07 pm** 1:07 pm
7	**6:22 pm** 3:22 pm	□♆	♋	7	10:00 pm
7	**6:22 pm** 3:22 pm	□♆	♋	8	**1:00 am**
10	**8:47 am** 5:47 am	☍♇	♌	10	**12:36 pm** 9:36 am
12	**11:06 am** 8:06 am	□♅	♍	12	10:18 pm
12	**11:06 am** 8:06 am	□♅	♍	13	**1:18 am**
15	**9:49 am** 6:49 am	△♇	♎	15	**1:44 pm** 10:44 am
17	**9:06 pm** 6:06 pm	□♇	♏	17	9:58 pm
17	**9:06 pm** 6:06 pm	□♇	♏	18	**12:58 am**
20	**6:21 am** 3:21 am	⚹♇	♐	20	**10:06 am** 7:06 am
22	**3:32 pm** 12:32 pm	□☉	♑	22	**4:20 pm** 1:20 pm
24	**4:05 pm** 1:05 pm	☌♇	♒	24	**7:29 pm** 4:29 pm
26	**8:38 am** 5:38 am	□♅	♓	26	**8:18 pm** 5:18 pm
28	**4:58 pm** 1:58 pm	⚹♇	♈	28	**8:17 pm** 5:17 pm
30	**5:50 pm** 2:50 pm	□♇	♉	30	**9:18 pm** 6:18 pm

☽ Phases & Eclipses phase	day	ET / hr:mn / PT
4th Quarter	6	**6:21 pm** 3:21 pm
New Moon	14	**9:40 pm** 6:40 pm
2nd Quarter	22	**3:32 pm** 12:32 pm
Full Moon	29	**5:58 am** 2:58 am

Planet Ingress	day	ET / hr:mn / PT
♀ ♎	13	**12:38 pm** 9:38 am
⚵ ♋	13	**7:28 pm** 4:28 pm
⚳ ♏	15	**8:50 am** 5:50 am
☉ ♎	22	11:50 pm
☉ ♎	23	**2:50 am**

Planetary Motion		day	ET / hr:mn / PT
♀	D	3	**9:20 pm** 6:20 pm
♃	℞	4	**10:10 am** 7:10 am
☿	D	15	**4:21 pm** 1:21 pm

1 FRIDAY
☽☌♆ **4:13 am** 1:13 am
☽⚹♇ **6:36 am** 3:36 am
☽☍♂ **2:50 pm** 11:50 am
☽⚺♄ **2:56 pm** 11:56 am
♂⚻♄ **5:01 pm** 2:01 pm
☽⚻☉ 9:46 pm

2 SATURDAY
☽⚻☉ **12:46 am**
☽△♀ **5:19 am** 2:19 am
☽⚺♃ **10:47 am** 7:47 am
☽⚻☿ **1:25 pm** 10:25 am
☽⚺♅ **11:15 pm** 8:15 pm

3 SUNDAY
☽⚺♆ **5:24 am** 2:24 am
☽□♇ **7:57 am** 4:57 am
☽⚹♄ **4:36 pm** 1:36 pm
☽⚻♂ **7:10 pm** 4:10 pm

4 MONDAY
☿△♃ **6:29 am** 3:29 am
☽△☉ **7:12 am** 4:12 am
☽□♀ **8:08 am** 5:08 am
☽△☿ **1:35 pm** 10:35 am
☽☌♃ **2:06 pm** 11:06 am
☉⚺♀ **8:42 pm** 5:42 pm

5 TUESDAY
☽☌♅ **3:28 am** 12:28 am
☽⚹♆ **9:59 am** 6:59 am

☽△♇ **12:46 pm** 9:46 am
☽□♄ **9:50 pm** 6:50 pm

6 WEDNESDAY
☽△♂ **3:45 am** 12:45 am
☉☌☿ **7:09 am** 4:09 am
☽⚹♀ **3:06 pm** 12:06 pm
☽□☿ **4:46 pm** 1:46 pm
☽□☉ **6:21 pm** 3:21 pm
☽⚺♃ **9:12 pm** 6:12 pm

7 THURSDAY
☽⚺♅ **11:30 am** 8:30 am
☿⚺♀ **12:18 pm** 9:18 am
☽□♆ **6:22 pm** 3:22 pm
☽⚻♇ **9:22 pm** 6:22 pm

8 FRIDAY
☽△♄ **6:43 am** 3:43 am
☉△♃ **7:13 am** 4:13 am
☽□♂ **4:34 pm** 1:34 pm
☽⚹☿ **10:57 pm** 7:57 pm
☽⚺♀ 11:02 pm

9 SATURDAY
☽⚺♀ **2:02 am**
☽⚹♃ **7:38 am** 4:38 am
☽⚹☉ **9:49 am** 6:49 am
☽⚹♅ **10:34 pm** 7:34 pm

10 SUNDAY
☽△♆ **5:36 am** 2:36 am
☽☍♇ **8:47 am** 5:47 am
☽⚻♄ **6:09 pm** 3:09 pm

11 MONDAY
☿⚺♂ **3:22 am** 12:22 am
☽⚺☿ **7:37 am** 4:37 am
☽⚹♂ **8:06 am** 5:06 am
☽☌♀ **3:32 pm** 12:32 pm
☽□♃ **7:54 pm** 4:54 pm

12 TUESDAY
☽⚺☉ **3:37 am** 12:37 am
☽□♅ **11:06 am** 8:06 am
☽⚻♆ **6:07 pm** 3:07 pm
☽⚻♇ **9:24 pm** 6:24 pm

13 WEDNESDAY
☽☍♄ **6:31 am** 3:31 am
☽☌☿ **6:04 pm** 3:04 pm
☽⚺♂ 9:22 pm

14 THURSDAY
☽⚺♂ **12:22 am**
☽⚺♀ **5:56 am** 2:56 am
☽△♃ **8:27 am** 5:27 am
☽☌☉ **9:40 pm** 6:40 pm
☽△♅ **11:38 pm** 8:38 pm

15 FRIDAY
☽☍♆ **6:30 am** 3:30 am
☽△♇ **9:49 am** 6:49 am
☽⚻♄ **6:32 pm** 3:32 pm
☉△♅ **9:24 pm** 6:24 pm

16 SATURDAY
☽⚺☿ **5:45 am** 2:45 am
☽☌♂ **3:53 pm** 12:53 pm
☽⚹♀ **7:57 pm** 4:57 pm
☽⚻♃ **8:12 pm** 5:12 pm
♀□♃ 11:10 pm

17 SUNDAY
♀□♃ **2:10 am**
☽⚻♅ **11:09 am** 8:09 am
☽⚺☉ **2:27 pm** 11:27 am
☽⚻♆ **5:47 pm** 2:47 pm
☽□♇ **9:06 pm** 6:06 pm

18 MONDAY
☽△♄ **5:19 am** 2:19 am
☽⚹☿ **5:52 pm** 2:52 pm

19 TUESDAY
☽⚺♂ **5:31 am** 2:31 am
☽☍♃ **6:16 am** 3:16 am
☉☍♆ **7:17 am** 4:17 am
☽□♀ **8:29 am** 5:29 am
♂⚻♃ **6:48 pm** 3:48 pm
☽☍♅ **8:46 pm** 5:46 pm

20 WEDNESDAY
☽△♆ **3:06 am** 12:06 am
☽⚹☉ **4:47 am** 1:47 am
☽⚹♇ **6:21 am** 3:21 am
☽□♄ **1:58 pm** 10:58 am
☉△♇ 10:21 pm

21 THURSDAY
☉△♇ **1:21 am**
☽□☿ **5:13 am** 2:13 am
☽⚻♃ **1:47 pm** 10:47 am
☽⚹♂ **4:12 pm** 1:12 pm
☽△♀ **6:25 pm** 3:25 pm

22 FRIDAY
☽⚻♅ **3:40 am** 12:40 am
☽□♆ **9:37 am** 6:37 am
☽⚺♇ **12:46 pm** 9:46 am
☽□☉ **3:32 pm** 12:32 pm
☽⚹♄ **7:44 pm** 4:44 pm

23 SATURDAY
☽△☿ **2:24 pm** 11:24 am
☽△♃ **6:12 pm** 3:12 pm
☽□♂ **11:17 pm** 8:17 pm
☽□⚷ 9:07 pm
☽⚻♀ 10:04 pm

24 SUNDAY
☽⚻♀ **1:04 am**
☽△♅ **7:27 am** 4:27 am
☽⚹♆ **1:03 pm** 10:03 am
☽☌♇ **4:05 pm** 1:05 pm
☽△☉ **10:26 pm** 7:26 pm
☽⚺♄ **10:29 pm** 7:29 pm
☉⚻♄ **11:10 pm** 8:10 pm

25 MONDAY
☿△♃ **8:10 am** 5:10 am
☽□♃ **7:49 pm** 4:49 pm
☽⚻☿ **9:02 pm** 6:02 pm

26 TUESDAY
☽△♂ **3:13 am** 12:13 am
☽☍♀ **4:47 am** 1:47 am
☽□♅ **8:38 am** 5:38 am
☽⚺♆ **2:00 pm** 11:00 am
☽⚺♇ **5:00 pm** 2:00 pm
☽☌♄ **11:01 pm** 8:01 pm
☽⚻☉ 11:33 pm

27 WEDNESDAY
☽⚻☉ **2:33 am**
☽⚹♃ **7:46 pm** 4:46 pm
☽☍☿ 11:18 pm

28 THURSDAY
☽☍☿ **2:18 am**
☽⚻♂ **5:30 am** 2:30 am
☽⚻♀ **7:06 am** 4:06 am
☽⚹♅ **8:35 am** 5:35 am
☽☌♆ **1:54 pm** 10:54 am
☽⚹♇ **4:58 pm** 1:58 pm
☽⚺♄ **10:49 pm** 7:49 pm

29 FRIDAY
☽☍☉ **5:58 am** 2:58 am
♀□♅ **1:53 pm** 10:53 am
☽⚺♃ **7:46 pm** 4:46 pm

30 SATURDAY
☿⚺♂ **4:35 am** 1:35 am
☽☍♂ **8:20 am** 5:20 am
☽⚻☿ **8:36 am** 5:36 am
☽⚺♅ **9:06 am** 6:06 am
☽△♀ **10:08 am** 7:08 am
☿△♅ **12:55 pm** 9:55 am
☽⚺♆ **2:35 pm** 11:35 am
☽□♇ **5:50 pm** 2:50 pm
☽⚹♄ **11:45 pm** 8:45 pm
♂⚻♅ 9:38 pm

Eastern time in bold type
Pacific time in medium type

SEPTEMBER 2023

DATE	SID.TIME	SUN	MOON	NODE	MERCURY	VENUS	MARS	JUPITER	SATURN	URANUS	NEPTUNE	PLUTO	CERES	PALLAS	JUNO	VESTA	CHIRON
1 F	22 39 36	8♍19 23	21♓36	25♉48R	18♍37R	12♋17R	2♎51	15♉34	3♓29R	23♉04R	26♓46R	28♑15R	24♎08	24♏10	8♌20	26♊16	19♈19R
2 Sa	22 43 33	9 17 24	6♈33	25 45	17 48	12 14	3 30	15 34	3 25	23 04	26 45	28 14	24 32	24 38	8 50	26 34	19 17
3 Su	22 47 29	10 15 27	21 07	25 43D	16 55	12 13D	4 09	15 35	3 20	23 04	26 43	28 13	24 56	25 05	9 21	26 52	19 15
4 M	22 51 26	11 13 32	5♉15	25 45	16 00	12 13	4 47	15 35R	3 16	23 04	26 42	28 12	25 20	25 33	9 51	27 10	19 13
5 T	22 55 23	12 11 39	18 54	25 45	15 02	12 15	5 26	15 35	3 11	23 03	26 40	28 11	25 44	26 01	10 21	27 28	19 11
6 W	22 59 19	13 09 48	2♊07	25 46R	14 04	12 18	6 05	15 35	3 07	23 03	26 38	28 10	26 08	26 28	10 50	27 46	19 09
7 Th	23 3 16	14 07 59	14 56	25 46	13 06	12 22	6 44	15 34	3 02	23 03	26 37	28 09	26 32	26 56	11 20	28 03	19 07
8 F	23 7 12	15 06 12	27 26	25 46	12 06	12 30	7 23	15 34	2 58	23 02	26 35	28 08	26 56	27 23	11 50	28 21	19 05
9 Sa	23 11 9	16 04 27	9♋41	25 43	11 16	12 40	8 02	15 33	2 53	23 02	26 34	28 08	27 20	27 51	12 20	28 38	19 03
10 Su	23 15 5	17 02 44	21 44	25 39	10 27	12 52	8 41	15 32	2 49	23 01	26 32	28 07	27 45	28 18	12 49	28 55	19 01
11 M	23 19 2	18 01 03	3♌40	25 33	9 44	13 07	9 20	15 31	2 45	23 00	26 30	28 06	28 09	28 46	13 18	29 11	18 58
12 T	23 22 58	18 59 24	15 32	25 26	9 07	13 23	9 59	15 29	2 40	23 00	26 29	28 05	28 33	29 13	13 48	29 28	18 56
13 W	23 26 55	19 57 47	27 23	25 20	8 37	13 41	10 38	15 28	2 36	22 59	26 27	28 05	28 58	29 41	14 17	29 44	18 54
14 Th	23 30 52	20 56 12	9♍15	25 13	8 16	14 01	11 17	15 26	2 32	22 58	26 25	28 04	29 22	0♐08	14 46	0♋01	18 51
15 F	23 34 48	21 54 39	21 09	25 08	8 04D	14 23	11 56	15 24	2 28	22 57	26 24	28 04	29 47	0 36	15 15	0 16	18 49
16 Sa	23 38 45	22 53 07	3♎08	25 05	8 00	14 47	12 36	15 22	2 24	22 57	26 22	28 03	0♏11	1 03	15 44	0 32	18 47
17 Su	23 42 41	23 51 38	15 13	25 03D	8 06	15 12	13 15	15 19	2 20	22 56	26 20	28 02	0 36	1 31	16 13	0 47	18 44
18 M	23 46 38	24 50 10	27 27	25 02	8 22	15 39	13 54	15 17	2 16	22 55	26 19	28 01	1 01	1 58	16 42	1 03	18 42
19 T	23 50 34	25 48 44	9♏51	25 03	8 47	16 08	14 34	15 14	2 12	22 54	26 17	28 00	1 26	2 26	17 10	1 18	18 39
20 W	23 54 31	26 47 20	22 28	25 05	9 21	16 39	15 13	15 11	2 08	22 53	26 15	28 00	1 50	2 53	17 39	1 33	18 37
21 Th	23 58 27	27 45 57	5♐21	25 07R	10 04	17 09	15 53	15 08	2 04	22 52	26 14	27 59	2 15	3 21	18 07	1 47	18 34
22 F	0 2 24	28 44 36	18 33	25 08	10 55	17 42	16 32	15 05	2 00	22 50	26 12	27 59	2 40	3 48	18 36	2 01	18 32
23 Sa	0 6 21	29 43 17	2♑05	25 07	11 54	18 16	17 12	15 01	1 56	22 49	26 10	27 58	3 05	4 16	19 04	2 16	18 29
24 Su	0 10 17	0♎42 00	16 01	25 05	13 00	18 52	17 52	14 57	1 53	22 48	26 09	27 58	3 30	4 43	19 32	2 29	18 27
25 M	0 14 14	1 40 44	0♒18	25 05	14 12	19 29	18 31	14 53	1 49	22 47	26 07	27 57	3 55	5 11	20 00	2 43	18 24
26 T	0 18 10	2 39 30	14 56	25 03	15 31	20 07	19 11	14 49	1 45	22 45	26 05	27 57	4 20	5 38	20 28	2 56	18 22
27 W	0 22 7	3 38 18	29 49	25 00	16 54	20 46	19 51	14 45	1 42	22 44	26 04	27 56	4 45	6 06	20 56	3 09	18 19
28 Th	0 26 3	4 37 07	14♓49	24 57	18 22	21 27	20 31	14 40	1 38	22 43	26 02	27 56	5 10	6 33	21 23	3 22	18 17
29 F	0 30 0	5 35 58	29 49	24 55	19 54	22 09	21 10	14 36	1 35	22 41	26 01	27 56	5 35	7 00	21 51	3 35	18 14
30 Sa	0 33 56	6 34 51	14♈40	24 54D	21 30	22 51	21 50	14 31	1 32	22 40	25 59	27 55	6 00	7 28	22 18	3 47	18 11

EPHEMERIS CALCULATED FOR 12 MIDNIGHT GREENWICH MEAN TIME. ALL OTHER DATA AND FACING ASPECTARIAN PAGE IN EASTERN TIME (**BOLD**) AND PACIFIC TIME (REGULAR).

OCTOBER 2023

☽ Last Aspect / ☽ Ingress

day	ET / hr:mn / PT	asp	sign day	ET / hr:mn / PT
2	9:20 pm 6:20 pm	△ ♀	♎ 2	
2	9:20 pm 6:20 pm	△ ♀	♏ 3	1:03 am
	11:34 am	* ♀	✕ 5	8:32 am 5:32 am
5	2:34 am	* ♃	♈ 5	8:32 am 5:32 am
7	3:12 pm 12:12 pm	□ ♀	♉ 7	7:24 am 4:24 am
10	5:37 am 2:37 am	* ♂	♊ 10	8:02 am 5:02 am
12	4:10 pm 1:10 pm	□ ♀	♋ 12	8:22 pm 5:22 pm
15	3:01 am 12:01 am	□ ♀	♌ 15	7:04 am 4:04 am
17	11:44 am 8:44 am	□ ♂	♍ 17	3:36 pm 12:36 pm
19	3:02 pm 12:02 pm	* ♀	♎ 19	9:55 pm 6:55 pm

☽ Last Aspect / ☽ Ingress

day	ET / hr:mn / PT	asp	sign day	ET / hr:mn / PT
21			♏ 21	11:00 pm
22	2:00 am		♏ 22	2:06 am
23	3:04 pm 12:04 pm		♐ 24	4:33 am 1:33 am
	11:39 pm		♑ 26	6:02 am 3:02 am
26	2:39 am		♒ 28	6:02 am 3:02 am
28	4:20 am 1:20 am		♓ 28	7:44 am 4:44 am
30	7:36 am 4:36 am		♈ 30	11:08 am 8:08 am

☽ Phases & Eclipses

phase	day	ET / hr:mn / PT
4th Quarter	6	9:48 am 6:48 am
New Moon	14	1:55 pm 10:55 am
2nd Quarter	21	11:29 pm 8:29 pm
Full Moon	28	4:24 pm 1:24 pm

Planet Ingress

planet	sign day	ET / hr:mn / PT
☿	♎	4	8:09 pm 5:09 pm
♀	♍	8	9:11 pm 6:11 pm
♂	♏	11	9:04 pm
♀	♏	11	12:04 am
♀	♍	17	9:27 am 6:27 am
☿	♏	21	11:49 pm
♀	♏	22	2:49 am
☉	♏	23	12:21 pm 9:21 am

Planetary Motion

	day	ET / hr:mn / PT
♀ D	10	9:10 pm 6:10 pm

Eastern time in bold type
Pacific time in medium type

OCTOBER 2023

DATE	SID. TIME	SUN	MOON	NODE	MERCURY	VENUS	MARS	JUPITER	SATURN	URANUS	NEPTUNE	PLUTO	CERES	PALLAS	JUNO	VESTA	CHIRON
1 Su	0 37 53	7♎53 47	29♍13	24♉54	23♍08	23♌35	22♎30	14♉26R	1♓29R	22♉38R	25♓57R	27♑55R	6♏25	7♎55	22♌46	3♋59	18♈09R
2 M	0 41 50	8 32 44	13♎24	24 55	24 48	24 20	23 10	14 21	1 25	22 37	25 56	27 55	6 50	8 22	23 13	4 11	18 06
3 T	0 45 46	9 31 44	27 10	24 55	26 31	25 05	23 50	14 16	1 22	22 35	25 54	27 55	7 16	8 50	23 40	4 22	18 03
4 W	0 49 43	10 30 46	10♏29	24 57	28 15	25 56	24 30	14 10	1 19	22 34	25 53	27 54	7 41	9 17	24 07	4 34	18 01
5 Th	0 53 39	11 29 50	23 24	24 58	29 59	26 39	25 11	14 04	1 16	22 32	25 51	27 54	8 06	9 44	24 34	4 45	17 58
6 F	0 57 36	12 28 57	5♐58	24 58R	1♎45	27 28	25 51	13 59	1 14	22 30	25 49	27 54	8 32	10 12	25 01	4 55	17 55
7 Sa	1 1 32	13 28 06	18 14	24 58	3 31	28 17	26 31	13 53	1 11	22 29	25 48	27 54	8 57	10 39	25 27	5 05	17 52
8 Su	1 5 29	14 27 17	0♑18	24 58	5 17	29 07	27 11	13 47	1 08	22 27	25 46	27 54	9 22	11 06	25 54	5 15	17 50
9 M	1 9 25	15 26 31	12 13	24 57	7 04	29 57	27 52	13 40	1 05	22 25	25 45	27 54	9 48	11 33	26 20	5 25	17 47
10 T	1 13 22	16 25 46	24 04	24 56	8 50	0♍49	28 32	13 34	1 03	22 23	25 43	27 54	10 13	12 01	26 46	5 34	17 44
11 W	1 17 19	17 25 04	5♒55	24 55	10 36	1 41	29 13	13 28	1 01	22 21	25 42	27 54D	10 38	12 28	27 12	5 43	17 41
12 Th	1 21 15	18 24 24	17 49	24 54	12 22	2 34	29 53	13 21	0 58	22 19	25 40	27 54	11 04	12 55	27 38	5 52	17 39
13 F	1 25 12	19 23 47	29 49	24 53	14 08	3 28	0♏34	13 14	0 56	22 17	25 39	27 54	11 29	13 22	28 04	6 00	17 36
14 Sa	1 29 8	20 23 11	11♓57	24 52	15 53	4 22	1 14	13 07	0 54	22 15	25 37	27 54	11 55	13 49	28 30	6 09	17 33
15 Su	1 33 5	21 22 38	24 16	24 52D	17 37	5 17	1 55	13 00	0 52	22 13	25 36	27 54	12 20	14 17	28 55	6 16	17 31
16 M	1 37 1	22 22 06	6♈45	24 52	19 21	6 12	2 36	12 53	0 50	22 11	25 34	27 54	12 46	14 44	29 21	6 24	17 28
17 T	1 40 58	23 21 37	19 28	24 53	21 04	7 08	3 16	12 46	0 48	22 09	25 33	27 54	13 12	15 11	29 46	6 30	17 25
18 W	1 44 54	24 21 10	2♉23	24 53R	22 47	8 04	3 57	12 39	0 46	22 07	25 31	27 54	13 37	15 38	0♍11	6 37	17 22
19 Th	1 48 51	25 20 44	15 32	24 53	24 29	9 01	4 38	12 31	0 44	22 05	25 30	27 54	14 03	16 05	0 36	6 43	17 20
20 F	1 52 47	26 20 20	28 55	24 53	26 11	9 59	5 19	12 24	0 43	22 03	25 29	27 55	14 28	16 32	1 01	6 49	17 17
21 Sa	1 56 44	27 19 58	11♊33	24 52	27 51	10 57	6 00	12 16	0 41	22 01	25 27	27 55	14 54	16 59	1 25	6 55	17 14
22 Su	2 0 41	28 19 38	26 26	24 52D	29 32	11 56	6 41	12 08	0 40	21 58	25 26	27 55	15 20	17 26	1 50	7 00	17 12
23 M	2 4 37	29 19 20	10♋33	24 52	1♏11	12 55	7 22	12 01	0 39	21 56	25 25	27 56	15 45	17 53	2 14	7 05	17 09
24 T	2 8 34	0♏19 03	24 52	24 53	2 50	13 54	8 03	11 53	0 37	21 54	25 23	27 56	16 11	18 20	2 39	7 09	17 06
25 W	2 12 30	1 18 47	9♌20	24 53R	4 29	14 54	8 44	11 45	0 36	21 52	25 22	27 57	16 37	18 47	3 03	7 13	17 04
26 Th	2 16 27	2 18 34	23 54	24 54	6 06	15 55	9 25	11 37	0 35	21 49	25 21	27 57	17 02	19 14	3 26	7 16	17 01
27 F	2 20 23	3 18 22	8♍29	24 54	7 44	16 55	10 07	11 29	0 34	21 47	25 20	27 57	17 28	19 41	3 50	7 20	16 59
28 Sa	2 24 20	4 18 12	22 59	24 55R	9 20	17 57	10 48	11 21	0 34	21 45	25 18	27 58	17 54	20 07	4 14	7 22	16 56
29 Su	2 28 16	5 18 03	7♎17	24 54	10 57	18 58	11 29	11 13	0 33	21 42	25 17	27 58	18 19	20 34	4 37	7 25	16 53
30 M	2 32 13	6 17 57	21 19	24 54	12 32	20 00	12 11	11 05	0 32	21 40	25 16	27 59	18 45	21 01	5 00	7 27	16 51
31 T	2 36 10	7 17 53	5♏01	24 55R	14 08	21 03	12 52	10 57	0 32	21 38	25 15	27 59	19 11	21 28	5 23	7 28	16 48

EPHEMERIS CALCULATED FOR 12 MIDNIGHT GREENWICH MEAN TIME. ALL OTHER DATA AND FACING ASPECTARIAN PAGE IN **EASTERN TIME (BOLD)** AND PACIFIC TIME (REGULAR).

NOVEMBER 2023

☽ Last Aspect day	ET / hr:mn / PT		asp	☽ Ingress sign	day	ET / hr:mn / PT	
1	**8:36 am**	5:36 am	□♆	♋	1	**5:30 pm**	2:30 pm
3	**11:28 pm**	8:28 pm	☍♇	♌	4	**3:21 am**	12:21 am
5		11:25 pm	□☿	♍	6	**2:39 pm**	11:39 am
6	**2:25 am**		□☿	♍	6	**2:39 pm**	11:39 am
8	**11:55 pm**	8:55 pm	⚹☿	♎	9	**3:08 am**	12:08 am
11	**10:05 am**	7:05 am	□♇	♏	11	**1:39 pm**	10:39 am
13	**6:03 pm**	3:03 pm	⚹♇	♐	13	**9:23 pm**	6:23 pm
15	**5:57 pm**	2:57 pm	□♆	♑	15		11:41 pm
15	**5:57 pm**	2:57 pm	□♆	♑	16	**2:41 am**	
18	**3:27 am**	12:27 am	☌♇	♒	18	**6:28 am**	3:28 am

☽ Last Aspect day	ET / hr:mn / PT		asp	☽ Ingress sign	day	ET / hr:mn / PT	
20	**5:50 am**	2:50 am	□☉	♓	20	**9:29 am**	6:29 am
22	**10:10 am**	7:10 am	△♂	♈	22	**12:19 pm**	9:19 am
24	**12:40 pm**	9:40 am	□♇	♉	24	**3:29 pm**	12:29 pm
26	**4:52 pm**	1:52 pm	△♇	♊	26	**7:40 pm**	4:40 pm
28	**8:03 pm**	5:03 pm	☍☿	♋	28		10:54 pm
28	**8:03 pm**	5:03 pm	☍☿	♋	29	**1:54 am**	

☽ Phases & Eclipses phase	day	ET / hr:mn / PT	
4th Quarter	5	**3:37 am**	1:37 am
New Moon	13	**4:27 am**	1:27 am
2nd Quarter	20	**5:50 am**	2:50 am
Full Moon	27	**4:16 am**	1:16 am

Planet Ingress		day	ET / hr:mn / PT	
♀	♎	8	**4:30 am**	1:30 am
☿	♐	9		10:25 pm
☿	♐	10	**1:25 am**	
♀	♏	19	**4:03 am**	1:03 am
☉	♐	22	**9:03 am**	6:03 am
♂	♐	24	**5:15 am**	2:15 am
⚳	♐	24		9:14 pm
⚳	♐	25	**12:14 am**	

Planetary Motion		day	ET / hr:mn / PT	
⚵	℞	2	**9:50 pm**	6:50 pm
♄	D	4	**3:03 am**	12:03 am

1 WEDNESDAY
- ☽ ⚺ ♅ **1:53 am**
- ☽ □ ♀ **3:26 am** 12:26 am
- ☽ □ ♆ **8:36 am** 5:36 am
- ☽ ⚻ ♇ **1:47 pm** 10:47 am
- ☽ △ ♄ **6:29 pm** 3:29 pm

2 THURSDAY
- ☽ △ ☉ **12:23 pm** 9:23 am
- ☽ ⚹ ♃ **1:31 pm** 10:31 am
- ☽ △ ♂ **10:01 pm** 7:01 pm
- ☉ ☍ ♃ 10:02 pm

3 FRIDAY
- ☉ ☍ ♃ **1:02 am**
- ☽ △ ☿ **6:49 am** 3:49 am
- ☽ ⚹ ♅ **10:36 am** 7:36 am
- ☽ ⚹ ♀ **5:49 pm** 2:49 pm
- ☽ △ ♆ **5:50 pm** 2:50 pm
- ♀ ☍ ♆ **6:06 pm** 3:06 pm
- ☽ ☍ ♇ **11:28 pm** 8:28 pm

4 SATURDAY
- ☽ ⚻ ♄ **4:22 am** 1:22 am
- ☿ ☍ ♅ **12:07 pm** 9:07 am
- ☽ □ ♃ **11:46 pm** 8:46 pm

5 SUNDAY
- ☽ □ ☉ **3:37 am** 1:37 am
- ☽ □ ♂ **12:00 pm** 9:00 am
- ☽ □ ♅ **9:11 pm** 6:11 pm
- ☽ □ ☿ 11:25 pm

6 MONDAY
- ☽ □ ☿ **2:25 am**
- ☽ ⚻ ♆ **4:48 am** 1:48 am
- ♀ △ ♇ **9:38 am** 6:38 am
- ☽ ⚻ ♇ **10:44 am** 7:44 am
- ☽ ⚺ ♀ **10:50 am** 7:50 am
- ☽ ☍ ♄ **3:42 pm** 12:42 pm
- ☿ △ ♆ **8:37 pm** 5:37 pm

7 TUESDAY
- ☽ △ ♃ **10:43 am** 7:43 am
- ☽ ⚹ ☉ **9:54 pm** 6:54 pm

8 WEDNESDAY
- ☽ ⚹ ♂ **4:29 am** 1:29 am
- ☽ △ ♅ **9:40 am** 6:40 am
- ♀ ⚻ ♄ **4:13 pm** 1:13 pm
- ☽ ☍ ♆ **5:20 pm** 2:20 pm
- ☿ ⚹ ♇ **7:17 pm** 4:17 pm
- ☽ △ ♇ **11:20 pm** 8:20 pm
- ☽ ⚹ ☿ **11:55 pm** 8:55 pm

9 THURSDAY
- ☽ ⚻ ♄ **4:12 am** 1:12 am
- ☽ ☌ ♀ **5:23 am** 2:23 am
- ☽ ⚻ ♃ **10:05 pm** 7:05 pm

10 FRIDAY
- ☿ □ ♄ **10:07 am** 7:07 am
- ☽ ⚺ ☉ **2:51 pm** 11:51 am
- ☽ ⚺ ♂ **7:29 pm** 4:29 pm
- ☽ ⚻ ♅ **8:43 pm** 5:43 pm

11 SATURDAY
- ☽ ⚻ ♆ **4:13 am** 1:13 am
- ☽ □ ♇ **10:05 am** 7:05 am
- ☽ △ ♄ **2:43 pm** 11:43 am
- ♂ ☍ ♅ **4:11 pm** 1:11 pm
- ☽ ⚺ ☿ **6:34 pm** 3:34 pm
- ☽ ⚺ ♀ **9:22 pm** 6:22 pm

12 SUNDAY
- ☽ ☍ ♃ **7:09 am** 4:09 am

13 MONDAY
- ☽ ☌ ☉ **4:27 am** 1:27 am
- ☽ ☍ ♅ **5:05 am** 2:05 am
- ☽ ☌ ♂ **7:18 am** 4:18 am
- ☽ △ ♆ **12:20 pm** 9:20 am
- ☉ ☍ ♅ **12:21 pm** 9:21 am
- ☽ ⚹ ♇ **6:03 pm** 3:03 pm
- ☽ □ ♄ **10:28 pm** 7:28 pm

14 TUESDAY
- ☽ ☌ ☿ **9:04 am** 6:04 am
- ☽ ⚹ ♀ **9:44 am** 6:44 am
- ☽ ⚻ ♃ **1:32 pm** 10:32 am

15 WEDNESDAY
- ☿ ⚹ ♀ **7:48 am** 4:48 am
- ☽ ⚻ ♅ **10:52 am** 7:52 am
- ☽ ⚺ ☉ **2:44 pm** 11:44 am
- ☽ ⚺ ♂ **4:05 pm** 1:05 pm
- ☽ □ ♆ **5:57 pm** 2:57 pm
- ☿ ⚻ ♃ **10:35 pm** 7:35 pm
- ☽ ⚺ ♇ **11:33 pm** 8:33 pm
- ♀ ⚻ ♃ 11:48 pm

16 THURSDAY
- ♀ ⚻ ♃ **2:48 am**
- ☽ ⚹ ♄ **3:49 am** 12:49 am
- ☽ △ ♃ **5:48 pm** 2:48 pm
- ☽ □ ♀ **7:16 pm** 4:16 pm
- ☽ ⚺ ☿ **8:17 pm** 5:17 pm

17 FRIDAY
- ♂ △ ♆ **3:36 am** 12:36 am
- ☉ △ ♆ **9:52 am** 6:52 am
- ☽ △ ♅ **2:51 pm** 11:51 am
- ☽ ⚹ ♆ **9:52 pm** 6:52 pm
- ☽ ⚹ ☉ **10:49 pm** 7:49 pm
- ☽ ⚹ ♂ **10:51 pm** 7:51 pm
- ☉ ☌ ♂ 9:42 pm

18 SATURDAY
- ☉ ☌ ♂ **12:42 am**
- ☽ ☌ ♇ **3:27 am** 12:27 am
- ☽ ⚺ ♄ **7:38 am** 4:38 am
- ☽ □ ♃ **8:50 pm** 5:50 pm

19 SUNDAY
- ☽ △ ♀ **3:12 am** 12:12 am
- ☽ ⚹ ☿ **5:39 am** 2:39 am
- ☽ □ ♅ **5:53 pm** 2:53 pm
- ☽ ⚺ ♆ 9:57 pm

20 MONDAY
- ☽ ⚺ ♆ **12:57 am**
- ☽ □ ♂ **4:38 am** 1:38 am
- ☽ □ ☉ **5:50 am** 2:50 am
- ☽ ⚺ ♇ **6:34 am** 3:34 am
- ☽ ☌ ♄ **10:45 am** 7:45 am
- ☉ ⚹ ♇ **4:26 pm** 1:26 pm
- ☽ ⚹ ♃ **11:20 pm** 8:20 pm

21 TUESDAY
- ☽ ⚻ ♀ **10:32 am** 7:32 am
- ☽ □ ☿ **2:16 pm** 11:16 am
- ♂ ⚹ ♇ **8:18 pm** 5:18 pm
- ☽ ⚹ ♅ **8:35 pm** 5:35 pm

22 WEDNESDAY
- ☽ ☌ ♆ **3:45 am** 12:45 am
- ☽ ⚹ ♇ **9:29 am** 6:29 am
- ☽ △ ♂ **10:10 am** 7:10 am
- ☽ △ ☉ **12:35 pm** 9:35 am
- ☽ ⚺ ♄ **1:42 pm** 10:42 am
- ☽ ⚺ ♃ 10:47 pm

23 THURSDAY
- ☽ ⚺ ♃ **1:47 am**
- ☉ □ ♄ **4:47 am** 1:47 am
- ☽ ☍ ♀ **5:57 pm** 2:57 pm
- ☽ △ ☿ **10:52 pm** 7:52 pm
- ☽ ⚺ ♅ **11:26 pm** 8:26 pm

24 FRIDAY
- ☿ ⚻ ♅ **4:27 am** 1:27 am
- ☽ ⚺ ♆ **6:47 am** 3:47 am
- ☽ □ ♇ **12:40 pm** 9:40 am
- ☽ ⚻ ♂ **4:02 pm** 1:02 pm
- ☽ ⚹ ♄ **5:00 pm** 2:00 pm
- ☽ ⚻ ☉ **7:43 pm** 4:43 pm

25 SATURDAY
- ☽ ☌ ♃ **4:43 am** 1:43 am
- ♂ □ ♄ **11:57 am** 8:57 am
- ☽ ⚻ ♀ 11:19 pm

26 SUNDAY
- ☽ ⚻ ♀ **2:19 am**
- ☽ ☌ ♅ **3:03 am** 12:03 am
- ☽ ⚻ ☿ **8:21 am** 5:21 am
- ☽ ⚹ ♆ **10:42 am** 7:42 am
- ♀ ⚻ ♅ **10:49 am** 7:49 am
- ☽ △ ♇ **4:52 pm** 1:52 pm
- ☽ □ ♄ **9:22 pm** 6:22 pm
- ☽ ☍ ♂ **11:08 pm** 8:08 pm

27 MONDAY
- ☽ ☍ ☉ **4:16 am** 1:16 am
- ☿ □ ♆ **8:27 am** 5:27 am
- ☽ ⚺ ♃ **8:54 am** 5:54 am

28 TUESDAY
- ☽ ⚺ ♅ **8:22 am** 5:22 am
- ☽ △ ♀ **12:54 pm** 9:54 am
- ☽ □ ♆ **4:30 pm** 1:30 pm
- ☽ ☍ ☿ **8:03 pm** 5:03 pm
- ☽ ⚻ ♇ **11:03 pm** 8:03 pm

29 WEDNESDAY
- ☽ △ ♄ **3:51 am** 12:51 am
- ☽ ⚻ ♂ **8:43 am** 5:43 am
- ☉ ⚻ ♃ **12:38 pm** 9:38 am
- ☽ ⚹ ♃ **3:21 pm** 12:21 pm
- ☽ ⚻ ☉ **3:37 pm** 12:37 pm

30 THURSDAY
- ☿ ⚺ ♇ **3:34 am** 12:34 am
- ♀ ⚻ ♆ **5:13 am** 2:13 am
- ☽ ⚹ ♅ **4:20 pm** 1:20 pm
- ☽ △ ♆ 10:05 pm

Eastern time in bold type
Pacific time in medium type

NOVEMBER 2023

DATE	SID.TIME	SUN	MOON	NODE	MERCURY	VENUS	MARS	JUPITER	SATURN	URANUS	NEPTUNE	PLUTO	CERES	PALLAS	JUNO	VESTA	CHIRON
1 W	2 40 6	8♏17 52	18♊22	24♉51℞	15♏42	22♍05	13♏34	10♉49℞	0♓31℞	21♉35℞	25♓14℞	28♑00	19♍37	21♎55	5♏46	7♋29	16♈46℞
2 Th	2 44 3	9 17 51	1♋20	24 49	17 17	23 09	14 15	10 40	0 31	21 33	25 13	28 01	20 02	22 21	6 09	7 30	16 43
3 F	2 47 59	10 17 53	13 57	24 47	18 50	24 12	14 57	10 32	0 31	21 30	25 12	28 01	20 28	22 48	6 31	7 30℞	16 41
4 Sa	2 51 56	11 17 58	26 17	24 45	20 24	25 16	15 38	10 24	0 31D	21 28	25 11	28 02	20 54	23 15	6 54	7 30	16 38
5 Su	2 55 52	12 18 04	8♌22	24 45D	21 57	26 20	16 20	10 16	0 31	21 25	25 10	28 03	21 20	23 41	7 16	7 29	16 36
6 M	2 59 49	13 18 12	20 18	24 45	23 29	27 24	17 02	10 08	0 31	21 23	25 09	28 03	21 45	24 08	7 38	7 28	16 34
7 T	3 3 45	14 18 23	2♍09	24 46	25 01	28 29	17 44	10 00	0 32	21 20	25 08	28 04	22 11	24 34	8 00	7 27	16 31
8 W	3 7 42	15 18 35	14 00	24 47	26 33	29 34	18 26	9 52	0 32	21 18	25 07	28 05	22 37	25 01	8 21	7 25	16 29
9 Th	3 11 39	16 18 50	25 56	24 49	28 05	0♎39	19 07	9 43	0 33	21 16	25 06	28 06	23 03	25 27	8 42	7 22	16 27
10 F	3 15 35	17 19 06	8♎00	24 50	29 36	1 45	19 49	9 35	0 33	21 13	25 05	28 07	23 29	25 54	9 04	7 20	16 24
11 Sa	3 19 32	18 19 24	20 17	24 51℞	1♐06	2 51	20 31	9 27	0 34	21 11	25 04	28 07	23 54	26 20	9 25	7 16	16 22
12 Su	3 23 28	19 19 44	2♏49	24 51	2 37	3 57	21 13	9 20	0 34	21 08	25 03	28 08	24 20	26 47	9 45	7 13	16 20
13 M	3 27 25	20 20 06	15 37	24 50	4 07	5 03	21 55	9 12	0 35	21 06	25 02	28 09	24 46	27 13	10 06	7 08	16 18
14 T	3 31 21	21 20 30	28 41	24 48	5 36	6 10	22 38	9 04	0 36	21 03	25 01	28 10	25 12	27 39	10 26	7 04	16 16
15 W	3 35 18	22 20 56	12♐02	24 43	7 05	7 17	23 20	8 56	0 37	21 01	25 00	28 11	25 37	28 06	10 46	6 59	16 14
16 Th	3 39 14	23 21 23	25 36	24 38	8 34	8 24	24 02	8 48	0 38	20 58	25 00	28 12	26 03	28 32	11 06	6 53	16 12
17 F	3 43 11	24 21 51	9♑23	24 34	10 02	9 31	24 44	8 41	0 39	20 56	24 59	28 13	26 29	28 58	11 26	6 47	16 10
18 Sa	3 47 8	25 22 21	23 19	24 30	11 30	10 39	25 27	8 33	0 41	20 53	24 58	28 14	26 55	29 24	11 45	6 41	16 08
19 Su	3 51 4	26 22 52	7♒23	24 27	12 58	11 47	26 09	8 26	0 42	20 51	24 58	28 15	27 20	29 50	12 05	6 34	16 06
20 M	3 55 1	27 23 25	21 28	24 25D	14 24	12 55	26 51	8 19	0 44	20 48	24 57	28 16	27 46	0♏16	12 24	6 27	16 04
21 T	3 58 57	28 23 59	5♓37	24 25	15 50	14 03	27 34	8 11	0 45	20 46	24 57	28 18	28 12	0 42	12 42	6 19	16 02
22 W	4 2 54	29 24 33	19 47	24 27	17 16	15 11	28 17	8 04	0 47	20 43	24 56	28 19	28 37	1 08	13 01	6 11	16 00
23 Th	4 6 50	0♐25 08	3♈56	24 29℞	18 41	16 20	28 59	7 57	0 49	20 41	24 56	28 20	29 03	1 34	13 19	6 02	15 58
24 F	4 10 47	1 25 45	18 02	24 29	20 05	17 28	29 42	7 51	0 51	20 38	24 56	28 22	29 29	2 00	13 37	5 53	15 57
25 Sa	4 14 44	2 26 23	2♉03	24 29	21 28	18 37	0♐24	7 44	0 53	20 36	24 55	28 23	29 54	2 26	13 55	5 44	15 55
26 Su	4 18 40	3 27 03	15 56	24 27	22 49	19 46	1 07	7 37	0 55	20 33	24 55	28 24	0♎20	2 51	14 12	5 34	15 53
27 M	4 22 37	4 27 43	29 37	24 23	24 10	20 55	1 50	7 31	0 58	20 31	24 55	28 25	0 46	3 17	14 30	5 24	15 52
28 T	4 26 33	5 28 26	13♊05	24 18	25 29	22 05	2 33	7 24	1 00	20 29	24 54	28 26	1 11	3 43	14 47	5 13	15 50
29 W	4 30 30	6 29 09	26 16	24 10	26 47	23 14	3 16	7 18	1 02	20 26	24 54	28 28	1 37	4 08	15 03	5 02	15 49
30 Th	4 34 26	7 29 54	9♋09	24 02	28 03	24 24	3 59	7 12	1 05	20 24	24 54	28 29	2 02	4 34	15 20	4 51	15 47

DECEMBER 2023

☽ Last Aspect / ☽ Ingress

day	ET / hr:mn / PT	asp	sign	day	ET / hr:mn / PT
1	**8:07 am** 5:07 am	⚹ ♀	♊	1	**11:00 am** 8:00 am
3	**9:11 pm** 6:11 pm	□ ♀	♋	3	**10:50 pm** 8:50 pm
6	**8:50 am** 5:50 am	△ ♀	♌	6	**11:35 am** 8:35 am
8	**8:05 pm** 5:05 pm	△ ♂	♍	8	**10:35 pm** 7:35 pm
11	**3:57 am** 12:57 am	□ ♀	♎	11	**6:11 am** 3:11 am
13	**1:48 am** 10:48 am	□ ♀	♏	13	**10:31 am** 7:31 am
15	**11:04 am** 8:04 am	△ ♂	♐	15	**12:56 pm** 9:56 am
17	**7:04 am** 4:04 am	□ ♂	♑	17	**2:50 pm** 11:50 am
19	**4:03 pm** 1:03 pm	⚹ ♀	♒	19	**3:47 pm** 2:47 pm

☽ Last Aspect / ☽ Ingress

day	ET / hr:mn / PT	asp	sign	day	ET / hr:mn / PT
21	**9:47 pm** 6:47 pm	△ ♀	♈	21	**9:50 pm** 6:50 pm
23	**1:40 am**	△ ♂	♉	24	**3:15 am** 12:15 am
26	**2:55 am**	⚹ ♀	♊	24	**3:15 am** 12:15 am
26	**5:57 pm** 2:57 pm	△ ♀	♋	26	**10:15 am** 7:15 am
30	**9:18 pm**	△ ♀	♌	28	**7:23 pm** 4:23 pm
31	**12:18 am**	□ ♀	♍	31	**6:53 am** 3:53 am

Phases & Eclipses

phase	day	ET / hr:mn / PT
4th Quarter	5	**12:49 am**
New Moon	12	**6:32 pm** 3:32 pm
2nd Quarter	19	**1:39 pm** 10:39 am
Full Moon	26	**7:33 pm** 4:33 pm

Planet Ingress

planet	sign	day	ET / hr:mn / PT
♀	♏	4	**6:31 am**
♂	♐	4	**1:51 pm** 10:51 am
☿	♑	1	
☉	♑	21	**10:27 pm** 7:27 pm
♀	♐	29	**10:18 pm**
☿ R		13	**1:18 am**
		23	**3:24 pm** 12:24 pm

Planetary Motion

	day	ET / hr:mn / PT
Ψ D	6	**8:20 am** 5:20 am
☿ R	12	**11:09 am**
♀	13	**2:09 am**
☿ R	20	**4:56 am** 1:56 am
♃	26	**10:10 pm** 7:10 pm
☿ D	30	**9:40 pm** 6:40 pm

---

1 FRIDAY
2 SATURDAY
3 SUNDAY
4 MONDAY
5 TUESDAY
6 WEDNESDAY
7 THURSDAY
8 FRIDAY
9 SATURDAY
10 SUNDAY
11 MONDAY
12 TUESDAY
13 WEDNESDAY
14 THURSDAY
15 FRIDAY
16 SATURDAY
17 SUNDAY
18 MONDAY
19 TUESDAY
20 WEDNESDAY
21 THURSDAY
22 FRIDAY
23 SATURDAY
24 SUNDAY
25 MONDAY
26 TUESDAY
27 WEDNESDAY
28 THURSDAY
29 FRIDAY
30 SATURDAY
31 SUNDAY

DECEMBER 2023

DATE	SID.TIME	SUN	MOON	NODE	MERCURY	VENUS	MARS	JUPITER	SATURN	URANUS	NEPTUNE	PLUTO	CERES	PALLAS	JUNO	VESTA	CHIRON
1 F	4 38 23	8♐30 40	21♋45	23♈54R	29♐17	25♎34	4♐42	7♉06R	1♓08	20♉22R	24♓54R	28♑30	2♌54	4♍59	15♍36	4♋39R	15♈46R
2 Sa	4 42 19	9 31 28	4♌05	23 48	0♑28	26 44	5 25	7 01	1 11	20 19	24 54	28 32	2 54	5 25	15 52	4 27	15 44
3 Su	4 46 16	10 32 17	16 10	23 42	1 36	27 54	6 08	6 55	1 13	20 17	24 53	28 33	3 19	5 50	16 08	4 15	15 43
4 M	4 50 13	11 33 07	28 06	23 39	2 42	29 05	6 51	6 50	1 16	20 15	24 53	28 34	3 45	6 15	16 23	4 02	15 42
5 T	4 54 9	12 33 59	9♍57	23 38D	3 44	0♏15	7 34	6 44	1 19	20 12	24 53	28 36	4 10	6 41	16 38	3 49	15 41
6 W	4 58 6	13 34 52	21 47	23 38	4 41	1 26	8 17	6 39	1 23	20 10	24 53D	28 37	4 36	7 06	16 53	3 36	15 39
7 Th	5 2 2	14 35 46	3♎42	23 41R	5 34	2 36	9 01	6 34	1 26	20 08	24 53	28 39	5 01	7 31	17 07	3 22	15 38
8 F	5 5 59	15 36 41	15 48	23 41	6 21	3 47	9 44	6 30	1 29	20 06	24 53	28 40	5 26	7 56	17 22	3 08	15 37
9 Sa	5 9 55	16 37 38	28 08	23 41	7 02	4 58	10 27	6 25	1 33	20 04	24 53	28 42	5 52	8 21	17 36	2 54	15 36
10 Su	5 13 52	17 38 36	10♏47	22 44	7 37	6 09	11 11	6 21	1 36	20 01	24 53	28 43	6 17	8 46	17 49	2 40	15 35
11 M	5 17 48	18 39 35	23 48	22 39	8 03	7 21	11 54	6 17	1 40	19 59	24 54	28 45	6 42	9 11	18 02	2 25	15 34
12 T	5 21 45	19 40 36	7♐12	22 36	8 21	8 32	12 38	6 13	1 43	19 57	24 54	28 47	7 08	9 36	18 15	2 10	15 33
13 W	5 25 42	20 41 37	20 57	22 37R	8 29R	9 43	13 21	6 09	1 47	19 55	24 54	28 48	7 33	10 00	18 28	1 55	15 33
14 Th	5 29 38	21 42 39	4♑59	22 37	8 27	10 55	14 05	6 05	1 51	19 53	24 54	28 50	7 58	10 25	18 40	1 40	15 32
15 F	5 33 35	22 43 42	19 15	22 35	8 14	12 07	14 49	6 02	1 55	19 51	24 55	28 51	8 24	10 50	18 52	1 25	15 31
16 Sa	5 37 31	23 44 45	3♒39	22 32	7 49	13 18	15 33	5 59	1 59	19 49	24 55	28 53	8 49	11 14	19 04	1 09	15 31
17 Su	5 41 28	24 45 49	18 03	22 31	7 13	14 30	16 16	5 56	2 03	19 47	24 55	28 55	9 14	11 39	19 15	0 54	15 30
18 M	5 45 24	25 46 53	2♓47	22 14	6 25	15 42	17 00	5 53	2 07	19 45	24 56	28 56	9 39	12 03	19 26	0 38	15 29
19 T	5 49 21	26 47 57	16 38	22 01	5 37	16 54	17 44	5 50	2 12	19 44	24 56	28 58	10 04	12 27	19 36	0 22	15 29
20 W	5 53 17	27 49 02	0♈43	21 48	4 19	18 06	18 28	5 48	2 16	19 42	24 56	29 00	10 29	12 51	19 46	0 07	15 29
21 Th	5 57 14	28 50 07	14 38	21 35	3 04	19 18	19 12	5 45	2 21	19 40	24 57	29 02	10 54	13 15	19 56	29♊51	15 28
22 F	6 1 11	29 51 12	28 23	21 22	1 44	20 30	19 56	5 43	2 25	19 38	24 57	29 03	11 19	13 39	20 06	29 35	15 28
23 Sa	6 5 7	0♑52 18	11♉59	21 22	0 22	21 43	20 40	5 42	2 30	19 37	24 58	29 05	11 44	14 03	20 15	29 19	15 28
24 Su	6 9 4	1 53 24	25 25	21 20	28♐59	22 55	21 24	5 40	2 34	19 35	24 59	29 07	12 09	14 27	20 23	29 03	15 27
25 M	6 13 0	2 54 30	8♊42	21 18	27 40	24 08	22 08	5 39	2 39	19 33	24 59	29 09	12 34	14 51	20 32	28 47	15 27
26 T	6 16 57	3 55 36	21 47	21 16	26 27	25 20	22 52	5 38	2 44	19 32	25 00	29 10	12 59	15 14	20 40	28 32	15 27
27 W	6 20 53	4 56 43	4♋40	21 15	25 20	26 33	23 37	5 37	2 49	19 30	25 01	29 12	13 23	15 38	20 47	28 16	15 27D
28 Th	6 24 50	5 57 50	17 21	21 14	24 23	27 45	24 21	5 36	2 54	19 29	25 01	29 14	13 48	16 01	20 54	28 00	15 27
29 F	6 28 47	6 58 57	29 48	21 13	23 36	28 58	25 05	5 36	2 59	19 27	25 02	29 16	14 13	16 25	21 01	27 45	15 27
30 Sa	6 32 43	8 00 04	12♌02	21 12	22 59	0♐11	25 50	5 35	3 04	19 26	25 03	29 18	14 37	16 48	21 08	27 30	15 27
31 Su	6 36 40	9 01 12	24 05	21 12	22 33	1 24	26 34	5 35D	3 09	19 24	25 04	29 20	15 02	17 11	21 14	27 15	15 28

EPHEMERIS CALCULATED FOR 12 MIDNIGHT GREENWICH MEAN TIME. ALL OTHER DATA AND FACING ASPECTARIAN PAGE IN **EASTERN TIME (BOLD)** AND PACIFIC TIME (REGULAR).

JANUARY 2024

D Last Aspect / D Ingress

day	ET / hr:mn / PT	asp	sign	day	ET / hr:mn / PT
2	6:36 pm 3:36 pm	△♀	♎	2	7:47 pm 4:47 pm
5	6:41 am 3:41 am	□♂	♏	5	7:39 am 4:39 am
7	3:22 pm 12:22 pm	✶♀	♐	7	4:08 pm 1:08 pm
9	1:24 am 10:24 am	□♄	♑	9	8:33 am 5:33 am
11	9:33 am 6:33 am	σⷱ♀	≈	11	10:01 am 7:01 am
13	4:59 am 1:59 am	✶♄	♓	13	10:29 am 7:29 am
15	11:33 am 8:33 am	σⷱ♄	♈	15	11:49 am 8:49 am
18	3:03 am 12:03 am	□♀	♉	18	3:12 am 12:12 am
20	8:57 am 5:57 am	□♀	♊	20	8:58 am 5:58 am
22	3:40 pm 12:40 pm	⊗♀	♋	22	4:51 pm 1:51 pm

day	ET / hr:mn / PT	asp	sign	day	ET / hr:mn / PT
24	5:58 pm 2:58 pm	△♀	♌	24	5:58 pm 2:58 pm
24	5:58 pm 2:58 pm	□♀	♍	26	4:19 pm 1:19 pm
26	4:19 pm 1:19 pm		♎	28	11:37 pm
29	6:29 am 3:29 am	△♀	♏	30	2:37 am

Planetary Motion

		day	ET / hr:mn / PT
♀	D	1	10:08 pm 7:08 pm
✶	R	0	11:55 pm 8:55 pm
☿	D	26	11:35 pm
♇	D	27	2:35 am

Planet Ingress

	day	ET / hr:mn / PT
♂ ♑	4	9:58 am 6:58 am
♀ ♑	13	8:49 pm 6:49 pm
☿ ≈	20	9:07 am 6:07 am
♀ ♑	23	3:50 pm 12:50 pm

D Phases & Eclipses

phase	day	ET / hr:mn / PT
4th Quarter	3	10:30 pm 7:30 pm
New Moon	11	6:57 am 3:57 am
2nd Quarter	17	10:53 pm 7:53 pm
Full Moon	25	12:54 am 9:54 am

---

1 MONDAY
D△♀ 3:59 am 12:59 am
D△♄ 8:26 am 5:26 am
D✶♀ 10:09 am 7:09 am

2 TUESDAY
D✶♀ 3:54 am 12:54 am
D□♄ 9:50 am 6:50 am
D✶✶ 6:36 am 3:36 am

3 WEDNESDAY
D△✶ 2:47 am
D✶✶ 3:05 am
D✶♄ 7:07 am 4:07 am
D✶✶ 7:15 am 4:15 am
D✶♀ 4:09 am 1:09 am
D△☿ 10:30 pm 7:30 pm

4 THURSDAY
D△✶ 10:37 am 7:37 am
D✶✶ 5:25 am 2:25 am
D✶♀ 10:08 am 7:08 am

5 FRIDAY
D✶✶ 6:41 am 3:41 am
D△♀ 9:03 am 6:03 am
D✶✶ 2:49 pm 11:49 am
D✶✶ 6:35 am 3:35 am

6 SATURDAY
D□♀ ⊙ 1:03 am
D✶✶ 2:12 pm 11:12 am
D✶✶ 8:24 am 5:24 am

7 SUNDAY
D✶✶ 5:15 am 2:15 am
D✶✶ 7:21 am 4:21 am
D△✶✶ 3:22 pm 12:22 pm
D✶♄ 5:47 pm 2:47 pm
D✶✶ 8:47 am 5:47 am
D✶✶ 2:11 pm 11:11 am

8 MONDAY
D✶♀ 2:23 am
D✶♄ 1:44 am
D✶✶ 8:24 am 5:24 am

9 TUESDAY
D✶✶⊙ 12:48 am
D✶✶ 2:16 am
D✶✶ 12:27 pm 9:27 am
D✶✶ 1:24 pm 10:24 am
D✶✶ 7:07 pm 4:07 pm
D✶♀ 9:40 pm 6:40 pm

10 WEDNESDAY
D△✶ 3:29 am 12:29 am
D✶✶ 3:45 am 12:45 am

11 THURSDAY
D△♀ 4:15 am 1:14 am
D✶♀ 9:27 am 6:27 am

12 FRIDAY
D✶♄ 5:01 am 2:01 am
D✶✶ 5:52 am 2:52 am
D✶✶ 8:47 am 5:47 am
D✶✶ 7:24 am 4:24 am
D✶♀ 11:32 pm

13 SATURDAY
D✶♄ 2:32 am
D✶✶ 11:55 am 8:55 am
D△✶ 4:29 pm 1:39 pm
D✶✶ 7:22 pm 4:22 pm
D△✶✶ 10:22 pm 7:22 pm

14 SUNDAY
D♂✶ 5:50 am 2:50 am
D✶✶ 8:03 am 5:03 am
D✶✶ 1:42 pm 10:42 am
D✶✶ 7:40 pm

15 MONDAY
D✶□ 2:47 am
D✶□ 7:48 am 4:48 am

16 TUESDAY
D✶✶ ⊙ 3:47 am
D✶✶♀ 4:03 pm 1:03 pm
D✶♀ 7:38 pm 4:38 pm
D✶✶ 11:33 pm 8:33 pm

17 WEDNESDAY
D□✶ 4:05 am 1:05 am
D✶✶ 7:47 am 4:47 am
D✶✶ 9:59 am 6:59 am
D✶✶ 3:14 pm 12:14 pm

18 THURSDAY
D△✶♀ 8:18 am 5:18 am
D✶✶♀ 3:22 pm 12:22 pm
D✶✶ 7:10 pm 4:10 pm
D✶✶ 10:53 pm 7:53 pm

19 FRIDAY
D□☿ 3:03 am 12:03 am
D✶✶ 11:57 am 8:57 am
D✶✶ 12:42 pm 9:42 am
D✶♀ 2:05 pm 11:05 am
D△✶ 10:26 pm 7:26 pm

20 SATURDAY
D✶♀ 4:31 am 1:31 am
D✶✶ 10:49 am 7:49 am
D✶♀ 1:11 am 10:11 am
D✶✶ 9:40 pm
D✶✶ 11:04 pm

D Ingress

day	ET / hr:mn / PT	asp
	3:14 am	
	6:27 pm	
	1:26 am	
	11:20 am	
	3:27 am	
	6:33 pm	
	2:01 am	
	2:42 am	
	4:29 am	
	4:34 am	
	11:32 pm	
	1:59 am	
	8:05 am	
	11:53 am	
	1:39 pm	
	7:07 pm	
	7:32 pm	
	2:50 am	
	8:08 am	
	8:08 am	
	10:42 am	
	2:47 am	
	4:48 am	

---

21 SUNDAY
D✶✶ ⊙ 8:46 am 5:45 am
D✶✶ 8:56 am 5:56 am
D△✶✶ 8:57 am 5:57 am
D✶♄ 6:32 pm 3:32 pm
D✶✶ 8:36 pm 5:36 pm

22 MONDAY
D✶✶♀ 12:45 pm 9:45 am
D✶♀ 8:23 am 5:23 am
D✶✶ 8:19 pm 5:19 pm

23 TUESDAY
D☿✶ 8:22 am 5:22 am
D✶✶ 3:49 pm 12:49 pm
D✶✶ 4:56 am 1:58 am
D✶♄ 9:43 pm 6:43 pm

24 WEDNESDAY
D□✶ 3:15 am 12:15 am
D✶♀ 5:13 am 2:13 am
D✶✶ 5:21 am 2:21 am
D✶✶ 3:53 pm 12:53 pm
D✶✶ 8:44 pm 5:44 pm

25 THURSDAY
D✶✶♀ 5:24 am 2:24 am
D✶✶ 5:58 am 2:58 am
D✶♄ 11:53 pm

Planet Ingress (times)

	day	ET / hr:mn / PT
D△✶		3:46 am 12:46 pm
		10:52 pm
26 FRIDAY		
D✶✶♀		1:52 am
D✶✶		6:56 am 6:56 am
D✶✶		4:19 pm 8:19 am
D✶✶		1:19 pm
D✶✶		11:18 pm
27 SATURDAY		
D✶✶		2:25 am
D✶♄		6:59 am
D✶✶		11:38 am
D△✶		10:03 pm
D✶✶		11:20 pm
D✶✶		11:28 pm
28 SUNDAY		
D✶✶♀		1:03 pm
D✶✶		2:20 am
D✶✶		2:28 am
D✶✶		4:10 am 1:10 am
D✶✶		6:23 am 3:23 am
D✶✶		4:07 pm 1:07 pm
D✶✶		8:02 pm 5:02 pm
29 MONDAY		
D✶✶♀		3:54 am 12:54 am
D✶✶		4:51 am 1:51 am
D✶✶		6:38 am 3:38 am
D✶✶		6:20 pm 3:20 pm
D✶✶		6:41 pm 3:41 pm

30 TUESDAY
D△✶ 3:41 am 12:41 am
D✶✶ 3:55 pm 12:55 pm
D✶✶♀ 5:40 pm 2:40 pm
D✶✶ 10:34 pm 7:34 pm
10:07 pm

31 WEDNESDAY
D△♀ 1:07 am
D△✶ 5:48 pm 2:48 pm
D✶♂ 9:00 pm 6:00 pm

Eastern time in **bold type**
Pacific time in medium type

JANUARY 2024

DATE	SID.TIME	SUN	MOON	NODE	MERCURY	VENUS	MARS	JUPITER	SATURN	URANUS	NEPTUNE	PLUTO	CERES	PALLAS	JUNO	VESTA	CHIRON
1 M	6 40 36	10♑02 20	6♍02	21♈06R	22♐17R	2♐37	27♐19	5♉35	3♓15	19♉23R	25♓05	29♑21	15♐27	17♍34	21♍19	27♎00	15♈28
2 T	6 44 33	11 03 29	17 49	21 00	22 11D	3 50	28 03	28 48	5 35	3 20	19 22	25 05	29 23	15 51	17 57	21 24	26 45	15 28
3 W	6 48 29	12 04 38	29 37	20 58	22 14	5 03	28 48	5 36	3 25	19 21	25 06	29 25	16 15	18 20	21 29	26 30	15 29
4 Th	6 52 26	13 05 47	11♎30	20 57	22 26	6 16	29 32	5 37	3 31	19 19	25 07	29 27	16 40	18 43	21 33	26 16	15 29
5 F	6 56 22	14 06 56	23 33	20 57	22 46	7 29	0♑17	5 38	3 36	19 18	25 08	29 29	17 04	19 05	21 37	26 02	15 30
6 Sa	7 0 19	15 08 06	5♏51	20 57	23 13	8 42	1 01	5 40	3 42	19 17	25 09	29 31	17 28	19 28	21 41	25 48	15 30
7 Su	7 4 16	16 09 16	18 31	20 54	23 46	9 56	1 46	5 41	3 48	19 16	25 10	29 33	17 53	19 50	21 44	25 34	15 30
8 M	7 8 12	17 10 26	1♐35	20 49	24 26	11 09	2 31	5 43	3 53	19 15	25 11	29 35	18 17	20 12	21 46	25 21	15 31
9 T	7 12 9	18 11 36	15 06	20 42	25 10	12 22	3 16	5 45	3 59	19 14	25 13	29 37	18 41	20 34	21 48	25 08	15 32
10 W	7 16 5	19 12 46	29 05	20 31	25 59	13 36	4 01	5 47	4 05	19 13	25 14	29 39	19 05	20 56	21 50	24 56	15 32
11 Th	7 20 2	20 13 57	13♑27	20 19	26 52	14 49	4 46	5 50	4 11	19 12	25 15	29 40	19 29	21 18	21 51	24 43	15 33
12 F	7 23 58	21 15 07	28 08	20 07	27 49	16 03	5 31	5 52	4 17	19 11	25 16	29 42	19 53	21 40	21 52	24 31	15 34
13 Sa	7 27 55	22 16 16	12♒59	19 55	28 49	17 16	6 16	5 55	4 23	19 11	25 17	29 44	20 17	22 02	21 52R	24 20	15 35
14 Su	7 31 51	23 17 25	27 51	19 46	29 52	18 30	7 01	5 58	4 29	19 10	25 19	29 46	20 41	22 23	21 52	24 08	15 36
15 M	7 35 48	24 18 33	12♓36	19 39	0♑58	19 43	7 46	6 01	4 35	19 09	25 20	29 48	21 04	22 45	21 51	23 58	15 37
16 T	7 39 45	25 19 41	27 07	19 36	2 06	20 57	8 31	6 04	4 41	19 09	25 21	29 50	21 28	23 06	21 50	23 47	15 38
17 W	7 43 41	26 20 48	11♈22	19 34D	3 17	22 10	9 16	6 08	4 48	19 08	25 23	29 52	21 52	23 27	21 49	23 37	15 39
18 Th	7 47 38	27 21 54	25 18	19 34R	4 29	23 24	10 01	6 12	4 54	19 08	25 24	29 54	22 15	23 48	21 47	23 27	15 40
19 F	7 51 34	28 23 00	8♉57	19 34	5 43	24 38	10 46	6 15	5 00	19 07	25 25	29 56	22 39	24 08	21 45	23 18	15 42
20 Sa	7 55 31	29 24 04	22 20	19 32	6 59	25 51	11 32	6 20	5 07	19 07	25 27	29 58	23 02	24 29	21 42	23 09	15 43
21 Su	7 59 27	0♒25 08	5♊28	19 28	8 16	27 05	12 17	6 24	5 13	19 06	25 28	0♒00	23 26	24 50	21 38	23 01	15 44
22 M	8 3 24	1 26 11	18 24	19 21	9 35	28 19	13 02	6 28	5 19	19 06	25 30	0 02	23 49	25 10	21 35	22 53	15 45
23 T	8 7 20	2 27 13	1♋06	19 10	10 55	29 33	13 48	6 33	5 26	19 06	25 31	0 04	24 12	25 30	21 30	22 45	15 47
24 W	8 11 17	3 28 14	13 42	18 58	12 16	0♑47	14 33	6 38	5 33	19 06	25 33	0 06	24 35	25 50	21 26	22 38	15 48
25 Th	8 15 14	4 29 14	26 06	18 44	13 38	2 01	15 18	6 43	5 39	19 05	25 34	0 08	24 58	26 10	21 21	22 31	15 50
26 F	8 19 10	5 30 14	8♌21	18 31	15 01	3 14	16 04	6 48	5 46	19 05	25 36	0 10	25 21	26 30	21 15	22 25	15 52
27 Sa	8 23 7	6 31 13	20 26	18 18	16 25	4 28	16 49	6 54	5 52	19 05D	25 38	0 12	25 44	26 49	21 09	22 19	15 53
28 Su	8 27 3	7 32 10	2♍23	18 07	17 50	5 42	17 35	6 59	5 59	19 05	25 39	0 14	26 07	27 08	21 03	22 14	15 55
29 M	8 31 0	8 33 08	14 15	17 59	19 16	6 56	18 20	7 05	6 06	19 05	25 41	0 16	26 29	27 28	20 56	22 09	15 57
30 T	8 34 56	9 34 04	26 02	17 54	20 43	8 10	19 06	7 11	6 13	19 06	25 43	0 17	26 52	27 47	20 48	22 05	15 58
31 W	8 38 53	10 34 59	7♎50	17 52	22 10	9 24	19 52	7 17	6 20	19 06	25 44	0 19	27 15	28 05	20 41	22 01	16 00

EPHEMERIS CALCULATED FOR 12 MIDNIGHT GREENWICH MEAN TIME. ALL OTHER DATA AND FACING ASPECTARIAN PAGE IN EASTERN TIME (BOLD) AND PACIFIC TIME (REGULAR).

FEBRUARY 2024

☽ Last Aspect day	ET / hr:mn / PT	asp	☽ Ingress sign day	ET / hr:mn / PT
1	**4:03 am** 1:03 am	□☿	♏ 1	**3:37 pm** 12:37 pm
3	**10:24 pm** 7:24 pm	⚹☿	♐ 3	10:28 pm
3	**10:24 pm** 7:24 pm	⚹☿	♐ 4	**1:28 am**
5	9:06 pm	□♆	♑ 6	**7:08 am** 4:08 am
6	**12:06 am**	□♆	♑ 6	**7:08 am** 4:08 am
7	11:52 pm	☌♂	♒ 8	**8:59 am** 5:59 am
8	**2:52 am**	☌♂	♒ 8	**8:59 am** 5:59 am
9	**5:59 pm** 2:59 pm	☌☉	♓ 10	**8:42 am** 5:42 am
12	**7:32 am** 4:32 am	⚹♂	♈ 12	**8:26 am** 5:26 am
14	**5:21 am** 2:21 am	□♀	♉ 14	**10:02 am** 7:02 am
16	**10:01 am** 7:01 am	□☉	♊ 16	**2:39 pm** 11:39 am
18	**10:21 pm** 7:21 pm	△☉	♋ 18	**10:25 pm** 7:25 pm
20	10:38 pm	△♆	♌ 21	**8:40 am** 5:40 am
21	**1:38 am**	△♆	♌ 21	**8:40 am** 5:40 am
22	**11:18 pm** 8:18 pm	□♅	♍ 23	**8:38 pm** 5:38 pm
25	11:35 pm	☍♆	♎ 26	**9:29 am** 6:29 am
26	**2:35 am**	☍♆	♎ 26	**9:29 am** 6:29 am
27	**1:22 pm** 10:22 am	△♀	♏ 28	**10:09 pm** 7:09 pm

☽ Phases & Eclipses phase	day	ET / hr:mn / PT
4th Quarter	2	**6:18 pm** 3:18 pm
New Moon	9	**5:59 pm** 2:59 pm
2nd Quarter	16	**10:01 am** 7:01 am
Full Moon	24	**7:30 am** 4:30 am

Planet Ingress	day	ET / hr:mn / PT
☿ ♒	4	9:10 pm
☿ ♒	5	**12:10 am**
♀ ♐	6	**3:09 am** 12:09 am
⚳ ♑	7	**6:11 am** 3:11 am
♂ ♒	12	10:05 pm
♂ ♒	13	**1:05 am**
♀ ♒	16	**11:05 am** 8:05 am
☉ ♓	18	**11:13 pm** 8:13 pm
☿ ♓	22	11:29 pm
☿ ♓	23	**2:29 am**

Planetary Motion	day	ET / hr:mn / PT
⚵ D	8	**4:41 am** 1:41 am

1 THURSDAY
☽ □ ☿ **4:03 am** 1:03 am
☽ ⚻ ♆ **7:13 am** 4:13 am
☽ □ ♇ **4:23 pm** 1:23 pm

2 FRIDAY
☽ △ ♄ **4:39 am** 1:39 am
☿ ⚹ ♆ **5:55 am** 2:55 am
☽ ☍ ♃ **6:17 am** 3:17 am
☽ ⚹ ♀ **5:09 pm** 2:09 pm
☽ □ ☉ **6:18 pm** 3:18 pm

3 SATURDAY
☽ ☍ ♅ **4:55 am** 1:55 am
☽ ⚹ ♂ **11:42 am** 8:42 am
☽ △ ♆ **5:42 pm** 2:42 pm
☽ ⚹ ☿ **10:24 pm** 7:24 pm
☽ ⚹ ♇ 11:19 pm

4 SUNDAY
☽ ⚹ ♇ **2:19 am**
☽ □ ♄ **2:10 pm** 11:10 am
☽ ⚻ ♃ **3:39 pm** 12:39 pm

5 MONDAY
☉ ⚺ ♀ **4:03 am** 1:03 am
☽ ⚹ ☉ **6:55 am** 3:55 am
☽ ⚺ ♀ **6:58 am** 3:58 am
☿ ☌ ♇ **7:58 am** 4:58 am
☽ ⚻ ♅ **12:11 pm** 9:11 am
☽ ⚺ ♂ **9:40 pm** 6:40 pm
☽ □ ♆ 9:06 pm

6 TUESDAY
☽ □ ♆ **12:06 am**
☽ ⚺ ♇ **8:03 am** 5:03 am
☽ ⚺ ☿ **10:59 am** 7:59 am
☽ ⚹ ♄ **7:18 pm** 4:18 pm
☽ △ ♃ **8:41 pm** 5:41 pm

7 WEDNESDAY
☽ ⚺ ☉ **2:14 pm** 11:14 am
☽ ☌ ♀ **3:12 pm** 12:12 pm
☽ △ ♅ **3:19 pm** 12:19 pm
♀ △ ♅ **4:25 pm** 1:25 pm
♂ ⚹ ♆ **7:20 pm** 4:20 pm
☽ ⚹ ♆ 11:30 pm
☽ ☌ ♂ 11:52 pm

8 THURSDAY
☽ ⚹ ♆ **2:30 am**
☽ ☌ ♂ **2:52 am**
☉ □ ♅ **5:46 am** 2:46 am
☽ ☌ ♇ **9:57 am** 6:57 am
☽ ☌ ☿ **6:25 pm** 3:25 pm
☽ ⚺ ♄ **8:51 pm** 5:51 pm
☽ □ ♃ **10:10 pm** 7:10 pm

9 FRIDAY
☽ □ ♅ **3:35 pm** 12:35 pm
☽ ☌ ☉ **5:59 pm** 2:59 pm
☿ ⚺ ♄ **6:59 pm** 3:59 pm
☽ ⚺ ♀ **7:44 pm** 4:44 pm
☽ ⚺ ♆ 11:29 pm

10 SATURDAY
☽ ⚺ ♆ **2:29 am**
☽ ⚺ ♂ **5:17 am** 2:17 am
☿ □ ♃ **8:25 am** 5:25 am
☽ ⚺ ♇ **9:45 am** 6:45 am
☽ ☌ ♄ **8:45 pm** 5:45 pm
☽ ⚹ ♃ **10:05 pm** 7:05 pm
☽ ⚺ ☿ **11:34 pm** 8:34 pm

11 SUNDAY
☽ ⚹ ♅ **3:07 pm** 12:07 pm
☽ ⚺ ☉ **8:55 pm** 5:55 pm
☽ ⚹ ♀ **11:31 pm** 8:31 pm
☽ ☌ ♆ 11:11 pm

12 MONDAY
☽ ☌ ♆ **2:11 am**
☽ ⚹ ♂ **7:32 am** 4:32 am
☽ ⚹ ♇ **9:36 am** 6:36 am
☽ ⚺ ♄ **9:11 pm** 6:11 pm
☽ ⚺ ♃ **10:36 pm** 7:36 pm

13 TUESDAY
☽ ⚹ ☿ **5:44 am** 2:44 am
♀ ⚹ ♆ **8:36 am** 5:36 am
☽ ⚺ ♅ **3:55 pm** 12:55 pm
♂ ☌ ♇ 10:06 pm
☽ ⚹ ☉ 10:40 pm

14 WEDNESDAY
♂ ☌ ♇ **1:06 am**
☽ ⚹ ☉ **1:40 am**
☽ ⚺ ♆ **3:35 am** 12:35 am
☽ □ ♀ **5:21 am** 2:21 am
☽ □ ♇ **11:22 am** 8:22 am
☽ □ ♂ **11:56 am** 8:56 am
☽ ⚹ ♄ **11:57 pm** 8:57 pm
☽ ☌ ♃ 10:31 pm

15 THURSDAY
☽ ☌ ♃ **1:31 am**
☉ ⚺ ♆ **5:28 am** 2:28 am
☽ □ ☿ **3:36 pm** 12:36 pm
☽ ☌ ♅ **7:27 pm** 4:27 pm

16 FRIDAY
☽ ⚹ ♆ **7:55 am** 4:55 am
☽ □ ☉ **10:01 am** 7:01 am
☽ △ ♀ **3:02 pm** 12:02 pm
☽ △ ♇ **4:11 pm** 1:11 pm
☽ △ ♂ **7:56 pm** 4:56 pm
☿ □ ♅ **10:53 pm** 7:53 pm

17 SATURDAY
♀ ☌ ♇ **3:48 am** 12:48 am
☽ □ ♄ **5:57 am** 2:57 am
☽ ⚺ ♃ **7:42 am** 4:42 am
☽ ⚺ ♅ 11:12 pm

18 SUNDAY
☽ ⚺ ♅ **2:12 am**
☽ △ ☿ **6:22 am** 3:22 am
☽ □ ♆ **3:28 pm** 12:28 pm
☽ △ ☉ **10:21 pm** 7:21 pm
☽ ⚻ ♇ 9:10 pm

19 MONDAY
☽ ⚻ ♇ **12:10 am**
☽ ⚻ ♀ **4:53 am** 1:53 am
☽ ⚻ ♂ **7:38 am** 4:38 am
☽ △ ♄ **3:02 pm** 12:02 pm
☽ ⚹ ♃ **5:00 pm** 2:00 pm
☉ ⚺ ♇ **9:39 pm** 6:39 pm

20 TUESDAY
☽ ⚹ ♅ **11:45 am** 8:45 am
☽ ⚻ ☿ 10:32 pm
☽ △ ♆ 10:38 pm
☿ ⚺ ♆ 11:10 pm

21 WEDNESDAY
☽ ⚻ ☿ **1:32 am**
☽ △ ♆ **1:38 am**
☿ ⚺ ♆ **2:10 am**
☽ ☍ ♇ **10:37 am** 7:37 am
☽ ⚻ ☉ **1:53 pm** 10:53 am
☽ ☍ ♀ **10:03 pm** 7:03 pm
☽ ☍ ♂ **10:13 pm** 7:13 pm
♀ ☌ ♂ 11:14 pm
☽ ⚻ ♄ 11:28 pm

22 THURSDAY
♀ ☌ ♂ **2:14 am**
☽ ⚻ ♄ **2:28 am**
☽ □ ♃ **4:39 am** 1:39 am
☽ □ ♅ **11:18 pm** 8:18 pm

23 FRIDAY
☽ ⚻ ♆ **1:36 pm** 10:36 am
☿ ⚺ ♇ **4:31 pm** 1:31 pm
♀ ⚺ ♄ **9:26 pm** 6:26 pm
☽ ⚻ ♇ **10:46 pm** 7:46 pm
☽ ☍ ☿ **11:52 pm** 8:52 pm

24 SATURDAY
☽ ☍ ☉ **7:30 am** 4:30 am
☽ ⚻ ♂ **2:39 pm** 11:39 am
☽ ☍ ♄ **3:24 pm** 12:24 pm
☽ ⚻ ♀ **5:18 pm** 2:18 pm
☽ △ ♃ **5:49 pm** 2:49 pm
♀ □ ♃ **11:01 pm** 8:01 pm

25 SUNDAY
♂ ⚺ ♄ **4:20 am** 1:20 am
☽ △ ♅ **12:04 pm** 9:04 am
☽ ☍ ♆ 11:35 pm

26 MONDAY
☽ ☍ ♆ **2:35 am**
☽ △ ♇ **11:47 am** 8:47 am
☽ ⚻ ☿ **11:54 pm** 8:54 pm
☽ ⚻ ☉ 11:06 pm

27 TUESDAY
☽ ⚻ ☉ **2:06 am**
♂ □ ♃ **3:30 am** 12:30 am
☽ ⚻ ♄ **4:59 am** 1:59 am
☽ ⚻ ♃ **7:38 am** 4:38 am
☽ △ ♂ **7:51 am** 4:51 am
☽ △ ♀ **1:22 pm** 10:22 am
☽ ⚻ ♅ 10:06 pm

28 WEDNESDAY
☽ ⚻ ♅ **1:06 am**
☉ ☌ ☿ **3:43 am** 12:43 am
☿ ☌ ♄ **10:08 am** 7:08 am
☽ ⚻ ♆ **3:32 pm** 12:32 pm
☉ ☌ ♄ **4:25 pm** 1:25 pm
☽ □ ♇ 9:33 pm

29 THURSDAY
☽ □ ♇ **12:33 am**
☿ ⚹ ♃ **4:53 am** 1:53 am
☽ △ ♄ **5:52 pm** 2:52 pm
☽ △ ☉ **7:53 pm** 4:53 pm
☽ ☍ ♃ **8:40 pm** 5:40 pm
☽ △ ☿ **11:18 pm** 8:18 pm
☽ □ ♂ 9:08 pm

Eastern time in bold type
Pacific time in medium type

FEBRUARY 2024

DATE	SID.TIME	SUN	MOON	NODE	MERCURY	VENUS	MARS	JUPITER	SATURN	URANUS	NEPTUNE	PLUTO	CERES	PALLAS	JUNO	VESTA	CHIRON
1 Th	8 42 49	11♒35 54	19♋42	17♈51	23♑39	10♑38	20♑37	7♉17	6♓24	19♉06	25♓46	0♒21	27♐37	28♏24	20♏33R	21♊57R	16♈02
2 F	8 46 46	12 36 48	1♌58	17 52R	25 08	11 52	21 23	7 23	6 33	19 06	25 48	0 23	27 59	28 42	20 24	21 54	16 04
3 Sa	8 50 43	13 37 41	13 58	17 52	26 38	13 06	22 09	7 30	6 40	19 06	25 50	0 25	28 22	29 01	20 15	21 51	16 06
4 Su	8 54 39	14 38 34	26 33	17 51	28 09	14 20	22 55	7 36	6 47	19 07	25 51	0 27	28 44	29 19	20 06	21 49	16 08
5 M	8 58 36	15 39 26	9♍58	17 48	29 40	15 34	23 41	7 43	6 54	19 07	25 53	0 29	29 06	29 36	19 56	21 47	16 10
6 T	9 2 32	16 40 17	23 00	17 43	1♒13	16 49	24 26	7 50	7 01	19 08	25 55	0 31	29 28	29 54	19 46	21 46	16 12
7 W	9 6 29	17 41 07	6♎58	17 36	2 46	18 03	25 12	7 57	7 08	19 08	25 57	0 33	29 50	0♐11	19 35	21 45	16 14
8 Th	9 10 25	18 41 56	21 24	17 27	4 19	19 17	25 58	8 04	7 15	19 09	25 59	0 35	0♑12	0 29	19 24	21 45D	16 16
9 F	9 14 22	19 42 44	6♏14	17 18	5 54	20 31	26 44	8 11	7 22	19 10	26 01	0 36	0 33	0 46	19 13	21 45	16 19
10 Sa	9 18 19	20 43 31	21 19	17 09	7 30	21 45	27 30	8 19	7 30	19 10	26 03	0 38	0 55	1 02	19 02	21 45	16 21
11 Su	9 22 15	21 44 16	6♐31	17 01	9 06	22 59	28 16	8 27	7 37	19 11	26 05	0 40	1 16	1 19	18 50	21 46	16 23
12 M	9 26 12	22 45 00	21 38	16 56	10 43	24 13	29 02	8 35	7 44	19 12	26 07	0 42	1 38	1 35	18 38	21 48	16 25
13 T	9 30 8	23 45 42	6♑31	16 54D	12 21	25 28	29 48	8 42	7 51	19 13	26 09	0 44	1 59	1 51	18 25	21 49	16 28
14 W	9 34 5	24 46 23	21 05	16 53	13 59	26 42	0♒34	8 51	7 58	19 14	26 11	0 46	2 20	2 07	18 12	21 52	16 30
15 Th	9 38 1	25 47 02	5♒15	16 55	15 39	27 56	1 21	8 59	8 05	19 15	26 13	0 47	2 41	2 23	17 59	21 54	16 33
16 F	9 41 58	26 47 40	19 01	16 55R	17 19	29 10	2 07	9 07	8 13	19 16	26 15	0 49	3 02	2 38	17 46	21 57	16 35
17 Sa	9 45 54	27 48 15	2♓24	16 55	19 00	0♒24	2 53	9 16	8 20	19 17	26 17	0 51	3 23	2 53	17 32	22 01	16 38
18 Su	9 49 51	28 48 49	15 27	16 54	20 42	1 39	3 39	9 25	8 27	19 18	26 19	0 53	3 44	3 08	17 18	22 05	16 40
19 M	9 53 48	29 49 22	28 12	16 50	22 25	2 53	4 25	9 33	8 34	19 19	26 21	0 55	4 04	3 22	17 04	22 09	16 43
20 T	9 57 44	0♓49 52	10♈44	16 45	24 09	4 07	5 11	9 42	8 42	19 20	26 23	0 56	4 25	3 37	16 50	22 14	16 46
21 W	10 1 41	1 50 21	23 03	16 37	25 54	5 21	5 58	9 51	8 49	19 21	26 25	0 58	4 45	3 51	16 36	22 19	16 48
22 Th	10 5 37	2 50 48	5♉13	16 29	27 40	6 36	6 44	10 01	8 56	19 23	26 27	1 00	5 05	4 05	16 21	22 24	16 51
23 F	10 9 34	3 51 13	17 15	16 20	29 27	7 50	7 30	10 10	9 04	19 24	26 29	1 01	5 25	4 18	16 06	22 30	16 54
24 Sa	10 13 30	4 51 36	29 12	16 12	1♓14	9 04	8 17	10 20	9 11	19 25	26 31	1 03	5 45	4 32	15 52	22 36	16 57
25 Su	10 17 27	5 51 58	11♊03	16 06	3 03	10 18	9 03	10 29	9 18	19 27	26 34	1 05	6 05	4 44	15 37	22 43	16 59
26 M	10 21 23	6 52 18	22 52	16 01	4 52	11 33	9 49	10 39	9 25	19 28	26 36	1 07	6 25	4 57	15 22	22 50	17 02
27 T	10 25 20	7 52 36	4♋41	15 59D	6 43	12 47	10 36	10 49	9 33	19 30	26 38	1 08	6 44	5 09	15 07	22 57	17 05
28 W	10 29 16	8 52 53	16 31	15 58	8 34	14 01	11 22	10 59	9 40	19 31	26 40	1 10	7 04	5 21	14 51	23 05	17 08
29 Th	10 33 13	9 53 09	28 26	15 59	10 26	15 15	12 09	11 09	9 47	19 33	26 42	1 11	7 23	5 33	14 36	23 13	17 11

EPHEMERIS CALCULATED FOR 12 MIDNIGHT GREENWICH MEAN TIME. ALL OTHER DATA AND FACING ASPECTARIAN PAGE IN **EASTERN TIME (BOLD)** AND PACIFIC TIME (REGULAR).

MARCH 2024

☽ Last Aspect day	ET	PT	asp	☽ Ingress sign	day	ET	PT
1		11:47 pm	△♆	♐	2	**8:56 am**	5:56 am
2	**2:47 am**		△♆	♐	2	**8:56 am**	5:56 am
4	**10:41 am**	7:41 am	□♆	♑	4	**4:15 pm**	1:15 pm
6	**2:35 pm**	11:35 am	⚹♆	♒	6	**7:38 pm**	4:38 pm
8	**1:56 pm**	10:56 am	☌♀	♓	8	**8:03 pm**	5:03 pm
10	**3:45 pm**	12:45 pm	☌♆	♈	10	**8:19 pm**	5:19 pm
12	**7:08 am**	4:08 am	⚹♂	♉	12	**8:28 pm**	5:28 pm
14	**6:29 pm**	3:29 pm	⚹♆	♊	14	**11:16 pm**	8:16 pm
16		9:43 pm	□♆	♋	17	**5:40 am**	2:40 am
17	**12:43 am**		□♆	♋	17	**5:40 am**	2:40 am
19	**2:52 pm**	11:52 am	△☉	♌	19	**3:33 pm**	12:33 pm
21		11:34 pm	☍♂	♍	22	**3:42 am**	12:42 am
22	**2:34 am**		☍♂	♍	22	**3:42 am**	12:42 am
24	**11:49 am**	8:49 am	☍♆	♎	24	**4:37 pm**	1:37 pm
26	**7:09 pm**	4:09 pm	☍☿	♏	27	**5:03 am**	2:03 am
29	**11:40 am**	8:40 am	△♆	♐	29	**3:52 pm**	12:52 pm
31	**8:16 pm**	5:16 pm	□♆	♑	31		9:05 pm
31	**8:16 pm**	5:16 pm	□♆	♑	4/1	**12:05 am**	

☽ Phases & Eclipses phase	day	ET	PT
4th Quarter	3	**10:23 am**	7:23 am
New Moon	10	**5:00 am**	1:00 am
2nd Quarter	16		9:11 pm
2nd Quarter	17	**12:11 am**	
Full Moon	25	**3:00 am**	12:00 am
●	25	5° ♎ 07'	

Planet Ingress		day	ET	PT
☿	♈	9	**11:03 pm**	8:03 pm
♀	♓	11	**5:50 pm**	2:50 pm
☉	♈	19	**11:06 pm**	8:06 pm
♂	♓	22	**7:47 pm**	4:47 pm
⚳	♋	31	**7:02 am**	4:02 am

Planetary Motion		day	ET	PT
⚴	℞	29	**9:17 am**	6:17 am

1 FRIDAY
- ☽ □ ♂ 12:08 am
- ☉ ⚹ ♃ **7:15 am** 4:15 am
- ☿ ⚺ ♂ **7:41 am** 4:41 am
- ☽ □ ♀ **8:09 am** 5:09 am
- ☽ ☍ ♅ **12:53 pm** 9:53 am
- ☽ △ ♆ 11:47 pm

2 SATURDAY
- ☽ △ ♆ **2:47 am**
- ☽ ⚹ ♇ **11:20 am** 8:20 am

3 SUNDAY
- ☽ □ ♄ **4:12 am** 1:12 am
- ☽ ⚻ ♃ **7:04 am** 4:04 am
- ♀ □ ♅ **8:17 am** 5:17 am
- ☽ □ ☉ **10:23 am** 7:23 am
- ☽ ⚹ ♂ **1:11 pm** 10:11 am
- ☽ □ ☿ **6:39 pm** 3:39 pm
- ☽ ⚻ ♅ **9:39 pm** 6:39 pm
- ☽ ⚹ ♀ **11:01 pm** 8:01 pm

4 MONDAY
- ☽ □ ♆ **10:41 am** 7:41 am
- ☿ ⚹ ♅ **3:24 pm** 12:24 pm
- ☽ ⚺ ♇ **6:35 pm** 3:35 pm

5 TUESDAY
- ☽ ⚹ ♄ **10:38 am** 7:38 am
- ☽ △ ♃ **1:30 pm** 10:30 am
- ☽ ⚹ ☉ **8:01 pm** 5:01 pm
- ☽ ⚺ ♂ **9:37 pm** 6:37 pm
- ☽ △ ♅ 11:28 pm

6 WEDNESDAY
- ☽ △ ♅ **2:28 am**
- ☽ ⚹ ☿ **7:54 am** 4:54 am
- ☽ ⚺ ♀ **8:37 am** 5:37 am
- ☽ ⚹ ♆ **2:35 pm** 11:35 am
- ☿ ⚺ ♀ **9:00 pm** 6:00 pm
- ☽ ☌ ♇ **9:54 pm** 6:54 pm

7 THURSDAY
- ☽ ⚺ ♄ **1:14 pm** 10:14 am
- ☽ □ ♃ **4:08 pm** 1:08 pm
- ☽ ⚺ ☉ 10:12 pm
- ☽ ☌ ♂ 10:51 pm

8 FRIDAY
- ☽ ⚺ ☉ **1:12 am**
- ☽ ☌ ♂ **1:51 am**
- ☽ □ ♅ **3:50 am** 12:50 am
- ☿ ☌ ♆ **10:06 am** 7:06 am
- ☽ ☌ ♀ **1:56 pm** 10:56 am
- ☽ ⚺ ♆ **3:21 pm** 12:21 pm
- ☽ ⚺ ☿ **4:07 pm** 1:07 pm
- ☽ ⚺ ♇ **10:18 pm** 7:18 pm

9 SATURDAY
- ♀ ⚺ ♆ **7:49 am** 4:49 am
- ☽ ☌ ♄ **1:23 pm** 10:23 am
- ☽ ⚹ ♃ **4:24 pm** 1:24 pm
- ♂ □ ♅ **5:55 pm** 2:55 pm
- ☉ ⚹ ♅ **6:01 pm** 3:01 pm
- ☉ ⚺ ♂ **6:20 pm** 3:20 pm

10 SUNDAY
- ☽ ⚹ ♅ **4:22 am** 12:22 am
- ☽ ⚺ ♂ **4:52 am** 12:52 am
- ☽ ☌ ☉ **5:00 am** 1:00 am
- ☽ ☌ ♆ **3:45 pm** 12:45 pm
- ☿ ⚹ ♇ **6:21 pm** 3:21 pm
- ☽ ⚺ ♀ **6:25 pm** 3:25 pm
- ☽ ⚹ ♇ **10:38 pm** 7:38 pm
- ☽ ☌ ☿ **11:15 pm** 8:15 pm

11 MONDAY
- ☽ ⚺ ♄ **2:08 pm** 11:08 am
- ☽ ⚺ ♃ **5:24 pm** 2:24 pm

12 TUESDAY
- ☽ ⚺ ♅ **4:07 am** 1:07 am
- ☽ ⚹ ♂ **7:08 am** 4:08 am
- ☽ ⚺ ☉ **8:06 am** 5:06 am
- ☽ ⚺ ♆ **3:52 pm** 12:52 pm
- ☽ ⚹ ♀ **10:56 pm** 7:56 pm
- ☽ □ ♇ **10:57 pm** 7:57 pm
- ♀ ⚺ ♇ **11:11 pm** 8:11 pm

13 WEDNESDAY
- ☽ ⚺ ☿ **6:43 am** 3:43 am
- ☽ ⚹ ♄ **3:30 pm** 12:30 pm
- ☽ ☌ ♃ **7:13 pm** 4:13 pm

14 THURSDAY
- ☽ ☌ ♅ **6:00 am** 3:00 am
- ☽ □ ♂ **12:01 pm** 9:01 am
- ☽ ⚹ ☉ **1:57 pm** 10:57 am
- ☽ ⚹ ♆ **6:29 pm** 3:29 pm
- ☽ △ ♇ 11:00 pm

15 FRIDAY
- ☽ △ ♇ **2:00 am**
- ☽ □ ♀ **6:59 am** 3:59 am
- ☽ ⚹ ☿ **6:11 pm** 3:11 pm
- ☽ □ ♄ **8:06 pm** 5:06 pm
- ☽ ⚺ ♃ 9:22 pm

16 SATURDAY
- ☽ ⚺ ♃ **12:22 am**
- ☿ ⚺ ♄ **9:57 am** 6:57 am
- ☽ ⚺ ♅ **11:20 am** 8:20 am
- ☽ △ ♂ **9:02 pm** 6:02 pm
- ☽ □ ☉ 9:11 pm
- ☽ □ ♆ 9:43 pm

17 SUNDAY
- ☽ □ ☉ **12:11 am**
- ☽ □ ♆ **12:43 am**
- ☉ ☌ ♆ **7:22 am** 4:22 am
- ☽ ⚻ ♇ **8:42 am** 5:42 am
- ☽ △ ♀ **7:55 pm** 4:55 pm
- ☿ ⚺ ♃ 10:02 pm

18 MONDAY
- ☿ ⚺ ♃ **1:02 am**
- ☽ △ ♄ **4:29 am** 1:29 am
- ☽ ⚹ ♃ **9:24 am** 6:24 am
- ☽ □ ☿ **10:29 am** 7:29 am
- ☽ ⚹ ♅ **8:20 pm** 5:20 pm

19 TUESDAY
- ☽ ⚻ ♂ **10:20 am** 7:20 am
- ☽ △ ♆ **10:30 am** 7:30 am
- ♂ ⚺ ♆ **12:57 pm** 9:57 am
- ☽ △ ☉ **2:52 pm** 11:52 am
- ☽ ☍ ♇ **6:49 pm** 3:49 pm

20 WEDNESDAY
- ☽ ⚻ ♀ **1:13 pm** 10:13 am
- ☽ ⚻ ♄ **4:02 pm** 1:02 pm
- ☽ □ ♃ **9:35 pm** 6:35 pm

21 THURSDAY
- ☽ △ ☿ **5:57 am** 2:57 am
- ☽ □ ♅ **8:07 am** 5:07 am
- ☉ ⚹ ♇ **4:03 pm** 1:03 pm
- ♀ ☌ ♄ **7:09 pm** 4:09 pm
- ☽ ⚻ ♆ **10:42 pm** 7:42 pm
- ☿ ⚺ ♅ 11:27 pm
- ☽ ☍ ♂ 11:34 pm

22 FRIDAY
- ☿ ⚺ ♅ **2:27 am**
- ☽ ☍ ♂ **2:34 am**
- ☽ ⚻ ♇ **7:09 am** 4:09 am
- ☽ ⚻ ☉ **8:30 am** 5:30 am

23 SATURDAY
- ☽ ☍ ♄ **5:17 am** 2:17 am
- ☽ ☍ ♀ **8:54 am** 5:54 am
- ☽ △ ♃ **11:22 am** 8:22 am
- ☽ △ ♅ **9:10 pm** 6:10 pm
- ☽ ⚻ ☿ 10:37 pm

24 SUNDAY
- ☽ ⚻ ☿ **1:37 am**
- ☽ ☍ ♆ **11:49 am** 8:49 am
- ♀ ⚹ ♃ **12:37 pm** 9:37 am
- ☽ ⚻ ♂ **7:47 pm** 4:47 pm
- ☽ △ ♇ **8:11 pm** 5:11 pm
- ♂ ⚺ ♇ 10:58 pm

25 MONDAY
- ♂ ⚺ ♇ **1:58 am**
- ☽ ☍ ☉ **3:00 am** 12:00 am
- ☽ ⚻ ♄ **6:45 pm** 3:45 pm
- ☽ ⚻ ♃ 10:15 pm

26 TUESDAY
- ☽ ⚻ ♃ **1:15 am**
- ☽ ⚻ ♀ **4:47 am** 1:47 am
- ☽ ⚻ ♅ **10:06 am** 7:06 am
- ☽ ☍ ☿ **7:09 pm** 4:09 pm
- ☽ ⚻ ♆ 9:31 pm

27 WEDNESDAY
- ☽ ⚻ ♆ **12:31 am**
- ☽ □ ♇ **8:37 am** 5:37 am
- ☽ △ ♂ **12:18 pm** 9:18 am
- ☽ ⚻ ☉ **8:35 pm** 5:35 pm

28 THURSDAY
- ☽ △ ♄ **7:11 am** 4:11 am
- ♀ ⚹ ♅ **9:58 am** 6:58 am
- ☽ ☍ ♃ **1:59 pm** 10:59 am
- ☽ ☍ ♅ **9:46 pm** 6:46 pm
- ☽ △ ♀ **11:02 pm** 8:02 pm

29 FRIDAY
- ☽ ⚻ ☿ **9:10 am** 6:10 am
- ☽ △ ♆ **11:40 am** 8:40 am
- ☽ ⚹ ♇ **7:23 pm** 4:23 pm
- ☽ □ ♂ 11:43 pm

30 SATURDAY
- ☽ □ ♂ **2:43 am**
- ☽ △ ☉ **11:44 am** 8:44 am
- ☽ □ ♄ **5:29 pm** 2:29 pm
- ☽ ⚻ ♃ 9:26 pm

31 SUNDAY
- ☽ ⚻ ♃ **12:26 am**
- ☽ ⚻ ♅ **7:06 am** 4:06 am
- ☽ □ ♀ **2:06 pm** 11:06 am
- ☽ △ ☿ **6:54 pm** 3:54 pm
- ☽ □ ♆ **8:16 pm** 5:16 pm

Eastern time in bold type
Pacific time in medium type

MARCH 2024

DATE	SID.TIME	SUN	MOON	NODE	MERCURY	VENUS	MARS	JUPITER	SATURN	URANUS	NEPTUNE	PLUTO	CERES	PALLAS	JUNO	VESTA	CHIRON
1 F	10 37 10	10♓53 22	10♏22	16♈00	12♓19	16♒30	12♒55	11♉19	9♓55	19♉35	26♓44	1♒13	7♏42	5♐45	14♍21 R	23♊21	17♈14
2 Sa	10 41 6	11 53 35	22 45	16 02	14 13	17 44	13 42	11 29	10 02	19 36	26 47	1 15	8 01	5 56	14 06	23 30	17 17
3 Su	10 45 3	12 53 45	5♐18	16 03 R	16 08	18 58	14 28	11 40	10 09	19 38	26 49	1 16	8 20	6 07	13 50	23 39	17 20
4 M	10 48 59	13 53 55	18 13	16 03	18 03	20 12	15 15	11 50	10 17	19 40	26 51	1 18	8 39	6 17	13 35	23 49	17 23
5 T	10 52 56	14 54 02	1♑53	16 02	19 59	21 27	16 01	12 01	10 24	19 42	26 53	1 19	8 57	6 27	13 20	23 58	17 26
6 W	10 56 52	15 54 09	15 21	16 00	21 55	22 41	16 48	12 11	10 31	19 44	26 56	1 21	9 16	6 37	13 05	24 08	17 29
7 Th	11 0 49	16 54 13	29 37	15 56	23 52	23 55	17 34	12 22	10 39	19 46	26 58	1 22	9 34	6 46	12 50	24 19	17 32
8 F	11 4 45	17 54 17	14♒18	15 52	25 48	25 10	18 21	12 33	10 46	19 48	27 00	1 24	9 52	6 56	12 35	24 30	17 36
9 Sa	11 8 42	18 54 18	29 20	15 48	27 45	26 24	19 07	12 44	10 53	19 50	27 02	1 25	10 10	7 04	12 20	24 41	17 39
10 Su	11 12 39	19 54 17	14♓33	15 45	29 41	27 38	19 54	12 55	11 01	19 52	27 05	1 26	10 28	7 13	12 05	24 52	17 42
11 M	11 16 35	20 54 15	29 48	15 43	1♈36	28 52	20 41	13 07	11 08	19 54	27 07	1 28	10 46	7 21	11 51	25 04	17 45
12 T	11 20 32	21 54 10	14♈54	15 42 D	3 30	0♓07	21 27	13 18	11 15	19 56	27 09	1 29	11 03	7 28	11 37	25 16	17 48
13 W	11 24 28	22 54 04	29 43	15 43	5 23	1 21	22 14	13 29	11 22	19 58	27 11	1 31	11 20	7 36	11 22	25 28	17 52
14 Th	11 28 25	23 53 55	14♉09	15 44	7 13	2 35	23 00	13 41	11 30	20 01	27 14	1 32	11 37	7 42	11 08	25 40	17 55
15 F	11 32 21	24 53 44	28 08	15 45	9 02	3 49	23 47	13 52	11 37	20 03	27 16	1 33	11 54	7 49	10 55	25 53	17 58
16 Sa	11 36 18	25 53 31	11♊41	15 46	10 48	5 04	24 34	14 04	11 44	20 05	27 18	1 35	12 11	7 55	10 41	26 06	18 02
17 Su	11 40 14	26 53 16	24 49	15 47 R	12 31	6 18	25 20	14 16	11 51	20 08	27 20	1 36	12 28	8 01	10 28	26 20	18 05
18 M	11 44 11	27 52 59	7♋35	15 47	14 10	7 32	26 07	14 28	11 58	20 10	27 23	1 37	12 44	8 06	10 15	26 33	18 08
19 T	11 48 8	28 52 39	20 02	15 46	15 45	8 46	26 54	14 40	12 05	20 12	27 25	1 38	13 00	8 11	10 02	26 47	18 12
20 W	11 52 4	29 52 17	2♌15	15 44	17 15	10 01	27 40	14 52	12 13	20 15	27 27	1 39	13 16	8 15	9 50	27 01	18 15
21 Th	11 56 1	0♈51 53	14 17	15 42	18 40	11 15	28 27	15 04	12 20	20 17	27 30	1 41	13 32	8 19	9 37	27 16	18 19
22 F	11 59 57	1 51 26	26 12	15 39	20 00	12 29	29 14	15 16	12 27	20 20	27 32	1 42	13 48	8 23	9 26	27 30	18 22
23 Sa	12 3 54	2 50 58	8♍02	15 37	21 14	13 43	0♓00	15 28	12 34	20 23	27 34	1 43	14 03	8 26	9 14	27 45	18 25
24 Su	12 7 50	3 50 27	19 51	15 36	22 22	14 58	0 47	15 40	12 41	20 25	27 36	1 44	14 18	8 29	9 03	28 00	18 29
25 M	12 11 47	4 49 54	1♎40	15 35	23 23	16 12	1 34	15 53	12 48	20 28	27 39	1 45	14 33	8 31	8 52	28 16	18 32
26 T	12 15 43	5 49 19	13 32	15 34 D	24 17	17 26	2 20	16 05	12 55	20 30	27 41	1 46	14 48	8 33	8 41	28 31	18 36
27 W	12 19 40	6 48 42	25 28	15 34	25 04	18 40	3 07	16 18	13 02	20 33	27 43	1 47	15 02	8 34	8 31	28 47	18 39
28 Th	12 23 37	7 48 03	7♏02	15 35	25 44	19 54	3 54	16 30	13 09	20 36	27 45	1 48	15 17	8 35	8 21	29 03	18 43
29 F	12 27 33	8 47 22	19 45	15 36	26 17	21 08	4 41	16 43	13 16	20 39	27 48	1 49	15 31	8 36 R	8 11	29 19	18 46
30 Sa	12 31 30	9 46 39	2♐09	15 36	26 42	22 23	5 27	16 56	13 22	20 41	27 50	1 50	15 45	8 36	8 01	29 36	18 50
31 Su	12 35 26	10 45 55	14 49	15 37	27 00	23 37	6 14	17 08	13 29	20 44	27 52	1 51	15 59	8 35	7 53	29 52	18 53

EPHEMERIS CALCULATED FOR 12 MIDNIGHT GREENWICH MEAN TIME. ALL OTHER DATA AND FACING ASPECTARIAN PAGE IN EASTERN TIME (BOLD) AND PACIFIC TIME (REGULAR).

APRIL 2024

☽ Last Aspect day	ET / hr:mn / PT		asp	☽ Ingress sign	day	ET / hr:mn / PT	
3/31	**8:16 pm**	5:16 pm	□♆	♑	3/31		9:05 pm
3/31	**8:16 pm**	5:16 pm	□♆	♑	1	**12:05 am**	
2		10:40 pm	⚹♆	♒	3	**5:08 am**	2:08 am
3	**1:40 am**		⚹♆	♒	3	**5:08 am**	2:08 am
4		10:40 pm	⚹☿	♓	5	**7:13 am**	4:13 am
5	**1:40 am**		⚹☿	♓	5	**7:13 am**	4:13 am
7	**4:27 am**	1:27 am	☌♆	♈	7	**7:25 am**	4:25 am
8	**10:39 pm**	7:39 pm	☌☿	♉	9	**7:23 am**	4:23 am
11	**6:04 am**	3:04 am	⚹♆	♊	11	**8:59 am**	5:59 am
13	**10:46 am**	7:46 am	□♆	♋	13	**1:45 pm**	10:45 am
15	**7:22 pm**	4:22 pm	△♆	♌	15	**10:24 pm**	7:24 pm
18	**8:02 am**	5:02 am	△☉	♍	18	**10:10 am**	7:10 am
20	**8:20 pm**	5:20 pm	☍♆	♎	20	**11:08 pm**	8:08 pm
22	**7:24 pm**	4:24 pm	☍♀	♏	23	**11:20 am**	8:20 am
25	**7:17 pm**	4:17 pm	△♆	♐	25	**9:37 pm**	6:37 pm
28	**3:31 am**	12:31 am	□♆	♑	28	**5:37 am**	2:37 am
30	**11:19 am**	8:19 am	⚹♂	♒	30	**11:20 am**	8:20 am

☽ Phases & Eclipses phase	day	ET / hr:mn / PT	
4th Quarter	1	**11:15 pm**	8:15 pm
New Moon	8	**2:21 pm**	11:21 am
●	8	19° ♈ 24'	
2nd Quarter	15	**3:13 pm**	12:13 pm
Full Moon	23	**7:49 pm**	4:49 pm

Planet Ingress	day	ET / hr:mn / PT	
♀ ♈	4		9:00 pm
♀ ♈	5	**12:00 am**	
☉ ♉	19	**10:00 am**	7:00 am
♀ ♉	29	**7:31 am**	4:31 am
♂ ♈	30	**11:33 am**	8:33 am

Planetary Motion	day	ET / hr:mn / PT	
☿ ℞	1	**6:14 pm**	3:14 pm
⚵ D	21	**10:58 pm**	7:58 pm
☿ D	25	**8:54 am**	5:54 am

1 MONDAY
☽⚺♇ **3:29 am** 12:29 am
☽⚹♂ **1:49 pm** 10:49 am
☽□☉ **11:15 pm** 8:15 pm
☽⚹♄ 9:46 pm

2 TUESDAY
☽⚹♄ **12:46 am**
☽△♃ **7:44 am** 4:44 am
☽△♅ **1:20 pm** 10:20 am
☿⚺♀ **4:58 pm** 1:58 pm
☉⚺♄ **10:42 pm** 7:42 pm
☽□☿ 9:11 pm
☽⚹♀ 9:58 pm
☽⚹♆ 10:40 pm

3 WEDNESDAY
☽□☿ **12:11 am**
☽⚹♀ **12:58 am**
☽⚹♆ **1:40 am**
☽☌♇ **8:23 am** 5:23 am
♀☌♆ **9:10 am** 6:10 am
☽⚺♂ **9:04 pm** 6:04 pm

4 THURSDAY
☽⚺♄ **4:47 am** 1:47 am
☽⚹☉ **6:45 am** 3:45 am
☽□♃ **11:43 am** 8:43 am
☽□♅ **4:24 pm** 1:24 pm
☽⚹☿ 10:40 pm

Eastern time in bold type
Pacific time in medium type

5 FRIDAY
☽⚹☿ **1:40 am**
☽⚺♆ **4:03 am** 1:03 am
☽⚺♀ **7:52 am** 4:52 am
☽⚺♇ **10:21 am** 7:21 am
☽☌♂ 10:08 pm

6 SATURDAY
☽☌♂ **1:08 am**
☽☌♄ **6:10 am** 3:10 am
☽⚺☉ **11:08 am** 8:08 am
☽⚹♃ **1:13 pm** 10:13 am
♀⚹♇ **1:46 pm** 10:46 am
☽⚹♅ **5:11 pm** 2:11 pm
☽⚺☿ 9:36 pm

7 SUNDAY
☽⚺☿ **12:36 am**
☽☌♆ **4:27 am** 1:27 am
☽⚹♇ **10:31 am** 7:31 am
☽☌♀ **12:22 pm** 9:22 am

8 MONDAY
☉⚺♃ **3:11 am** 12:11 am
☽⚺♂ **3:39 am** 12:39 am
☽⚺♄ **6:23 am** 3:23 am
☽⚺♃ **1:46 pm** 10:46 am
☽☌☉ **2:21 pm** 11:21 am
☽⚺♅ **5:12 pm** 2:12 pm
☽☌☿ **10:39 pm** 7:39 pm

9 TUESDAY
☽⚺♆ **4:30 am** 1:30 am
☽□♇ **10:35 am** 7:35 am
☽⚺♀ **4:48 pm** 1:48 pm

10 WEDNESDAY
☽⚹♂ **6:49 am** 3:49 am
☽⚹♄ **7:16 am** 4:16 am
☉⚺♅ **12:00 pm** 9:00 am
☽☌♃ **3:19 pm** 12:19 pm
♂☌♄ **4:36 pm** 1:36 pm
☽☌♅ **6:18 pm** 3:18 pm
☽⚺☉ **6:44 pm** 3:44 pm
☽⚺☿ **9:31 pm** 6:31 pm

11 THURSDAY
☽⚹♆ **6:04 am** 3:04 am
☽△♇ **12:23 pm** 9:23 am
☉☌☿ **7:03 pm** 4:03 pm
☽⚹♀ **11:47 pm** 8:47 pm

12 FRIDAY
☽□♄ **10:39 am** 7:39 am
☽□♂ **12:51 pm** 9:51 am
☽⚺♃ **7:43 pm** 4:43 pm
☽⚺♅ **10:13 pm** 7:13 pm
☽⚹☿ **10:43 pm** 7:43 pm
☽⚹☉ 11:35 pm

13 SATURDAY
☽⚹☉ **2:35 am**
☿⚺♅ **6:47 am** 3:47 am
☽□♆ **10:46 am** 7:46 am
☽⚻♇ **5:26 pm** 2:26 pm

14 SUNDAY
☽□♀ **11:24 am** 8:24 am
☿⚺♃ **3:38 pm** 12:38 pm
☽△♄ **5:48 pm** 2:48 pm
☽△♂ **11:17 pm** 8:17 pm

15 MONDAY
☽□☿ **3:12 am** 12:12 am
☽⚹♃ **4:05 am** 1:05 am
☽⚹♅ **6:01 am** 3:01 am
☽□☉ **3:13 pm** 12:13 pm
☽△♆ **7:22 pm** 4:22 pm
☽☍♇ 11:23 pm

16 TUESDAY
☽☍♇ **2:23 am**
☿⚺♂ **10:46 am** 7:46 am

17 WEDNESDAY
☽△♀ **4:03 am** 1:03 am
☽⚻♄ **4:42 am** 1:42 am
♀⚺♄ **10:53 am** 7:53 am
☽△☿ **11:01 am** 8:01 am
☽⚻♂ **2:04 pm** 11:04 am
☽□♃ **4:11 pm** 1:11 pm
☽□♅ **5:20 pm** 2:20 pm
☉⚺♆ **9:31 pm** 6:31 pm

18 THURSDAY
☽⚻♆ **7:12 am** 4:12 am
☽△☉ **8:02 am** 5:02 am
☽⚻♇ **2:20 pm** 11:20 am

19 FRIDAY
☿☌♀ **4:59 am** 1:59 am
♂⚹♃ **11:28 am** 8:28 am
☽☍♄ **5:53 pm** 2:53 pm
♂⚹♅ **7:56 pm** 4:56 pm
☽⚻☿ **9:10 pm** 6:10 pm
☽⚻♀ **11:47 pm** 8:47 pm

20 SATURDAY
☽△♃ **6:14 am** 3:14 am
☽△♅ **6:28 am** 3:28 am
☽☍♂ **7:09 am** 4:09 am
☽☍♆ **8:20 pm** 5:20 pm
♃☌♅ **10:27 pm** 7:27 pm
☽⚻☉ 11:28 pm

21 SUNDAY
☽⚻☉ **2:28 am**
☽△♇ **3:20 am** 12:20 am
☉□♇ **1:02 pm** 10:02 am

22 MONDAY
☽⚻♄ **7:08 am** 4:08 am
☽☍☿ **8:10 am** 5:10 am
♀⚺♅ **6:25 pm** 3:25 pm
☽⚻♅ **7:18 pm** 4:18 pm
☽☍♀ **7:24 pm** 4:24 pm
☽⚻♃ **7:58 pm** 4:58 pm
☽⚻♂ **11:51 pm** 8:51 pm
♀⚺♃ 11:04 pm

23 TUESDAY
♀⚺♃ **2:04 am**
☽⚻♆ **8:45 am** 5:45 am
☽□♇ **3:27 pm** 12:27 pm
☽☍☉ **7:49 pm** 4:49 pm

24 WEDNESDAY
☿⚺♄ **5:14 am** 2:14 am
☽⚻☿ **6:41 pm** 3:41 pm
☽△♄ **6:52 pm** 3:52 pm

25 THURSDAY
☽☍♅ **6:26 am** 3:26 am
☽☍♃ **7:55 am** 4:55 am
☽⚻♀ **12:42 pm** 9:42 am
☽△♂ **2:25 pm** 11:25 am
☽△♆ **7:17 pm** 4:17 pm
☽⚹♇ 10:36 pm

26 FRIDAY
☽⚹♇ **1:36 am**
☽⚻☉ **10:36 am** 7:36 am

27 SATURDAY
☽△☿ **3:59 am** 12:59 am
☽□♄ **4:21 am** 1:21 am
♀⚺♂ **8:36 am** 5:36 am
☽⚻♅ **3:18 pm** 12:18 pm
☽⚻♃ **5:30 pm** 2:30 pm
☽□♂ 11:15 pm
☽△♀ 11:56 pm

28 SUNDAY
☽□♂ **2:15 am**
☽△♀ **2:56 am**
☽□♆ **3:31 am** 12:31 am
♀⚺♆ **9:13 am** 6:13 am
☽⚺♇ **9:27 am** 6:27 am
☿⚺♄ **6:49 pm** 3:49 pm
☽△☉ **10:28 pm** 7:28 pm
♂☌♆ 9:31 pm

29 MONDAY
♂☌♆ **12:31 am**
☽⚹♄ **11:28 am** 8:28 am
☽□☿ **11:45 am** 8:45 am
☽△♅ **9:49 pm** 6:49 pm
☽△♃ 9:39 pm

30 TUESDAY
☽△♃ **12:39 am**
☽⚹♆ **9:25 am** 6:25 am
☽⚹♂ **11:19 am** 8:19 am
☽□♀ **2:04 pm** 11:04 am
☽☌♇ **3:00 pm** 12:00 pm
♀□♇ 9:30 pm

APRIL 2024

DATE	SID. TIME	SUN	MOON	NODE	MERCURY	VENUS	MARS	JUPITER	SATURN	URANUS	NEPTUNE	PLUTO	CERES	PALLAS	JUNO	VESTA	CHIRON
1 M	12 39 23	11♈45 09	27♈46	15♈37	27♈10R	24♓51	7♓01	17♉21	13♓36	20♉47	27♓54	1♒52	16♉13	8♓34R	7♉45R	0♊09	18♈57
2 T	12 43 19	12 44 21	11♉03	15 37R	27 13	26 05	7 47	17 34	13 43	20 50	27 57	1 53	16 26	8 33	7 39	0 26	19 00
3 W	12 47 16	13 43 31	24 42	15 37	27 09	27 19	8 34	17 47	13 49	20 53	27 59	1 54	16 39	8 31	7 34	0 44	19 04
4 Th	12 51 12	14 42 40	8♊45	15 37D	26 58	28 33	9 21	18 00	13 56	20 56	28 01	1 55	16 52	8 29	7 29	1 01	19 07
5 F	12 55 9	15 41 47	23 09	15 37	26 41	29 48	10 07	18 13	14 03	20 59	28 03	1 55	17 04	8 26	7 22	1 19	19 11
6 Sa	12 59 6	16 40 52	7♋53	15 37	26 18	1♈02	10 54	18 26	14 09	21 02	28 05	1 56	17 17	8 23	7 15	1 37	19 15
7 Su	13 3 2	17 39 55	22 51	15 37	25 49	2 16	11 41	18 39	14 16	21 05	28 08	1 57	17 29	8 19	7 08	1 55	19 18
8 M	13 6 59	18 38 56	7♌54	15 37	25 16	3 30	12 27	18 53	14 22	21 08	28 10	1 58	17 41	8 14	7 02	2 13	19 22
9 T	13 10 55	19 37 55	22 56	15 36	24 39	4 44	13 14	19 06	14 29	21 11	28 12	1 58	17 52	8 10	6 57	2 31	19 25
10 W	13 14 52	20 36 52	7♍46	15 37	23 58	5 58	14 01	19 19	14 35	21 14	28 14	1 59	18 04	8 04	6 51	2 50	19 29
11 Th	13 18 48	21 35 48	22 18	15 37	23 15	7 12	14 47	19 33	14 42	21 17	28 16	2 00	18 15	7 59	6 46	3 09	19 32
12 F	13 22 45	22 34 41	6♎27	15 36	22 31	8 26	15 34	19 46	14 48	21 20	28 18	2 00	18 25	7 52	6 42	3 28	19 36
13 Sa	13 26 41	23 33 32	20 09	15 35	21 45	9 41	16 21	19 59	14 54	21 24	28 20	2 01	18 36	7 45	6 38	3 47	19 39
14 Su	13 30 38	24 32 20	3♏25	15 34	21 00	10 55	17 07	20 13	15 01	21 27	28 23	2 01	18 46	7 38	6 34	4 06	19 43
15 M	13 34 35	25 31 07	16 16	15 34D	20 16	12 09	17 54	20 26	15 07	21 30	28 25	2 02	18 56	7 31	6 31	4 26	19 46
16 T	13 38 31	26 29 51	28 46	15 34	19 34	13 23	18 40	20 40	15 13	21 33	28 27	2 02	19 06	7 22	6 28	4 45	19 50
17 W	13 42 28	27 28 33	10♐59	15 34	18 54	14 37	19 27	20 54	15 19	21 36	28 29	2 03	19 15	7 14	6 25	5 05	19 53
18 Th	13 46 24	28 27 12	22 59	15 35	18 17	15 51	20 13	21 07	15 25	21 40	28 31	2 03	19 25	7 04	6 23	5 25	19 57
19 F	13 50 21	29 25 50	4♑49	15 36	17 44	17 05	21 00	21 21	15 31	21 43	28 33	2 03	19 33	6 55	6 21	5 45	20 01
20 Sa	13 54 17	0♉24 25	16 39	15 37	17 15	18 19	21 46	21 35	15 37	21 46	28 35	2 04	19 42	6 45	6 20	6 05	20 04
21 Su	13 58 14	1 22 58	28 27	15 39	16 50	19 33	22 33	21 48	15 43	21 49	28 37	2 04	19 50	6 34	6 19	6 26	20 08
22 M	14 2 10	2 21 29	10♒24	15 39R	16 30	20 47	23 19	22 02	15 49	21 53	28 39	2 05	19 58	6 23	6 18	6 46	20 11
23 T	14 6 7	3 19 58	22 17	15 39	16 15	22 01	24 06	22 16	15 54	21 56	28 41	2 05	20 06	6 12	6 18D	7 07	20 14
24 W	14 10 3	4 18 26	4♓24	15 38	16 05	23 15	24 52	22 30	16 00	21 59	28 43	2 05	20 13	6 00	6 18	7 27	20 18
25 Th	14 14 0	5 16 51	16 41	15 36	16 00D	24 29	25 38	22 44	16 06	22 03	28 45	2 06	20 21	5 48	6 19	7 48	20 21
26 F	14 17 57	6 15 15	29 09	15 34	15 59	25 43	26 25	22 58	16 11	22 06	28 47	2 06	20 27	5 35	6 21	8 09	20 25
27 Sa	14 21 53	7 13 36	11♈50	15 30	16 04	26 57	27 11	23 11	16 17	22 10	28 48	2 06	20 34	5 22	6 22	8 31	20 28
28 Su	14 25 50	8 11 57	24 45	15 27	16 14	28 11	27 57	23 25	16 22	22 13	28 50	2 06	20 40	5 08	6 24	8 52	20 32
29 M	14 29 46	9 10 15	7♉54	15 24	16 28	29 25	28 44	23 39	16 28	22 16	28 52	2 06	20 46	4 54	6 27	9 13	20 35
30 T	14 33 43	10 08 33	21 18	15 22	16 47	0♉38	29 30	23 53	16 33	22 20	28 54	2 06	20 51	4 40	6 29	9 35	20 39

EPHEMERIS CALCULATED FOR 12 MIDNIGHT GREENWICH MEAN TIME. ALL OTHER DATA AND FACING ASPECTARIAN PAGE IN **EASTERN TIME (BOLD)** AND PACIFIC TIME (REGULAR).

MAY 2024

1 WEDNESDAY
☿ □ ♃ 12:30 am
♀ ⚹ ♇ 4:27 am 1:27 am
☿ △ ♄ 7:27 am
☿ ⚹ ♇ 7:27 am 4:17 pm
☿ △ ♃ 5:48 am 2:06 pm

2 THURSDAY
☿ △ ♀ 2:06 am
♀ □ ♃ 5:28 am 2:28 am
☿ ⚹ ♃ 1:08 pm 10:08 am
☿ △ ♇ 6:24 pm 3:24 pm
♀ ⚹ ♄ 10:21 pm 7:21 pm

3 FRIDAY
♂ ⚹ ♀ 5:06 am 2:06 am
♀ □ ♇ 7:55 pm 4:55 pm
♀ △ ♄ 10:18 pm

4 SATURDAY
♀ △ ♄ 4:28 am 1:28 am
♂ ☐ ♇ 8:22 am 5:22 am
☿ △ ♀ 3:06 pm 12:06 pm
♀ ⚹ ♇ 8:08 pm 5:08 pm
♂ ♂ ♀ 10:17 pm 7:17 pm

5 SUNDAY
♀ △ ⊙ 4:32 am 1:32 am
♀ ☐ ♀ 6:42 am 3:42 am
♀ △ ♇ 8:35 am 5:35 am
3:00 am

6 MONDAY
☿ ♂ ♀ 1:57 am
☿ ⚹ ♄ 5:46 am 2:46 am
♀ △ ♀ 10:14 am 7:14 am
♀ △ ♇ 9:08 pm 6:08 pm
11:01 pm

7 TUESDAY
⊙ ☐ ♀ 1:42 am
♀ ⚹ ♀ 2:01 am 7:05 am
☿ △ ♄ 10:05 am 7:02 pm
☿ △ ♇ 10:02 pm 8:22 pm
☿ ♂ ♀ 11:22 pm

8 WEDNESDAY
☿ ♂ ♀ 6:14 am 3:14 am
♀ ⚹ ♇ 7:19 am 4:19 am
♀ △ ♇ 12:30 pm 9:30 am
♀ △ ♄ 5:55 pm 2:55 pm
☿ ☐ ♇ 10:52 pm 7:52 pm
9:17 pm

9 THURSDAY
☿ ⚹ ♀ 12:17 am
♀ ⚹ ♄ 6:47 am 3:47 am
5:08 pm 2:08 pm
10:03 pm

10 FRIDAY
♀ ☐ ♇ 1:03 am
♀ △ ♄ 6:00 am 3:00 am
2:06 pm
4:47 pm
8:45 pm

11 SATURDAY
☿ ⚹ ♀ 10:4 am 7:44 am
☿ ⚹ ♄ 1:3 pm 10:13 am
♀ △ ♇ 4:54 pm 1:54 pm
♀ ☐ ♇ 9:9 pm 6:49 pm
11:57 pm

12 SUNDAY
☿ ⚹ ♄ 2:57 am 11:36 am
♀ △ ♀ 2:38 pm 12:57 am
☿ ⚹ ♇ 3:7 am 4:11 am
♀ △ ♄ 7:1 am 4:24 pm
♀ ♂ ♀ 5:29 pm 1:34 pm
9:00 pm
9:56 pm

13 MONDAY
♀ ⚹ ♀ 12:1 am 12:57 am
☿ △ ♇ 12:1 pm 4:11 am
☿ ☐ ♇ 5:1 am 1:34 am
♀ △ ♀ 5:4 am 2:48 am
♀ ♂ ♇ 3:5 pm 12:15 pm
11:49 pm

14 TUESDAY
♀ △ ♇ 12:17 am
☿ ⚹ ♀ 5:0 pm 2:09 am
♀ ♂ ♀ 7:9 pm 4:41 am
☿ △ ♄ 11:0 pm 7:32 am
11:29 am
11:45 am

15 WEDNESDAY
☿ ☐ ♀ 3:58 am 12:58 am
♀ □ ♄ 7:48 am 4:48 am
♀ ⚹ ♀ 12:41 pm 9:41 am
☿ ♂ ♇ 6:04 pm 3:04 pm
☿ △ ♄ 9:42 pm 6:42 pm

16 THURSDAY
♀ ♂ ♀ 6:48 pm 3:46 pm

17 FRIDAY
♀ △ ♄ 3:44 am 12:44 am
♀ ☐ ♀ 5:48 am 2:48 am
♀ ♂ ♇ 3:15 pm 12:15 pm
☿ ⚹ ♀ 4:53 pm 1:53 pm

18 SATURDAY
♀ △ ♀ 1:53 am
☿ △ ♇ 5:42 am 2:42 am
♀ ♂ ♄ 7:41 am 4:41 am
♀ ⚹ ♇ 10:32 am 7:32 am
♀ △ ♄ 2:29 pm 11:29 am
♀ ☐ ♀ 2:45 pm 11:45 am

19 SUNDAY
♀ ♂ ♀ 11:48 am 8:48 am
⊙ ⚹ ♀ 6:45 pm 3:45 pm
♀ ☐ ♄ 6:52 pm 3:52 pm

20 MONDAY
♀ △ ♀ 5:43 am 2:43 am
♀ ☐ ♇ 7:41 am 4:41 am
♀ △ ♄ 4:11 pm 1:11 pm
♀ ⚹ ♀ 5:29 pm 2:29 pm
♀ ⊙ ♊ 7:23 pm 4:23 pm
♀ □ ♇ 10:34 pm 7:34 pm

21 TUESDAY
♀ △ ♀ 10:18 pm 7:18 am
11:49 pm

22 WEDNESDAY
♀ △ ♇ 2:49 am
♀ ⚹ ♄ 6:03 am 3:03 am
☿ △ ♀ 11:14 am 8:14 am
☿ ♂ ♀ 4:24 pm 1:24 pm

23 THURSDAY
♀ △ ♀ 3:07 am 12:07 am
♀ ☐ ♀ 3:13 pm 12:13 pm
♀ ☐ ♇ 4:28 pm 1:28 pm
♀ △ ♄ 6:50 pm 3:50 pm
☿ ⊙ ♀ 8:10 pm 5:10 pm
♂ □ ♄ 9:53 pm 6:53 pm
☿ ♂ ♀ 5:44 pm 2:44 pm

24 FRIDAY
♀ △ ♀ 3:05 am 12:05 am
♀ ♂ ♇ 12:23 pm 9:23 am
♀ △ ♄ 2:29 pm 11:29 am
♀ □ ♀ 2:36 pm 11:36 am
9:21 pm

25 SATURDAY
♀ ⚹ ♀ 12:21 am
☿ ☐ ♀ 10:47 am 7:47 am
♀ △ ♀ 11:28 am 8:28 am
♀ ⚹ ♇ 3:58 pm 12:58 pm
♀ ♂ ♄ 9:06 pm 6:06 pm
4:16 pm
7:47 pm

26 SUNDAY
♀ △ ♀ 4:49 am 1:49 am
♀ ⚹ ♄ 8:33 pm 5:33 pm
♀ △ ♇ 11:37 pm 8:37 pm

27 MONDAY
♀ △ ♀ 6:05 am 3:05 am
♀ ⚹ ♄ 4:02 pm 1:02 pm
♀ □ ♀ 5:32 pm 2:32 pm
8:10 pm 5:10 pm
11:22 pm 8:22 pm
11:10 pm

28 TUESDAY
♀ △ ♀ 2:10 am
☿ △ ♇ 5:54 am 2:54 am
10:00 pm

29 WEDNESDAY
♀ △ ♀ 1:00 am
♀ □ ♀ 4:36 am 1:36 am
♀ ⚹ ♄ 6:46 am 3:45 am
♀ ☐ ♇ 10:20 am 7:20 am
♀ △ ♀ 7:55 pm 4:55 pm

30 THURSDAY
♀ △ ♀ 10:12 pm 7:12 pm
♀ ⚹ ♇ 11:51 pm 8:51 pm

31 FRIDAY
♀ △ ♀ 1:54 am
♀ ♂ ♇ 4:24 am 1:24 am
♀ ☐ ♄ 12:45 pm 9:45 am
♀ ♂ ♀ 1:36 pm 10:36 am
☿ ⚹ ♄ 3:19 pm 12:19 pm
♀ △ ♇ 10:55 pm 7:55 pm
10:57 pm
11:41 pm

Eastern time in bold type
Pacific time in medium type

MAY 2024

DATE	SID.TIME	SUN	MOON	NODE	MERCURY	VENUS	MARS	JUPITER	SATURN	URANUS	NEPTUNE	PLUTO	CERES	PALLAS	JUNO	VESTA	CHIRON
1 W	14 37 39	11♉06 48	4≈58	15♈21D	17♈11	1♉52	0♈16	24♉07	16♓38	22♉23	28♓56	2≈06	20♑56	4♈25R	6♊32	9♋57	20♈42
2 Th	14 41 36	12 05 02	18 53	15 21	17 39	3 06	1 03	24 21	16 43	22 27	28 58	2 06R	21 01	4 10	6 36	10 18	20 45
3 F	14 45 33	13 03 15	3♓03	15 22	18 11	4 20	1 49	24 35	16 49	22 30	28 59	2 06	21 06	3 55	6 39	10 40	20 49
4 Sa	14 49 29	14 01 26	17 27	15 23	18 47	5 34	2 35	24 49	16 54	22 34	29 01	2 06	21 10	3 39	6 43	11 02	20 52
5 Su	14 53 26	14 59 36	2♈02	15 24R	19 26	6 48	3 21	25 04	16 59	22 37	29 03	2 06	21 14	3 23	6 48	11 25	20 55
6 M	14 57 22	15 57 44	16 43	15 25	20 10	8 02	4 07	25 18	17 04	22 41	29 04	2 06	21 17	3 07	6 52	11 47	20 59
7 T	15 1 19	16 55 51	1♉24	15 24	20 57	9 16	4 53	25 32	17 09	22 44	29 06	2 06	21 20	2 51	6 57	12 09	21 02
8 W	15 5 15	17 53 56	16 00	15 21	21 48	10 30	5 39	25 46	17 13	22 47	29 08	2 06	21 23	2 34	7 03	12 32	21 05
9 Th	15 9 12	18 52 00	0♊23	15 17	22 42	11 44	6 25	26 00	17 18	22 51	29 09	2 06	21 26	2 17	7 08	12 54	21 08
10 F	15 13 8	19 50 02	14 29	15 12	23 39	12 57	7 11	26 14	17 23	22 54	29 11	2 05	21 28	2 00	7 14	13 17	21 12
11 Sa	15 17 5	20 48 02	28 12	15 07	24 39	14 11	7 57	26 28	17 27	22 58	29 13	2 05	21 29	1 42	7 21	13 40	21 15
12 Su	15 21 2	21 46 00	11♋30	15 01	25 42	15 25	8 43	26 42	17 32	23 01	29 14	2 05	21 31	1 25	7 27	14 03	21 18
13 M	15 24 58	22 43 57	24 25	14 57	26 48	16 39	9 29	26 57	17 36	23 05	29 16	2 05	21 32	1 07	7 34	14 26	21 21
14 T	15 28 55	23 41 52	6♌58	14 54	27 56	17 53	10 15	27 11	17 41	23 08	29 17	2 04	21 32	0 49	7 41	14 49	21 24
15 W	15 32 51	24 39 45	19 12	14 53	29 08	19 07	11 01	27 25	17 45	23 12	29 19	2 04	21 33R	0 31	7 49	15 12	21 27
16 Th	15 36 48	25 37 37	1♍13	14 53	0♉22	20 20	11 46	27 39	17 49	23 15	29 20	2 04	21 32	0 13	7 56	15 36	21 30
17 F	15 40 44	26 35 26	13 05	14 54	1 38	21 34	12 32	27 53	17 53	23 19	29 22	2 03	21 32	29♓55	8 04	15 59	21 33
18 Sa	15 44 41	27 33 14	24 54	14 55	2 57	22 48	13 18	28 07	17 57	23 22	29 23	2 03	21 31	29 37	8 13	16 23	21 36
19 Su	15 48 37	28 31 01	6≏43	14 56R	4 19	24 02	14 03	28 21	18 01	23 26	29 24	2 03	21 30	29 19	8 21	16 46	21 39
20 M	15 52 34	29 28 45	18 39	14 57	5 43	25 16	14 49	28 36	18 05	23 29	29 26	2 02	21 28	29 00	8 30	17 10	21 42
21 T	15 56 31	0♊26 28	0♏44	14 55	7 09	26 29	15 35	28 50	18 09	23 33	29 27	2 01	21 27	28 42	8 39	17 34	21 45
22 W	16 0 27	1 24 10	13 01	14 52	8 38	27 43	16 20	29 04	18 12	23 36	29 28	2 01	21 24	28 24	8 48	17 58	21 48
23 Th	16 4 24	2 21 50	25 33	14 46	10 09	28 57	17 06	29 18	18 16	23 40	29 30	2 00	21 22	28 06	8 58	18 22	21 51
24 F	16 8 20	3 19 30	8♐21	14 39	11 42	0♊11	17 51	29 32	18 20	23 43	29 31	2 00	21 19	27 48	9 08	18 46	21 54
25 Sa	16 12 17	4 17 07	21 23	14 31	13 18	1 25	18 36	29 46	18 23	23 47	29 32	1 59	21 15	27 30	9 18	19 10	21 57
26 Su	16 16 13	5 14 44	4♑41	14 23	14 56	2 38	19 22	0♊00	18 26	23 50	29 33	1 59	21 11	27 13	9 28	19 34	22 00
27 M	16 20 10	6 12 20	18 11	14 15	16 36	3 52	20 07	0 15	18 30	23 53	29 35	1 58	21 07	26 55	9 39	19 58	22 02
28 T	16 24 6	7 09 55	1≈52	14 08	18 19	5 06	20 52	0 29	18 33	23 57	29 36	1 58	21 03	26 38	9 49	20 22	22 05
29 W	16 28 3	8 07 28	15 43	14 04	20 04	6 20	21 37	0 43	18 36	24 00	29 37	1 57	20 58	26 20	10 00	20 47	22 08
30 Th	16 31 59	9 05 01	29 41	14 02D	21 51	7 33	22 23	0 57	18 39	24 04	29 38	1 56	20 53	26 03	10 11	21 11	22 11
31 F	16 35 56	10 02 33	13♓46	14 02	23 41	8 47	23 08	1 11	18 42	24 07	29 39	1 55	20 47	25 46	10 23	21 36	22 13

EPHEMERIS CALCULATED FOR 12 MIDNIGHT GREENWICH MEAN TIME. ALL OTHER DATA AND FACING ASPECTARIAN PAGE IN **EASTERN TIME (BOLD)** AND PACIFIC TIME (REGULAR).

JUNE 2024

☽ Last Aspect day	ET / hr:mn / PT	asp	☽ Ingress sign day	ET / hr:mn / PT
2	**6:04 pm** 3:04 pm	☌ ♂	♉ 2	10:55 pm
2	**6:04 pm** 3:04 pm	☌ ♂	♉ 3	**1:55 am**
5	**4:09 am** 1:09 am	⚹ ♆	♊ 5	**4:36 am** 1:36 am
7	**8:16 am** 5:16 am	□ ♆	♋ 7	**8:41 am** 5:41 am
9	**3:05 pm** 12:05 pm	△ ♆	♌ 9	**3:29 pm** 12:29 pm
11	**3:16 pm** 12:16 pm	□ ♅	♍ 11	10:39 pm
11	**3:16 pm** 12:16 pm	□ ♅	♍ 12	**1:39 am**
14	**1:54 pm** 10:54 am	☍ ♆	♎ 14	**2:12 pm** 11:12 am
16	11:05 pm	△ ☿	♏ 16	11:38 pm
17	**2:05 am**	△ ☿	♏ 17	**2:38 am**
19	**12:19 pm** 9:19 am	△ ♆	♐ 19	**12:32 pm** 9:32 am
21	**6:58 pm** 3:58 pm	□ ♆	♑ 21	**7:08 pm** 4:08 pm
23	**11:05 pm** 8:05 pm	⚹ ♆	♒ 23	**11:14 pm** 8:14 pm
25	**6:30 pm** 3:30 pm	□ ♅	♓ 25	11:08 pm
25	**6:30 pm** 3:30 pm	□ ♅	♓ 26	**2:08 am**
28	**4:45 am** 1:45 am	☌ ♆	♈ 28	**4:52 am** 1:52 am
29	9:56 pm	□ ☿	♉ 30	**8:00 am** 5:00 am
30	**12:56 am**	□ ☿	♉ 30	**8:00 am** 5:00 am

☽ Phases & Eclipses phase	day	ET / hr:mn / PT
New Moon	6	**8:38 am** 5:38 am
2nd Quarter	13	10:18 pm
2nd Quarter	14	**1:18 am**
Full Moon	21	**9:08 pm** 6:08 pm
4th Quarter	28	**5:53 pm** 2:53 pm

Planet Ingress	day	ET / hr:mn / PT
☿ ♊	3	**3:37 am** 12:37 am
♂ ♉	8	9:35 pm
♂ ♉	9	**12:35 am**
♀ ♋	16	11:20 pm
♀ ♋	17	**2:20 am**
☿ ♋	17	**5:07 am** 2:07 am
⚵ ♌	19	**6:11 pm** 3:11 pm
☉ ♋	20	**4:51 pm** 1:51 pm

Planetary Motion	day	ET / hr:mn / PT
♄ ℞	29	**3:07 pm** 12:07 pm

1 SATURDAY
☽ ⚹ ♃ **1:57 am**
☽ ⚹ ♇ **2:41 am**
♂ ⚺ ♅ **6:07 am** 3:07 am
☽ ⚹ ♀ **6:15 pm** 3:15 pm
☽ ⚹ ☉ **7:35 pm** 4:35 pm

2 SUNDAY
☽ ⚺ ♄ **7:08 am** 4:08 am
☽ ⚺ ♅ **4:18 pm** 1:18 pm
☽ ☌ ♂ **6:04 pm** 3:04 pm
♃ △ ♇ **8:13 pm** 5:13 pm
☿ ⚹ ♆ **11:57 pm** 8:57 pm
☽ ⚺ ♆ 10:25 pm
☽ ⚺ ☿ 10:39 pm

3 MONDAY
☽ ⚺ ♆ **1:25 am**
☽ ⚺ ☿ **1:39 am**
☽ □ ♇ **5:05 am** 2:05 am
☽ ⚺ ♃ **5:14 am** 2:14 am
☽ ⚺ ♀ 10:27 pm
☽ ⚺ ☉ 10:39 pm
☿ △ ♇ 11:12 pm

4 TUESDAY
☽ ⚺ ♀ **1:27 am**
☽ ⚺ ☉ **1:39 am**
☿ △ ♇ **2:12 am**
☿ ☌ ♃ **6:23 am** 3:23 am
☽ ⚹ ♄ **9:46 am** 6:46 am
☉ ☌ ♀ **11:32 am** 8:32 am

☽ ☌ ♅ **7:04 pm** 4:04 pm
☽ ⚺ ♂ **11:28 pm** 8:28 pm

5 WEDNESDAY
☽ ⚹ ♆ **4:09 am** 1:09 am
☽ △ ♇ **7:46 am** 4:46 am
☽ ☌ ♃ **8:49 am** 5:49 am
☽ ☌ ☿ **12:46 pm** 9:46 am

6 THURSDAY
☽ ☌ ☉ **8:38 am** 5:38 am
☽ ☌ ♀ **9:36 am** 6:36 am
☽ □ ♄ **1:19 pm** 10:19 am
☽ ⚺ ♅ **10:59 pm** 7:59 pm

7 FRIDAY
☽ ⚹ ♂ **6:22 am** 3:22 am
☽ □ ♆ **8:16 am** 5:16 am
☽ ⚻ ♇ **11:55 am** 8:55 am
☽ ⚺ ♃ **2:00 pm** 11:00 am
☽ ⚺ ☿ 11:55 pm

8 SATURDAY
☽ ⚺ ☿ **2:55 am**
♀ □ ♄ **4:25 am** 1:25 am
♂ ⚺ ♆ **5:33 pm** 2:33 pm
☽ ⚺ ☉ **6:15 pm** 3:15 pm
☽ △ ♄ **7:08 pm** 4:08 pm
☽ ⚺ ♀ **8:37 pm** 5:37 pm

9 SUNDAY
☽ ⚹ ♅ **5:26 am** 2:26 am
☉ □ ♄ **6:36 am** 3:36 am

☽ △ ♆ **3:05 pm** 12:05 pm
☽ □ ♂ **4:24 pm** 1:24 pm
☽ ☍ ♇ **6:50 pm** 3:50 pm
☽ ⚹ ♃ **10:09 pm** 7:09 pm

10 MONDAY
☽ ⚹ ☿ **10:35 pm** 7:35 pm

11 TUESDAY
☽ ⚻ ♄ **4:14 am** 1:14 am
☽ ⚹ ☉ **7:58 am** 4:58 am
♂ □ ♇ **9:21 am** 6:21 am
☽ ⚹ ♀ **12:02 pm** 9:02 am
☽ □ ♅ **3:16 pm** 12:16 pm
☽ ⚻ ♆ 10:17 pm

12 WEDNESDAY
☽ ⚻ ♆ **1:17 am**
☽ ⚻ ♇ **5:07 am** 2:07 am
☽ △ ♂ **6:26 am** 3:26 am
☿ □ ♄ **6:47 am** 3:47 am
☽ □ ♃ **9:49 am** 6:49 am
♀ ⚺ ♅ **9:24 pm** 6:24 pm

13 THURSDAY
☽ ☍ ♄ **4:18 pm** 1:18 pm
☽ □ ☿ **11:51 pm** 8:51 pm
☽ □ ☉ 10:18 pm

14 FRIDAY
☽ □ ☉ **1:18 am**
☽ △ ♅ **3:50 am** 12:50 am
☽ □ ♀ **7:13 am** 4:13 am
☉ ☌ ☿ **12:33 pm** 9:33 am
☽ ☍ ♆ **1:54 pm** 10:54 am

☽ △ ♇ **5:39 pm** 2:39 pm
☿ ⚺ ♅ **9:41 pm** 6:41 pm
☽ ⚻ ♂ **11:08 pm** 8:08 pm
☽ △ ♃ **11:44 pm** 8:44 pm

15 SATURDAY
☉ ⚺ ♅ **10:16 am** 7:16 am
♂ ⚺ ♃ **12:37 pm** 9:37 am

16 SUNDAY
☽ ⚻ ♄ **5:14 am** 2:14 am
☽ ⚻ ♅ **4:45 pm** 1:45 pm
☽ △ ☉ **7:14 pm** 4:14 pm
♀ □ ♆ **11:46 pm** 8:46 pm
☽ △ ☿ 11:05 pm
☽ ⚻ ♆ 11:22 pm
☽ △ ♀ 11:40 pm

17 MONDAY
☽ △ ☿ **2:05 am**
☽ ⚻ ♆ **2:22 am**
☽ △ ♀ **2:40 am**
☿ □ ♆ **3:41 am** 12:41 am
☽ □ ♇ **5:54 am** 2:54 am
☿ ☌ ♀ **8:43 am** 5:43 am
☽ ⚻ ♃ **1:02 pm** 10:02 am
☽ ☍ ♂ **3:10 pm** 12:10 pm
☿ ⚻ ♇ **11:13 pm** 8:13 pm

18 TUESDAY
♀ ⚻ ♇ **10:12 am** 7:12 am
☽ △ ♄ **4:19 pm** 1:19 pm

19 WEDNESDAY
☽ ☍ ♅ **3:24 am** 12:24 am
☽ ⚻ ☉ **10:15 am** 7:15 am
☽ △ ♆ **12:19 pm** 9:19 am
☽ ⚹ ♇ **3:32 pm** 12:32 pm
☽ ⚻ ♀ **6:41 pm** 3:41 pm
☿ ⚺ ♃ **9:40 pm** 6:40 pm
☽ ☍ ♃ **11:22 pm** 8:22 pm
☽ ⚻ ☿ **11:40 pm** 8:40 pm

20 THURSDAY
☽ ⚻ ♂ **3:47 am** 12:47 am
☉ □ ♆ **2:12 pm** 11:12 am
☽ □ ♄ 9:08 pm

21 FRIDAY
☽ □ ♄ **12:08 am**
☽ ⚻ ♅ **10:44 am** 7:44 am
☿ ⚹ ♂ **12:23 pm** 9:23 am
☽ □ ♆ **6:58 pm** 3:58 pm
☽ ☍ ☉ **9:08 pm** 6:08 pm
☽ ⚺ ♇ **9:55 pm** 6:55 pm

22 SATURDAY
♀ ⚺ ♃ **5:56 am** 2:56 am
☽ ⚻ ♃ **6:18 am** 3:18 am
☽ ☍ ♀ **6:20 am** 3:20 am
☉ ⚻ ♇ **8:01 am** 5:01 am
☽ △ ♂ **12:37 pm** 9:37 am
☽ ☍ ☿ **3:25 pm** 12:25 pm

23 SUNDAY
☽ ⚹ ♄ **5:02 am** 2:02 am
☽ △ ♅ **3:20 pm** 12:20 pm

☽ ⚹ ♆ **11:05 pm** 8:05 pm
☽ ☌ ♇ 10:50 pm

24 MONDAY
☽ ☌ ♇ **1:50 am**
☽ ⚻ ☉ **4:57 am** 1:57 am
☽ △ ♃ **10:52 am** 7:52 am
☽ ⚻ ♀ **3:00 pm** 12:00 pm
☽ □ ♂ **6:58 pm** 3:58 pm

25 TUESDAY
☽ ⚻ ☿ **3:27 am** 12:27 am
☽ ⚺ ♄ **8:14 am** 5:14 am
☽ □ ♅ **6:30 pm** 3:30 pm
☽ ⚺ ♆ 11:00 pm

26 WEDNESDAY
☽ ⚺ ♆ **2:00 am**
☽ ⚺ ♇ **4:37 am** 1:37 am
☽ △ ☉ **11:26 am** 8:26 am
☿ △ ♄ **2:10 pm** 11:10 am
☽ □ ♃ **2:27 pm** 11:27 am
☽ △ ♀ **10:33 pm** 7:33 pm
☽ ⚹ ♂ 9:26 pm

27 THURSDAY
☽ ⚹ ♂ **12:26 am**
☽ ☌ ♄ **10:57 am** 7:57 am
☽ △ ☿ **2:11 pm** 11:11 am
☽ ⚹ ♅ **9:23 pm** 6:23 pm

28 FRIDAY
☽ ☌ ♆ **4:45 am** 1:45 am
☽ ⚹ ♇ **7:18 am** 4:18 am
☽ □ ☉ **5:53 pm** 2:53 pm

☽ ⚹ ♃ **6:03 pm** 3:03 pm
☉ ⚺ ♃ **8:54 pm** 5:54 pm
♀ ⚹ ♂ 9:49 pm

29 SATURDAY
♀ ⚹ ♂ **12:49 am**
☽ ⚺ ♂ **6:04 am** 3:04 am
☽ □ ♀ **6:16 am** 3:16 am
☽ ⚺ ♄ **1:55 pm** 10:55 am
☿ ⚹ ♅ **10:20 pm** 7:20 pm
☽ ⚺ ♅ 9:37 pm
☽ □ ☿ 9:56 pm

30 SUNDAY
☽ ⚺ ♅ **12:37 am**
☽ □ ☿ **12:56 am**
☽ ⚺ ♆ **7:53 am** 4:53 am
☽ □ ♇ **10:23 am** 7:23 am
☽ ⚺ ♃ **10:09 pm** 7:09 pm
☽ ⚹ ☉ 9:57 pm

Eastern time in bold type
Pacific time in medium type

JUNE 2024

DATE	SID.TIME	SUN	MOON	NODE	MERCURY	VENUS	MARS	JUPITER	SATURN	URANUS	NEPTUNE	PLUTO	CERES	PALLAS	JUNO	VESTA	CHIRON
1 Sa	16 39 53	11♊00 04	27♈57	14♈03	25♉32	10♊02	23♈53	1♊25	18♓45	24♉10	29♓40	1♒55R	20♑41R	25♏30R	10♍34	22♋00	22♈16
2 Su	16 43 49	11 57 35	12♉11	14 02	27 26	11 15	24 38	1 39	18 48	24 14	29 41	1 54	20 35	25 13	10 46	22 25	22 18
3 M	16 47 46	12 55 05	26 29	14 00	29 23	12 28	25 23	1 53	18 50	24 17	29 42	1 53	20 28	24 57	10 58	22 50	22 21
4 T	16 51 42	13 52 34	10♊45	13 55	1♊21	13 42	26 08	2 07	18 53	24 20	29 43	1 52	20 22	24 41	11 11	23 15	22 23
5 W	16 55 39	14 50 02	24 57	13 47	3 22	14 56	26 53	2 21	18 55	24 24	29 44	1 51	20 14	24 26	11 23	23 40	22 26
6 Th	16 59 35	15 47 29	8♋59	13 37	5 24	16 10	27 37	2 35	18 58	24 27	29 45	1 51	20 07	24 11	11 36	24 05	22 28
7 F	17 3 32	16 44 56	22 49	13 27	7 28	17 23	28 22	2 49	19 00	24 30	29 45	1 50	19 59	23 56	11 49	24 30	22 31
8 Sa	17 7 29	17 42 22	6♌21	13 17	9 34	18 37	29 07	3 03	19 02	24 34	29 46	1 49	19 50	23 42	12 02	24 55	22 33
9 Su	17 11 25	18 39 47	19 32	13 07	11 42	19 51	29 51	3 17	19 04	24 37	29 47	1 48	19 42	23 27	12 15	25 21	22 35
10 M	17 15 22	19 37 10	2♍24	13 00	13 51	21 04	0♉36	3 30	19 06	24 40	29 48	1 47	19 33	23 14	12 28	25 46	22 37
11 T	17 19 18	20 34 33	14 55	12 55	16 01	22 18	1 21	3 44	19 08	24 43	29 48	1 46	19 24	23 00	12 42	26 11	22 40
12 W	17 23 15	21 31 55	27 09	12 52	18 12	23 32	2 05	3 58	19 10	24 47	29 49	1 45	19 14	22 47	12 56	26 37	22 42
13 Th	17 27 11	22 29 16	9♎10	12 51D	20 23	24 46	2 49	4 12	19 12	24 50	29 49	1 44	19 04	22 35	13 09	27 02	22 44
14 F	17 31 8	23 26 35	21 02	12 52R	22 35	25 59	3 34	4 25	19 13	24 53	29 50	1 43	18 54	22 23	13 24	27 28	22 46
15 Sa	17 35 4	24 23 54	2♏51	12 52	24 47	27 13	4 18	4 39	19 15	24 56	29 51	1 42	18 44	22 11	13 38	27 53	22 48
16 Su	17 39 1	25 21 12	14 42	12 52	26 59	28 27	5 02	4 53	19 16	24 59	29 52	1 41	18 34	22 00	13 52	28 19	22 50
17 M	17 42 58	26 18 29	26 40	12 51	29 11	29 41	5 46	5 06	19 18	25 02	29 52	1 40	18 23	21 49	14 07	28 45	22 52
18 T	17 46 54	27 15 46	8♐50	12 48	1♋21	0♋54	6 30	5 20	19 19	25 05	29 53	1 39	18 12	21 38	14 22	29 10	22 54
19 W	17 50 51	28 13 01	21 16	12 43	3 31	2 08	7 14	5 34	19 20	25 08	29 53	1 37	18 02	21 29	14 37	29 36	22 56
20 Th	17 54 47	29 10 16	4♑29	12 36	5 39	3 22	7 58	5 47	19 21	25 12	29 53	1 36	17 49	21 19	14 52	0♌02	22 58
21 F	17 58 44	0♋07 31	17 05	12 26	7 46	4 35	8 42	6 01	19 22	25 15	29 54	1 35	17 37	21 10	15 07	0 28	23 00
22 Sa	18 2 40	1 04 45	0♒29	12 14	9 52	5 49	9 26	6 14	19 23	25 18	29 54	1 33	17 25	21 01	15 22	0 54	23 01
23 Su	18 6 37	2 01 58	14 11	12 03	11 56	7 03	10 10	6 27	19 24	25 23	29 54	1 32	17 13	20 53	15 38	1 20	23 03
24 M	18 10 34	2 59 12	28 06	11 53	13 58	8 17	10 54	6 41	19 24	25 26	29 55	1 30	17 01	20 46	15 53	1 46	23 05
25 T	18 14 30	3 56 25	12♓12	11 43	15 59	9 30	11 37	6 54	19 25	25 29	29 55	1 29	16 49	20 38	16 09	2 12	23 06
26 W	18 18 27	4 53 37	26 22	11 36	17 57	10 44	12 21	7 07	19 25	25 32	29 55	1 27	16 36	20 30	16 25	2 38	23 08
27 Th	18 22 23	5 50 50	10♈35	11 31D	19 53	11 58	13 04	7 21	19 25	25 35	29 55	1 26	16 24	20 26	16 41	3 05	23 09
28 F	18 26 20	6 48 03	24 46	11 31R	21 48	13 11	13 48	7 34	19 26	25 38	29 56	1 25	16 11	20 20	16 57	3 31	23 11
29 Sa	18 30 16	7 45 15	8♉55	11 31	23 40	14 25	14 31	7 47	19 26R	25 40	29 56	1 24	15 58	20 14	17 13	3 57	23 12
30 Su	18 34 13	8 42 28	22 59	11 30	25 30	15 39	15 14	8 00	19 26	25 40	29 56	1 24	15 45	20 10	17 30	4 24	23 14

EPHEMERIS CALCULATED FOR 12 MIDNIGHT GREENWICH MEAN TIME. ALL OTHER DATA AND FACING ASPECTARIAN PAGE IN EASTERN TIME (BOLD) AND PACIFIC TIME (REGULAR).

JULY 2024

☽ Last Aspect day	ET / hr:mn / PT		asp	☽ Ingress sign	day	ET / hr:mn / PT	
2	**11:43 am**	8:43 am	⚹♆	♊	2	**11:50 am**	8:50 am
4	**4:44 pm**	1:44 pm	□♆	♋	4	**4:51 pm**	1:51 pm
6	**11:47 pm**	8:47 pm	△♆	♌	6	**11:56 pm**	8:56 pm
8		11:04 pm	□♅	♍	9	**9:48 am**	6:48 am
9	**2:04 am**		□♅	♍	9	**9:48 am**	6:48 am
11	**9:55 pm**	6:55 pm	☍♆	♎	11	**10:06 pm**	7:06 pm
13	**6:49 pm**	3:49 pm	□☉	♏	14	**10:53 am**	7:53 am
16	**9:10 pm**	6:10 pm	△♆	♐	16	**9:25 pm**	6:25 pm
19	**3:58 am**	12:58 am	□♆	♑	19	**4:14 am**	1:14 am
21	**7:26 am**	4:26 am	⚹♆	♒	21	**7:43 am**	4:43 am
23	**5:58 am**	2:58 am	☍☿	♓	23	**9:23 am**	6:23 am
25	**10:31 am**	7:31 am	☌♆	♈	25	**10:52 am**	7:52 am
26	**6:14 pm**	3:14 pm	△♀	♉	27	**1:23 pm**	10:23 am
29	**4:59 pm**	1:59 pm	⚹♆	♊	29	**5:28 pm**	2:28 pm
31	**10:46 pm**	7:46 pm	□♆	♋	31	**11:19 pm**	8:19 pm

☽ Phases & Eclipses phase	day	ET / hr:mn / PT	
New Moon	5	**6:57 pm**	3:57 pm
2nd Quarter	13	**6:49 pm**	3:49 pm
Full Moon	21	**6:17 am**	3:17 am
4th Quarter	27	**10:52 pm**	7:52 pm

Planet Ingress		day	ET / hr:mn / PT	
☿	♌	2	**8:50 am**	5:50 am
♀	♌	11	**12:19 pm**	9:19 am
♂	♊	20	**4:43 pm**	1:43 pm
☉	♌	22	**3:44 am**	12:44 am
☿	♍	25	**6:42 pm**	3:42 pm

Planetary Motion		day	ET / hr:mn / PT	
♆	℞	2	**6:40 am**	3:40 am
♀	D	9	**10:46 pm**	7:46 pm
⚷	℞	26	**9:59 am**	6:59 am

1 MONDAY
☽ ⚹ ☉ **12:57 am**
☽ ☌ ♂ **12:19 pm** 9:19 am
☽ ⚹ ♀ **2:42 pm** 11:42 am
☽ ⚹ ♄ **5:28 pm** 2:28 pm

2 TUESDAY
☽ ☌ ♅ **4:29 am** 1:29 am
☿ △ ♆ **7:53 am** 4:53 am
☽ ⚹ ♆ **11:43 am** 8:43 am
☽ ⚹ ☿ **12:16 pm** 9:16 am
☽ △ ♇ **2:11 pm** 11:11 am
♀ △ ♄ **9:41 pm** 6:41 pm

3 WEDNESDAY
☽ ☌ ♃ **3:05 am** 12:05 am
☿ ☍ ♇ **3:27 am** 12:27 am
☽ ⚺ ☉ **9:01 am** 6:01 am
☽ ⚺ ♂ **7:38 pm** 4:38 pm
☽ □ ♄ **9:58 pm** 6:58 pm
☽ ⚺ ♀ 9:24 pm

4 THURSDAY
☽ ⚺ ♀ **12:24 am**
☽ ⚺ ♅ **9:28 am** 6:28 am
☽ □ ♆ **4:44 pm** 1:44 pm
☽ ⚻ ♇ **7:11 pm** 4:11 pm
☽ ⚺ ☿ 9:57 pm

5 FRIDAY
☽ ⚺ ☿ **12:57 am**
☽ ⚺ ♃ **9:29 am** 6:29 am

♂ ⚹ ♄ **3:02 pm** 12:02 pm
☽ ☌ ☉ **6:57 pm** 3:57 pm

6 SATURDAY
☽ △ ♄ **4:10 am** 1:10 am
☽ ⚹ ♂ **4:56 am** 1:56 am
☽ ☌ ♀ **12:27 pm** 9:27 am
☽ ⚹ ♅ **4:24 pm** 1:24 pm
☽ △ ♆ **11:47 pm** 8:47 pm
☽ ☍ ♇ 11:16 pm

7 SUNDAY
☽ ☍ ♇ **2:16 am**
☽ ☌ ☿ **4:23 pm** 1:23 pm
☽ ⚹ ♃ **6:19 pm** 3:19 pm

8 MONDAY
♀ ⚹ ♅ **7:04 am** 4:04 am
☽ ⚺ ☉ **8:00 am** 5:00 am
☿ ⚹ ♃ **10:26 am** 7:26 am
☽ ⚻ ♄ **12:57 pm** 9:57 am
☽ □ ♂ **5:18 pm** 2:18 pm
☽ □ ♅ 11:04 pm

9 TUESDAY
☽ □ ♅ **2:04 am**
☽ ⚺ ♀ **4:07 am** 1:07 am
☽ ⚻ ♆ **9:38 am** 6:38 am
☽ ⚻ ♇ **12:08 pm** 9:08 am

10 WEDNESDAY
☽ □ ♃ **6:07 am** 3:07 am
☽ ⚺ ☿ **11:24 am** 8:24 am

☉ △ ♄ **11:05 pm** 8:05 pm
☽ ☍ ♄ 9:27 pm
☽ ⚹ ☉ 9:34 pm

11 THURSDAY
☽ ☍ ♄ **12:27 am**
☽ ⚹ ☉ **12:34 am**
☽ △ ♂ **8:51 am** 5:51 am
♀ △ ♆ **10:32 am** 7:32 am
☽ △ ♅ **2:20 pm** 11:20 am
☽ ☍ ♆ **9:55 pm** 6:55 pm
☽ ⚹ ♀ **11:15 pm** 8:15 pm
☽ △ ♇ 9:24 pm

12 FRIDAY
☽ △ ♇ **12:24 am**
♀ ☍ ♇ **10:12 am** 7:12 am
☽ △ ♃ **7:58 pm** 4:58 pm

13 SATURDAY
☽ ⚹ ☿ **8:18 am** 5:18 am
☽ ⚻ ♄ **1:16 pm** 10:16 am
☽ □ ☉ **6:49 pm** 3:49 pm
☽ ⚻ ♂ 10:35 pm

14 SUNDAY
☽ ⚻ ♂ **1:35 am**
☽ ⚻ ♅ **3:24 am** 12:24 am
☽ ⚻ ♆ **10:40 am** 7:40 am
☽ □ ♇ **1:01 pm** 10:01 am
☽ □ ♀ **6:55 pm** 3:55 pm

15 MONDAY
☿ ⚻ ♄ **4:57 am** 1:57 am
☽ ⚻ ♃ **9:15 am** 6:15 am

♂ ☌ ♅ **10:05 am** 7:05 am
☽ △ ♄ 9:45 pm
☽ □ ☿ 11:59 pm

16 TUESDAY
☽ △ ♄ **12:45 am**
☽ □ ☿ **2:59 am**
☽ △ ☉ **11:04 am** 8:04 am
☽ ☍ ♅ **2:31 pm** 11:31 am
☽ ☍ ♂ **4:06 pm** 1:06 pm
☽ △ ♆ **9:10 pm** 6:10 pm
☽ ⚹ ♇ **11:20 pm** 8:20 pm

17 WEDNESDAY
☽ △ ♀ **11:08 am** 8:08 am
☽ ☍ ♃ **7:20 pm** 4:20 pm

18 THURSDAY
☽ □ ♄ **8:49 am** 5:49 am
☉ ⚹ ♅ **10:00 am** 7:00 am
☽ △ ☿ **4:24 pm** 1:24 pm
☽ ⚻ ♅ **9:56 pm** 6:56 pm
☽ ⚻ ☉ **10:49 pm** 7:49 pm
☽ ⚻ ♂ 11:16 pm

19 FRIDAY
☽ ⚻ ♂ **2:16 am**
☽ □ ♆ **3:58 am** 12:58 am
☽ ⚺ ♇ **5:55 am** 2:55 am
☽ ⚻ ♀ **10:17 pm** 7:17 pm
☽ ⚻ ♃ 10:29 pm

20 SATURDAY
☽ ⚻ ♃ **1:29 am**
♂ ⚹ ♆ **11:17 am** 8:17 am

☽ ⚹ ♄ **1:15 pm** 10:15 am
☽ ⚻ ☿ 9:42 pm
☽ △ ♅ 10:53 pm

21 SUNDAY
☽ ⚻ ☿ **12:42 am**
☽ △ ♅ **1:53 am**
☽ ☍ ☉ **6:17 am** 3:17 am
☽ ⚹ ♆ **7:26 am** 4:26 am
☽ △ ♂ **8:29 am** 5:29 am
☽ ☌ ♇ **9:14 am** 6:14 am
♀ ⚹ ♃ **4:43 pm** 1:43 pm
☿ □ ♅ **6:21 pm** 3:21 pm
☉ △ ♆ **11:25 pm** 8:25 pm
♂ △ ♇ **11:48 pm** 8:48 pm

22 MONDAY
☽ △ ♃ **4:43 am** 1:43 am
☽ ☍ ♀ **5:39 am** 2:39 am
☽ ⚺ ♄ **3:16 pm** 12:16 pm
☉ ☍ ♇ 10:38 pm

23 TUESDAY
☉ ☍ ♇ **1:38 am**
☽ □ ♅ **3:47 am** 12:47 am
☽ ☍ ☿ **5:58 am** 2:58 am
☽ ⚺ ♆ **9:05 am** 6:05 am
☽ ⚺ ♇ **10:48 am** 7:48 am
☽ ⚻ ☉ **11:27 am** 8:27 am
☽ □ ♂ **12:36 pm** 9:36 am

24 WEDNESDAY
☽ □ ♃ **6:47 am** 3:47 am
☽ ⚻ ♀ **11:36 am** 8:36 am
☽ ☌ ♄ **4:31 pm** 1:31 pm

25 THURSDAY
☽ ⚹ ♅ **5:19 am** 2:19 am
☽ ⚻ ☿ **10:26 am** 7:26 am
☽ ☌ ♆ **10:31 am** 7:31 am
☿ ⚻ ♆ **12:00 pm** 9:00 am
☽ ⚹ ♇ **12:13 pm** 9:13 am
☽ △ ☉ **4:29 pm** 1:29 pm
☽ ⚹ ♂ **4:36 pm** 1:36 pm
☉ ⚹ ♂ **10:32 pm** 7:32 pm

26 FRIDAY
☽ ⚹ ♃ **9:16 am** 5:16 am
☽ △ ♀ **6:14 pm** 3:14 pm
☽ ⚺ ♄ **6:24 pm** 3:24 pm
♀ ⚻ ♄ **8:07 pm** 5:07 pm
☿ ⚻ ♇ **8:49 pm** 5:49 pm

27 SATURDAY
☽ ⚺ ♅ **7:47 am** 4:47 am
☽ ⚺ ♆ **12:58 pm** 9:58 am
☽ □ ♇ **2:41 pm** 11:41 am
☽ △ ☿ **3:36 pm** 12:36 pm
☽ ⚺ ♂ **9:52 pm** 6:52 pm
☽ □ ☉ **10:52 pm** 7:52 pm

28 SUNDAY
☽ ⚺ ♃ **1:08 pm** 10:08 am
☽ ⚹ ♄ **9:42 pm** 6:42 pm
☽ □ ♀ 11:45 pm

29 Monday
☽ □ ♀ **2:45 am**
☽ ☌ ♅ **11:47 am** 8:47 am
☽ ⚹ ♆ **4:59 pm** 1:59 pm

☽ △ ♇ **6:43 pm** 3:43 pm
☽ □ ☿ **10:00 pm** 7:00 pm

30 TUESDAY
☽ ☌ ♂ **5:01 am** 2:01 am
☽ ⚹ ☉ **7:15 am** 4:15 am
☽ ☌ ♃ **6:45 pm** 3:45 pm
☽ □ ♄ 11:42 pm

31 WEDNESDAY
☽ □ ♄ **2:42 am**
☽ ⚹ ♀ **1:33 pm** 10:33 am
☽ ⚺ ♅ **5:33 pm** 2:33 pm
☽ □ ♆ **10:46 pm** 7:46 pm
☽ ⚻ ♇ 9:31 pm

Eastern time in bold type
Pacific time in medium type

JULY 2024

DATE	SID.TIME	SUN	MOON	NODE	MERCURY	VENUS	MARS	JUPITER	SATURN	URANUS	NEPTUNE	PLUTO	CERES	PALLAS	JUNO	VESTA	CHIRON
1 M	18 38 9	9♋39 41	6♍59	11♈29R	27♋18	16♋53	15♉58	8♊13	19♓26R	25♉43	29♓56	1♒23R	15♍32R	20♍05R	17♍46	4♌50	23♈15
2 T	18 42 6	10 36 55	20 53	11 25	29 04	18 06	16 41	8 26	19 25	25 46	29 56R	1 22	15 19	20 01	18 03	5 16	23 16
3 W	18 46 3	11 34 08	4♎41	11 19	0♌48	19 20	17 24	8 39	19 25	25 49	29 56	1 20	15 06	19 58	18 20	5 43	23 18
4 Th	18 49 59	12 31 22	18 18	11 10	2 30	20 34	18 07	8 52	19 25	25 51	29 56	1 19	14 52	19 55	18 37	6 10	23 19
5 F	18 53 56	13 28 35	1♏45	10 59	4 09	21 47	18 50	9 05	19 24	25 54	29 56	1 18	14 39	19 52	18 54	6 36	23 20
6 Sa	18 57 52	14 25 49	14 57	10 57	5 47	23 01	19 33	9 17	19 24	25 56	29 56	1 16	14 26	19 50	19 11	7 03	23 21
7 Su	19 1 49	15 23 03	27 54	10 34	7 22	24 15	20 16	9 30	19 23	25 59	29 55	1 15	14 13	19 49	19 28	7 30	23 22
8 M	19 5 45	16 20 17	10♐35	10 22	8 55	25 29	20 58	9 43	19 22	26 02	29 55	1 14	13 59	19 47	19 45	7 56	23 23
9 T	19 9 42	17 17 30	22 59	10 13	10 26	26 42	21 41	9 55	19 21	26 04	29 55	1 12	13 46	19 47	20 03	8 23	23 24
10 W	19 13 38	18 14 44	5♑09	10 06	11 55	27 56	22 23	10 08	19 21	26 06	29 55	1 11	13 33	19 46D	20 20	8 50	23 25
11 Th	19 17 35	19 11 58	17 07	10 02	13 22	29 10	23 06	10 20	19 19	26 09	29 55	1 09	13 20	19 47	20 38	9 17	23 26
12 F	19 21 32	20 09 11	28 58	10 00D	14 46	0♌24	23 48	10 33	19 18	26 11	29 54	1 08	13 07	19 47	20 56	9 44	23 26
13 Sa	19 25 28	21 06 24	10♒46	10 00R	16 08	1 37	24 30	10 45	19 17	26 14	29 54	1 07	12 54	19 48	21 14	10 11	23 27
14 Su	19 29 25	22 03 38	22 36	10 00	17 28	2 51	25 13	10 57	19 16	26 16	29 54	1 05	12 41	19 50	21 32	10 38	23 28
15 M	19 33 21	23 00 51	4♓34	10 00	18 45	4 05	25 55	11 09	19 14	26 18	29 53	1 04	12 29	19 52	21 50	11 05	23 29
16 T	19 37 18	23 58 05	16 46	9 58	20 00	5 19	26 37	11 21	19 13	26 20	29 53	1 02	12 16	19 54	22 08	11 32	23 29
17 W	19 41 14	24 55 19	29 15	9 53	21 13	6 32	27 19	11 33	19 11	26 23	29 52	1 01	12 04	19 57	22 26	11 59	23 30
18 Th	19 45 11	25 52 33	12♈07	9 47	22 23	7 46	28 01	11 45	19 09	26 25	29 52	1 00	11 52	20 00	22 44	12 26	23 30
19 F	19 49 7	26 49 47	25 22	9 38	23 31	9 00	28 42	11 57	19 08	26 27	29 51	0 58	11 40	20 03	23 03	12 53	23 31
20 Sa	19 53 4	27 47 02	9♉01	9 27	24 36	10 13	29 24	12 09	19 06	26 29	29 51	0 57	11 28	20 07	23 21	13 21	23 31
21 Su	19 57 1	28 44 17	23 03	9 17	25 38	11 27	0♊06	12 21	19 04	26 31	29 50	0 55	11 16	20 11	23 40	13 48	23 31
22 M	20 0 57	29 41 32	7♊52	9 07	26 37	12 41	0 47	12 32	19 02	26 33	29 50	0 54	11 04	20 16	23 58	14 15	23 32
23 T	20 4 54	0♌38 48	21 52	8 58	27 33	13 55	1 29	12 44	18 59	26 35	29 49	0 53	10 53	20 22	24 17	14 42	23 32
24 W	20 8 50	1 36 04	6♋27	8 52	28 23	15 08	2 10	12 55	18 57	26 37	29 48	0 51	10 42	20 27	24 36	15 10	23 32
25 Th	20 12 47	2 33 22	21 01	8 49	29 16	16 22	2 51	13 07	18 55	26 39	29 48	0 50	10 31	20 32	24 55	15 37	23 32
26 F	20 16 43	3 30 40	5♍29	8 48D	0♍02	17 36	3 32	13 18	18 52	26 40	29 47	0 48	10 21	20 39	25 14	16 05	23 32R
27 Sa	20 20 40	4 27 59	19 46	8 48	0 45	18 49	4 13	13 29	18 50	26 42	29 46	0 47	10 10	20 45	25 33	16 32	23 32
28 Su	20 24 36	5 25 19	3♎52	8 48R	1 25	20 03	4 54	13 40	18 47	26 44	29 46	0 45	10 00	20 52	25 52	17 00	23 32
29 M	20 28 33	6 22 40	17 45	8 48	2 00	21 17	5 35	13 51	18 44	26 46	29 45	0 44	9 51	20 59	26 11	17 27	23 32
30 T	20 32 30	7 20 03	1♏26	8 46	2 32	22 30	6 16	14 02	18 42	26 47	29 44	0 43	9 41	21 07	26 30	17 55	23 32
31 W	20 36 26	8 17 26	14 55	8 41	2 59	23 44	6 57	14 13	18 39	26 49	29 43	0 41	9 32	21 15	26 50	18 22	23 32

EPHEMERIS CALCULATED FOR 12 MIDNIGHT GREENWICH MEAN TIME. ALL OTHER DATA AND FACING ASPECTARIAN PAGE IN **EASTERN TIME (BOLD)** AND PACIFIC TIME (REGULAR).

AUGUST 2024

☽ Last Aspect day	ET / hr:mn / PT		asp	☽ Ingress sign	day	ET / hr:mn / PT	
3	**6:31 am**	3:31 am	△♆	♌	3	**7:10 am**	4:10 am
5	**11:16 am**	8:16 am	□♅	♍	5	**5:17 pm**	2:17 pm
8	**4:40 am**	1:40 am	☍♆	♎	8	**5:31 am**	2:31 am
9	**5:45 pm**	2:45 pm	⚹☉	♏	10	**6:34 pm**	3:34 pm
13	**5:01 am**	2:01 am	△♆	♐	13	**6:01 am**	3:01 am
15	**12:52 pm**	9:52 am	△☿	♑	15	**1:51 pm**	10:51 am
17	**4:43 pm**	1:43 pm	⚹♆	♒	17	**5:45 pm**	2:45 pm
19	**2:26 pm**	11:26 am	☍☉	♓	19	**6:52 pm**	3:52 pm
21	**5:54 pm**	2:54 pm	☌♆	♈	21	**7:02 pm**	4:02 pm
23	**8:44 am**	5:44 am	△☿	♉	23	**8:00 pm**	5:00 pm
25	**9:40 pm**	6:40 pm	⚹♆	♊	25	**11:04 pm**	8:04 pm
28	**3:14 am**	12:14 am	□♆	♋	28	**4:47 am**	1:47 am
30	**11:24 am**	8:24 am	△♆	♌	30	**1:09 pm**	10:09 am

☽ Phases & Eclipses phase	day	ET / hr:mn / PT	
New Moon	4	**7:13 am**	4:13 am
2nd Quarter	12	**11:19 am**	8:19 am
Full Moon	19	**2:26 pm**	11:26 am
4th Quarter	26	**5:26 am**	2:26 am

Planet Ingress		day	ET / hr:mn / PT	
♀	♍	4	**10:23 pm**	7:23 pm
⚵	♎	9	**12:35 pm**	9:35 am
☿	♌	14	**8:16 pm**	5:16 pm
☉	♍	22	**10:55 am**	7:55 am
⚶	♍	24	**7:38 pm**	4:38 pm
♀	♎	29	**9:23 am**	6:23 am

Planetary Motion		day	ET / hr:mn / PT	
☿	℞	4		9:56 pm
☿	℞	5	**12:56 am**	
⚳	D	26	**3:37 am**	12:37 am
☿	D	28	**5:14 pm**	2:14 pm

1 THURSDAY
- ☽ ⚻ ♇ **12:31 am**
- ☽ ⚹ ☿ **5:43 am** 2:43 am
- ☽ ⚺ ♂ **2:15 pm** 11:15 am
- ☽ ⚺ ☉ **5:55 pm** 2:55 pm
- ☽ ⚺ ♃ 11:16 pm

2 FRIDAY
- ☽ ⚺ ♃ **2:16 am**
- ♀ □ ♅ **9:27 am** 6:27 am
- ☽ △ ♄ **9:32 am** 6:32 am
- ☽ ⚹ ♅ 10:17 pm
- ☽ ⚺ ♀ 11:57 pm

3 SATURDAY
- ☽ ⚹ ♅ **1:17 am**
- ☽ ⚺ ♀ **2:57 am**
- ☽ △ ♆ **6:31 am** 3:31 am
- ☽ ☍ ♇ **8:19 am** 5:19 am
- ☽ ⚺ ☿ **2:48 pm** 11:48 am
- ☽ ⚹ ♂ 10:54 pm

4 SUNDAY
- ☽ ⚹ ♂ **1:54 am**
- ☽ ☌ ☉ **7:13 am** 4:13 am
- ☽ ⚹ ♃ **12:01 pm** 9:01 am
- ♀ ⚻ ♆ **3:24 pm** 12:24 pm
- ☽ ⚻ ♄ **6:31 pm** 3:31 pm

5 MONDAY
- ♀ ⚻ ♇ **9:18 am** 6:18 am
- ☽ □ ♅ **11:16 am** 8:16 am
- ☽ ⚻ ♆ **4:32 pm** 1:32 pm
- ☽ ⚻ ♇ **6:22 pm** 3:22 pm
- ☽ ☌ ♀ **7:24 pm** 4:24 pm
- ☽ ☌ ☿ 10:19 pm

6 TUESDAY
- ☽ ☌ ☿ **1:19 am**
- ☽ □ ♂ **4:15 pm** 1:15 pm
- ☽ ⚺ ☉ **11:27 pm** 8:27 pm
- ☽ □ ♃ 9:08 pm

7 WEDNESDAY
- ☽ □ ♃ **12:08 am**
- ☽ ☍ ♄ **5:44 am** 2:44 am
- ☉ ⚹ ♃ **9:37 am** 6:37 am
- ☿ ☌ ♀ **11:12 pm** 8:12 pm
- ☽ △ ♅ **11:27 pm** 8:27 pm

8 THURSDAY
- ☽ ☍ ♆ **4:40 am** 1:40 am
- ☽ △ ♇ **6:32 am** 3:32 am
- ☽ ⚺ ☿ **12:47 pm** 9:47 am
- ☽ ⚺ ♀ **2:43 pm** 11:43 am

9 FRIDAY
- ☽ △ ♂ **8:40 am** 5:40 am
- ☽ △ ♃ **1:55 pm** 10:55 am
- ☽ ⚹ ☉ **5:45 pm** 2:45 pm
- ☽ ⚻ ♄ **6:24 pm** 3:24 pm
- ☉ ⚻ ♄ 10:26 pm

10 SATURDAY
- ☉ ⚻ ♄ **1:26 am**
- ☽ ⚻ ♅ **12:36 pm** 9:36 am
- ☽ ⚻ ♆ **5:37 pm** 2:37 pm
- ☽ □ ♇ **7:27 pm** 4:27 pm
- ☽ ⚹ ☿ **11:42 pm** 8:42 pm

11 SUNDAY
- ☽ ⚹ ♀ **10:40 am** 7:40 am
- ☽ ⚻ ♂ 9:48 pm

12 MONDAY
- ☽ ⚻ ♂ **12:48 am**
- ☽ ⚻ ♃ **3:14 am** 12:14 am
- ☽ △ ♄ **6:29 am** 3:29 am
- ☽ □ ☉ **11:19 am** 8:19 am
- ☽ ☍ ♅ 9:24 pm

13 TUESDAY
- ☽ ☍ ♅ **12:24 am**
- ☽ △ ♆ **5:01 am** 2:01 am
- ☽ ⚹ ♇ **6:45 am** 3:45 am
- ☽ □ ☿ **8:09 am** 5:09 am

14 WEDNESDAY
- ☽ □ ♀ **3:33 am** 12:33 am
- ☿ ⚻ ♇ **9:03 am** 6:03 am
- ♂ ☌ ♃ **11:22 am** 8:22 am
- ☽ ☍ ♃ **1:35 pm** 10:35 am
- ☽ ☍ ♂ **1:40 pm** 10:40 am
- ☽ □ ♄ **3:38 pm** 12:38 pm
- ☽ △ ☉ 9:57 pm

15 THURSDAY
- ☽ △ ☉ **12:57 am**
- ☽ ⚻ ♅ **8:42 am** 5:42 am
- ☽ □ ♆ **12:50 pm** 9:50 am
- ☽ △ ☿ **12:52 pm** 9:52 am
- ☿ ⚻ ♆ **1:19 pm** 10:19 am
- ☽ ⚺ ♇ **2:27 pm** 11:27 am
- ♂ □ ♄ 10:30 pm

16 FRIDAY
- ♂ □ ♄ **1:30 am**
- ☽ △ ♀ **3:08 pm** 12:08 pm
- ☽ ⚻ ♃ **7:45 pm** 4:45 pm
- ☽ ⚹ ♄ **8:49 pm** 5:49 pm
- ☽ ⚻ ♂ **9:51 pm** 6:51 pm

17 SATURDAY
- ☽ ⚻ ☉ **9:33 am** 6:33 am
- ☽ △ ♅ **12:59 pm** 9:59 am
- ☽ ⚻ ☿ **1:57 pm** 10:57 am
- ☽ ⚹ ♆ **4:43 pm** 1:43 pm
- ☽ ☌ ♇ **6:13 pm** 3:13 pm

18 SUNDAY
- ☿ □ ♅ **5:47 am** 2:47 am
- ☉ ☌ ☿ **9:58 pm** 6:58 pm
- ☽ ⚻ ♀ **10:05 pm** 7:05 pm
- ☽ △ ♃ **10:22 pm** 7:22 pm
- ☽ ⚺ ♄ **10:38 pm** 7:38 pm
- ♀ □ ♃ 10:53 pm
- ☽ △ ♂ 11:08 pm

19 MONDAY
- ♀ □ ♃ **1:53 am**
- ☽ △ ♂ **2:08 am**
- ♀ ☍ ♄ **4:30 am** 1:30 am
- ☽ ☍ ☿ **12:32 pm** 9:32 am
- ☉ □ ♅ **12:45 pm** 9:45 am
- ☽ □ ♅ **2:19 pm** 11:19 am
- ☽ ☍ ☉ **2:26 pm** 11:26 am
- ♃ □ ♄ **5:46 pm** 2:46 pm
- ☽ ⚺ ♆ **5:48 pm** 2:48 pm
- ☽ ⚺ ♇ **7:15 pm** 4:15 pm

20 TUESDAY
- ☽ ☌ ♄ **10:45 pm** 7:45 pm
- ☽ □ ♃ **11:10 pm** 8:10 pm
- ☽ ☍ ♀ 11:44 pm

21 WEDNESDAY
- ☽ ☍ ♀ **2:44 am**
- ☽ □ ♂ **4:34 am** 1:34 am
- ☽ ⚻ ☿ **10:15 am** 7:15 am
- ☽ ⚹ ♅ **2:32 pm** 11:32 am
- ☉ ⚻ ♆ **5:29 pm** 2:29 pm
- ☽ ☌ ♆ **5:54 pm** 2:54 pm
- ☽ ⚻ ☉ **5:56 pm** 2:56 pm
- ☽ ⚹ ♇ **7:21 pm** 4:21 pm

22 THURSDAY
- ☉ ⚻ ♇ **3:34 pm** 12:34 pm
- ☽ ⚺ ♄ **10:58 pm** 7:58 pm
- ♀ □ ♂ **11:20 pm** 8:20 pm
- ☽ ⚹ ♃ 9:05 pm

23 FRIDAY
- ☽ ⚹ ♃ **12:05 am**
- ☽ ⚹ ♂ **7:21 am** 4:21 am
- ☽ ⚻ ♀ **7:43 am** 4:43 am
- ☽ △ ☿ **8:44 am** 5:44 am
- ☽ ⚺ ♅ **3:24 pm** 12:24 pm
- ☿ ⚺ ♀ **4:15 pm** 1:15 pm
- ☽ ⚺ ♆ **6:46 pm** 3:46 pm
- ☽ □ ♇ **8:17 pm** 5:17 pm
- ☽ △ ☉ **10:22 pm** 7:22 pm
- ☿ ⚹ ♂ 9:31 pm

24 SATURDAY
- ☿ ⚹ ♂ **12:31 am**
- ☽ ⚹ ♄ 9:46 pm
- ☽ ⚺ ♃ 11:40 pm

25 SUNDAY
- ☽ ⚹ ♄ **12:46 am**
- ☽ ⚺ ♃ **2:40 am**
- ☽ □ ☿ **9:25 am** 6:25 am
- ☽ ⚺ ♂ **12:12 pm** 9:12 am
- ☽ △ ♀ **3:03 pm** 12:03 pm
- ☽ ☌ ♅ **6:15 pm** 3:15 pm
- ☽ ⚹ ♆ **9:40 pm** 6:40 pm
- ☽ △ ♇ **11:17 pm** 8:17 pm

26 MONDAY
- ☽ □ ☉ **5:26 am** 2:26 am

27 TUESDAY
- ♀ △ ♅ **3:24 am** 12:24 am
- ☽ □ ♄ **5:02 am** 2:02 am
- ☽ ☌ ♃ **7:50 am** 4:50 am
- ☽ ⚹ ☿ **1:17 pm** 10:17 am
- ☽ ☌ ♂ **8:00 pm** 5:00 pm
- ☽ ⚺ ♅ **11:45 pm** 8:45 pm
- ☽ □ ♀ 10:50 pm

28 WEDNESDAY
- ☽ □ ♀ **1:50 am**
- ☽ □ ♆ **3:14 am** 12:14 am
- ☽ ⚻ ♇ **4:56 am** 1:56 am
- ☽ ⚹ ☉ **3:50 pm** 12:50 pm
- ♀ ☍ ♆ **4:25 pm** 1:25 pm

29 THURSDAY
- ♀ △ ♇ **10:32 am** 7:32 am
- ☽ △ ♄ **11:57 am** 8:57 am
- ☽ ⚺ ♃ **3:46 pm** 12:46 pm
- ☽ ⚺ ☿ **8:56 pm** 5:56 pm

30 FRIDAY
- ☽ ⚺ ♂ **6:52 am** 3:52 am
- ☽ ⚹ ♅ **7:54 am** 4:54 am
- ☽ △ ♆ **11:24 am** 8:24 am
- ☽ ☍ ♇ **1:14 pm** 10:14 am
- ☽ ⚹ ♀ **4:10 pm** 1:10 pm

31 SATURDAY
- ♂ ⚺ ♅ **3:52 am** 12:52 am
- ☽ ⚺ ☉ **5:30 am** 2:30 am
- ☽ ⚻ ♄ **9:18 pm** 6:18 pm
- ☽ ⚹ ♃ 11:10 pm

Eastern time in bold type
Pacific time in medium type

AUGUST 2024

DATE	SID.TIME	SUN	MOON	NODE	MERCURY	VENUS	MARS	JUPITER	SATURN	URANUS	NEPTUNE	PLUTO	CERES	PALLAS	JUNO	VESTA	CHIRON
1 Th	20 40 23	9♌14 51	28♊11	8♈34 R	3♍22	24♌58	7♊37	14♊24	18♓36 R	26♉51	29♓42 R	0≈40 R	9♋23 R	21♍23	27♍09	18♌50	23♈31 R
2 F	20 44 19	10 12 16	11♋15	8 25	3 40	26 12	8 18	14 35	18 33	26 52	29 41	0 38	9 14	21 31	27 28	19 18	23 31
3 Sa	20 48 16	11 09 43	24 06	8 15	3 54	27 25	8 58	14 45	18 30	26 54	29 40	0 37	9 06	21 40	27 48	19 45	23 31
4 Su	20 52 12	12 07 10	6♌44	8 05	4 03	28 39	9 39	14 56	18 27	26 55	29 39	0 36	8 58	21 49	28 07	20 13	23 30
5 M	20 56 9	13 04 38	19 09	7 56	4 06 R	29 53	10 19	15 06	18 23	26 56	29 38	0 34	8 50	21 59	28 27	20 41	23 30
6 T	21 0 6	14 02 08	1♍23	7 48	4 05	1♍08	10 59	15 16	18 20	26 58	29 37	0 33	8 43	22 09	28 47	21 08	23 29
7 W	21 4 2	14 59 38	13 25	7 43	4 00	2 20	11 39	15 27	18 17	26 59	29 36	0 32	8 36	22 19	29 07	21 36	23 29
8 Th	21 7 59	15 57 09	25 19	7 40	3 48	3 34	12 19	15 37	18 13	27 00	29 35	0 30	8 29	22 29	29 26	22 04	23 28
9 F	21 11 55	16 54 41	7≏07	7 39 D	3 28	4 47	12 58	15 47	18 10	27 01	29 34	0 29	8 23	22 40	29 46	22 32	23 27
10 Sa	21 15 52	17 52 14	18 53	7 40	3 05	6 01	13 38	15 56	18 06	27 03	29 33	0 27	8 17	22 51	0≏06	23 00	23 27
11 Su	21 19 48	18 49 47	0♏43	7 41	2 37	7 15	14 18	16 06	18 02	27 04	29 32	0 26	8 11	23 02	0 26	23 28	23 26
12 M	21 23 45	19 47 22	12 40	7 42 R	2 05	8 28	14 57	16 16	17 59	27 05	29 31	0 25	8 06	23 14	0 46	23 56	23 25
13 T	21 27 41	20 44 58	24 50	7 42	1 27	9 42	15 36	16 26	17 55	27 06	29 30	0 23	8 01	23 26	1 06	24 23	23 24
14 W	21 31 38	21 42 34	7♐19	7 41	0 46	10 56	16 15	16 35	17 51	27 07	29 28	0 22	7 56	23 38	1 26	24 51	23 23
15 Th	21 35 35	22 40 12	20 10	7 38	0 01	12 09	16 55	16 44	17 47	27 08	29 27	0 21	7 52	23 50	1 47	25 19	23 22
16 F	21 39 31	23 37 50	3♑27	7 33	29♋13	13 23	17 33	16 53	17 43	27 08	29 26	0 20	7 48	24 03	2 07	25 47	23 21
17 Sa	21 43 28	24 35 30	17 11	7 27	28 23	14 37	18 12	17 02	17 39	27 09	29 25	0 18	7 45	24 15	2 27	26 15	23 20
18 Su	21 47 24	25 33 10	1≈21	7 20	27 31	15 50	18 51	17 11	17 35	27 10	29 23	0 17	7 42	24 28	2 47	26 44	23 19
19 M	21 51 21	26 30 52	15 54	7 14	27 04	17 04	19 30	17 20	17 31	27 11	29 22	0 16	7 39	24 42	3 08	27 12	23 18
20 T	21 55 17	27 28 35	0♓43	7 09	26 49	18 17	20 08	17 28	17 27	27 11	29 21	0 15	7 36	24 55	3 28	27 40	23 17
21 W	21 59 14	28 26 19	15 40	7 06	25 49	19 31	20 47	17 37	17 23	27 12	29 19	0 13	7 34	25 09	3 49	28 08	23 15
22 Th	22 3 10	29 24 05	0♈36	7 04 D	25 00	20 44	21 25	17 45	17 19	27 13	29 18	0 12	7 33	25 23	4 09	28 36	23 14
23 F	22 7 7	0♍21 52	15 25	7 04	24 14	21 58	22 03	17 53	17 14	27 13	29 16	0 11	7 31	25 37	4 30	29 04	23 13
24 Sa	22 11 3	1 19 42	0♉00	7 05	23 32	23 11	22 41	18 02	17 10	27 14	29 15	0 10	7 30	25 52	4 50	29 32	23 11
25 Su	22 15 0	2 17 32	14 17	7 07	22 55	24 25	23 19	18 10	17 06	27 14	29 14	0 09	7 30	26 06	5 11	0♍00	23 10
26 M	22 18 57	3 15 25	28 17	7 08 R	22 23	25 39	23 56	18 18	17 01	27 14	29 12	0 08	7 29 D	26 21	5 31	0 29	23 08
27 T	22 22 53	4 13 20	11♊52	7 08	21 57	26 52	24 34	18 25	16 57	27 15	29 11	0 06	7 29	26 36	5 52	0 57	23 07
28 W	22 26 50	5 11 16	25 12	7 06	21 39	28 06	25 12	18 33	16 53	27 15	29 09	0 05	7 30	26 52	6 13	1 25	23 05
29 Th	22 30 46	6 09 14	8♋09	7 03	21 30	29 19	25 49	18 40	16 48	27 15	29 08	0 04	7 31	27 07	6 34	1 53	23 04
30 F	22 34 43	7 07 14	21 00	7 01	21 30	0≏33	26 26	18 47	16 44	27 15	29 06	0 03	7 32	27 23	6 54	2 22	23 02
31 Sa	22 38 39	8 05 16	3♌39	6 59	21 43	1 46	26 26	18 54	16 39	27 15	29 05	0 02	7 33	27 39	7 15	2 50	23 00

SEPTEMBER 2024

☽ Last Aspect day	ET / hr:mn / PT		asp	☽ Ingress sign	day	ET / hr:mn / PT	
1	**8:25 pm**	5:25 pm	⚹♂	♍	1	**11:48 pm**	8:48 pm
4	**12:06 pm**	9:06 am	△♇	♎	4	**12:12 pm**	9:12 am
6		10:08 pm	□♇	♏	6		10:18 pm
7	**1:08 am**		□♇	♏	7	**1:18 am**	
9	**1:11 pm**	10:11 am	⚹♇	♐	9	**1:26 pm**	10:26 am
11	**8:21 pm**	5:21 pm	□♆	♑	11	**10:38 pm**	7:38 pm
14	**3:35 am**	12:35 am	☌♇	♒	14	**3:53 am**	12:53 am
15		10:04 pm	□♅	♓	16	**5:39 am**	2:39 am
16	**1:04 am**		□♅	♓	16	**5:39 am**	2:39 am
18	**5:02 am**	2:02 am	⚹♇	♈	18	**5:24 am**	2:24 am
20	**4:39 am**	1:39 am	□♇	♉	20	**5:03 am**	2:03 am
22	**6:14 am**	3:14 am	△☉	♊	22	**6:24 am**	3:24 am
24	**7:59 am**	4:59 am	□♆	♋	24	**10:50 am**	7:50 am
26	**6:12 pm**	3:12 pm	☍♇	♌	26	**6:47 pm**	3:47 pm
28	**11:36 pm**	8:36 pm	□♅	♍	29	**5:42 am**	2:42 am

☽ Phases & Eclipses phase	day	ET / hr:mn / PT	
New Moon	2	**9:56 pm**	6:56 pm
2nd Quarter	10		11:06 pm
2nd Quarter	11	**2:06 am**	
Full Moon	17	**10:34 pm**	7:34 pm
●	17	25° ♓ 41'	
4th Quarter	24	**2:50 pm**	11:50 am

Planet Ingress		day	ET / hr:mn / PT	
♇	♑	1	**8:10 pm**	5:10 pm
♂	♋	4	**3:46 pm**	12:46 pm
♀	♐	8	**6:29 am**	3:29 am
☿	♍	8		11:50 pm
☿	♍	9	**2:50 am**	
☉	♎	22	**8:44 am**	5:44 am
♀	♏	22	**10:36 pm**	7:36 pm
☿	♎	26	**4:09 am**	1:09 am

Planetary Motion		day	ET / hr:mn / PT	
♅	℞	1	**11:18 am**	8:18 am

1 SUNDAY

☽ ⚹ ♃	**2:10 am**	
☽ ☌ ☿	**8:36 am**	5:36 am
☽ □ ♅	**6:22 pm**	3:22 pm
☽ ⚹ ♂	**8:25 pm**	5:25 pm
☽ ⚻ ♆	**9:52 pm**	6:52 pm
☽ ⚻ ♇	**11:48 pm**	8:48 pm

2 MONDAY

☽ ⚺ ♀	**9:35 am**	6:35 am
☽ ☌ ☉	**9:56 pm**	6:56 pm
♂ □ ♆		9:10 pm

3 TUESDAY

♂ □ ♆	**12:10 am**	
☽ ☍ ♄	**8:37 am**	5:37 am
☽ □ ♃	**2:34 pm**	11:34 am
☽ ⚺ ☿		9:17 pm

4 WEDNESDAY

☽ ⚺ ☿	**12:17 am**	
☽ △ ♅	**6:37 am**	3:37 am
☽ ☍ ♆	**10:05 am**	7:05 am
☽ □ ♂	**12:00 pm**	9:00 am
☽ △ ♇	**12:06 pm**	9:06 am
♂ ⚻ ♇	**1:59 pm**	10:59 am

5 Thursday

☽ ☌ ♀	**5:12 am**	2:12 am
☽ ⚺ ☉	**4:12 pm**	1:12 pm
☽ ⚻ ♄	**9:11 pm**	6:11 pm

6 FRIDAY

☽ △ ♃	**4:08 am**	1:08 am
☽ ⚹ ☿	**7:11 pm**	4:11 pm
☽ ⚻ ♅	**7:42 pm**	4:42 pm
☽ ⚻ ♆	**11:04 pm**	8:04 pm
☿ □ ♅		9:21 pm
☽ □ ♇		10:08 pm

7 SATURDAY

☿ □ ♅	**12:21 am**	
☽ □ ♇	**1:08 am**	
☽ △ ♂	**4:24 am**	1:24 am
☉ ☍ ♄		9:35 pm
☽ ⚺ ♀		10:14 pm

8 SUNDAY

☉ ☍ ♄	**12:35 am**	
☽ ⚺ ♀	**1:14 am**	
☿ ⚻ ♆	**6:52 am**	3:52 am
☽ △ ♄	**9:37 am**	6:37 am
☽ ⚹ ☉	**10:29 am**	7:29 am
☽ ⚻ ♃	**5:20 pm**	2:20 pm
☿ ⚻ ♇		9:55 pm

9 MONDAY

☿ ⚻ ♇	**12:55 am**	
☽ ☍ ♅	**7:58 am**	4:58 am
☽ △ ♆	**11:07 am**	8:07 am
☽ ⚹ ♇	**1:11 pm**	10:11 am
☽ □ ☿	**2:50 pm**	11:50 am
☽ ⚻ ♂	**7:28 pm**	4:28 pm

10 TUESDAY

☽ ⚹ ♀	**6:48 pm**	3:48 pm
☽ □ ♄	**8:02 pm**	5:02 pm
☽ □ ☉		11:06 pm

11 WEDNESDAY

☽ □ ☉	**2:06 am**	
☽ ☍ ♃	**4:07 am**	1:07 am
♀ ⚻ ♄	**6:52 am**	3:52 am
☽ ⚻ ♅	**5:28 pm**	2:28 pm
☽ □ ♆	**8:21 pm**	5:21 pm
☽ ⚺ ♇	**10:21 pm**	7:21 pm
☿ ⚹ ♂	**11:42 pm**	8:42 pm

12 THURSDAY

☉ □ ♃	**6:53 am**	3:53 am
☽ ☍ ♂	**6:56 am**	3:56 am
☽ △ ☿	**7:36 am**	4:36 am
☽ ⚹ ♄		11:53 pm

13 FRIDAY

☽ ⚹ ♄	**2:53 am**	
☽ □ ♀	**7:30 am**	4:30 am
☽ ⚻ ♃	**11:02 am**	8:02 am
☽ △ ☉	**1:01 pm**	10:01 am
☽ △ ♅	**11:04 pm**	8:04 pm
☽ ⚹ ♆		10:40 pm

14 SATURDAY

☽ ⚹ ♆	**1:40 am**	
☽ ☌ ♇	**3:35 am**	12:35 am
☽ ⚻ ♂	**1:52 pm**	10:52 am
☽ ⚻ ☿	**7:21 pm**	4:21 pm
♀ △ ♃		10:34 pm

15 SUNDAY

♀ △ ♃	**1:34 am**	
☽ ⚺ ♄	**5:55 am**	2:55 am
☽ △ ♃	**2:05 pm**	11:05 am
☽ △ ♀	**3:09 pm**	12:09 pm
☽ ⚻ ☉	**7:15 pm**	4:15 pm
☽ □ ♅		10:04 pm

16 MONDAY

☽ □ ♅	**1:04 am**	
☽ ⚺ ♆	**3:27 am**	12:27 am
☽ ⚺ ♇	**5:19 am**	2:19 am
☽ △ ♂	**5:03 pm**	2:03 pm
☽ ☍ ☿		11:55 pm

17 TUESDAY

☽ ☍ ☿	**2:55 am**	
☽ ☌ ♄	**6:11 am**	3:11 am
☽ □ ♃	**2:30 pm**	11:30 am
☽ ⚻ ♀	**7:31 pm**	4:31 pm
☽ ☍ ☉	**10:34 pm**	7:34 pm
☽ ⚹ ♅		9:53 pm

18 WEDNESDAY

☽ ⚹ ♅	**12:53 am**	
☽ ☌ ♆	**3:10 am**	12:10 am
☿ ☍ ♄	**4:50 am**	1:50 am
☽ ⚹ ♇	**5:02 am**	2:02 am
☽ □ ♂	**6:27 pm**	3:27 pm

19 THURSDAY

☽ ⚺ ♄	**5:24 am**	2:24 am
☽ ⚻ ☿	**8:57 am**	5:57 am
☉ △ ♅	**10:04 am**	7:04 am
☽ ⚹ ♃	**2:11 pm**	11:11 am
☽ ☍ ♀	**11:14 pm**	8:14 pm
☽ ⚺ ♅		9:25 pm
☽ ⚻ ☉		10:26 pm
☽ ⚺ ♆		11:41 pm

20 FRIDAY

☽ ⚺ ♅	**12:25 am**	
☽ ⚻ ☉	**1:26 am**	
☽ ⚺ ♆	**2:41 am**	
☽ □ ♇	**4:39 am**	1:39 am
♀ ⚻ ♅	**1:36 pm**	10:36 am
☉ ☍ ♆	**8:17 pm**	5:17 pm
☽ ⚹ ♂	**8:18 pm**	5:18 pm

21 SATURDAY

☿ □ ♃	**4:50 am**	1:50 am
☽ ⚹ ♄	**5:28 am**	2:28 am
☽ ⚺ ♃	**3:03 pm**	12:03 pm
☽ △ ☿	**4:30 pm**	1:30 pm
♀ ⚻ ♆	**4:53 pm**	1:53 pm
☽ ☌ ♅		10:29 pm
☉ △ ♇		11:12 pm

22 SUNDAY

☽ ☌ ♅	**1:29 am**	
☉ △ ♇	**2:12 am**	
☽ ⚹ ♆	**3:50 am**	12:50 am
☽ ⚻ ♀	**4:53 am**	1:53 am
☽ △ ♇	**5:57 am**	2:57 am
☽ △ ☉	**6:14 am**	3:14 am
♀ □ ♇	**5:15 pm**	2:15 pm
☽ ⚺ ♂		9:37 pm

23 MONDAY

☽ ⚺ ♂	**12:37 am**	
☽ □ ♄	**7:58 am**	4:58 am
☽ ☌ ♃	**6:39 pm**	3:39 pm

24 TUESDAY

☽ □ ☿	**4:13 am**	1:13 am
☽ ⚺ ♅	**5:31 am**	2:31 am
☽ □ ♆	**7:59 am**	4:59 am
☽ ⚻ ♇	**10:19 am**	7:19 am
☿ △ ♅	**1:27 pm**	10:27 am
☽ △ ♀	**2:30 pm**	11:30 am
☽ □ ☉	**2:50 pm**	11:50 am

25 WEDNESDAY

☿ ☍ ♆	**7:07 am**	4:07 am
☉ ⚺ ♀	**7:27 am**	4:27 am
☽ ☌ ♂	**8:40 am**	5:40 am
☽ △ ♄	**1:52 pm**	10:52 am
☿ △ ♇		9:14 pm
☽ ⚺ ♃		10:45 pm

26 THURSDAY

☿ △ ♇	**12:14 am**	
☽ ⚺ ♃	**1:45 am**	
☽ ⚹ ♅	**1:02 pm**	10:02 am
☽ △ ♆	**3:38 pm**	12:38 pm
☽ ☍ ♇	**6:12 pm**	3:12 pm
☽ ⚹ ☿	**9:18 pm**	6:18 pm

27 FRIDAY

☽ ⚹ ☉	**3:51 am**	12:51 am
☽ □ ♀	**4:47 am**	1:47 am
☽ ⚺ ♂	**8:33 pm**	5:33 pm
☽ ⚻ ♄	**11:04 pm**	8:04 pm

28 SATURDAY

☽ ⚹ ♃	**12:05 pm**	9:05 am
☽ □ ♅	**11:36 pm**	8:36 pm
☽ ⚻ ♆		11:16 pm

29 SUNDAY

☽ ⚻ ♆	**2:16 am**	
☽ ⚻ ♇	**5:03 am**	2:03 am
☽ ⚺ ☿	**6:48 pm**	3:48 pm
☽ ⚺ ☉	**8:25 pm**	5:25 pm
☽ ⚹ ♀	**10:49 pm**	7:49 pm
♂ △ ♄		9:06 pm

30 MONDAY

♂ △ ♄	**12:06 am**	
☽ ☍ ♄	**10:38 am**	7:38 am
☽ ⚹ ♂	**11:11 am**	8:11 am
☉ ☌ ☿	**5:09 pm**	2:09 pm
☽ □ ♃		9:30 pm

Eastern time in bold type
Pacific time in medium type

SEPTEMBER 2024

DATE	SID.TIME	SUN	MOON	NODE	MERCURY	VENUS	MARS	JUPITER	SATURN	URANUS	NEPTUNE	PLUTO	CERES	PALLAS	JUNO	VESTA	CHIRON
1 Su	22 42 36	9♍03 20	15♌54	6♈50R	22♌05	2♎59	27♊40	19♊01	16♓35R	27♉15R	29♓03R	0♒01R	7♈35	27♍55	7♎36	3♍18	22♈58R
2 M	22 46 33	10 01 25	28 05	6 46	23 13	4 13	28 17	19 08	16 30	27 15	29 02	0 00	7 37	28 11	7 57	3 47	22 55
3 T	22 50 29	10 59 32	10♍07	6 42	24 53	5 26	28 54	19 15	16 25	27 15	29 00	29♑59	7 40	28 28	8 18	4 15	22 53
4 W	22 54 26	11 57 40	22 01	6 40	25 54	6 40	29 30	19 21	16 21	27 15	28 59	29 57	7 43	28 44	8 39	4 43	22 51
5 Th	22 58 22	12 55 51	3♎50	6 39D	27 02	7 53	0♋06	19 28	16 16	27 15	28 57	29 56	7 46	29 01	9 00	5 12	22 49
6 F	23 2 19	13 54 02	15 37	6 39	28 16	9 07	0 43	19 34	16 12	27 15	28 55	29 55	7 49	29 18	9 21	5 40	22 47
7 Sa	23 6 15	14 52 16	27 23	6 40	29 36	10 20	1 19	19 40	16 07	27 15	28 54	29 55	7 53	29 35	9 42	6 09	22 45
8 Su	23 10 12	15 50 31	9♏14	6 42	1♍02	11 33	1 54	19 46	16 03	27 14	28 52	29 54	7 57	29 52	10 03	6 37	22 45
9 M	23 14 8	16 48 47	21 12	6 43	2 32	12 47	2 30	19 52	15 58	27 14	28 51	29 53	8 02	0♎10	10 24	7 05	22 43
10 T	23 18 5	17 47 06	3♐21	6 45	4 07	14 00	3 06	19 57	15 53	27 14	28 49	29 53	8 07	0 28	10 45	7 34	22 41
11 W	23 22 1	18 45 25	15 48	6 45R	5 45	15 13	3 41	20 03	15 49	27 13	28 47	29 52	8 12	0 45	11 06	8 02	22 39
12 Th	23 25 58	19 43 47	28 35	6 45	7 27	16 27	4 16	20 08	15 44	27 13	28 46	29 51	8 17	1 03	11 27	8 31	22 37
13 F	23 29 55	20 42 10	11♑46	6 44	9 11	17 40	4 51	20 13	15 40	27 12	28 44	29 50	8 23	1 21	11 48	8 59	22 34
14 Sa	23 33 51	21 40 34	25 25	6 43	10 57	18 53	5 26	20 18	15 35	27 12	28 43	29 49	8 29	1 40	12 09	9 28	22 32
15 Su	23 37 48	22 39 00	9♒31	6 41	12 45	20 07	6 01	20 23	15 30	27 11	28 41	29 49	8 36	1 58	12 31	9 56	22 30
16 M	23 41 44	23 37 28	24 03	6 39	14 35	21 20	6 35	20 27	15 26	27 10	28 39	29 48	8 42	2 17	12 52	10 25	22 28
17 T	23 45 41	24 35 57	8♓56	6 38	16 25	22 33	7 10	20 32	15 21	27 09	28 38	29 47	8 49	2 35	13 13	10 53	22 25
18 W	23 49 37	25 34 28	24 03	6 37D	18 16	23 46	7 44	20 36	15 17	27 09	28 36	29 46	8 57	2 54	13 34	11 22	22 23
19 Th	23 53 34	26 33 01	9♈15	6 37	20 07	25 00	8 18	20 40	15 12	27 08	28 34	29 45	9 04	3 13	13 55	11 50	22 21
20 F	23 57 30	27 31 36	24 21	6 37	21 59	26 13	8 52	20 44	15 08	27 07	28 33	29 45	9 12	3 32	14 17	12 19	22 18
21 Sa	0 1 27	28 30 13	9♉15	6 38	23 50	27 26	9 26	20 47	15 04	27 05	28 31	29 45	9 20	3 51	14 38	12 47	22 16
22 Su	0 5 24	29 28 53	23 49	6 38	25 42	28 39	9 59	20 51	14 59	27 04	28 29	29 44	9 29	4 10	14 59	13 16	22 13
23 M	0 9 20	0♎27 34	5♊03	6 39R	27 32	29 52	10 32	20 54	14 55	27 03	28 28	29 44	9 37	4 30	15 21	13 44	22 11
24 T	0 13 17	1 26 18	21 43	6 39	29 23	1♏05	11 05	20 57	14 51	27 02	28 26	29 43	9 46	4 50	15 42	14 13	22 08
25 W	0 17 13	2 25 05	6♋00	6 39	1♎12	2 18	11 38	21 00	14 46	27 01	28 24	29 43	9 56	5 09	16 03	14 41	22 06
26 Th	0 21 10	3 23 53	18 00	6 39	3 01	3 31	12 11	21 03	14 42	27 00	28 23	29 42	10 05	5 29	16 24	15 10	22 03
27 F	0 25 6	4 22 44	0♌38	6 39	4 50	4 44	12 43	21 05	14 38	26 59	28 21	29 42	10 15	5 49	16 46	15 38	22 00
28 Sa	0 29 3	5 21 37	13 00	6 39	6 37	5 57	13 16	21 08	14 34	26 58	28 19	29 41	10 25	6 09	17 07	16 07	21 58
29 Su	0 32 59	6 20 32	25 08	6 39D	8 24	7 10	13 48	21 10	14 30	26 57	28 18	29 41	10 35	6 29	17 29	16 35	21 55
30 M	0 36 56	7 19 29	7♍08	6 39	10 09	8 23	14 19	21 12	14 26	26 56	28 16	29 41	10 46	6 49	17 50	17 04	21 53

EPHEMERIS CALCULATED FOR 12 MIDNIGHT GREENWICH MEAN TIME. ALL OTHER DATA AND FACING ASPECTARIAN PAGE IN **EASTERN TIME (BOLD)** AND PACIFIC TIME (REGULAR).

OCTOBER 2024

☽ Last Aspect day	ET / hr:mn / PT	asp	☽ Ingress sign	day	ET / hr:mn / PT
1	**5:39 pm** 2:39 pm	△♇	♎	1	**6:20 pm** 3:20 pm
4	**6:40 am** 3:40 am	□♇	♏	4	**7:22 am** 4:22 am
6	**6:52 pm** 3:52 pm	⚹♇	♐	6	**7:34 pm** 4:34 pm
8	10:54 pm	□♆	♑	9	**5:38 am** 2:38 am
9	**1:54 am**	□♆	♑	9	**5:38 am** 2:38 am
11	**11:53 am** 8:53 am	☌♇	♒	11	**12:31 pm** 9:31 am
13	**10:11 am** 7:11 am	□♅	♓	13	**3:55 pm** 12:55 pm
15	**4:00 pm** 1:00 pm	⚹♇	♈	15	**4:34 pm** 1:34 pm
17	**3:26 pm** 12:26 pm	□♇	♉	17	**4:00 pm** 1:00 pm
19	**3:33 pm** 12:33 pm	△♇	♊	19	**4:07 pm** 1:07 pm
21	**5:00 pm** 2:00 pm	△☉	♋	21	**6:50 pm** 3:50 pm
23	9:47 pm	☍♇	♌	23	10:24 pm
24	**12:47 am**	☍♇	♌	24	**1:24 am**
26	**4:04 am** 1:04 am	□♅	♍	26	**11:47 am** 8:47 am
28	**11:54 pm** 8:54 pm	△♇	♎	28	9:30 pm
28	**11:54 pm** 8:54 pm	△♇	♎	29	**12:30 am**
31	**12:57 pm** 9:57 am	□♇	♏	31	**1:29 pm** 10:29 am

☽ Phases & Eclipses phase	day	ET / hr:mn / PT
New Moon	2	**2:49 pm** 11:49 am
●	2	10° ♎ 04′
2nd Quarter	10	**2:55 pm** 11:55 am
Full Moon	17	**7:26 am** 4:26 am
4th Quarter	24	**4:03 am** 1:03 am

Planet Ingress	day	ET / hr:mn / PT
☿ ♏	13	**3:23 pm** 12:23 pm
♀ ♐	17	**3:28 pm** 12:28 pm
☉ ♏	22	**6:15 pm** 3:15 pm
⚶ ♎	26	11:35 pm
⚶ ♎	27	**2:35 am**

Planetary Motion	day	ET / hr:mn / PT
♃ ℞	9	**3:05 am** 12:05 am
♇ D	11	**8:34 pm** 5:34 pm

1 TUESDAY
☽ □ ♃ **12:30 am**
☽ △ ♅ **12:00 pm** 9:00 am
☽ ☍ ♆ **2:42 pm** 11:42 am
☽ △ ♇ **5:39 pm** 2:39 pm

2 WEDNESDAY
☽ ☌ ☉ **2:49 pm** 11:49 am
☽ ☌ ☿ **6:22 pm** 3:22 pm
☽ ⚺ ♀ **6:43 pm** 3:43 pm
☽ ⚻ ♄ **11:17 pm** 8:17 pm
☿ ⚺ ♀ 10:26 pm

3 THURSDAY
☿ ⚺ ♀ **1:26 am**
☽ □ ♂ **3:00 am** 12:00 am
☽ △ ♃ **1:40 pm** 10:40 am
☽ ⚻ ♅ 9:56 pm
☿ ⚻ ♄ 11:46 pm

4 FRIDAY
☽ ⚻ ♅ **12:56 am**
☿ ⚻ ♄ **2:46 am**
☽ ⚻ ♆ **3:37 am** 12:37 am
☽ □ ♇ **6:40 am** 3:40 am
♀ △ ♄ **1:04 pm** 10:04 am

5 SATURDAY
☽ ⚺ ☉ **9:13 am** 6:13 am
☽ △ ♄ **11:46 am** 8:46 am
☽ ☌ ♀ **2:28 pm** 11:28 am
☽ ⚺ ☿ **5:30 pm** 2:30 pm
☽ △ ♂ **6:27 pm** 3:27 pm
☽ ⚻ ♃ 11:19 pm
☿ □ ♂ 11:37 pm

6 SUNDAY
☽ ⚻ ♃ **2:19 am**
☿ □ ♂ **2:37 am**
☽ ☍ ♅ **1:09 pm** 10:09 am
☉ ⚻ ♄ **2:28 pm** 11:28 am
☽ △ ♆ **3:47 pm** 12:47 pm
☽ ⚹ ♇ **6:52 pm** 3:52 pm

7 MONDAY
☽ □ ♄ **10:50 pm** 7:50 pm
☽ ⚹ ☉ 10:49 pm

8 TUESDAY
☽ ⚹ ☉ **1:49 am**
♀ △ ♂ **6:22 am** 3:22 am
☽ ⚻ ♂ **8:02 am** 5:02 am
☽ ⚺ ♀ **8:09 am** 5:09 am
☿ △ ♃ **8:23 am** 5:23 am
☽ ☍ ♃ **1:10 pm** 10:10 am
☽ ⚹ ☿ **1:54 pm** 10:54 am
☽ ⚻ ♅ **11:23 pm** 8:23 pm
☽ □ ♆ 10:54 pm

9 WEDNESDAY
☽ □ ♆ **1:54 am**
☽ ⚺ ♇ **4:58 am** 1:58 am

10 THURSDAY
☽ ⚹ ♄ **7:16 am** 4:16 am
♀ ⚻ ♃ **11:44 am** 8:44 am
☽ □ ☉ **2:5 pm** 11:55 am
☽ ☍ ♂ **6:2 pm** 3:22 pm
☽ ⚻ ♃ **9:_ pm** 6:02 pm
☽ ⚹ ♀ **9:5 pm** 6:58 pm

11 FRIDAY
☽ □ ☿ **5:3 am** 2:35 am
☽ △ ♅ **6:3 am** 3:31 am
☽ ⚹ ♆ **8:5 am** 5:54 am
☽ ☌ ♇ **11:5 am** 8:53 am
☿ ⚻ ♅ **1:1 pm** 10:11 am

12 SATURDAY
☿ ⚻ ♆ **8:41 am** 5:41 am
☽ ⚺ ♄ **12:19 pm** 9:19 am
☽ △ ☉ **11:39 pm** 8:39 pm
☽ ⚻ ♂ 9:44 pm
☽ △ ♃ 10:22 pm

13 SUNDAY
☽ ⚻ ♂ **12:44 am**
☽ △ ♃ **1:22 am**
☽ □ ♀ **7:08 am** 4:08 am
☿ □ ♇ **10:03 am** 7:03 am
☽ □ ♅ **10:11 am** 7:11 am
☽ ⚺ ♆ **12:26 pm** 9:26 am
☽ ⚺ ♇ **3:19 pm** 12:19 pm
☽ △ ☿ **3:59 pm** 12:59 pm
♂ ⚺ ♃ **7:08 pm** 4:08 pm
☉ △ ♃ **11:52 pm** 8:52 pm

14 MONDAY
☉ □ ♂ **4:15 am** 1:15 am
☽ ☌ ♄ **2:09 pm** 11:09 am
♀ ☍ ♅ **6:22 pm** 3:22 pm
☽ □ ♃ 11:38 pm

15 TUESDAY
☽ □ ♃ **2:38 am**
☽ △ ♂ **3:41 am** 12:41 am
☽ ⚻ ☉ **4:34 am** 1:34 am
☽ ⚹ ♅ **10:59 am** 7:59 am
☽ △ ♀ **12:28 pm** 9:28 am
☽ ☌ ♆ **1:09 pm** 10:09 am
☽ ⚹ ♇ **4:00 pm** 1:00 pm
♀ △ ♆ **8:49 pm** 5:49 pm
☽ ⚻ ☿ **10:22 pm** 7:22 pm

16 WEDNESDAY
☽ ⚺ ♄ **1:52 pm** 10:52 am
☽ ⚹ ♃ 11:09 pm

17 THURSDAY
☽ ⚹ ♃ **2:09 am**
☽ □ ♂ **4:44 am** 1:44 am
☽ ☍ ☉ **7:26 am** 4:26 am
♀ ⚹ ♇ **8:30 am** 5:30 am
☽ ⚺ ♅ **10:21 am** 7:21 am
☽ ⚺ ♆ **12:32 pm** 9:32 am
☽ □ ♇ **3:26 pm** 12:26 pm
☽ ⚻ ♀ **4:02 pm** 1:02 pm

18 FRIDAY
☽ ☍ ☿ **3:15 am** 12:15 am
☽ ⚹ ♄ **1:13 pm** 10:13 am
☽ ⚺ ♃ 10:46 pm
☉ ⚻ ♅ 11:40 pm

19 SATURDAY
☽ ⚺ ♃ **1:46 am**
☉ ⚻ ♅ **2:40 am**
☽ ⚹ ♂ **6:00 am** 3:00 am
☽ ☌ ♅ **10:11 am** 7:11 am
☽ ⚻ ☉ **10:44 am** 7:44 am
☽ ⚹ ♆ **12:28 pm** 9:28 am
☽ △ ♇ **3:33 pm** 12:33 pm
☽ ☍ ♀ **8:30 pm** 5:30 pm

20 SUNDAY
☽ ⚻ ☿ **9:39 am** 6:39 am
☉ ⚻ ♆ **11:44 am** 8:44 am
☽ □ ♄ **2:07 pm** 11:07 am

21 MONDAY
☽ ☌ ♃ **3:25 am** 12:25 am
☽ ⚺ ♂ **9:39 am** 6:39 am
☽ ⚺ ♅ **12:22 pm** 9:22 am
☽ □ ♆ **2:50 pm** 11:50 am
☽ △ ☉ **5:00 pm** 2:00 pm
☽ ⚻ ♇ **6:15 pm** 3:15 pm
☿ △ ♄ 11:35 pm

22 TUESDAY
☿ △ ♄ **2:35 am**
☽ ⚻ ♀ **4:30 am** 1:30 am
☉ □ ♇ **10:15 am** 7:15 am
☽ △ ♄ **6:17 pm** 3:17 pm
☽ △ ☿ **8:22 pm** 5:22 pm

23 WEDNESDAY
☽ ⚺ ♃ **8:36 am** 5:36 am
☽ ☌ ♂ **5:20 pm** 2:20 pm
☽ ⚹ ♅ **6:16 pm** 3:16 pm
☽ △ ♆ **9:00 pm** 6:00 pm
☽ ☍ ♇ 9:47 pm

24 THURSDAY
☽ ☍ ♇ **12:47 am**
☽ □ ☉ **4:03 am** 1:03 am
☽ △ ♀ **5:43 pm** 2:43 pm
♂ ⚹ ♅ **8:13 pm** 5:13 pm
☽ ⚻ ♄ 11:27 pm

25 FRIDAY
☽ ⚻ ♄ **2:27 am**
☽ □ ☿ **12:41 pm** 9:41 am
☽ ⚹ ♃ **5:42 pm** 2:42 pm

26 SATURDAY
☽ □ ♅ **4:04 am** 1:04 am
☽ ⚺ ♂ **5:16 am** 2:16 am
☽ ⚻ ♆ **7:02 am** 4:02 am
☽ ⚻ ♇ **11:11 am** 8:11 am
☽ ⚹ ☉ **7:54 pm** 4:54 pm

27 SUNDAY
☿ ⚻ ♃ **4:50 am** 1:50 am
☽ □ ♀ **11:39 am** 8:39 am
☽ ☍ ♄ **1:56 pm** 10:56 am

28 MONDAY
☽ □ ♃ **5:37 am** 2:37 am
♂ △ ♆ **8:31 am** 5:31 am
☽ ⚹ ☿ **9:16 am** 6:16 am
♀ □ ♄ **9:35 am** 6:35 am
☽ △ ♅ **4:23 pm** 1:23 pm
☽ ☍ ♆ **7:31 pm** 4:31 pm
☽ ⚹ ♂ **7:55 pm** 4:55 pm
☽ △ ♇ **11:54 pm** 8:54 pm

29 TUESDAY
☽ ⚺ ☉ **2:24 pm** 11:24 am
☽ ⚻ ♄ 11:50 pm

30 WEDNESDAY
☽ ⚻ ♄ **2:50 am**
☽ ⚹ ♀ **7:39 am** 4:39 am
☿ ☍ ♅ **6:15 pm** 3:15 pm
☽ △ ♃ **6:22 pm** 3:22 pm

31 THURSDAY
☽ ⚻ ♅ **5:15 am** 2:15 am
☽ ⚺ ☿ **6:47 am** 3:47 am
☽ ⚻ ♆ **8:27 am** 5:27 am
☽ □ ♂ **10:57 am** 7:57 am
☽ □ ♇ **12:57 pm** 9:57 am
☿ △ ♆ **8:33 pm** 5:33 pm

Eastern time in bold type
Pacific time in medium type

OCTOBER 2024

DATE	SID.TIME	SUN	MOON	NODE	MERCURY	VENUS	MARS	JUPITER	SATURN	URANUS	NEPTUNE	PLUTO	CERES	PALLAS	JUNO	VESTA	CHIRON
1 T	0 40 53	8≏18 28	19♈01	6♈39	8≏24	9♏36	14♋51	21Ⅱ13	14♓22R	26♉54R	28♓14R	29♑40R	10♌57	7♏10	18≏11	17♍33	21♈50R
2 W	0 44 49	9 17 30	1♉30	6 39R	10 10	10 49	15 22	21 15	14 18	26 53	28 13	29 40	11 08	7 30	18 33	18 01	21 48
3 Th	0 48 46	10 16 33	12 36	6 39	11 55	12 02	15 53	21 16	14 14	26 51	28 11	29 40	11 19	7 51	18 54	18 30	21 45
4 F	0 52 42	11 15 39	24 24	6 38	13 39	13 15	16 24	21 17	14 10	26 49	28 10	29 39	11 31	8 11	19 15	18 58	21 42
5 Sa	0 56 39	12 14 46	6♊14	6 38	15 23	14 28	16 55	21 18	14 06	26 48	28 08	29 39	11 42	8 32	19 37	19 27	21 39
6 Su	1 0 35	13 13 56	18 10	6 37	17 06	15 41	17 25	21 19	14 02	26 46	28 06	29 39	11 54	8 53	19 58	19 55	21 37
7 M	1 4 32	14 13 07	0♋13	6 36	18 47	16 54	17 56	21 20	13 59	26 45	28 05	29 39	12 07	9 14	20 19	20 24	21 34
8 T	1 8 28	15 12 21	12 27	6 35	20 28	18 07	18 25	21 20	13 55	26 43	28 03	29 39	12 19	9 35	20 41	20 52	21 31
9 W	1 12 25	16 11 36	24 55	6 34	22 09	19 20	18 55	21 20R	13 52	26 42	28 02	29 39	12 32	9 56	21 02	21 21	21 28
10 Th	1 16 22	17 10 53	7♌40	6 34D	23 48	20 32	19 24	21 20	13 48	26 40	28 00	29 39	12 45	10 17	21 24	21 49	21 26
11 F	1 20 18	18 10 12	20 46	6 34	25 27	21 45	19 53	21 20	13 45	26 38	27 59	29 39	12 58	10 39	21 45	22 18	21 23
12 Sa	1 24 15	19 09 32	4♍15	6 34	27 05	22 58	20 22	21 20	13 41	26 36	27 57	29 39D	13 11	11 00	22 06	22 46	21 20
13 Su	1 28 11	20 08 54	18 09	6 35	28 42	24 11	20 51	21 19	13 38	26 35	27 56	29 39	13 25	11 22	22 28	23 15	21 17
14 M	1 32 8	21 08 18	2♎28	6 36	0♏18	25 23	21 19	21 18	13 35	26 33	27 54	29 39	13 38	11 43	22 49	23 44	21 15
15 T	1 36 4	22 07 44	17 10	6 37	1 54	26 36	21 47	21 17	13 32	26 31	27 53	29 39	13 52	12 05	23 10	24 12	21 12
16 W	1 40 1	23 07 11	2♏09	6 38R	3 29	27 49	22 15	21 16	13 29	26 29	27 51	29 39	14 07	12 26	23 32	24 40	21 09
17 Th	1 43 57	24 06 41	17 20	6 36	5 04	29 01	22 42	21 14	13 26	26 27	27 50	29 39	14 21	12 48	23 53	25 09	21 06
18 F	1 47 54	25 06 12	2♐32	6 36	6 38	0♐14	23 09	21 13	13 23	26 25	27 48	29 39	14 35	13 10	24 14	25 37	21 04
19 Sa	1 51 51	26 05 46	17 35	6 35	8 11	1 26	23 36	21 11	13 20	26 23	27 47	29 39	14 50	13 32	24 35	26 05	21 01
20 Su	1 55 47	27 05 21	2♑22	6 32	9 44	2 39	24 02	21 09	13 18	26 21	27 45	29 39	15 05	13 54	24 57	26 34	20 58
21 M	1 59 44	28 04 59	16 45	6 29	11 16	3 51	24 29	21 07	13 15	26 19	27 44	29 40	15 20	14 16	25 18	27 02	20 56
22 T	2 3 40	29 04 40	0♒40	6 26	12 47	5 04	24 54	21 04	13 13	26 16	27 43	29 40	15 35	14 38	25 39	27 31	20 53
23 W	2 7 37	0♏04 22	14 07	6 23D	14 18	6 16	25 20	21 01	13 10	26 14	27 41	29 40	15 51	15 00	26 00	27 59	20 50
24 Th	2 11 33	1 04 07	27 08	6 23	15 48	7 28	25 45	20 59	13 08	26 12	27 40	29 41	16 06	15 22	26 22	28 27	20 47
25 F	2 15 30	2 03 54	10♓04	6 23	17 18	8 41	26 10	20 56	13 06	26 09	27 39	29 41	16 22	15 45	26 43	28 56	20 45
26 Sa	2 19 26	3 03 43	22 03	6 24	18 47	9 53	26 34	20 52	13 04	26 08	27 37	29 41	16 38	16 07	27 04	29 24	20 42
27 Su	2 23 23	4 03 34	4♈06	6 26	20 15	11 05	26 58	20 49	13 01	26 06	27 36	29 42	16 54	16 30	27 25	29 52	20 39
28 M	2 27 20	5 03 28	16 00	6 28	21 43	12 18	27 22	20 45	13 00	26 03	27 35	29 43	17 11	16 52	27 46	0≏21	20 37
29 T	2 31 16	6 03 23	27 48	6 29	23 10	13 30	27 45	20 42	12 58	26 01	27 34	29 43	17 27	17 15	28 07	0 49	20 34
30 W	2 35 13	7 03 21	9♉34	6 30	24 37	14 42	28 08	20 38	12 56	25 59	27 32	29 43	17 44	17 37	28 28	1 17	20 31
31 Th	2 39 9	8 03 22	21 22	6 32	26 03	15 54	28 31	20 33	12 54	25 56	27 31	29 44	18 01	18 00	28 49	1 45	20 29

EPHEMERIS CALCULATED FOR 12 MIDNIGHT GREENWICH MEAN TIME. ALL OTHER DATA AND FACING ASPECTARIAN PAGE IN **EASTERN TIME (BOLD)** AND PACIFIC TIME (REGULAR).

NOVEMBER 2024

☽ Last Aspect			☽ Ingress		
day	ET / hr:mn / PT	asp	sign day	ET / hr:mn / PT	
2	9:51 pm	⚹♇	♐ 2		10:19 pm
3	**12:51 am**	⚹♇	♐ 3	**1:19 am**	
5	**5:23 am** 2:23 am	□♆	♑ 5	**10:17 am**	7:17 am
7	**5:38 pm** 2:38 pm	☌♇	♒ 7	**5:58 pm**	2:58 pm
9	**7:23 pm** 4:23 pm	⚹♀	♓ 9	**11:00 pm**	8:00 pm
11	10:13 pm	⚹♇	♈ 11		10:26 pm
12	**1:13 am**	⚹♇	♈ 12	**1:26 am**	
13	10:50 pm	□♇	♉ 13		10:59 pm
14	**1:50 am**	□♇	♉ 14	**1:59 am**	
15	11:03 pm	△♇	♊ 15		11:09 pm
16	**2:03 am**	△♇	♊ 16	**2:09 am**	
17	**11:09 pm** 8:09 pm	⚼♆	♋ 18	**3:50 am**	12:50 am
20	**6:20 am** 3:20 am	△☉	♌ 20	**8:51 am**	5:51 am
22	**8:15 am** 5:15 am	⚼♅	♍ 22	**6:01 pm**	3:01 pm
24	9:35 pm	☍♆	♎ 25	**6:20 am**	3:20 am
25	**12:35 am**	☍♆	♎ 25	**6:20 am**	3:20 am
27	**4:14 am** 1:14 am	⚹☿	♏ 27	**7:21 pm**	4:21 pm
29	10:19 pm	△♆	♐ 30	**6:53 am**	3:53 am
30	**1:19 am**	△♆	♐ 30	**6:53 am**	3:53 am

☽ Phases & Eclipses			
phase	day	ET / hr:mn / PT	
New Moon	1	**8:47 am**	5:47 am
2nd Quarter	8		9:55 pm
2nd Quarter	9	**12:55 am**	
Full Moon	15	**4:28 pm**	1:28 pm
4th Quarter	22	**8:28 pm**	5:28 pm
New Moon	30		10:21 pm
New Moon	12/1	**1:21 am**	

Planet Ingress			
	day	ET / hr:mn / PT	
☿ ♐	2	**3:18 pm**	12:18 pm
⚵ ♏	3	**3:35 am**	1:35 am
♂ ♌	3	**11:10 pm**	8:10 pm
♀ ♑	11	**1:26 pm**	10:26 am
♇ ♒	19	**3:29 pm**	12:29 pm
☉ ♐	21	**2:56 pm**	11:56 am
♀ ♑	30	**5:37 pm**	2:37 pm

Planetary Motion				
		day	ET / hr:mn / PT	
♄	D	15	**9:20 am**	6:20 am
☿	℞	25	**9:42 pm**	6:42 pm

1 FRIDAY
☽☌☉ **8:47 am** 5:47 am
☽△♄ **3:20 pm** 12:20 pm
☽⚺♀ 11:53 pm

2 SATURDAY
☽⚺♀ **2:53 am**
☿△♂ **4:21 am** 1:21 am
☽⚻♃ **6:18 am** 3:18 am
☿⚹♇ **11:03 am** 8:03 am
☽☍♅ **5:06 pm** 2:06 pm
☽△♆ **8:20 pm** 5:20 pm
☽△♂ 9:40 pm
☽⚹♇ 9:51 pm
☽☌☿ 11:37 pm

3 SUNDAY
☽△♂ **12:40 am**
☽⚹♇ **12:51 am**
☽☌☿ **1:37 am**
♂☍♇ **6:37 am** 3:37 am
♀☍♃ **10:25 am** 7:25 am
☽⚺☉ 9:18 pm
☽□♄ 10:19 pm

4 MONDAY
☽⚺☉ **12:18 am**
☽□♄ **1:19 am**
☉△♄ **12:36 pm** 9:36 am
☽☍♃ **3:32 pm** 12:32 pm
☽☌♀ **6:51 pm** 3:51 pm
☽⚻♅ 11:10 pm

5 TUESDAY
☽⚻♅ **2:10 am**
☽□♆ **5:23 am** 2:23 am
☽⚺♇ **9:53 am** 6:53 am
☽⚻♂ **11:15 am** 8:15 am
☽⚺☿ **6:30 pm** 3:30 pm

6 WEDNESDAY
☽⚹♄ **10:17 am** 7:17 am
☽⚹☉ **2:11 pm** 11:11 am
☽⚻♃ **11:38 pm** 8:38 pm

7 THURSDAY
☽⚺♀ **8:51 am** 5:51 am
☽△♅ **10:01 am** 7:01 am
☽⚹♆ **1:12 pm** 10:12 am
☽☌♇ **5:38 pm** 2:38 pm
☽☍♂ **8:15 pm** 5:15 pm
♀⚻♅ **9:20 pm** 6:20 pm

8 FRIDAY
☽⚹☿ **7:52 am** 4:52 am
☽⚺♄ **4:48 pm** 1:48 pm
☽□☉ 9:55 pm

9 SATURDAY
☽□☉ **12:55 am**
☽△♃ **5:12 am** 2:12 am
♀□♆ **8:15 am** 5:15 am
☽□♅ **3:17 pm** 12:17 pm
☽⚺♆ **6:25 pm** 3:25 pm
☽⚹♀ **7:23 pm** 4:23 pm
☽⚺♇ **10:44 pm** 7:44 pm
☽⚻♂ 11:21 pm

10 SUNDAY
☽⚻♂ **2:21 am**
☽□☿ **5:20 pm** 2:20 pm
☽☌♄ **8:39 pm** 5:39 pm

11 MONDAY
☉⚻♃ **6:08 am** 3:08 am
☽□♃ **8:07 am** 5:07 am
☽△☉ **8:17 am** 5:17 am
♀⚺♇ **10:44 am** 7:44 am
☽⚹♅ **5:56 pm** 2:56 pm
☽☌♆ **9:01 pm** 6:01 pm
☽⚹♇ 10:13 pm
☽□♀ 11:29 pm

12 TUESDAY
☽⚹♇ **1:13 am**
☽□♀ **2:29 am**
☽△♂ **5:37 am** 2:37 am
☿□♄ **8:22 am** 5:22 am
☽⚺♄ **10:08 pm** 7:08 pm
☽△☿ **11:19 pm** 8:19 pm

13 WEDNESDAY
☽⚹♃ **8:51 am** 5:51 am
☽⚻☉ **12:54 pm** 9:54 am
☽⚺♅ **6:34 pm** 3:34 pm
☽⚺♆ **9:38 pm** 6:38 pm
☽□♇ 10:50 pm

14 THURSDAY
☽□♇ **1:50 am**
♀⚻♂ **3:02 am** 12:02 am
☽□♂ **6:57 am** 3:57 am
☽△♀ **7:13 am** 4:13 am
☽⚹♄ **10:18 pm** 7:18 pm

15 FRIDAY
☽⚻☿ **3:20 am** 12:20 am
☽⚺♃ **8:36 am** 5:36 am
☽☍☉ **4:28 pm** 1:28 pm
☽☌♅ **6:32 pm** 3:32 pm
☽⚹♆ **9:43 pm** 6:43 pm
☽△♇ 11:03 pm

16 SATURDAY
☽△♇ **2:03 am**
☽⚹♂ **8:00 am** 5:00 am
☽⚻♀ **11:41 am** 8:41 am
☉☍♅ **9:45 pm** 6:45 pm
☽□♄ **10:52 pm** 7:52 pm

17 SUNDAY
☽☍☿ **7:41 am** 4:41 am
☽☌♃ **9:07 am** 6:07 am
☽⚺♅ **7:42 pm** 4:42 pm
☽⚻☉ **9:27 pm** 6:27 pm
☽□♆ **11:09 pm** 8:09 pm

18 MONDAY
☽⚻♇ **3:47 am** 12:47 am
☿☍♃ **3:55 am** 12:55 am
☽⚺♂ **10:49 am** 7:49 am
☽☍♀ **6:35 pm** 3:35 pm
☉△♆ **9:07 pm** 6:07 pm
☽△♄ 10:48 pm

19 TUESDAY
☽△♄ **1:48 am**
☽⚺♃ **12:17 pm** 9:17 am
☽⚻☿ **2:43 pm** 11:43 am
☽⚹♅ **11:56 pm** 8:56 pm

20 WEDNESDAY
☽△♆ **3:46 am** 12:46 am
☽△☉ **6:20 am** 3:20 am
☽☍♇ **8:52 am** 5:52 am
☽☌♂ **5:15 pm** 2:15 pm

21 THURSDAY
☽⚻♀ **6:20 am** 3:20 am
☽⚻♄ **8:36 am** 5:36 am
☉⚹♇ **3:49 pm** 12:49 pm
☽⚹♃ **7:21 pm** 4:21 pm
☽△☿ 10:36 pm

22 FRIDAY
☽△☿ **1:36 am**
♀⚹♄ **6:55 am** 3:55 am
☽□♅ **8:15 am** 5:15 am
☽⚻♆ **12:31 pm** 9:31 am
☽⚻♇ **6:08 pm** 3:08 pm
☽□☉ **8:28 pm** 5:28 pm

23 SATURDAY
☽⚺♂ **3:53 am** 12:53 am
☽☍♄ **7:24 pm** 4:24 pm
☽△♀ **11:21 pm** 8:21 pm

24 SUNDAY
☽□♃ **6:04 am** 3:04 am
☽□☿ **3:10 pm** 12:10 pm
☽△♅ **7:59 pm** 4:59 pm
☽☍♆ 9:35 pm

25 MONDAY
☽☍♆ **12:35 am**
☽△♇ **6:33 am** 3:33 am
☽⚹☉ **2:32 pm** 11:32 am
☽⚹♂ **5:18 pm** 2:18 pm

26 TUESDAY
☽⚻♄ **8:25 am** 5:25 am
♀⚻♃ **1:08 pm** 10:08 am
☽△♃ **6:27 pm** 3:27 pm
☽□♀ **7:06 pm** 4:06 pm

27 WEDNESDAY
☉△♂ **3:06 am** 12:06 am
☽⚹☿ **4:14 am** 1:14 am
☽⚻♅ **8:51 am** 5:51 am
☽⚻♆ **1:36 pm** 10:36 am
☽□♇ **7:40 pm** 4:40 pm

28 THURSDAY
☽□♂ **6:49 am** 3:49 am
☽⚺☉ **9:05 am** 6:05 am
☽△♄ **9:07 pm** 6:07 pm

29 FRIDAY
☽⚻♃ **6:08 am** 3:08 am
☽⚹♀ **1:51 pm** 10:51 am
☽⚺☿ **2:13 pm** 11:13 am
☿⚺♀ **4:26 pm** 1:26 pm
☽☍♅ **8:32 pm** 5:32 pm
☽△♆ 10:19 pm

30 SATURDAY
☽△♆ **1:19 am**
☽⚹♇ **7:18 am** 4:18 am
☽△♂ **6:23 pm** 3:23 pm
☽☌☉ 10:21 pm

Eastern time in bold type
Pacific time in medium type

NOVEMBER 2024

DATE	SID.TIME	SUN	MOON	NODE	MERCURY	VENUS	MARS	JUPITER	SATURN	URANUS	NEPTUNE	PLUTO	CERES	PALLAS	JUNO	VESTA	CHIRON
1 F	2 43 6	9♏03 22	3♍14	6♈26R	27♏28	17♐06	28♋53	20♊29R	12♓53R	25♉54R	27♓30R	29♑44	18♑18	18♐23	29♎10	2♎13	20♈26R
2 Sa	2 47 2	10 03 26	15 12	6 21	28 53	18 18	29 14	20 24	12 51	25 52	27 29	29 45	18 35	18 45	29 32	2 41	20 24
3 Su	2 50 59	11 03 31	27 18	6 15	0♐39	19 30	29 36	20 20	12 50	25 49	27 28	29 45	18 52	19 08	29 53	3 10	20 21
4 M	2 54 55	12 03 39	9♎33	6 09	1 39	20 42	29 56	20 15	12 49	25 47	27 27	29 46	19 09	19 31	0♏13	3 38	20 19
5 T	2 58 52	13 03 48	21 59	6 02	3 01	21 54	0♌17	20 10	12 47	25 44	27 26	29 47	19 27	19 54	0 34	4 06	20 16
6 W	3 2 49	14 03 58	4♏37	5 56	4 22	23 06	0 37	20 05	12 46	25 42	27 25	29 47	19 45	20 17	0 55	4 34	20 14
7 Th	3 6 45	15 04 11	17 28	5 51	5 42	24 18	0 56	19 59	12 45	25 40	27 24	29 48	20 02	20 40	1 16	5 02	20 11
8 F	3 10 42	16 04 25	0♐42	5 48	7 01	25 30	1 15	19 54	12 45	25 37	27 23	29 49	20 20	21 03	1 37	5 30	20 09
9 Sa	3 14 38	17 04 40	13 58	5 47D	8 19	26 42	1 34	19 48	12 44	25 35	27 22	29 50	20 38	21 26	1 58	5 58	20 07
10 Su	3 18 35	18 04 57	27 41	5 47	9 35	27 53	1 51	19 42	12 43	25 32	27 21	29 51	20 57	21 49	2 19	6 26	20 04
11 M	3 22 31	19 05 15	11♑44	5 48	10 50	29 05	2 09	19 36	12 43	25 30	27 20	29 51	21 15	22 12	2 39	6 53	20 02
12 T	3 26 28	20 05 34	26 06	5♈50R	12 04	0♑17	2 26	19 30	12 42	25 27	27 19	29 52	21 34	22 35	3 00	7 21	20 00
13 W	3 30 24	21 05 55	10♒46	5 50	13 13	1 28	2 42	19 24	12 42	25 25	27 18	29 53	21 52	22 59	3 21	7 49	19 57
14 Th	3 34 21	22 06 17	25 39	5 48	14 22	2 40	2 58	19 17	12 42D	25 22	27 17	29 54	22 11	23 22	3 41	8 17	19 55
15 F	3 38 18	23 06 41	10♓38	5 44	15 28	3 51	3 14	19 11	12 42	25 20	27 17	29 55	22 30	23 45	4 02	8 44	19 53
16 Sa	3 42 14	24 07 07	25 35	5 38	16 31	5 02	3 28	19 04	12 42	25 17	27 16	29 56	22 49	24 09	4 22	9 12	19 51
17 Su	3 46 11	25 07 34	10♈21	5 31	17 31	6 14	3 43	18 57	12 42	25 15	27 15	29 57	23 08	24 32	4 43	9 40	19 49
18 M	3 50 7	26 08 03	24 47	5 22	18 28	7 25	3 56	18 50	12 42	25 12	27 15	29 58	23 27	24 55	5 03	10 07	19 46
19 T	3 54 4	27 08 33	8♉49	5 14	19 20	8 36	4 10	18 43	12 42	25 10	27 14	29 59	23 46	25 19	5 24	10 35	19 44
20 W	3 58 0	28 09 05	22 23	5 07	20 08	9 47	4 22	18 36	12 43	25 07	27 13	0♒00	24 06	25 42	5 44	11 02	19 42
21 Th	4 1 57	29 09 39	5♊29	5 02	20 50	10 58	4 34	18 29	12 43	25 05	27 13	0 01	24 25	26 06	6 04	11 30	19 40
22 F	4 5 53	0♐10 15	18 10	4 59	21 27	12 09	4 45	18 21	12 44	25 02	27 12	0 02	24 45	26 29	6 25	11 57	19 38
23 Sa	4 9 50	1 10 52	0♋30	4 59D	21 57	13 20	4 56	18 14	12 44	25 00	27 12	0 04	25 05	26 53	6 45	12 24	19 37
24 Su	4 13 47	2 11 31	12 33	4 59	22 20	14 30	5 06	18 06	12 45	24 57	27 11	0 05	25 25	27 16	7 05	12 52	19 35
25 M	4 17 43	3 12 12	24 26	5 00R	22 34	15 41	5 15	17 59	12 46	24 55	27 11	0 06	25 45	27 40	7 25	13 19	19 33
26 T	4 21 40	4 12 54	6♌13	5 00	22 40R	16 52	5 24	17 51	12 47	24 52	27 10	0 07	26 05	28 03	7 45	13 46	19 31
27 W	4 25 36	5 13 38	17 59	4 59	22 36	18 03	5 32	17 43	12 48	24 50	27 10	0 08	26 25	28 27	8 05	14 13	19 29
28 Th	4 29 33	6 14 23	29 50	4 56	22 22	19 13	5 39	17 35	12 50	24 47	27 09	0 10	26 45	28 50	8 25	14 40	19 28
29 F	4 33 29	7 15 10	11♍46	4 42	21 59	20 23	5 45	17 27	12 51	24 45	27 09	0 11	27 06	29 14	8 45	15 07	19 26
30 Sa	4 37 26	8 15 58	23 55	4 42	21 21	21 33	5 51	17 19	12 53	24 43	27 09	0 12	27 26	29 38	9 05	15 34	19 24

EPHEMERIS CALCULATED FOR 12 MIDNIGHT GREENWICH MEAN TIME. ALL OTHER DATA AND FACING ASPECTARIAN PAGE IN EASTERN TIME (**BOLD**) AND PACIFIC TIME (REGULAR).

DECEMBER 2024

☽ Last Aspect day	ET / hr:mn / PT		asp	☽ Ingress sign	day	ET / hr:mn / PT	
2	**10:47 am**	7:47 am	□♆	♑	2	**4:09 pm**	1:09 pm
4	**6:34 pm**	3:34 pm	☌♀	♒	4	**11:21 pm**	8:21 pm
6	**7:01 pm**	4:01 pm	□♅	♓	7	**4:49 am**	1:49 am
9	**3:45 am**	12:45 am	☌♆	♈	9	**8:38 am**	5:38 am
10	**5:13 pm**	2:13 pm	△☉	♉	11	**10:55 am**	7:55 am
13	**7:39 am**	4:39 am	⚹♆	♊	13	**12:22 pm**	9:22 am
15	**9:32 am**	6:32 am	□♆	♋	15	**2:21 pm**	11:21 am
17	**1:33 pm**	10:33 am	△♆	♌	17	**6:39 pm**	3:39 pm
19		9:19 pm	△☉	♍	19		11:37 pm
20	**12:19 am**		△☉	♍	20	**2:37 am**	
22	**8:27 am**	5:27 am	☍♆	♎	22	**2:08 pm**	11:08 am
24	**5:44 am**	2:44 am	△♀	♏	25	**3:06 am**	12:06 am
27	**9:24 am**	6:24 am	△♆	♐	27	**2:46 pm**	11:46 am
29	**6:34 pm**	3:34 pm	□♆	♑	29	**11:37 pm**	8:37 pm
31		10:02 pm	⚹♆	♒	1/1	**5:50 am**	2:50 am
1/1	**1:02 am**		⚹♆	♒	1/1	**5:50 am**	2:50 am

☽ Phases & Eclipses phase	day	ET / hr:mn / PT	
New Moon	11/30		10:21 pm
New Moon	1	**1:21 am**	
2nd Quarter	8	**10:27 am**	7:27 am
Full Moon	15	**4:02 am**	1:02 am
4th Quarter	22	**5:18 pm**	2:18 pm
New Moon	30	**5:27 pm**	2:27 pm

Planet Ingress		day	ET / hr:mn / PT	
♀	♒	6		10:13 pm
♀	♒	7	**1:13 am**	
⚳	♒	7	**4:16 am**	1:16 am
☉	♑	21	**4:21 am**	1:21 am

Planetary Motion		day	ET / hr:mn / PT	
♂	℞	6	**6:33 pm**	3:33 pm
♆	D	7	**6:43 pm**	3:43 pm
☿	D	15	**3:56 am**	12:56 pm
⚷	D	29	**4:13 pm**	1:13 pm

1 SUNDAY
☽ ☌ ☉ **1:21 am**
☽ □ ♄ **7:49 am** 4:49 am
☽ ☍ ♃ **3:45 pm** 12:45 pm
☽ ☌ ☿ **8:29 pm** 5:29 pm

2 MONDAY
☽ ⚺ ♀ **5:39 am** 2:39 am
☽ ⚻ ♅ **6:02 am** 3:02 am
♀ △ ♅ **9:43 am** 6:43 am
☽ □ ♆ **10:47 am** 7:47 am
☽ ⚺ ♇ **4:39 pm** 1:39 pm

3 TUESDAY
☽ ⚻ ♂ **3:30 am** 12:30 am
☽ ⚺ ☉ **2:43 pm** 11:43 am
☽ ⚹ ♄ **4:17 pm** 1:17 pm
☽ ⚻ ♃ **11:13 pm** 8:13 pm
☽ ⚺ ☿ **11:43 pm** 8:43 pm

4 WEDNESDAY
☿ ☍ ♃ **5:16 am** 2:16 am
☉ □ ♄ **11:18 am** 8:18 am
☽ △ ♅ **1:24 pm** 10:24 am
♀ ⚹ ♆ **1:52 pm** 10:52 am
☽ ⚹ ♆ **6:09 pm** 3:09 pm
☽ ☌ ♀ **6:34 pm** 3:34 pm
☽ ☌ ♇ **11:56 pm** 8:56 pm

5 THURSDAY
☽ ☍ ♂ **10:28 am** 7:28 am
☉ ☌ ☿ **9:18 pm** 6:18 pm
☽ ⚺ ♄ **10:50 pm** 7:50 pm
☽ ⚹ ☿ 9:56 pm
☽ ⚹ ☉ 10:38 pm

6 FRIDAY
☽ ⚹ ☿ **12:56 am**
☽ ⚹ ☉ **1:38 am**
☽ △ ♃ **4:53 am** 1:53 am
☽ □ ♅ **7:01 pm** 4:01 pm
☿ □ ♄ **8:53 pm** 5:53 pm
☽ ⚺ ♆ **11:46 pm** 8:46 pm

7 SATURDAY
☽ ⚺ ♀ **5:09 am** 2:09 am
☽ ⚺ ♇ **5:29 am** 2:29 am
♀ ☌ ♇ **9:08 am** 6:08 am
☽ ⚻ ♂ **3:36 pm** 12:36 pm
☉ ☍ ♃ **3:58 pm** 12:58 pm
☽ □ ☿ 9:58 pm

8 SUNDAY
☽ □ ☿ **12:58 am**
☽ ☌ ♄ **3:43 am** 12:43 am
☽ □ ♃ **8:56 am** 5:56 am
☽ □ ☉ **10:27 am** 7:27 am
☽ ⚹ ♅ **11:00 pm** 8:00 pm

9 MONDAY
☽ ☌ ♆ **3:45 am** 12:45 am
☽ ⚹ ♇ **9:22 am** 6:22 am
☽ ⚹ ♀ **1:33 pm** 10:33 am
☽ △ ♂ **6:59 pm** 3:59 pm
☽ △ ☿ 9:19 pm

10 TUESDAY
☽ △ ☿ **12:19 am**
☽ ⚺ ♄ **6:59 am** 3:59 am
☽ ⚹ ♃ **11:24 am** 8:24 am
☽ △ ☉ **5:13 pm** 2:13 pm
☽ ⚺ ♅ 10:25 pm

11 WEDNESDAY
☽ ⚺ ♅ **1:25 am**
☽ ⚺ ♆ **6:10 am** 3:10 am
☽ □ ♇ **11:43 am** 8:43 am
☽ □ ♀ **8:01 pm** 5:01 pm
☽ □ ♂ **8:50 pm** 5:50 pm
☽ ⚻ ☿ **11:29 pm** 8:29 pm

12 THURSDAY
♀ ☍ ♂ **5:46 am** 2:46 am
☽ ⚹ ♄ **8:55 am** 5:55 am
☽ ⚺ ♃ **12:39 pm** 9:39 am
☽ ⚻ ☉ **10:34 pm** 7:34 pm
☿ ⚹ ♀ 11:45 pm
☽ ☌ ♅ 11:49 pm

13 FRIDAY
☿ ⚹ ♀ **2:45 am**
☽ ☌ ♅ **2:49 am**
☽ ⚹ ♆ **7:39 am** 4:39 am
☽ △ ♇ **1:15 pm** 10:15 am
☽ ⚹ ♂ **9:58 pm** 6:58 pm
☽ ☍ ☿ **11:20 pm** 8:20 pm
☽ △ ♀ 10:40 pm

14 SATURDAY
☽ △ ♀ **1:40 am**
☽ □ ♄ **10:34 am** 7:34 am
☽ ☌ ♃ **1:43 pm** 10:43 am

15 SUNDAY
☽ ☍ ☉ **4:02 am** 1:02 am
☽ ⚺ ♅ **4:27 am** 1:27 am
☽ □ ♆ **9:32 am** 6:32 am
☉ ⚻ ♅ **9:44 am** 6:44 am
☽ ⚻ ♇ **3:22 pm** 12:22 pm
☽ ⚺ ♂ **11:52 pm** 8:52 pm
☽ ⚻ ☿ 10:16 pm

16 MONDAY
☽ ⚻ ☿ **1:16 am**
☽ ⚻ ♀ **8:34 am** 5:34 am
☽ △ ♄ **1:34 pm** 10:34 am
☽ ⚺ ♃ **4:11 pm** 1:11 pm

17 TUESDAY
☽ ⚹ ♅ **8:02 am** 5:02 am
☽ ⚻ ☉ **11:56 am** 8:56 am
☽ △ ♆ **1:33 pm** 10:33 am
☽ ☍ ♇ **7:50 pm** 4:50 pm

18 WEDNESDAY
☽ ☌ ♂ **4:13 am** 1:13 am
☽ △ ☿ **7:15 am** 4:15 am
☉ □ ♆ **9:29 am** 6:29 am
☽ ☍ ♀ **7:10 pm** 4:10 pm
☽ ⚻ ♄ **7:39 pm** 4:39 pm
☽ ⚹ ♃ **9:40 pm** 6:40 pm
♀ ⚺ ♄ 9:52 pm

19 THURSDAY
♀ ⚺ ♄ **12:52 am**
☽ □ ♅ **3:04 pm** 12:04 pm
☽ ⚻ ♆ **9:10 pm** 6:10 pm
♀ △ ♃ **9:11 pm** 6:11 pm
☽ △ ☉ 9:19 pm

20 FRIDAY
☽ △ ☉ **12:19 am**
☽ ⚻ ♇ **4:01 am** 1:01 am
☽ ⚺ ♂ **12:05 pm** 9:05 am
☽ □ ☿ **6:46 pm** 3:46 pm

21 SATURDAY
☽ ☍ ♄ **5:39 am** 2:39 am
☽ □ ♃ **6:55 am** 3:55 am
☽ ⚻ ♀ **10:45 am** 7:45 am
☉ ⚺ ♇ **10:32 pm** 7:32 pm
☽ △ ♅ 10:50 pm

22 SUNDAY
☽ △ ♅ **1:50 am**
☽ ☍ ♆ **8:27 am** 5:27 am
☽ △ ♇ **3:44 pm** 12:44 pm
☽ □ ☉ **5:18 pm** 2:18 pm
☽ ⚹ ♂ **10:59 pm** 7:59 pm

23 Monday
☽ ⚹ ☿ **11:22 am** 8:22 am
☽ ⚻ ♄ **6:30 pm** 3:30 pm
☽ △ ♃ **6:51 pm** 3:51 pm

24 TUESDAY
☽ △ ♀ **5:44 am** 2:44 am
☽ ⚻ ♅ **2:35 pm** 11:35 am
♃ □ ♄ **4:59 pm** 1:59 pm
☽ ⚻ ♆ **9:28 pm** 6:28 pm
☉ ⚻ ♂ 9:00 pm

25 WEDNESDAY
☉ ⚻ ♂ **12:00 am**
☽ □ ♇ **4:51 am** 1:51 am
☽ □ ♂ **10:44 am** 7:44 am
☽ ⚹ ☉ **12:00 pm** 9:00 am

26 THURSDAY
☽ ⚺ ☿ **5:43 am** 2:43 am
☽ ⚻ ♃ **6:55 am** 3:55 am
☽ △ ♄ **7:31 am** 4:31 am
☿ ☍ ♃ **5:48 pm** 2:48 pm
☽ □ ♀ 9:08 pm
☿ □ ♄ 11:29 pm
☽ ☍ ♅ 11:34 pm

27 FRIDAY
☽ □ ♀ **12:08 am**
☿ □ ♄ **2:29 am**
☽ ☍ ♅ **2:34 am**
☽ △ ♆ **9:24 am** 6:24 am
☽ ⚹ ♇ **4:36 pm** 1:36 pm
☽ △ ♂ **8:50 pm** 5:50 pm
♀ □ ♅ 11:42 pm

28 SATURDAY
♀ □ ♅ **2:42 am**
☽ ⚺ ☉ **4:35 am** 1:35 am
☽ ☍ ♃ **4:50 pm** 1:50 pm
☽ □ ♄ **6:15 pm** 3:15 pm
☽ ☌ ☿ **10:01 pm** 7:01 pm

29 SUNDAY
☽ ⚻ ♅ **11:55 am** 8:55 am
☽ ⚹ ♀ **3:03 pm** 12:03 pm
☽ □ ♆ **6:34 pm** 3:34 pm
☽ ⚺ ♇ 10:29 pm

30 MONDAY
☽ ⚺ ♇ **1:29 am**
☽ ⚻ ♂ **4:07 am** 1:07 am
☽ ☌ ☉ **5:27 pm** 2:27 pm
☽ ⚻ ♃ **11:56 pm** 8:56 pm
☽ ⚹ ♄ 11:03 pm

31 TUESDAY
☽ ⚹ ♄ **2:03 am**
♀ ⚺ ♆ **9:38 am** 6:38 am
☽ ⚺ ☿ **11:00 am** 8:00 am
☽ △ ♅ **6:30 pm** 3:30 pm
☽ ⚹ ♆ 10:02 pm
☽ ⚺ ♀ 11:21 pm

Eastern time in bold type
Pacific time in medium type

DECEMBER 2024

DATE	SID.TIME	SUN	MOON	NODE	MERCURY	VENUS	MARS	JUPITER	SATURN	URANUS	NEPTUNE	PLUTO	CERES	PALLAS	JUNO	VESTA	CHIRON
1 Su	4 41 22	9♐16 48	6♈15	4♈31R	20♐35R	22♑43	5♌56	17♊11R	12♓56	24♉40R	27♓09R	0♒14	27♏47	0♏47	9♍25	16♎01	19♈23R
2 M	4 45 19	10 17 39	18 47	4 18	19 37	23 53	6 00	17 03	12 58	24 38	27 08	0 15	28 07	0 25	9 44	16 28	19 21
3 T	4 49 16	11 18 31	1♉31	4 06	18 31	25 03	6 04	16 55	12 58	24 35	27 08	0 16	28 28	0 49	10 04	16 55	19 20
4 W	4 53 12	12 19 24	14 28	3 54	17 17	26 13	6 07	16 47	12 59	24 33	27 08	0 18	28 49	1 12	10 24	17 21	19 18
5 Th	4 57 9	13 20 18	27 36	3 44	15 57	27 23	6 09	16 39	13 01	24 31	27 08	0 19	29 10	1 36	10 43	17 48	19 17
6 F	5 1 5	14 21 12	10♊55	3 37	14 35	28 33	6 10R	16 31	13 04	24 28	27 08	0 21	29 31	2 00	11 03	18 15	19 16
7 Sa	5 5 2	15 22 08	24 25	3 33	13 12	29 42	6 10	16 23	13 06	24 26	27 08D	0 22	29 52	2 24	11 22	18 41	19 15
8 Su	5 8 58	16 23 04	8♋07	3♈31D	11 52	0♒51	6 10	16 14	13 08	24 24	27 08	0 23	0♐13	2 47	11 41	19 07	19 13
9 M	5 12 55	17 24 01	22 01	3 31R	10 37	2 01	6 09	16 06	13 10	24 22	27 08	0 25	0 34	3 11	12 01	19 34	19 12
10 T	5 16 51	18 24 58	6♌07	3 31	9 30	3 10	6 07	15 58	13 13	24 19	27 08	0 26	0 56	3 35	12 20	20 00	19 11
11 W	5 20 48	19 25 56	20 25	3 30	8 32	4 19	6 04	15 50	13 15	24 17	27 09	0 28	1 17	3 59	12 39	20 26	19 10
12 Th	5 24 45	20 26 54	4♍53	3 27	7 44	5 27	6 00	15 42	13 18	24 15	27 09	0 30	1 38	4 22	12 58	20 52	19 09
13 F	5 28 41	21 27 54	19 27	3 21	7 08	6 36	5 56	15 34	13 21	24 13	27 09	0 31	2 00	4 46	13 17	21 18	19 08
14 Sa	5 32 38	22 28 54	4♎01	3 12	6 42	7 44	5 50	15 26	13 24	24 11	27 09	0 33	2 21	5 10	13 36	21 44	19 07
15 Su	5 36 34	23 29 54	18 29	3 01	6 28D	8 53	5 44	15 18	13 27	24 09	27 09	0 34	2 43	5 34	13 54	22 10	19 06
16 M	5 40 31	24 30 56	2♏44	2 49	6 24	10 01	5 37	15 10	13 30	24 07	27 09	0 36	3 05	5 57	14 13	22 36	19 05
17 T	5 44 27	25 31 58	16 39	2 36	6 30	11 09	5 29	15 02	13 33	24 05	27 09	0 38	3 27	6 21	14 32	23 01	19 05
18 W	5 48 24	26 33 00	0♐12	2 25	6 45	12 16	5 20	14 54	13 36	24 03	27 10	0 39	3 49	6 45	14 50	23 27	19 04
19 Th	5 52 21	27 34 04	13 19	2 16	7 09	13 24	5 11	14 46	13 40	24 01	27 10	0 41	4 10	7 09	15 09	23 52	19 03
20 F	5 56 17	28 35 08	26 02	2 10	7 40	14 31	5 01	14 38	13 43	23 59	27 10	0 43	4 32	7 32	15 27	24 18	19 03
21 Sa	6 0 14	29 36 13	8♑25	2 07	8 18	15 39	4 49	14 31	13 47	23 57	27 11	0 44	4 55	7 56	15 45	24 43	19 02
22 Su	6 4 10	0♑37 19	20 30	2 06	9 02	16 46	4 37	14 23	13 50	23 55	27 11	0 46	5 17	8 20	16 03	25 08	19 02
23 M	6 8 7	1 38 25	2♒24	2 06	9 51	17 52	4 25	14 15	13 54	23 53	27 12	0 48	5 39	8 43	16 21	25 33	19 01
24 T	6 12 3	2 39 33	14 12	2 05	10 45	18 59	4 11	14 08	13 58	23 51	27 12	0 50	6 01	9 07	16 39	25 58	19 01
25 W	6 16 0	3 40 40	26 00	2 04	11 43	20 05	3 57	14 01	14 02	23 49	27 13	0 51	6 23	9 31	16 57	26 23	19 01
26 Th	6 19 56	4 41 49	7♓55	2 02	12 45	21 11	3 41	13 54	14 06	23 48	27 14	0 53	6 46	9 54	17 15	26 47	19 00
27 F	6 23 53	5 42 58	19 55	1 54	13 50	22 17	3 25	13 47	14 10	23 46	27 14	0 55	7 08	10 18	17 33	27 12	19 00
28 Sa	6 27 50	6 44 07	2♈11	1 45	14 58	23 23	3 09	13 40	14 14	23 44	27 15	0 57	7 30	10 42	17 50	27 37	19 00
29 Su	6 31 46	7 45 17	14 42	1 33	16 09	24 28	2 51	13 33	14 18	23 43	27 16	0 58	7 53	11 05	18 08	28 01	19 00D
30 M	6 35 43	8 46 28	27 30	1 19	17 21	25 33	2 33	13 26	14 23	23 41	27 16	1 00	8 16	11 29	18 25	28 25	19 00
31 T	6 39 39	9 47 38	10♉35	1 06	18 36	26 38	2 14	13 19	14 27	23 40	27 17	1 02	8 38	11 53	18 42	28 49	19 00

EPHEMERIS CALCULATED FOR 12 MIDNIGHT GREENWICH MEAN TIME. ALL OTHER DATA AND FACING ASPECTARIAN PAGE IN **EASTERN TIME (BOLD)** AND PACIFIC TIME (REGULAR).

JANUARY 2025

☽ Last Aspect day	ET / hr:mn / PT		asp	☽ Ingress sign day	ET / hr:mn / PT	
12/31		10:02 pm	⚹♆	≈ 1	**5:50 am**	2:50 am
1	**1:02 am**		⚹♆	≈ 1	**5:50 am**	2:50 am
2	**11:13 pm**	8:13 pm	□♅	♓ 3	**10:21 am**	7:21 am
5	**9:30 am**	6:30 am	☌♆	♈ 5	**2:01 pm**	11:01 am
7	**4:16 pm**	1:16 pm	□♂	♉ 7	**5:11 pm**	2:11 pm
9	**5:50 pm**	2:50 pm	⚹♂	♊ 9	**8:07 pm**	5:07 pm
11	**7:03 pm**	4:03 pm	□♆	♋ 11	**11:24 pm**	8:24 pm
13	**11:46 pm**	8:46 pm	△♆	♌ 14	**4:12 am**	1:12 am
15	**11:10 pm**	8:10 pm	□♅	♍ 16	**11:46 am**	8:46 am
18	**9:01 pm**	6:01 pm	△☉	♎ 18	**10:33 pm**	7:33 pm
20	**11:34 pm**	8:34 pm	□♂	♏ 21	**11:20 am**	8:20 am
23	**7:03 pm**	4:03 pm	△♆	♐ 23	**11:29 pm**	8:29 pm
26	**4:40 am**	1:40 am	□♆	♑ 26	**8:43 am**	5:43 am
28	**10:48 am**	7:48 am	⚹♆	≈ 28	**2:31 pm**	11:31 am
30	**6:29 am**	3:29 am	□♅	♓ 30	**5:52 pm**	2:52 pm

☽ Phases & Eclipses phase	day	ET / hr:mn / PT	
2nd Quarter	6	**6:56 pm**	3:56 pm
Full Moon	13	**5:27 pm**	2:27 pm
4th Quarter	21	**3:31 pm**	12:31 pm
New Moon	29	**7:36 am**	4:36 am

Planet Ingress	day	ET / hr:mn / PT	
⯓ ♏	2	**6:15 pm**	3:15 pm
♀ ♓	2	**10:24 pm**	7:24 pm
♂ ♋	6	**5:44 am**	2:44 am
☿ ♑	8	**5:30 am**	2:30 am
☉ ≈	19	**3:00 pm**	12:00 pm
☿ ≈	27	**9:53 pm**	6:53 pm

Planetary Motion		day	ET / hr:mn / PT	
♅	D	30	**11:22 am**	8:22 am

1 WEDNESDAY
- ☽ ⚹ ♆ **1:02 am**
- ☽ ⚺ ♀ **2:21 am**
- ☽ ☌ ♇ **7:45 am** 4:45 am
- ☽ ☍ ♂ **8:53 am** 5:53 am

2 THURSDAY
- ☽ ⚺ ☉ **3:19 am** 12:19 am
- ☽ △ ♃ **4:51 am** 1:51 am
- ☽ ⚺ ♄ **7:37 am** 4:37 am
- ☽ ⚹ ☿ **9:34 pm** 6:34 pm
- ☉ ⚻ ♃ **10:18 pm** 7:18 pm
- ☽ □ ♅ **11:13 pm** 8:13 pm
- ♂ ☍ ♇ 11:21 pm

3 FRIDAY
- ♂ ☍ ♇ **2:21 am**
- ☽ ⚺ ♆ **5:44 am** 2:44 am
- ☽ ☌ ♀ **11:21 am** 8:21 am
- ☽ ⚻ ♂ **12:05 pm** 9:05 am
- ☽ ⚺ ♇ **12:21 pm** 9:21 am
- ☿ ⚻ ♅ **2:19 pm** 11:19 am
- ♀ ⚻ ♂ **6:41 pm** 3:41 pm
- ♀ ⚺ ♇ 9:47 pm

4 SATURDAY
- ♀ ⚺ ♇ **12:47 am**
- ☽ □ ♃ **8:34 am** 5:34 am
- ☽ ⚹ ☉ **11:32 am** 8:32 am
- ☽ ☌ ♄ **11:56 am** 8:56 am
- ☉ ⚹ ♄ **5:36 pm** 2:36 pm
- ☽ ⚹ ♅ 11:56 pm

5 SUNDAY
- ☽ ⚹ ♅ **2:56 am**
- ☽ □ ☿ **6:57 am** 3:57 am
- ☽ ☌ ♆ **9:30 am** 6:30 am
- ☽ △ ♂ **2:25 pm** 11:25 am
- ☽ ⚹ ♇ **4:06 pm** 1:06 pm
- ☽ ⚺ ♀ **7:11 pm** 4:11 pm

6 MONDAY
- ☿ □ ♆ **8:56 am** 5:56 am
- ☽ ⚹ ♃ **11:38 am** 8:38 am
- ☽ ⚺ ♄ **3:38 pm** 12:38 pm
- ☽ □ ☉ **6:56 pm** 3:56 pm

7 TUESDAY
- ☽ ⚺ ♅ **6:07 am** 3:07 am
- ☽ ⚺ ♆ **12:46 pm** 9:46 am
- ☽ △ ☿ **3:49 pm** 12:49 pm
- ☽ □ ♂ **4:16 pm** 1:16 pm
- ☽ □ ♇ **7:22 pm** 4:22 pm
- ☿ ⚻ ♂ **7:28 pm** 4:28 pm
- ☽ ⚹ ♀ 11:23 pm

8 WEDNESDAY
- ☽ ⚹ ♀ **2:23 am**
- ☽ ⚺ ♃ **2:21 pm** 11:21 am
- ☽ ⚹ ♄ **6:57 pm** 3:57 pm
- ☽ △ ☉ 10:53 pm

9 THURSDAY
- ☽ △ ☉ **1:53 am**
- ☿ ⚺ ♇ **3:48 am** 12:48 am
- ☽ ☌ ♅ **9:00 am** 6:00 am
- ☽ ⚹ ♆ **3:46 pm** 12:46 pm
- ☽ ⚹ ♂ **5:50 pm** 2:50 pm
- ☽ △ ♇ **10:24 pm** 7:24 pm
- ☽ ⚻ ☿ 9:28 pm

10 FRIDAY
- ☽ ⚻ ☿ **12:28 am**
- ☽ □ ♀ **9:18 am** 6:18 am
- ☽ ☌ ♃ **5:01 pm** 2:01 pm
- ☽ □ ♄ **10:15 pm** 7:15 pm

11 SATURDAY
- ☽ ⚻ ☉ **8:56 am** 5:56 am
- ☽ ⚺ ♅ **12:04 pm** 9:04 am
- ☽ □ ♆ **7:03 pm** 4:03 pm
- ☽ ⚺ ♂ **7:40 pm** 4:40 pm
- ☽ ⚻ ♇ 10:51 pm

12 SUNDAY
- ☽ ⚻ ♇ **1:51 am**
- ☽ ☍ ☿ **9:53 am** 6:53 am
- ♂ △ ♆ **4:16 pm** 1:16 pm
- ☽ △ ♀ **4:56 pm** 1:56 pm
- ☽ ⚺ ♃ **8:28 pm** 5:28 pm
- ☽ △ ♄ 11:30 pm

13 MONDAY
- ☽ △ ♄ **2:30 am**
- ☉ △ ♅ **3:13 am** 12:13 am
- ☽ ⚹ ♅ **4:22 pm** 1:22 pm
- ☽ ☍ ☉ **5:27 pm** 2:27 pm
- ☽ ☌ ♂ **10:48 pm** 7:48 pm
- ☽ △ ♆ **11:46 pm** 8:46 pm

14 TUESDAY
- ☽ ☍ ♇ **6:53 am** 3:53 am
- ♀ □ ♃ **2:48 pm** 11:48 am
- ☽ ⚻ ☿ **9:56 pm** 6:56 pm
- ☽ ⚹ ♃ 10:58 pm
- ☽ ⚻ ♀ 11:57 pm

15 WEDNESDAY
- ☽ ⚹ ♃ **1:58 am**
- ☽ ⚻ ♀ **2:57 am**
- ☽ ⚻ ♄ **8:59 am** 5:59 am
- ☉ ☍ ♂ **9:39 pm** 6:39 pm
- ☽ □ ♅ **11:10 pm** 8:10 pm

16 THURSDAY
- ☽ ⚺ ♂ **4:21 am** 1:21 am
- ☽ ⚻ ☉ **5:10 am** 2:10 am
- ☽ ⚻ ♆ **7:09 am** 4:09 am
- ☿ ⚻ ♃ **7:51 am** 4:51 am
- ☽ ⚻ ♇ **2:45 pm** 11:45 am

17 FRIDAY
- ☉ ⚹ ♆ **6:20 am** 3:20 am
- ☽ □ ♃ **10:33 am** 7:33 am
- ☽ △ ☿ **2:28 pm** 11:28 am
- ☽ ☍ ♀ **4:46 pm** 1:46 pm
- ☽ ☍ ♄ **6:43 pm** 3:43 pm

18 SATURDAY
- ☽ △ ♅ **9:13 am** 6:13 am
- ☽ ⚹ ♂ **12:53 pm** 9:53 am
- ☽ ☍ ♆ **5:48 pm** 2:48 pm
- ♀ ☌ ♄ **8:26 pm** 5:26 pm
- ☽ △ ☉ **9:01 pm** 6:01 pm
- ☽ △ ♇ 10:51 pm
- ☿ ⚹ ♄ 11:38 pm

19 SUNDAY
- ☽ △ ♇ **1:51 am**
- ☿ ⚹ ♄ **2:38 am**
- ☿ ⚹ ♀ **11:32 am** 8:32 am
- ☽ △ ♃ **10:06 pm** 7:06 pm

20 MONDAY
- ☽ ⚻ ♄ **7:21 am** 4:21 am
- ☽ ⚻ ♀ **10:03 am** 7:03 am
- ☽ □ ☿ **11:23 am** 8:23 am
- ☽ ⚻ ♅ **9:43 pm** 6:43 pm
- ☽ □ ♂ **11:34 pm** 8:34 pm

21 TUESDAY
- ☽ ⚻ ♆ **6:38 am** 3:38 am
- ☉ ☌ ♇ **7:29 am** 4:29 am
- ☽ □ ♇ **2:50 pm** 11:50 am
- ☽ □ ☉ **3:31 pm** 12:31 pm

22 WEDNESDAY
- ☽ ⚻ ♃ **10:44 am** 7:44 am
- ☽ △ ♄ **8:39 pm** 5:39 pm

23 THURSDAY
- ☽ △ ♀ **3:51 am** 12:51 am
- ☽ ⚹ ☿ **9:10 am** 6:10 am
- ♂ ⚹ ♅ **10:08 am** 7:08 am
- ☽ △ ♂ **10:12 am** 7:12 am
- ☽ ☍ ♅ **10:13 am** 7:13 am
- ☿ ☍ ♂ **3:49 pm** 12:49 pm
- ☿ △ ♅ **5:07 pm** 2:07 pm
- ☽ △ ♆ **7:03 pm** 4:03 pm

24 FRIDAY
- ☽ ⚹ ♇ **3:01 am** 12:01 am
- ☽ ⚹ ☉ **8:55 am** 5:55 am
- ☽ ☍ ♃ **9:45 pm** 6:45 pm

25 SATURDAY
- ☽ □ ♄ **7:51 am** 4:51 am
- ☽ □ ♀ **6:34 pm** 3:34 pm
- ☽ ⚻ ♂ **6:36 pm** 3:36 pm
- ♀ △ ♂ **6:54 pm** 3:54 pm
- ☽ ⚻ ♅ **8:11 pm** 5:11 pm

26 SUNDAY
- ☽ ⚺ ☿ **3:25 am** 12:25 am
- ☽ □ ♆ **4:40 am** 1:40 am
- ☽ ⚺ ♇ **12:11 pm** 9:11 am
- ☿ ⚹ ♆ **1:33 pm** 10:33 am
- ♀ ⚹ ♅ **6:11 pm** 3:11 pm
- ☽ ⚺ ☉ **10:20 pm** 7:20 pm

27 MONDAY
- ☽ ⚻ ♃ **5:30 am** 2:30 am
- ☽ ⚹ ♄ **3:33 pm** 12:33 pm
- ☽ ☍ ♂ **11:52 pm** 8:52 pm
- ☽ △ ♅ 11:42 pm

28 TUESDAY
- ☽ △ ♅ **2:42 am**
- ☽ ⚹ ♀ **4:53 am** 1:53 am
- ☽ ⚹ ♆ **10:48 am** 7:48 am
- ☽ ☌ ☿ **4:45 pm** 1:45 pm
- ☽ ☌ ♇ **5:56 pm** 2:56 pm
- ☿ ☌ ♇ 11:52 pm

29 WEDNESDAY
- ☿ ☌ ♇ **2:52 am**
- ☽ ☌ ☉ **7:36 am** 4:36 am
- ☽ △ ♃ **10:08 am** 7:08 am
- ☽ ⚺ ♄ **8:12 pm** 5:12 pm
- ☽ ⚻ ♂ 11:36 pm

30 THURSDAY
- ☽ ⚻ ♂ **2:36 am**
- ☽ □ ♅ **6:29 am** 3:29 am
- ☽ ⚺ ♀ **11:48 am** 8:48 am
- ☽ ⚺ ♆ **2:23 pm** 11:23 am
- ☉ △ ♃ **5:59 pm** 2:59 pm
- ☽ ⚺ ♇ **9:17 pm** 6:17 pm
- ☽ ⚺ ☿ 11:43 pm

31 FRIDAY
- ☽ ⚺ ☿ **2:43 am**
- ☽ □ ♃ **12:52 pm** 9:52 am
- ☽ ⚺ ☉ **2:20 pm** 11:20 am
- ☽ ☌ ♄ **11:09 pm** 8:09 pm

Eastern time in bold type
Pacific time in medium type

JANUARY 2025

DATE	SID.TIME	SUN	MOON	NODE	MERCURY	VENUS	MARS	JUPITER	SATURN	URANUS	NEPTUNE	PLUTO	CERES	PALLAS	JUNO	VESTA	CHIRON
1 W	6 43 36	10♑48 49	23♒55	0♈53R	19♐52	27♒43	1♌55R	13♊13R	14♓31	23♉38R	27♓18	1♒04	9♒01	12♈16	18♍59	29♎13	19♈00
2 Th	6 47 32	11 50 00	7♓27	0 42	21 10	28 47	1 35	13 07	14 36	23 37	27 19	1 06	9 23	12 40	19 16	29 37	19 00
3 F	6 51 29	12 51 10	21 10	0 34	22 29	29 51	1 15	13 00	14 41	23 35	27 20	1 08	9 46	13 03	19 33	0♏01	19 01
4 Sa	6 55 25	13 52 21	5♈00	0 29	23 50	0♓55	0 54	12 54	14 45	23 34	27 20	1 09	10 09	13 27	19 50	0 24	19 01
5 Su	6 59 22	14 53 31	18 55	0 26D	25 12	1 58	0 32	12 49	14 50	23 33	27 21	1 11	10 32	13 50	20 07	0 48	19 01
6 M	7 3 19	15 54 40	2♉55	0 26R	26 35	3 01	0 10	12 43	14 55	23 31	27 22	1 13	10 55	14 14	20 23	1 11	19 01
7 T	7 7 15	16 55 50	16 58	0 26	27 58	4 04	29♋48	12 37	15 00	23 30	27 23	1 15	11 18	14 37	20 40	1 34	19 01
8 W	7 11 12	17 56 59	1♊04	0 26	29 23	5 06	29 26	12 32	15 05	23 29	27 24	1 17	11 40	15 01	20 56	1 57	19 02
9 Th	7 15 8	18 58 07	15 12	0 23	0♑48	6 08	29 02	12 27	15 10	23 28	27 26	1 19	12 03	15 24	21 12	2 20	19 02
10 F	7 19 5	19 59 15	29 21	0 18	2 14	7 09	28 38	12 22	15 15	23 27	27 27	1 21	12 26	15 47	21 28	2 43	19 03
11 Sa	7 23 1	21 00 22	13♋27	0 10	3 41	8 10	28 15	12 17	15 21	23 26	27 28	1 23	12 49	16 11	21 44	3 05	19 04
12 Su	7 26 58	22 01 29	27 27	0 00	5 08	9 11	27 51	12 12	15 26	23 25	27 29	1 25	13 13	16 34	22 00	3 28	19 04
13 M	7 30 55	23 02 36	11♌17	29♓48	6 37	10 11	27 27	12 07	15 31	23 24	27 30	1 27	13 36	16 57	22 15	3 50	19 05
14 T	7 34 51	24 03 42	24 52	29 26	8 05	11 11	27 03	12 03	15 37	23 23	27 31	1 28	13 59	17 21	22 31	4 12	19 06
15 W	7 38 48	25 04 48	8♍12	29 26	9 35	12 10	26 39	11 59	15 42	23 22	27 33	1 30	14 22	17 44	22 46	4 34	19 06
16 Th	7 42 44	26 05 53	21 08	29 26	11 05	13 09	26 15	11 55	15 48	23 21	27 34	1 32	14 45	18 07	23 01	4 55	19 07
17 F	7 46 41	27 06 58	3♎47	29 12	12 35	14 07	25 51	11 51	15 54	23 21	27 35	1 34	15 08	18 30	23 16	5 17	19 08
18 Sa	7 50 37	28 08 03	16 08	29 09	14 06	15 05	25 27	11 48	15 59	23 20	27 37	1 36	15 32	18 53	23 31	5 38	19 09
19 Su	7 54 34	29 09 07	28 14	29 08D	15 38	16 02	25 04	11 44	16 05	23 19	27 38	1 38	15 55	19 16	23 46	5 59	19 10
20 M	7 58 30	0♒10 10	10♏09	29 08	17 10	16 59	24 40	11 41	16 11	23 19	27 39	1 40	16 18	19 39	24 00	6 20	19 11
21 T	8 2 27	1 11 14	21 58	29 09R	18 43	17 55	24 17	11 38	16 17	23 18	27 41	1 42	16 41	20 02	24 15	6 41	19 12
22 W	8 6 24	2 12 17	3♐47	29 08	20 16	18 50	23 54	11 35	16 23	23 18	27 42	1 44	17 05	20 25	24 29	7 02	19 14
23 Th	8 10 20	3 13 19	15 40	29 08	21 50	19 45	23 31	11 32	16 29	23 17	27 44	1 46	17 28	20 48	24 43	7 22	19 15
24 F	8 14 17	4 14 22	27 43	29 05	23 24	20 39	23 09	11 30	16 35	23 17	27 45	1 48	17 51	21 11	24 57	7 42	19 16
25 Sa	8 18 13	5 15 23	10♑02	29 00	24 59	21 33	22 47	11 28	16 41	23 17	27 47	1 50	18 15	21 34	25 11	8 02	19 18
26 Su	8 22 10	6 16 25	22 38	28 53	26 35	22 26	22 25	11 26	16 47	23 16	27 48	1 52	18 38	21 57	25 24	8 22	19 19
27 M	8 26 6	7 17 25	5♒36	28 44	28 11	23 18	22 04	11 24	16 53	23 16	27 50	1 54	19 02	22 19	25 38	8 41	19 20
28 T	8 30 3	8 18 25	18 55	28 35	29 48	24 09	21 44	11 23	17 00	23 16	27 51	1 56	19 25	22 42	25 51	9 01	19 22
29 W	8 33 59	9 19 24	2♓34	28 26	1♒26	25 00	21 24	11 21	17 06	23 16	27 53	1 57	19 49	23 05	26 04	9 20	19 23
30 Th	8 37 56	10 20 22	16 31	28 18	3 04	25 50	21 05	11 20	17 12	23 16D	27 55	1 59	20 12	23 27	26 17	9 38	19 25
31 F	8 41 53	11 21 19	0♈40	28 13	4 43	26 39	20 46	11 19	17 19	23 16	27 56	2 01	20 36	23 50	26 29	9 57	19 28

EPHEMERIS CALCULATED FOR 12 MIDNIGHT GREENWICH MEAN TIME. ALL OTHER DATA AND FACING ASPECTARIAN PAGE IN **EASTERN TIME (BOLD)** AND PACIFIC TIME (REGULAR).

FEBRUARY 2025

☽ Last Aspect day	ET / hr:mn / PT		asp	☽ Ingress sign	day	ET / hr:mn / PT	
1	5:06 pm	2:06 pm	☌ ♀	♈	1	8:10 pm	5:10 pm
3	5:19 am	2:19 am	□ ♂	♉	3	10:33 pm	7:33 pm
5	10:29 pm	7:29 pm	⚹ ♆	♊	5		10:44 pm
5	10:29 pm	7:29 pm	⚹ ♆	♊	6	1:44 am	
7		11:52 pm	□ ♆	♋	8	6:04 am	3:04 am
8	2:52 am		□ ♆	♋	8	6:04 am	3:04 am
10	8:49 am	5:49 am	△ ♆	♌	10	12:01 pm	9:01 am
12	2:12 pm	11:12 am	☍ ☿	♍	12	8:07 pm	5:07 pm
15	3:36 am	12:36 am	☍ ♆	♎	15	6:45 am	3:45 am
17	6:24 pm	3:24 pm	△ ☉	♏	17	7:19 pm	4:19 pm
20	5:06 am	2:06 am	△ ♆	♐	20	7:55 am	4:55 am
22	3:38 pm	12:38 pm	□ ♆	♑	22	6:09 pm	3:09 pm
24	10:28 pm	7:28 pm	⚹ ♆	♒	24		9:40 pm
24	10:28 pm	7:28 pm	⚹ ♆	♒	25	12:40 am	
26	5:04 pm	2:04 pm	□ ♅	♓	27	3:46 am	12:46 am

☽ Phases & Eclipses

phase	day	ET / hr:mn / PT	
2nd Quarter	5	3:02 am	12:02 am
Full Moon	12	8:53 am	5:53 am
4th Quarter	20	12:33 pm	9:33 am
New Moon	27	7:45 pm	4:45 pm

Planet Ingress

		day	ET / hr:mn / PT	
♀	♈	3		11:57 pm
♀	♈	4	2:57 am	
☿	♓	14	7:06 am	4:06 am
♀	♒	16	2:26 pm	11:26 am
☉	♓	18	5:07 am	2:07 am
⚵	♐	19	10:30 pm	7:30 pm
⚳	♓	23	5:55 pm	2:55 pm

Planetary Motion

		day	ET / hr:mn / PT	
♃	D	4	4:40 am	1:40 am
♂	D	23	9:00 pm	6:00 pm

1 SATURDAY

☽ △ ♂	4:02 am	1:02 am
☽ ⚹ ♅	8:54 am	5:54 am
♀ ☌ ♆	11:33 am	8:33 am
☽ ☌ ♆	4:49 pm	1:49 pm
☽ ☌ ♀	5:06 pm	2:06 pm
☽ ⚹ ♇	11:40 pm	8:40 pm

2 SUNDAY

☽ ⚹ ☿	11:35 am	8:35 am
☽ ⚹ ♃	3:03 pm	12:03 pm
☽ ⚹ ☉	8:23 pm	5:23 pm
☽ ⚺ ♄		10:47 pm

3 MONDAY

☽ ⚺ ♄	1:47 am	
☽ □ ♂	5:19 am	2:19 am
☽ ⚺ ♅	11:12 am	8:12 am
☿ △ ♃	4:52 pm	1:52 pm
☽ ⚺ ♆	7:16 pm	4:16 pm
☽ ⚺ ♀	10:19 pm	7:19 pm
☽ □ ♇		11:12 pm

4 TUESDAY

☽ □ ♇	2:12 am	
☽ ⚺ ♃	5:41 pm	2:41 pm
☽ □ ☿	9:06 pm	6:06 pm

5 WEDNESDAY

☽ □ ☉	3:02 am	12:02 am
☽ ⚹ ♄	4:59 am	1:59 am
☽ ⚹ ♂	7:16 am	4:16 am
☽ ☌ ♅	2:10 pm	11:10 am
☽ ⚹ ♆	10:29 pm	7:29 pm

6 THURSDAY

☽ ⚹ ♀	4:17 am	1:17 am
☽ △ ♇	5:34 am	2:34 am
☉ ⚺ ♄	9:10 am	6:10 am
☽ ☌ ♃	9:16 pm	6:16 pm

7 FRIDAY

☉ ⚻ ♂	3:42 am	12:42 am
♀ ⚹ ♇	7:14 am	4:14 am
☽ △ ☿	8:11 am	5:11 am
☽ □ ♄	9:14 am	6:14 am
☽ ⚺ ♂	10:18 am	7:18 am
☽ △ ☉	10:57 am	7:57 am
☿ ⚺ ♄	4:57 pm	1:57 pm
☽ ⚺ ♅	6:15 pm	3:15 pm
☿ ⚻ ♂	11:15 pm	8:15 pm
☽ □ ♆		11:52 pm

8 SATURDAY

☽ □ ♆	2:52 am	
☽ ⚻ ♇	10:08 am	7:08 am
☽ □ ♀	11:28 am	8:28 am
☽ ⚺ ♃		11:12 pm

9 SUNDAY

☽ ⚺ ♃	2:12 am	
☉ ☌ ☿	7:08 am	4:08 am
♂ △ ♄	8:15 am	5:15 am
☽ ☌ ♂	2:48 pm	11:48 am
☽ △ ♄	2:57 pm	11:57 am
☽ ⚻ ☉	8:39 pm	5:39 pm
☽ ⚻ ☿	9:33 pm	6:33 pm
☽ ⚹ ♅	11:49 pm	8:49 pm

10 MONDAY

☽ △ ♆	8:49 am	5:49 am
☿ □ ♅	2:28 pm	11:28 am
☽ ☍ ♇	4:21 pm	1:21 pm
☽ △ ♀	8:21 pm	5:21 pm

11 TUESDAY

☽ ⚹ ♃	8:59 am	5:59 am
☉ □ ♅	2:30 pm	11:30 am
☽ ⚺ ♂	9:16 pm	6:16 pm
☽ ⚻ ♄	10:39 pm	7:39 pm

12 WEDNESDAY

☽ □ ♅	7:26 am	4:26 am
☽ ☍ ☉	8:53 am	5:53 am
☽ ☍ ☿	2:12 pm	11:12 am
☽ ⚻ ♆	4:56 pm	1:56 pm
☽ ⚻ ♇		9:47 pm

13 THURSDAY

☽ ⚻ ♇	12:47 am	
☽ ⚻ ♀	7:34 am	4:34 am
☿ ⚺ ♆	9:30 am	6:30 am
☽ □ ♃	6:10 pm	3:10 pm

14 FRIDAY

☽ ⚹ ♂	6:14 am	3:14 am
☽ ☍ ♄	8:53 am	5:53 am
☽ △ ♅	5:34 pm	2:34 pm
☽ ⚻ ☉		9:20 pm

15 SATURDAY

☽ ⚻ ☉	12:20 am	
☽ ☍ ♆	3:36 am	12:36 am
☽ ⚻ ☿	11:00 am	8:00 am
☽ △ ♇	11:46 am	8:46 am
☿ ⚺ ♇	3:58 pm	12:58 pm
☽ ☍ ♀	9:19 pm	6:19 pm

16 SUNDAY

☽ △ ♃	5:52 am	2:52 am
☉ ⚺ ♆	4:38 pm	1:38 pm
☽ □ ♂	5:37 pm	2:37 pm
☽ ⚻ ♄	9:30 pm	6:30 pm

17 MONDAY

☽ ⚻ ♅	5:54 am	2:54 am
☽ ⚻ ♆	4:16 pm	1:16 pm
☽ △ ☉	6:24 pm	3:24 pm
☽ □ ♇		9:34 pm

18 TUESDAY

☽ □ ♇	12:34 am	
☽ △ ☿	10:55 am	7:55 am
☽ ⚻ ♀	12:28 pm	9:28 am
☽ ⚻ ♃	6:57 pm	3:57 pm
☿ ⚺ ♀	11:02 pm	8:02 pm

19 WEDNESDAY

☽ △ ♂	6:07 am	3:07 am
☽ △ ♄	10:59 am	7:59 am
☽ ☍ ♅	6:47 pm	3:47 pm

20 THURSDAY

☽ △ ♆	5:06 am	2:06 am
☽ □ ☉	12:33 pm	9:33 am
☽ ⚹ ♇	1:12 pm	10:12 am
☿ □ ♃	3:13 pm	12:13 pm
☉ ⚺ ♇	8:35 pm	5:35 pm
☽ △ ♀		11:28 pm

21 FRIDAY

☽ △ ♀	2:28 am	
☽ ☍ ♃	7:09 am	4:09 am
☽ □ ☿	9:53 am	6:53 am
☽ ⚻ ♂	5:25 pm	2:25 pm
☽ □ ♄	10:50 pm	7:50 pm

22 SATURDAY

☽ ⚻ ♅	5:48 am	2:48 am
☽ □ ♆	3:38 pm	12:38 pm
☽ ⚺ ♇	11:15 pm	8:15 pm

23 SUNDAY

☽ ⚹ ☉	3:26 am	12:26 am
☿ △ ♂	11:58 am	8:58 am
☽ □ ♀	12:52 pm	9:52 am
☽ ⚻ ♃	4:15 pm	1:15 pm
☽ ☍ ♂		10:32 pm

24 MONDAY

☽ ☍ ♂	1:32 am	
☽ ⚹ ☿	3:41 am	12:41 am
☽ ⚹ ♄	7:10 am	4:10 am
☽ △ ♅	1:14 pm	10:14 am
☽ ⚹ ♆	10:28 pm	7:28 pm

25 TUESDAY

☽ ☌ ♇	5:33 am	2:33 am
☿ ☌ ♄	7:02 am	4:02 am
☽ ⚺ ☉	1:33 pm	10:33 am
☽ ⚹ ♀	6:54 pm	3:54 pm
☽ △ ♃	9:33 pm	6:33 pm

26 WEDNESDAY

☽ ⚻ ♂	6:03 am	3:03 am
☽ ⚺ ♄	11:44 am	8:44 am
☽ ⚺ ☿	3:30 pm	12:30 pm
☽ □ ♅	5:04 pm	2:04 pm
☽ ⚺ ♆		10:50 pm

27 THURSDAY

☽ ⚺ ♆	1:50 am	
☿ ⚹ ♅	4:38 am	1:38 am
☽ ⚺ ♇	8:30 am	5:30 am
☽ ☌ ☉	7:45 pm	4:45 pm
☽ ⚺ ♀	9:32 pm	6:32 pm
☽ □ ♃	11:54 pm	8:54 pm

28 FRIDAY

☽ △ ♂	7:57 am	4:57 am
☽ ☌ ♄	1:42 pm	10:42 am
☽ ⚹ ♅	6:32 pm	3:32 pm
☉ ⚺ ♀	11:08 pm	8:08 pm
☽ ☌ ☿	11:19 pm	8:19 pm

Eastern time in bold type
Pacific time in medium type

FEBRUARY 2025

DATE	SID.TIME	SUN	MOON	NODE	MERCURY	VENUS	MARS	JUPITER	SATURN	URANUS	NEPTUNE	PLUTO	CERES	PALLAS	JUNO	VESTA	CHIRON
1 Sa	8 45 49	12≈22 15	14×58	28×10D	6≈23	27×27	20⊚28R	11Ⅱ18R	17×25	23♉16	27×58	2≈03	20≈59	24√12	26Ⅲ42	10Ⅲ15	19♈30
2 Su	8 49 46	13 23 10	29 18	28 09	8 03	28 14	20 10	11 17	17 32	23 16	28 00	2 05	21 23	24 35	26 54	10 33	19 32
3 M	8 53 42	14 24 03	13♈38	28 10	9 44	29 00	19 54	11 17	17 39	23 16	28 02	2 07	21 46	24 57	27 06	10 51	19 34
4 T	8 57 39	15 24 55	27 54	28 11	11 26	29 45	19 38	11 17 D	17 45	23 16	28 03	2 09	22 10	25 20	27 18	11 09	19 36
5 W	9 1 35	16 25 46	12♉03	28 12 R	13 08	0♈29	19 22	11 17	17 52	23 16	28 05	2 11	22 33	25 42	27 30	11 26	19 38
6 Th	9 5 32	17 26 35	26 05	28 12	14 52	1 13	19 08	11 17	17 58	23 17	28 07	2 13	22 57	26 04	27 41	11 43	19 40
7 F	9 9 28	18 27 22	9Ⅱ59	28 12	16 36	1 55	18 54	11 17	18 05	23 17	28 09	2 15	23 20	26 26	27 53	12 00	19 42
8 Sa	9 13 25	19 28 09	23 43	28 06	18 20	2 35	18 41	11 18	18 12	23 18	28 11	2 16	23 44	26 48	28 04	12 17	19 44
9 Su	9 17 22	20 28 53	7⊚17	28 01	20 06	3 15	18 29	11 19	18 19	23 18	28 13	2 18	24 08	27 10	28 14	12 33	19 46
10 M	9 21 18	21 29 37	20 39	27 55	21 52	3 53	18 18	11 20	18 26	23 19	28 14	2 20	24 31	27 32	28 25	12 49	19 48
11 T	9 25 15	22 30 18	3♌49	27 48	23 39	4 30	18 07	11 21	18 33	23 19	28 16	2 22	24 55	27 54	28 36	13 04	19 50
12 W	9 29 11	23 30 59	16 44	27 43	25 27	5 06	17 57	11 23	18 40	23 20	28 18	2 24	25 18	28 16	28 46	13 20	19 52
13 Th	9 33 8	24 31 37	29 25	27 38	27 16	5 40	17 47	11 24	18 46	23 20	28 20	2 26	25 42	28 38	28 56	13 35	19 55
14 F	9 37 4	25 32 15	11♍52	27 35	29 05	6 13	17 40	11 26	18 53	23 21	28 22	2 27	26 05	28 59	29 05	13 50	19 57
15 Sa	9 41 1	26 32 51	24 05	27 34 D	0×54	6 44	17 33	11 28	19 00	23 22	28 24	2 29	26 29	29 21	29 15	14 04	19 59
16 Su	9 44 57	27 33 25	6≏07	27 34	2 45	7 14	17 26	11 30	19 08	23 23	28 26	2 31	26 53	29 43	29 24	14 18	20 02
17 M	9 48 54	28 33 59	18 01	27 36	4 36	7 42	17 20	11 33	19 15	23 24	28 28	2 33	27 16	0≈04	29 33	14 32	20 04
18 T	9 52 51	29 34 31	29 51	27 38	6 27	8 08	17 15	11 35	19 22	23 25	28 30	2 35	27 40	0 25	29 42	14 45	20 07
19 W	9 56 47	0×35 01	11♏40	27 41 R	8 18	8 33	17 11	11 38	19 29	23 26	28 32	2 36	28 03	0 47	29 51	14 59	20 09
20 Th	10 0 44	1 35 31	23 33	27 41	10 10	8 56	17 07	11 41	19 36	23 27	28 34	2 38	28 27	1 08	29 59	15 11	20 12
21 F	10 4 40	2 35 59	5♐35	27 41	12 01	9 17	17 04	11 44	19 43	23 28	28 36	2 40	28 50	1 29	0♐07	15 24	20 15
22 Sa	10 8 37	3 36 26	17 52	27 40	13 53	9 36	17 01	11 48	19 50	23 29	28 39	2 42	29 14	1 50	0 15	15 36	20 17
23 Su	10 12 33	4 36 52	0♒27	27 38	15 43	9 53	17 01	11 51	19 58	23 30	28 41	2 43	29 38	2 11	0 22	15 48	20 20
24 M	10 16 30	5 37 16	13 25	27 35	17 33	10 07	17 01 D	11 55	20 05	23 31	28 43	2 45	0×01	2 32	0 29	15 59	20 23
25 T	10 20 26	6 37 39	26 47	27 32	19 22	10 20	17 01	11 59	20 12	23 33	28 45	2 47	0 25	2 53	0 36	16 10	20 25
26 W	10 24 23	7 38 00	10≈34	27 29	21 09	10 31	17 02	12 03	20 19	23 34	28 47	2 48	0 48	3 14	0 43	16 21	20 28
27 Th	10 28 20	8 38 20	24 44	27 27	22 54	10 39	17 04	12 07	20 27	23 36	28 49	2 50	1 12	3 35	0 50	16 31	20 31
28 F	10 32 16	9 38 38	9×13	27 25	24 37	10 45	17 07	12 12	20 34	23 37	28 51	2 52	1 35	3 55	0 56	16 41	20 34

EPHEMERIS CALCULATED FOR 12 MIDNIGHT GREENWICH MEAN TIME. ALL OTHER DATA AND FACING ASPECTARIAN PAGE IN **EASTERN TIME (BOLD)** AND PACIFIC TIME (REGULAR).

MARCH 2025

☽ Last Aspect day	ET / hr:mn / PT	asp	☽ Ingress sign	day	ET / hr:mn / PT
1	**3:05 am** 12:05 am	☌♆	♈	1	**4:52 am** 1:52 am
2	**8:52 am** 5:52 am	□♂	♉	3	**5:37 am** 2:37 am
5	**5:53 am** 2:53 am	✶♆	♊	5	**7:29 am** 4:29 am
7	**9:57 am** 6:57 am	□♆	♋	7	**11:29 am** 8:29 am
9	**5:32 pm** 2:32 pm	△♆	♌	9	**6:59 pm** 3:59 pm
11	**4:16 pm** 1:16 pm	□♅	♍	12	**3:56 am** 12:56 am
14	**1:47 pm** 10:47 am	☍♆	♎	14	**2:59 pm** 11:59 am
16	**5:53 am** 2:53 am	□♂	♏	17	**3:30 am** 12:30 am
19	**3:28 pm** 12:28 pm	△♆	♐	19	**4:17 pm** 1:17 pm
21	11:53 pm	□♆	♑	22	**3:29 am** 12:29 am
22	**2:53 am**	□♆	♑	22	**3:29 am** 12:29 am
24	**11:01 am** 8:01 am	✶♆	♒	24	**11:25 am** 8:25 am
26	**6:15 am** 3:15 am	□♅	♓	26	**3:31 pm** 12:31 pm
28	**4:30 pm** 1:30 pm	☌♆	♈	28	**4:36 pm** 1:36 pm
30	**5:18 am** 2:18 am	□♂	♉	30	**4:16 pm** 1:16 pm

☽ Phases & Eclipses phase	day	ET / hr:mn / PT
2nd Quarter	6	**11:32 am** 8:32 am
Full Moon	13	11:55 pm
Full Moon	14	**2:55 am**
●	14	23° ♍ 57'
4th Quarter	22	**7:29 am** 4:29 am
New Moon	29	**6:58 am** 3:58 am
●	29	9° ♈ 00'

Planet Ingress	day	ET / hr:mn / PT
☿ ♈	3	**4:04 am** 1:04 am
☉ ♈	20	**5:01 am** 2:01 am
♀ ♓	27	**4:41 am** 1:41 am
☿ ♓	29	**10:18 pm** 7:18 pm
♆ ♈	30	**8:00 am** 5:00 am

Planetary Motion	day	ET / hr:mn / PT
♀ R	1	**7:36 pm** 4:36 pm
☿ R	14	11:46 pm
☿ R	15	**2:46 am**
⚵ R	19	**2:00 pm** 11:00 am
⯗ R	21	**6:10 am** 3:10 am

1 SATURDAY
☽☌♆ **3:05 am** 12:05 am
☽✶♇ **9:34 am** 6:34 am
☽☌♀ **10:26 pm** 7:26 pm
☽⊻☉ 9:06 pm
☽✶♃ 9:55 pm

2 SUNDAY
☽⊻☉ **12:06 am**
☽✶♃ **12:55 am**
☽□♂ **8:52 am** 5:52 am
☿☌♆ **11:22 am** 8:22 am
☉□♃ **1:19 pm** 10:19 am
☽⊻♄ **2:47 pm** 11:47 am
☽⊻♅ **7:18 pm** 4:18 pm

3 MONDAY
☽⊻♆ **3:57 am** 12:57 am
☽⊻☿ **5:47 am** 2:47 am
☽□♇ **10:27 am** 7:27 am
☽⊻♀ **11:16 pm** 8:16 pm
☽⊻♃ 11:16 pm

4 TUESDAY
☽⊻♃ **2:16 am**
☽✶☉ **4:47 am** 1:47 am
☽✶♂ **10:25 am** 7:25 am
☽✶♄ **4:37 pm** 1:37 pm
☽☌♅ **8:56 pm** 5:56 pm

5 WEDNESDAY
☽✶♆ **5:53 am** 2:53 am
☿✶♇ **8:13 am** 5:13 am
☽△♇ **12:36 pm** 9:36 am
☽✶☿ **1:01 pm** 10:01 am
☽✶♀ 10:21 pm

6 THURSDAY
☽✶♀ **1:21 am**
☽☌♃ **5:17 am** 2:17 am
☽□☉ **11:32 am** 8:32 am
☽⊻♂ **1:52 pm** 10:52 am
☽□♄ **8:23 pm** 5:23 pm
☽⊻♅ 9:33 pm

7 FRIDAY
☽⊻♅ **12:33 am**
☽□♆ **9:57 am** 6:57 am
☽⊼♇ **4:56 pm** 1:56 pm
☽□☿ **10:05 pm** 7:05 pm
☉△♂ 9:13 pm

8 SATURDAY
☉△♂ **12:13 am**
☽□♀ **5:20 am** 2:20 am
☽⊻♃ **10:43 am** 7:43 am
☽☌♂ **7:52 pm** 4:52 pm
☽△☉ **9:16 pm** 6:16 pm
☽△♄ 11:40 pm

9 SUNDAY
☽△♄ **3:40 am**
☽✶♅ **7:39 am** 4:39 am
☽△♆ **5:32 pm** 2:32 pm
☽☍♇ 9:48 pm

10 MONDAY
☽☍♇ **12:48 am**
☽△☿ **9:56 am** 6:56 am
☽△♀ **12:21 pm** 9:21 am
☽✶♃ **7:46 pm** 4:46 pm

11 TUESDAY
☽⊻♂ **5:35 am** 2:35 am
☽⊼☉ **11:10 am** 8:10 am
☽⊼♄ **12:32 pm** 9:32 am
☽□♅ **4:16 pm** 1:16 pm
☿☌♀ **6:55 pm** 3:55 pm
☽⊼♆ 11:36 pm

12 WEDNESDAY
☽⊼♆ **2:36 am**
☉☌♄ **6:29 am** 3:29 am
☽⊼♇ **10:05 am** 7:05 am
☽⊼♀ **8:10 pm** 5:10 pm
☽⊼☿ **9:55 pm** 6:55 pm

13 THURSDAY
☽□♃ **6:13 am** 3:13 am
☽✶♂ **4:45 pm** 1:45 pm
☽☍♄ **11:40 pm** 8:40 pm
☽☍☉ 11:55 pm

14 FRIDAY
☽☍☉ **2:55 am**
☽△♅ **3:06 am** 12:06 am
☉✶♅ **5:16 am** 2:16 am
☽☍♆ **1:47 pm** 10:47 am
☽△♇ **9:27 pm** 6:27 pm

15 SATURDAY
☽☍♀ **5:24 am** 2:24 am
☽☍☿ **10:12 am** 7:12 am
☽△♃ **6:38 pm** 3:38 pm

16 SUNDAY
☽□♂ **5:53 am** 2:53 am
☽⊼♄ **12:32 pm** 9:32 am
☽⊼♅ **3:35 pm** 12:35 pm
☽⊼☉ **8:45 pm** 5:45 pm
☽⊼♆ 11:29 pm

17 MONDAY
☽⊼♆ **2:29 am**
☽□♇ **10:11 am** 7:11 am
☽⊼♀ **3:25 pm** 12:25 pm
☽⊼☿ **9:54 pm** 6:54 pm

18 TUESDAY
☽⊼♃ **8:06 am** 5:06 am
☽△♂ **7:56 pm** 4:56 pm
☽△♄ 11:03 pm

19 WEDNESDAY
☽△♄ **2:03 am**
☽☍♅ **4:38 am** 1:38 am
☽△☉ **3:08 pm** 12:08 pm
☽△♆ **3:28 pm** 12:28 pm
☉☌♆ **7:25 pm** 4:25 pm
☽✶♇ **10:59 pm** 7:59 pm
☽△♀ 10:09 pm

20 THURSDAY
☽△♀ **1:09 am**
☽△☿ **7:56 am** 4:56 am
☽☍♃ **9:01 pm** 6:01 pm

21 FRIDAY
☽⊼♂ **9:06 am** 6:06 am
☽□♄ **2:23 pm** 11:23 am
☽⊼♅ **4:29 pm** 1:29 pm
♀✶♇ **5:32 pm** 2:32 pm
☽□♆ 11:53 pm

22 SATURDAY
☽□♆ **2:53 am**
☽□☉ **7:29 am** 4:29 am
☽□♀ **9:10 am** 6:10 am
☽⊻♇ **9:59 am** 6:59 am
☽□☿ **3:13 pm** 12:13 pm
☉☌♀ **9:07 pm** 6:07 pm

23 SUNDAY
☽⊼♃ **7:25 am** 4:25 am
☉✶♇ **3:32 pm** 12:32 pm
☽☍♂ **7:23 pm** 4:23 pm
☽✶♄ **11:41 pm** 8:41 pm
☽△♅ 10:18 pm

24 MONDAY
☽△♅ **1:18 am**
☽✶♆ **11:01 am** 8:01 am
☽✶♀ **2:15 pm** 11:15 am
☉☌☿ **3:48 pm** 12:48 pm
☽☌♇ **5:34 pm** 2:34 pm
☽✶☿ **7:06 pm** 4:06 pm
☽✶☉ **7:36 pm** 4:36 pm

25 TUESDAY
☽△♃ **2:01 pm** 11:01 am
☿✶♇ **6:02 pm** 3:02 pm
☽⊼♂ 10:40 pm

26 WEDNESDAY
☽⊼♂ **1:40 am**
☽⊻♄ **5:04 am** 2:04 am
☽□♅ **6:15 am** 3:15 am
☽⊻♆ **3:17 pm** 12:17 pm
☽⊻♀ **4:03 pm** 1:03 pm
☽⊻☿ **7:44 pm** 4:44 pm
☽⊻♇ **9:20 pm** 6:20 pm
☽⊻☉ 11:58 pm

27 THURSDAY
☽⊻☉ **2:58 am**
♀☌♆ **9:13 am** 6:13 am
☽□♃ **4:56 pm** 1:56 pm

28 FRIDAY
☽△♂ **4:27 am** 1:27 am
☽☌♄ **7:03 am** 4:03 am
☽✶♅ **7:55 am** 4:55 am
☽☌♀ **3:17 pm** 12:17 pm
☽☌♆ **4:30 pm** 1:30 pm
☽☌☿ **6:02 pm** 3:02 pm
☽✶♇ **10:12 pm** 7:12 pm

29 SATURDAY
☽☌☉ **6:58 am** 3:58 am
☽✶♃ **5:32 pm** 2:32 pm
☿☌♆ **10:47 pm** 7:47 pm

30 SUNDAY
☽□♂ **5:18 am** 2:18 am
☽⊻♄ **7:14 am** 4:14 am
☽⊻♅ **7:50 am** 4:50 am
☽⊻♀ **1:20 pm** 10:20 am
☽⊻☿ **3:28 pm** 12:28 pm
☽⊻♆ **4:17 pm** 1:17 pm
☽□♇ **9:53 pm** 6:53 pm

31 MONDAY
☽⊻☉ **9:55 am** 6:55 am
☽⊻♃ **5:42 pm** 2:42 pm

Eastern time in bold type
Pacific time in medium type

MARCH 2025

DATE	SID. TIME	SUN	MOON	NODE	MERCURY	VENUS	MARS	JUPITER	SATURN	URANUS	NEPTUNE	PLUTO	CERES	PALLAS	JUNO	VESTA	CHIRON
1 Sa	10 36 13	10♓38 54	23♋55	27♈24D	26♓17	10♈49	17♋10	12Ⅱ16	20♓41	23♉38	28♓54	2≈53	1♓59	4≈16	1♐02	16♏50	20♈37
2 Su	10 40 9	11 39 08	8♌43	27 24	27 54	10 50R	17 14	12 21	20 49	23 40	28 56	2 55	2 22	4 36	1 07	16 59	20 40
3 M	10 44 6	12 39 21	23 30	27 25	29 26	10 49	17 18	12 26	20 56	23 43	28 58	2 56	2 45	4 57	1 13	17 08	20 43
4 T	10 48 2	13 39 31	8♍09	27 26	0♈54	10 45	17 24	12 31	21 03	23 43	29 00	2 58	3 09	5 17	1 18	17 16	20 45
5 W	10 51 59	14 39 40	22 35	27 27	2 17	10 39	17 29	12 37	21 11	23 45	29 02	2 59	3 32	5 37	1 22	17 24	20 48
6 Th	10 55 55	15 39 46	6♎46	27 28R	3 34	10 31	17 36	12 42	21 18	23 46	29 05	3 01	3 56	5 57	1 27	17 31	20 52
7 F	10 59 52	16 39 50	20 39	27 28	4 45	10 19	17 43	12 48	21 26	23 48	29 07	3 03	4 19	6 17	1 31	17 38	20 55
8 Sa	11 3 49	17 39 52	4♏13	27 28	5 49	10 06	17 51	12 54	21 33	23 50	29 09	3 04	4 42	6 37	1 35	17 45	20 58
9 Su	11 7 45	18 39 52	17 31	27 27	6 46	9 49	18 00	13 00	21 40	23 52	29 11	3 05	5 06	6 57	1 38	17 51	21 01
10 M	11 11 42	19 39 50	0♐23	27 26	7 35	9 31	18 09	13 06	21 48	23 54	29 14	3 07	5 29	7 17	1 42	17 56	21 04
11 T	11 15 38	20 39 45	13 20	27 25	8 16	9 10	18 18	13 12	21 55	23 56	29 16	3 08	5 52	7 36	1 45	18 02	21 07
12 W	11 19 35	21 39 39	25 54	27 24	8 49	8 46	18 29	13 19	22 03	23 58	29 18	3 10	6 15	7 56	1 47	18 06	21 10
13 Th	11 23 31	22 39 30	8♑07	27 23	9 13	8 21	18 39	13 26	22 10	24 00	29 20	3 11	6 39	8 15	1 50	18 11	21 13
14 F	11 27 28	23 39 20	20 08	27 23D	9 28	7 53	18 51	13 32	22 17	24 02	29 23	3 13	7 02	8 34	1 52	18 14	21 17
15 Sa	11 31 24	24 39 07	2≈31	27 23	9 35R	7 24	19 02	13 39	22 25	24 04	29 25	3 14	7 25	8 53	1 53	18 18	21 20
16 Su	11 35 21	25 38 52	14 27	27 23	9 33	6 52	19 15	13 46	22 32	24 06	29 27	3 15	7 48	9 12	1 55	18 21	21 23
17 M	11 39 18	26 38 35	26 18	27 23R	9 23	6 20	19 28	13 54	22 39	24 08	29 29	3 16	8 11	9 31	1 56	18 23	21 27
18 T	11 43 14	27 38 17	8♓07	27 23	9 05	5 45	19 41	14 01	22 47	24 10	29 32	3 18	8 34	9 50	1 56	18 25	21 30
19 W	11 47 11	28 37 57	19 57	27 23	8 39	5 10	19 55	14 09	22 54	24 13	29 34	3 19	8 57	10 09	1 57R	18 26	21 33
20 Th	11 51 7	29 37 35	1♈51	27 23	8 07	4 33	20 09	14 16	23 02	24 15	29 36	3 20	9 20	10 27	1 57	18 27	21 37
21 F	11 55 4	0♈37 12	13 53	27 23	7 29	3 56	20 24	14 24	23 09	24 17	29 38	3 21	9 43	10 46	1 57	18 28R	21 40
22 Sa	11 59 0	1 36 46	26 08	27 23D	6 46	3 19	20 40	14 32	23 16	24 20	29 41	3 23	10 06	11 04	1 56	18 28	21 43
23 Su	12 2 57	2 36 19	8♉39	27 23	5 58	2 41	20 55	14 40	23 23	24 22	29 43	3 24	10 29	11 22	1 55	18 27	21 47
24 M	12 6 53	3 35 50	21 32	27 23	5 08	2 03	21 12	14 48	23 31	24 24	29 46	3 25	10 52	11 40	1 54	18 26	21 50
25 T	12 10 50	4 35 20	4Ⅱ48	27 24	4 16	1 26	21 28	14 57	23 39	24 27	29 48	3 26	11 15	11 58	1 52	18 25	21 54
26 W	12 14 47	5 34 47	18 31	27 24	3 23	0 49	21 45	15 05	23 46	24 30	29 50	3 27	11 38	12 16	1 50	18 23	21 57
27 Th	12 18 43	6 34 13	2♋40	27 25	2 30	0 13	22 03	15 14	23 53	24 32	29 52	3 28	12 01	12 34	1 48	18 20	22 00
28 F	12 22 40	7 33 37	17 14	27 26R	1 39	29♓38	22 21	15 22	24 00	24 35	29 54	3 29	12 23	12 51	1 46	18 17	22 04
29 Sa	12 26 36	8 32 59	2♌07	27 26	0 50	29 04	22 39	15 31	24 08	24 37	29 57	3 30	12 46	13 09	1 43	18 13	22 07
30 Su	12 30 33	9 32 19	17 13	27 25	0 04	28 32	22 58	15 40	24 15	24 40	29 59	3 31	13 09	13 26	1 39	18 09	22 11
31 M	12 34 29	10 31 37	2♍21	27 24	29♓22	28 01	23 17	15 49	24 22	24 43	0♈01	3 32	13 31	13 43	1 36	18 05	22 14

EPHEMERIS CALCULATED FOR 12 MIDNIGHT GREENWICH MEAN TIME. ALL OTHER DATA AND FACING ASPECTARIAN PAGE IN **EASTERN TIME (BOLD)** AND PACIFIC TIME (REGULAR).

APRIL 2025

☽ Last Aspect day	ET / hr:mn	PT	asp	☽ Ingress sign	day	ET / hr:mn	PT
1	1:43 pm	10:43 am	✶☿	♊	1	4:26 pm	1:26 pm
3	2:26 pm	11:26 am	□☿	♋	3	6:50 pm	3:50 pm
5	6:54 pm	3:54 pm	△☿	♌	5		9:34 pm
5	6:54 pm	3:54 pm	△☿	♌	6	12:34 am	
7		9:08 pm	□♅	♍	8	9:40 am	6:40 am
8	12:08 am		□♅	♍	8	9:40 am	6:40 am
10	3:49 pm	12:49 pm	☍☿	♎	10	9:12 pm	6:12 pm
13	6:01 am	3:01 am	□♂	♏	13	9:54 am	6:54 am
15	10:24 pm	7:24 pm	△☿	♐	15	10:37 pm	7:37 pm
18	7:38 am	4:38 am	△☉	♑	18	10:12 am	7:12 am
20	1:21 pm	10:21 am	✶♄	♒	20	7:22 pm	4:22 pm
22	5:55 pm	2:55 pm	□♅	♓	22		10:07 pm
22	5:55 pm	2:55 pm	□♅	♓	23	1:07 am	
24	10:57 pm	7:57 pm	☌♀	♈	25	3:24 am	12:24 am
26	12:18 pm	9:18 am	✶♃	♉	27	3:17 am	12:17 am
28		10:18 pm	✶♀	♊	28		11:34 pm
29	1:18 am		✶♀	♊	29	2:34 am	
30	11:49 pm	8:49 pm	□♄	♋	5/1	3:23 am	12:23 am

☽ Phases & Eclipses phase	day	ET / hr:mn	PT
2nd Quarter	4	10:15 pm	7:15 pm
Full Moon	12	8:22 pm	5:22 pm
4th Quarter	20	9:36 pm	6:36 pm
New Moon	27	3:31 pm	12:31 pm

Planet Ingress		day	ET / hr:mn	PT
⚵	♏	14		11:30 pm
⚵	♏	15	2:30 am	
☿	♈	15		11:25 pm
☿	♈	16	2:25 am	
♂	♌	17		9:21 pm
♂	♌	18	12:21 am	
☉	♉	19	3:56 pm	12:56 pm
♀	♈	30	1:16 pm	10:16 am

Planetary Motion		day	ET / hr:mn	PT
☿	D	7	7:08 am	4:08 am
♀	D	12	9:02 pm	6:02 pm

1 TUESDAY
☽✶♂ **6:15 am** 3:15 am
☽✶♄ **7:33 am** 4:33 am
☽☌♅ **7:56 am** 4:56 am
☽✶♀ **11:54 am** 8:54 am
☽✶☿ **1:43 pm** 10:43 am
☽✶♆ **4:34 pm** 1:34 pm
☽△♇ **10:17 pm** 7:17 pm

2 WEDNESDAY
☽✶☉ **2:20 pm** 11:20 am
☽☌♃ **7:25 pm** 4:25 pm

3 THURSDAY
☽⚺♂ **9:17 am** 6:17 am
☽□♄ **9:52 am** 6:52 am
☽⚺♅ **10:01 am** 7:01 am
☽□♀ **12:37 pm** 9:37 am
☽□☿ **2:26 pm** 11:26 am
☽□♆ **7:07 pm** 4:07 pm
☽⚻♇ 10:06 pm

4 FRIDAY
☽⚻♇ **1:06 am**
♄✶♅ **12:21 pm** 9:21 am
♂✶♅ **7:05 pm** 4:05 pm
♂△♄ **9:08 pm** 6:08 pm
☽□☉ **10:15 pm** 7:15 pm
☽⚺♃ 9:12 pm

5 SATURDAY
☽⚺♃ **12:12 am**
☽✶♅ **3:20 pm** 12:20 pm
☽△♄ **3:29 pm** 12:29 pm
☽☌♂ **3:49 pm** 12:49 pm
☽△♀ **4:36 pm** 1:36 pm
☽△☿ **6:54 pm** 3:54 pm
☽△♆ 10:02 pm

6 SUNDAY
☽△♆ **1:02 am**
☉✶♃ **5:44 am** 2:44 am
☽☍♇ **7:19 am** 4:19 am
♀△♂ **8:13 am** 5:13 am

7 MONDAY
♀☌♄ **7:01 am** 4:01 am
☽✶♃ **8:37 am** 5:37 am
☽△☉ **10:31 am** 7:31 am
☽□♅ 9:08 pm
☽⚻♀ 9:09 pm
☽⚻♄ 9:37 pm
♀✶♅ 9:48 pm
☽⚺♂ 11:07 pm

8 TUESDAY
☽□♅ **12:08 am**
☽⚻♀ **12:09 am**
☽⚻♄ **12:37 am**
♀✶♅ **12:48 am**
☽⚺♂ **2:07 am**
☽⚻☿ **3:33 am** 12:33 am
☽⚻♆ **10:19 am** 7:19 am
☽⚻♇ **4:50 pm** 1:50 pm

9 WEDNESDAY
☽□♃ **8:04 pm** 5:04 pm
☽⚻☉ 11:26 pm

10 THURSDAY
☽⚻☉ **2:26 am**
☽☍♀ **10:39 am** 7:39 am
☽△♅ **11:36 am** 8:36 am
☽☍♄ **12:26 pm** 9:26 am
☽✶♂ **3:19 pm** 12:19 pm
☽☍☿ **3:49 pm** 12:49 pm
☽☍♆ **10:03 pm** 7:03 pm

11 FRIDAY
☽△♇ **4:38 am** 1:38 am

12 SATURDAY
☽△♃ **9:20 am** 6:20 am
☽☍☉ **8:22 pm** 5:22 pm
☽⚻♀ **11:00 pm** 8:00 pm
☽⚻♅ 9:28 pm
☽⚻♄ 10:38 pm

13 SUNDAY
☽⚻♅ **12:28 am**
☽⚻♄ **1:38 am**
☽□♂ **6:01 am** 3:01 am
☽⚻☿ **6:32 am** 3:32 am
☽⚻♆ **10:57 am** 7:57 am
☽□♇ **5:27 pm** 2:27 pm

14 MONDAY
☉⚺♀ **4:52 am** 1:52 am
☽⚻♃ **11:06 pm** 8:06 pm
☉⚺♅ 9:20 pm

15 TUESDAY
☉⚺♅ **12:20 am**
☽△♀ **12:04 pm** 9:04 am
☽☍♅ **1:31 pm** 10:31 am
☽⚻☉ **2:38 pm** 11:38 am
☽△♄ **3:00 pm** 12:00 pm
☉⚺♄ **7:32 pm** 4:32 pm
☽△♂ **8:52 pm** 5:52 pm
☽△☿ **10:24 pm** 7:24 pm
☽△♆ **11:50 pm** 8:50 pm

16 WEDNESDAY
☽✶♇ **6:08 am** 3:08 am
☿☌♆ 9:11 pm

17 THURSDAY
☿☌♆ **12:11 am**
☽☍♃ **12:11 pm** 9:11 am
☽□♀ 9:40 pm
☽⚻♅ 10:37 pm

18 FRIDAY
☽□♀ **12:40 am**
☽⚻♅ **1:37 am**
☽□♄ **3:21 am** 12:21 am
☽△☉ **7:38 am** 4:38 am
☽⚻♂ **10:33 am** 7:33 am
☽□♆ **11:33 am** 8:33 am
☽□☿ **1:50 pm** 10:50 am
☽⚺♇ **5:31 pm** 2:31 pm

19 SATURDAY
♂△♆ **6:53 pm** 3:53 pm
☽⚻♃ **11:16 pm** 8:16 pm

20 SUNDAY
☉⚺♆ **10:35 am** 7:35 am
☽✶♀ **11:23 am** 8:23 am
☽△♅ **11:27 am** 8:27 am
☽✶♄ **1:21 pm** 10:21 am
♀✶♅ **2:21 pm** 11:21 am
☿✶♇ **5:40 pm** 2:40 pm
☽✶♆ **8:48 pm** 5:48 pm
☉□♂ **9:34 pm** 6:34 pm
☽☍♂ **9:35 pm** 6:35 pm
☽□☉ **9:36 pm** 6:36 pm
☽☌♇ 11:20 pm

21 MONDAY
☽☌♇ **2:20 am**
☽✶☿ **3:00 am** 12:00 am

22 TUESDAY
☽△♃ **7:04 am** 4:04 am
☽□♅ **5:55 pm** 2:55 pm
☽⚺♀ **6:56 pm** 3:56 pm
☽⚺♄ **7:55 pm** 4:55 pm
☽⚺♆ 11:35 pm

23 WEDNESDAY
☽⚺♆ **2:35 am**
☽⚻♂ **4:54 am** 1:54 am
☽✶☉ **7:14 am** 4:14 am
☽⚺♇ **7:38 am** 4:38 am
☽⚺☿ **12:24 pm** 9:24 am
☉□♇ **1:10 pm** 10:10 am

24 THURSDAY
☽□♃ **11:10 am** 8:10 am
♀☌♄ **8:02 pm** 5:02 pm
☽✶♅ **8:50 pm** 5:50 pm
☽☌♄ **10:54 pm** 7:54 pm
☽☌♀ **10:57 pm** 7:57 pm

25 FRIDAY
☽☌♆ **4:53 am** 1:53 am
☽△♂ **8:29 am** 5:29 am
☽✶♇ **9:34 am** 6:34 am
☽⚺☉ **12:40 pm** 9:40 am
☽☌☿ **6:04 pm** 3:04 pm

26 SATURDAY
☽✶♃ **12:18 pm** 9:18 am
♂☍♇ **9:05 pm** 6:05 pm
☽⚺♅ **9:07 pm** 6:07 pm
☽⚺♄ **11:16 pm** 8:16 pm
☽⚺♀ 9:25 pm

27 SUNDAY
☽⚺♀ **12:25 am**
☽⚺♆ **4:49 am** 1:49 am
☽□♇ **9:16 am** 6:16 am
☽□♂ **9:38 am** 6:38 am
☽☌☉ **3:31 pm** 12:31 pm
☽⚺☿ **9:39 pm** 6:39 pm

28 MONDAY
☽⚺♃ **12:10 pm** 9:10 am
☽☌♅ **8:33 pm** 5:33 pm
☽✶♄ **10:51 pm** 7:51 pm
☽✶♀ 10:18 pm

29 TUESDAY
☽✶♀ **1:18 am**
☽✶♆ **4:14 am** 1:14 am
☽△♇ **8:39 am** 5:39 am
☽✶♂ **10:29 am** 7:29 am
☽⚺☉ **6:19 pm** 3:19 pm
☽✶☿ 10:50 pm

30 WEDNESDAY
☽✶☿ **1:50 am**
☽☌♃ **12:58 pm** 9:58 am
☽⚺♅ **9:15 pm** 6:15 pm
☽□♄ **11:49 pm** 8:49 pm

Eastern time in bold type
Pacific time in medium type

APRIL 2025

DATE	SID.TIME	SUN	MOON	NODE	MERCURY	VENUS	MARS	JUPITER	SATURN	URANUS	NEPTUNE	PLUTO	CERES	PALLAS	JUNO	VESTA	CHIRON
1 T	12 38 26	11♈30 53	17♐23	27♈22R	28♓45R	27♓32R	23♋36	15♊59	24♓29	24♉45	0♈03	3♒33	13♉54	14♒00	1♐32R	18♍00R	22♈18
2 W	12 42 22	12♈30 06	2♑11	27 21	28 12	27 05	23 56	16 08	24 37	24 48	0 06	3 35	14 16	14 17	1 28	17 54	22 22
3 Th	12 46 19	13♈29 18	16♑38	27 19	27 45	26 40	24 16	16 18	24 44	24 51	0 08	3 35	14 39	14 33	1 23	17 48	22 25
4 F	12 50 15	14♈28 27	0♒40	27 19	27 23	26 17	24 36	16 27	24 51	24 54	0 10	3 36	15 01	14 50	1 18	17 42	22 29
5 Sa	12 54 12	15♈27 34	14♒18	27 17D	27 06	25 56	24 57	16 37	24 58	24 57	0 12	3 37	15 24	15 06	1 13	17 35	22 32
6 Su	12 58 9	16♈26 38	27♒31	27 18	26 55	25 38	25 19	16 47	25 05	25 00	0 14	3 38	15 46	15 23	1 07	17 28	22 36
7 M	13 2 5	17♈25 40	10♓24	27 19	26 50D	25 22	25 40	16 56	25 12	25 02	0 17	3 38	16 08	15 39	1 01	17 20	22 39
8 T	13 6 2	18♈24 40	22♓58	27 20	26 50	25 08	26 02	17 06	25 19	25 05	0 19	3 40	16 30	15 55	0 55	17 11	22 43
9 W	13 9 58	19♈23 37	5♈17	27 22	26 56	24 57	26 24	17 17	25 26	25 08	0 21	3 40	16 53	16 10	0 48	17 03	22 46
10 Th	13 13 55	20♈22 32	17♈25	27 23R	27 07	24 49	26 46	17 27	25 33	25 11	0 23	3 41	17 15	16 26	0 41	16 53	22 50
11 F	13 17 51	21♈21 25	29♈24	27 23	27 22	24 43	27 09	17 37	25 40	25 14	0 25	3 41	17 37	16 41	0 34	16 44	22 54
12 Sa	13 21 48	22♈20 16	11♉18	27 22	27 43	24 39	27 32	17 48	25 47	25 17	0 28	3 42	17 59	16 57	0 27	16 34	22 57
13 Su	13 25 44	23♈19 05	23♉09	27 20	28 08	24 37D	27 55	17 58	25 54	25 20	0 30	3 42	18 21	17 12	0 19	16 23	23 01
14 M	13 29 41	24♈17 52	4♊59	27 17	28 38	24 39	28 19	18 09	26 01	25 23	0 32	3 43	18 43	17 27	0 11	16 13	23 04
15 T	13 33 38	25♈16 37	16♊49	27 12	29 11	24 42	28 43	18 19	26 08	25 27	0 34	3 44	19 04	17 41	0 02	16 02	23 08
16 W	13 37 34	26♈15 20	28♊42	27 07	29 49	24 48	29 07	18 30	26 14	25 30	0 36	3 44	19 26	17 56	29♏54	15 50	23 11
17 Th	13 41 31	27♈14 02	10♋40	27 02	0♈31	24 56	29 31	18 41	26 21	25 33	0 38	3 45	19 48	18 10	29 45	15 38	23 15
18 F	13 45 27	28♈12 41	22♋46	26 57	1 16	25 06	29 56	18 52	26 28	25 36	0 40	3 45	20 10	18 25	29 35	15 26	23 19
19 Sa	13 49 24	29♈11 19	5♌02	26 54	2 05	25 18	0♌20	19 03	26 34	25 39	0 42	3 46	20 31	18 39	29 26	15 13	23 22
20 Su	13 53 20	0♉09 56	17♌33	26 51	2 57	25 33	0 45	19 14	26 41	25 43	0 44	3 46	20 53	18 52	29 16	15 01	23 26
21 M	13 57 17	1♉08 30	0♍28	26 51D	3 52	25 49	1 11	19 26	26 48	25 46	0 46	3 47	21 14	19 06	29 06	14 48	23 29
22 T	14 1 13	2♉07 03	13♍30	26 52	4 50	26 07	1 36	19 37	26 54	25 49	0 48	3 47	21 36	19 19	28 55	14 34	23 33
23 W	14 5 10	3♉05 35	27♍15	26 54	5 51	26 28	2 02	19 48	27 01	25 52	0 50	3 48	21 58	19 33	28 45	14 21	23 36
24 Th	14 9 7	4♉04 04	11♎03	26 55R	6 55	26 50	2 28	20 00	27 07	25 56	0 52	3 48	22 18	19 46	28 34	14 07	23 40
25 F	14 13 3	5♉02 32	25♎23	26 54	8 01	27 13	2 54	20 11	27 14	25 59	0 54	3 48	22 39	19 59	28 23	13 53	23 43
26 Sa	14 17 0	6♉00 59	10♏38	26 52	9 10	27 39	3 20	20 23	27 20	26 02	0 56	3 48	23 00	20 11	28 12	13 38	23 47
27 Su	14 20 56	6♉59 24	25♏23	26 52	10 22	28 06	3 47	20 35	27 26	26 06	0 58	3 49	23 21	20 24	28 00	13 24	23 50
28 M	14 24 53	7♉57 47	10♐38	26 47	11 36	28 35	4 14	20 46	27 32	26 09	1 00	3 49	23 42	20 36	27 48	13 10	23 54
29 T	14 28 49	8♉56 08	25♐23	26 41	12 52	29 05	4 41	20 58	27 39	26 12	1 02	3 49	24 03	20 48	27 36	12 57	23 57
30 W	14 32 46	9♉54 27	10♑53	26 35	14 10	29 36	5 08	21 10	27 45	26 16	1 04	3 49	24 24	21 00	27 24	12 40	24 01

EPHEMERIS CALCULATED FOR 12 MIDNIGHT GREENWICH MEAN TIME. ALL OTHER DATA AND FACING ASPECTARIAN PAGE IN **EASTERN TIME (BOLD)** AND PACIFIC TIME (REGULAR).

MAY 2025

D Last Aspect / D Ingress

D Last Aspect			D Ingress		
day	ET / hr:mn / PT	asp	sign	day	ET / hr:mn / PT
4/30	11:49 am 8:49 am	□ ♄	♋	1	3:23 am 12:23 am
4	4:02 am 1:02 am	⚹ ♆	♌	3	7:29 am 4:29 am
5	9:03 am 6:03 am	□ ♇	♍	5	3:40 pm 12:40 pm
	9:11 pm		♎	8	3:06 am 12:06 am
8	12:11 am		♏	10	3:58 pm 12:58 pm
9	11:17 pm		♐	13	4:35 am 1:35 am
10	2:17 am		♑	15	3:58 am 12:58 am
12	2:37 am				
13					
15	2:29 am 11:29 am				

D Last Aspect			D Ingress		
day	ET / hr:mn / PT	asp	sign	day	ET / hr:mn / PT
17	10:29		♒	17	9:27 am
18	1:29 am		♓	18	11:32
	8:28 am		♈	20	5:28 am
22	12:06 pm 9:06 am		♉	22	12:26 pm 9:26 am
24	1:38 pm 10:38 am		♊	24	10:38 am
	1:21 pm 10:21 am		♋	26	10:33 am
26	1:33 pm 10:33 am		♌	28	
30	4:17 pm 1:17 pm		♍	30	

D Phases & Eclipses

phase	day	ET / hr:mn / PT
2nd Quarter	4	9:52 am 6:52 am
Full Moon	12	12:56 pm 9:56 am
4th Quarter	20	7:59 am 4:59 am
New Moon	26	11:02 pm 8:02 pm

Planet Ingress

	day	ET / hr:mn / PT
♀ ♉	10	8:15 am 5:15 am
♀ ♈	16	2:23 pm 11:23 am
☉ ♊	20	2:55 pm 11:55 am
♆ ♈	24	11:35 pm 8:35 pm
♀ ♉	25	8:59 pm 5:59 pm

Planetary Motion

	day	ET / hr:mn / PT
♇ R	4	11:27 am 8:27 am

---

1 THURSDAY
- △ ♄ 3:57 am 12:57 am
- □ 5:14 am 2:14 am
- △ 9:48 am 6:48 am
- □ 1:22 pm 10:22 am
- 11:45 pm 8:45 pm

2 FRIDAY
- △ 9:38 am 6:38 am
- □ 1:07 pm 10:07 am
- ⚹ 4:45 pm 1:45 pm

3 SATURDAY
- △ 1:06 am
- △ 4:02 am 1:02 am
- △ 9:37 am 6:37 am
- □ 10:33 am 7:33 am
- △ 2:25 pm 11:25 am
- □ 8:13 pm 5:13 pm

4 SUNDAY
- △ ☉ 9:52 am 6:52 am
- △ 11:14 am 8:14 am
- 9:43 pm

5 MONDAY
- ⚹ 12:43 am
- △ 9:03 am 6:03 am
- □ 9:24 am 6:24 am
- △ 1:21 pm 10:21 am
- ⚹ 6:04 pm 3:04 pm

6 TUESDAY
- 7:34 am 4:34 am
- 2:31 pm 2:31 pm
- 9:50 pm

7 WEDNESDAY
- 12:50 am
- 12:30 pm
- 6:38 pm 3:38 pm
- 8:30 pm

8 THURSDAY
- 12:11 am
- 5:45 am 2:45 am
- 8:56 am 5:56 am
- 10:48 am 7:48 am
- 1:22 pm 10:22 am
- 10:07 pm 7:07 pm

9 FRIDAY
- 1:31 pm 10:31 am
- 8:43 pm 3:43 pm
- 11:17 pm

10 SATURDAY
- 2:17 am
- 9:36 am 6:36 am
- 1:31 pm 10:31 am
- 5:15 pm 2:15 pm

11 SUNDAY
- △ ♇ 6:47 4:34 am
- 11:52 2:31 pm
- 3:18 pm
- 1:9 pm

12 MONDAY
- 9:56 am
- 10:23 am
- 1:09 pm
- 10:25 pm
- 11:37

13 TUESDAY
- 4:29 am
- 9:11 am
- 9:18 am
- 10:46 pm 7:48 pm

14 WEDNESDAY
- 1:28 am
- 12:09 pm

15 THURSDAY
- 1:54 am
- 2:49 am
- 7:24 am
- 11:29 am
- 3:55 pm
- 8:20 pm

16 FRIDAY
- 1:29 pm 10:29 am
- 1:45 pm 10:45 am
- 4:24 pm 1:24 pm
- 5:37 pm 2:37 pm

17 SATURDAY
- 3:50 am 12:50 am
- 7:32 am 4:32 am
- 8:24 pm 5:24 pm
- 8:28 pm 5:28 pm
- 9:36

18 SUNDAY
- 12:27 am
- 12:36 am
- 4:27 am 1:27 am
- 8:34 am 5:34 am
- 11:18

19 MONDAY
- 2:18 am
- 4:23 am 1:23 am
- 8:00 am 5:00 am
- 9:13

20 TUESDAY
- 12:13 am
- 3:53 am 12:53 am
- 5:38 am 2:38 am
- 9:54 am 4:49 am
- 7:49 am 4:59 am
- 7:59 am

21 WEDNESDAY
- △ ♈ 11:23 am 8:23 am
- 3:09 pm 12:09 pm

22 THURSDAY
- 11:32 am 8:32 am
- 9:58 am 6:58 am
- 10:21 7:21

23 FRIDAY
- 3:42 am 12:42 am
- 5:27 am 2:27 am
- 8:40 am 5:40 am
- 12:06 pm 9:06 am
- 3:15 pm 12:15 pm
- 3:43 pm 12:43 pm
- 6:42 pm 3:42 pm

24 SATURDAY
- 4:13 pm 1:13 pm
- 5:13 pm 2:13 pm

25 SUNDAY
- △ ♇ 6:06 pm 3:06 pm
- 8:25 pm 5:25 pm
- 9:46 pm 6:46 pm

26 MONDAY
- 8:15 am 5:15 am
- 9:52 am 6:52 am
- 1:33 pm 10:33 am
- 4:05 pm 1:05 pm
- 4:10 pm 1:10 pm
- 4:37 pm 1:37 pm
- 7:14 pm 4:14 pm
- 11:02 pm 8:02 pm

27 TUESDAY
- 1:56 pm 10:56 am
- 7:35 pm 4:35 pm
- 11:21 pm 8:21 pm

28 WEDNESDAY
- 9:01 am 6:01 am
- 10:08 am 7:08 am
- 1:59 pm 10:59 am
- 4:31 pm 1:31 pm
- 7:36 pm 4:36 pm
- 9:54 pm

29 THURSDAY
- 12:54 am
- 3:02 am 12:02 am
- 11:05 am 8:05 am
- 9:13 pm

30 FRIDAY
- △ 12:13 pm
- 4:45 am 1:45 am
- 12:16 pm 9:16 am
- 12:50 pm 9:50 am
- 5:00 pm 2:00 pm
- 7:31 pm 4:31 pm
- 10:43 pm 7:43 pm

31 SATURDAY
- ⚹ 10:46 am 7:46 am
- ♀ 2:38 pm 11:38 am

MAY 2025

DATE	SID.TIME	SUN	MOON	NODE	MERCURY	VENUS	MARS	JUPITER	SATURN	URANUS	NEPTUNE	PLUTO	CERES	PALLAS	JUNO	VESTA	CHIRON
1 Th	14 36 42	10♉52 45	25♊34	26♈29R	15♈31	0♈09	5♌36	21♊22	27♓51	26♉19	1♈06	3≈49	24♊45	21♒11	27♏12R	12♍25R	24♈04
2 F	14 40 39	11 51 01	9♋49	26 23	16 54	0 44	6 03	21 36	27 57	26 22	1 08	3 49	25 05	21 23	27 00	12 10	24 08
3 Sa	14 44 36	12 49 14	23 35	26 20	18 18	1 19	6 31	21 46	28 03	26 25	1 09	3 49	25 26	21 34	26 47	11 56	24 11
4 Su	14 48 32	13 47 25	6♌52	26 18D	19 45	1 56	6 59	21 59	28 09	26 29	1 11	3 49R	25 47	21 45	26 34	11 41	24 15
5 M	14 52 29	14 45 35	19 44	26 18	21 14	2 34	7 27	22 11	28 15	26 33	1 13	3 49	26 07	21 55	26 21	11 26	24 18
6 T	14 56 25	15 43 42	2♍14	26 19	22 45	3 13	7 55	22 23	28 21	26 36	1 15	3 49	26 27	22 06	26 08	11 11	24 21
7 W	15 0 22	16 41 48	14 27	26 20R	24 18	3 53	8 24	22 35	28 26	26 40	1 16	3 49	26 47	22 16	25 55	10 56	24 25
8 Th	15 4 18	17 39 51	26 28	26 21	25 53	4 34	8 53	22 48	28 32	26 44	1 18	3 49	27 08	22 26	25 42	10 42	24 28
9 F	15 8 15	18 37 53	8♎21	26 20	27 30	5 17	9 21	23 00	28 38	26 47	1 20	3 49	27 28	22 35	25 29	10 27	24 31
10 Sa	15 12 11	19 35 53	20 11	26 17	29 09	6 00	9 50	23 13	28 43	26 50	1 22	3 49	27 48	22 45	25 16	10 13	24 35
11 Su	15 16 8	20 33 51	1♏59	26 12	0♉50	6 44	10 20	23 26	28 49	26 53	1 23	3 48	28 07	22 54	25 02	9 59	24 38
12 M	15 20 5	21 31 48	13 49	26 04	2 32	7 29	10 49	23 38	28 54	26 57	1 25	3 48	28 27	23 03	24 49	9 45	24 41
13 T	15 24 1	22 29 43	25 43	25 55	4 17	8 15	11 18	23 51	29 00	27 00	1 26	3 48	28 47	23 11	24 35	9 31	24 45
14 W	15 27 58	23 27 36	7♐43	25 44	6 04	9 02	11 48	24 04	29 05	27 04	1 28	3 48	29 06	23 20	24 22	9 17	24 48
15 Th	15 31 54	24 25 28	19 50	25 33	7 53	9 49	12 18	24 16	29 10	27 07	1 30	3 48	29 26	23 28	24 08	9 04	24 51
16 F	15 35 51	25 23 19	2♑04	25 23	9 44	10 38	12 48	24 29	29 16	27 11	1 31	3 47	29 45	23 36	23 55	8 51	24 54
17 Sa	15 39 47	26 21 09	14 29	25 15	11 37	11 27	13 18	24 42	29 21	27 14	1 33	3 47	0♋04	23 43	23 41	8 38	24 57
18 Su	15 43 44	27 18 57	27 05	25 08	13 31	12 17	13 48	24 55	29 26	27 18	1 34	3 47	0 24	23 51	23 28	8 25	25 01
19 M	15 47 40	28 16 44	9≈56	25 05	15 28	13 07	14 18	25 08	29 31	27 21	1 36	3 46	0 43	23 58	23 14	8 13	25 04
20 T	15 51 37	29 14 30	23 03	25 03D	17 27	13 58	14 48	25 21	29 36	27 24	1 37	3 46	1 02	24 04	23 01	8 01	25 07
21 W	15 55 34	0♊12 15	6♓30	25 03	19 27	14 50	15 19	25 34	29 41	27 28	1 38	3 45	1 20	24 11	22 47	7 49	25 10
22 Th	15 59 30	1 09 58	20 19	25 03R	21 29	15 43	15 50	25 47	29 45	27 32	1 40	3 45	1 39	24 17	22 34	7 38	25 13
23 F	16 3 27	2 07 41	4♈31	25 03	23 33	16 36	16 20	26 00	29 50	27 35	1 41	3 45	1 58	24 23	22 21	7 27	25 16
24 Sa	16 7 23	3 05 23	19 06	25 01	25 39	17 29	16 51	26 13	29 55	27 39	1 42	3 44	2 16	24 28	22 08	7 17	25 19
25 Su	16 11 20	4 03 04	3♉58	24 57	27 46	18 23	17 23	26 27	29 59	27 42	1 44	3 43	2 35	24 34	21 55	7 07	25 22
26 M	16 15 16	5 00 43	19 03	24 50	29 55	19 18	17 54	26 40	0♈04	27 46	1 45	3 43	2 53	24 39	21 42	6 57	25 25
27 T	16 19 13	5 58 22	4♊11	24 41	2♊04	20 13	18 25	26 53	0 08	27 49	1 46	3 42	3 11	24 43	21 29	6 48	25 28
28 W	16 23 9	6 55 59	19 12	24 30	4 15	21 09	18 57	27 06	0 13	27 53	1 47	3 42	3 29	24 48	21 17	6 39	25 31
29 Th	16 27 6	7 53 36	3♋56	24 20	6 26	22 05	19 28	27 20	0 17	27 56	1 49	3 41	3 47	24 52	21 04	6 30	25 34
30 F	16 31 3	8 51 11	18 16	24 11	8 38	23 01	20 00	27 33	0 21	28 00	1 50	3 40	4 05	24 55	20 52	6 22	25 36
31 Sa	16 34 59	9 48 44	2♌07	24 04	10 50	23 58	20 32	27 47	0 25	28 03	1 51	3 40	4 22	24 59	20 40	6 15	25 39

JUNE 2025

☽ Last Aspect				☽ Ingress			
day	ET / hr:mn / PT		asp	sign	day	ET / hr:mn / PT	
1	**7:38 pm**	4:38 pm	⚹ ♃	♍	1	**11:00 pm**	8:00 pm
4	**7:11 am**	4:11 am	□ ♃	♎	4	**9:38 am**	6:38 am
6	**9:04 pm**	6:04 pm	△ ♃	♏	6	**10:23 pm**	7:23 pm
9	**8:06 am**	5:06 am	☍ ♅	♐	9	**10:56 am**	7:56 am
11	**3:58 pm**	12:58 pm	△ ♂	♑	11	**9:55 pm**	6:55 pm
14	**4:52 am**	1:52 am	△ ♅	♒	14	**7:00 am**	4:00 am
16	**1:31 pm**	10:31 am	☍ ♂	♓	16	**2:09 pm**	11:09 am
18	**5:34 pm**	2:34 pm	⚹ ♅	♈	18	**7:08 pm**	4:08 pm
20	**9:49 pm**	6:49 pm	⚹ ☉	♉	20	**9:53 pm**	6:53 pm
22	**9:50 pm**	6:50 pm	☌ ♅	♊	22	**10:57 pm**	7:57 pm
23	**4:26 am**	1:26 am	□ ♂	♋	24	**11:44 pm**	8:44 pm
26		10:16 pm	⚹ ♅	♌	26		11:05 pm
27	**1:16 am**		⚹ ♅	♌	27	**2:05 am**	
29	**7:03 am**	4:03 am	□ ♅	♍	29	**7:44 am**	4:44 am

☽ Phases & Eclipses			
phase	day	ET / hr:mn / PT	
2nd Quarter	2	**11:41 pm**	8:41 pm
Full Moon	11	**3:44 am**	12:44 am
4th Quarter	18	**3:19 pm**	12:19 pm
New Moon	25	**6:32 am**	3:32 am

Planet Ingress			
	day	ET / hr:mn / PT	
♀ ♉	5		9:43 pm
♀ ♉	6	**12:43 am**	
☿ ♋	8	**6:58 pm**	3:58 pm
⚶ ♋	9	**5:02 pm**	2:02 pm
♂ ♍	17	**4:35 am**	1:35 am
☉ ♋	20	**10:42 pm**	7:42 pm
☿ ♌	26	**3:09 pm**	12:09 pm

Planetary Motion			
	day	ET / hr:mn / PT	
♇ R	9	**5:40 am**	2:40 am
⚷ D	14	**2:00 pm**	11:00 am

1 SUNDAY
☽ ☌ ♂ **6:41 am** 3:41 am
♃ ⚺ ♅ **11:48 am** 8:48 am
☽ △ ♀ **2:52 pm** 11:52 am
☽ □ ♅ **7:32 pm** 4:32 pm
☽ ⚹ ♃ **7:38 pm** 4:38 pm
☽ ⚻ ♄ 9:04 pm
☽ ⚻ ♆ 11:35 pm

2 MONDAY
☽ ⚻ ♄ **12:04 am**
☽ ⚻ ♆ **2:35 am**
☽ ⚻ ♇ **5:55 am** 2:55 am
☽ □ ☉ **11:41 pm** 8:41 pm

3 TUESDAY
☽ □ ☿ **11:23 am** 8:23 am
☽ ⚺ ♂ **6:58 pm** 3:58 pm

4 WEDNESDAY
☽ ⚻ ♀ **6:08 am** 3:08 am
☽ △ ♅ **6:15 am** 3:15 am
☽ □ ♃ **7:11 am** 4:11 am
♀ ⚺ ♅ **7:33 am** 4:33 am
☽ ☍ ♄ **11:04 am** 8:04 am
☽ ☍ ♆ **1:30 pm** 10:30 am
☽ △ ♇ **4:52 pm** 1:52 pm
♀ ⚹ ♃ **10:32 pm** 7:32 pm

5 THURSDAY
☽ △ ☉ **4:46 pm** 1:46 pm
☿ ⚹ ♂ **6:10 pm** 3:10 pm

6 FRIDAY
☽ ⚹ ♂ **10:19 am** 7:19 am
☽ △ ☿ **12:56 pm** 9:56 am
☽ ⚻ ♅ **7:13 pm** 4:13 pm
☽ △ ♃ **9:04 pm** 6:04 pm
♀ ⚺ ♄ **9:32 pm** 6:32 pm
☽ ⚻ ♄ 9:09 pm
☽ ☍ ♀ 9:22 pm
☽ ⚻ ♆ 11:23 pm

7 SATURDAY
☽ ⚻ ♄ **12:09 am**
☽ ☍ ♀ **12:22 am**
☽ ⚻ ♆ **2:23 am**
☽ □ ♇ **5:37 am** 2:37 am
♀ ⚺ ♆ 9:23 pm
☿ ⚺ ♅ 10:32 pm

8 SUNDAY
♀ ⚺ ♆ **12:23 am**
☿ ⚺ ♅ **1:32 am**
☽ ⚻ ☉ **10:59 am** 7:59 am
☿ ☌ ♃ **4:12 pm** 1:12 pm
☽ □ ♂ 10:57 pm

9 MONDAY
☽ □ ♂ **1:57 am**
☿ □ ♄ **6:48 am** 3:48 am
☽ ☍ ♅ **8:06 am** 5:06 am
☽ ⚻ ♃ **10:48 am** 7:48 am
☽ △ ♄ **12:56 pm** 9:56 am
♀ □ ♇ **1:20 pm** 10:20 am
☽ ⚻ ☿ **2:08 pm** 11:08 am
☽ △ ♆ :55 pm 11:55 am
☽ ⚹ ♇ :58 pm 2:58 pm
☽ ⚻ ♀ :23 pm 3:23 pm
☿ □ ♆ :54 pm 3:54 pm

10 TUESDAY
☿ ⚻ ♇ :13 pm 10:13 am

11 WEDNESDAY
☽ ☍ ☉ :44 am 12:44 am
☿ ⚹ ♀ :41 pm 12:41 pm
☽ △ ♂ :58 pm 12:58 pm
☽ ⚻ ♅ :27 pm 4:27 pm
☽ ☍ ♃ 1:54 pm 7:54 pm
☽ □ ♄ 9:07 pm
☽ □ ♆ 10:51 pm

12 THURSDAY
☽ □ ♄ 1:07 am
☽ □ ♆ :51 am
☽ ⚺ ♇ :39 am 1:39 am
☽ △ ♀ 1:22 am 7:22 am
☽ ☍ ☿ 1:56 am 8:56 am

13 FRIDAY
☽ ⚻ ☉ :06 pm 3:06 pm

14 SATURDAY
☽ ⚻ ♂ :50 am 12:50 am
☽ △ ♅ :52 am 1:52 am
☽ ⚻ ♃ :59 am 5:59 am
☽ ⚹ ♄ :21 am 6:21 am
☽ ⚹ ♆ 1:52 am 7:52 am
☽ ☌ ♇ 1:27 pm 10:27 am
☽ □ ♀ 1:57 pm 8:57 pm

15 SUNDAY
♂ □ ♅ **5:47 am** 2:47 am
☽ ⚻ ☿ **5:55 am** 2:55 am
♃ □ ♄ **10:36 am** 7:36 am

16 MONDAY
☽ △ ☉ **6:02 am** 3:02 am
☽ □ ♅ **12:18 pm** 9:18 am
☽ ☍ ♂ **1:31 pm** 10:31 am
☽ ⚺ ♄ **4:35 pm** 1:35 pm
☽ △ ♃ **5:01 pm** 2:01 pm
☽ ⚺ ♆ **5:54 pm** 2:54 pm
☽ ⚺ ♇ **8:17 pm** 5:17 pm

17 TUESDAY
☽ ⚹ ♀ **11:02 am** 8:02 am
☽ △ ☿ **8:09 pm** 5:09 pm

18 WEDNESDAY
☽ □ ☉ **3:19 pm** 12:19 pm
☽ ⚹ ♅ **5:34 pm** 2:34 pm
☽ ⚻ ♂ **8:45 pm** 5:45 pm
☽ ☌ ♄ **9:38 pm** 6:38 pm
☽ □ ♃ **10:46 pm** 7:46 pm
☽ ☌ ♆ **10:46 pm** 7:46 pm
♃ □ ♆ **11:16 pm** 8:16 pm
☽ ⚹ ♇ 9:57 pm

19 THURSDAY
☽ ⚹ ♇ **12:57 am**
☽ ⚺ ♀ **7:19 pm** 4:19 pm
♂ ⚻ ♄ **8:08 pm** 5:08 pm
☉ ⚺ ♅ 10:47 pm

20 FRIDAY
☉ ⚺ ♅ **1:47 am**
☽ □ ☿ **6:32 am** 3:32 am
☽ ⚺ ♅ **8:34 pm** 5:34 pm
☽ ⚹ ☉ **9:49 pm** 6:49 pm
♂ ⚻ ♆ **11:14 pm** 8:14 pm
☽ ⚺ ♄ 9:25 pm
☽ ⚺ ♆ 10:24 pm
☽ △ ♂ 10:29 pm
☽ ⚹ ♃ 11:10 pm

21 SATURDAY
☽ ⚺ ♄ **12:25 am**
☽ ⚺ ♆ **1:24 am**
☽ △ ♂ **1:29 am**
☽ ⚹ ♃ **2:10 am**
☽ □ ♇ **3:24 am** 12:24 am
☽ ☌ ♀ 10:02 pm

22 SUNDAY
☽ ☌ ♀ **1:02 am**
♂ ⚹ ♃ **6:32 am** 3:32 am
☽ ⚹ ☿ **1:44 pm** 10:44 am
☉ □ ♄ **2:36 pm** 11:36 am
☽ ☌ ♅ **9:50 pm** 6:50 pm
♂ ⚻ ♇ 10:00 pm
☽ ⚹ ♄ 10:33 pm
☽ ⚺ ☉ 11:17 pm
☽ ⚹ ♆ 11:25 pm

23 MONDAY
♂ ⚻ ♇ **1:00 am**
☽ ⚹ ♄ **1:33 am**
☽ ⚺ ☉ **2:17 am**
☽ ⚹ ♆ **2:25 am**
☽ ⚺ ♃ **3:55 am** 12:55 am
☽ △ ♇ **4:18 am** 1:18 am
☽ □ ♂ **4:26 am** 1:26 am
☉ □ ♆ **4:29 am** 1:29 am
♃ ⚻ ♇ 11:16 pm

24 TUESDAY
♃ ⚻ ♇ **2:16 am**
☽ ⚺ ♀ **5:32 am** 2:32 am
☉ ⚻ ♇ **8:59 am** 5:59 am
☉ ☌ ♃ **11:17 am** 8:17 am
☽ ⚺ ☿ **7:44 pm** 4:44 pm
☽ ⚺ ♅ **10:47 pm** 7:47 pm
☽ □ ♄ 11:28 pm

25 WEDNESDAY
☽ □ ♄ **2:28 am**
☽ □ ♆ **3:16 am** 12:16 am
☽ ⚻ ♇ **5:05 am** 2:05 am
☽ ☌ ♃ **5:33 am** 2:33 am
☽ ☌ ☉ **6:32 am** 3:32 am
☽ ⚹ ♂ **7:17 am** 4:17 am

26 THURSDAY
☿ ⚹ ♅ **5:45 am** 2:45 am
☉ ⚹ ♂ **10:11 am** 7:11 am
☽ ⚹ ♀ **11:08 am** 8:08 am
☽ ⚹ ♅ 10:16 pm

27 FRIDAY
☽ ⚹ ♅ **1:16 am**
☽ ☌ ☿ **3:13 am** 12:13 am
☽ △ ♄ **5:04 am** 2:04 am
☽ △ ♆ **5:50 am** 2:50 am
☽ ☍ ♇ **7:39 am** 4:39 am
☽ ⚺ ♃ **9:04 am** 6:04 am
☽ ⚺ ♂ **12:15 pm** 9:15 am
☽ ⚺ ☉ **1:02 pm** 10:02 am
☿ △ ♄ **11:53 pm** 8:53 pm

28 SATURDAY
☿ △ ♆ **7:58 am** 4:58 am
☽ □ ♀ **8:23 pm** 5:23 pm

29 SUNDAY
☿ ☍ ♇ **3:57 am** 12:57 am
☽ □ ♅ **7:03 am** 4:03 am
☽ ⚻ ♄ **11:02 am** 8:02 am
☽ ⚻ ♆ **11:45 am** 8:45 am
☽ ⚻ ♇ **1:37 pm** 10:37 am
☽ ⚺ ☿ **2:37 pm** 11:37 am
☽ ⚹ ♃ **4:13 pm** 1:13 pm
☽ ☌ ♂ **9:14 pm** 6:14 pm
☽ ⚹ ☉ **11:54 pm** 8:54 pm

30 MONDAY
☿ ⚺ ♃ **12:16 pm** 9:16 am

Eastern time in bold type
Pacific time in medium type

JUNE 2025

DATE	SID.TIME	SUN	MOON	NODE	MERCURY	VENUS	MARS	JUPITER	SATURN	URANUS	NEPTUNE	PLUTO	CERES	PALLAS	JUNO	VESTA	CHIRON
1 Su	16 38 56	10♊46 17	15♌30	23♈59R	13♊02	24♉56	21♌03	28♊00	0♈29	28♉07	1♈52	3♒39R	4♈40R	25♒02	20♏28R	6♏08R	25♈42
2 M	16 42 52	11 43 48	28 25	23 57	15 14	25 53	21 36	28 13	0 33	28 10	1 53	3 38	4 57	25 04	20 16	6 01	25 45
3 T	16 46 49	12 41 17	10♍57	23 57D	17 25	26 52	22 08	28 27	0 37	28 13	1 54	3 38	5 14	25 07	20 05	5 55	25 47
4 W	16 50 45	13 38 45	23 10	23 57R	19 35	27 50	22 40	28 40	0 41	28 17	1 55	3 37	5 31	25 09	19 53	5 50	25 50
5 Th	16 54 42	14 36 13	5≏10	23 56	21 44	28 49	23 12	28 54	0 44	28 20	1 56	3 36	5 48	25 10	19 42	5 45	25 53
6 F	16 58 39	15 33 38	17 01	23 54	23 52	29 48	23 45	29 07	0 48	28 24	1 57	3 35	6 05	25 12	19 31	5 40	25 55
7 Sa	17 2 35	16 31 03	28 50	23 50	25 58	0♊48	24 17	29 21	0 52	28 27	1 58	3 34	6 22	25 13	19 21	5 36	25 58
8 Su	17 6 32	17 28 27	10♏39	23 44	28 03	1 48	24 50	29 35	0 55	28 30	1 59	3 33	6 38	25 13	19 10	5 33	26 00
9 M	17 10 28	18 25 50	22 33	23 34	0♋05	2 48	25 23	29 48	0 58	28 34	2 00	3 33	6 55	25 14R	19 00	5 29	26 03
10 T	17 14 25	19 23 12	4♐33	23 22	2 06	3 49	25 55	0♋02	1 02	28 37	2 01	3 32	7 11	25 14	18 50	5 27	26 05
11 W	17 18 21	20 20 33	16 42	23 09	4 04	4 50	26 28	0 15	1 05	28 40	2 01	3 31	7 27	25 13	18 41	5 25	26 08
12 Th	17 22 18	21 17 53	29 01	22 56	6 01	5 51	27 01	0 29	1 08	28 44	2 02	3 30	7 43	25 13	18 31	5 23	26 10
13 F	17 26 14	22 15 13	11♑29	22 43	7 55	6 52	27 35	0 43	1 11	28 47	2 03	3 29	7 58	25 12	18 22	5 22	26 12
14 Sa	17 30 11	23 12 32	24 08	22 33	9 46	7 54	28 08	0 56	1 14	28 50	2 03	3 28	8 14	25 10	18 14	5 21D	26 15
15 Su	17 34 8	24 09 50	6≈58	22 24	11 36	8 56	28 41	1 10	1 17	28 53	2 04	3 27	8 29	25 08	18 05	5 21	26 17
16 M	17 38 4	25 07 08	20 00	22 19	13 22	9 58	29 15	1 24	1 19	28 57	2 05	3 26	8 45	25 06	17 57	5 22	26 19
17 T	17 42 1	26 04 26	3♓15	22 16	15 07	11 01	29 48	1 37	1 22	29 00	2 05	3 25	9 00	25 04	17 49	5 23	26 21
18 W	17 45 57	27 01 43	16 45	22 16	16 49	12 04	0♍22	1 51	1 24	29 03	2 06	3 24	9 14	25 01	17 41	5 24	26 23
19 Th	17 49 54	27 59 00	0♈30	22 16	18 29	13 07	0 55	2 05	1 27	29 06	2 06	3 23	9 29	24 57	17 34	5 26	26 25
20 F	17 53 50	28 56 16	14 33	22 15	20 06	14 10	1 29	2 18	1 29	29 09	2 07	3 22	9 44	24 54	17 27	5 28	26 27
21 Sa	17 57 47	29 53 33	28 52	22 13	21 41	15 14	2 03	2 32	1 31	29 12	2 07	3 20	9 58	24 50	17 20	5 31	26 29
22 Su	18 1 43	0♋50 49	13♉26	22 08	23 13	16 17	2 37	2 46	1 34	29 16	2 08	3 19	10 12	24 45	17 14	5 34	26 31
23 M	18 5 40	1 48 06	28 11	22 01	24 43	17 21	3 11	2 59	1 36	29 19	2 08	3 18	10 26	24 41	17 08	5 38	26 33
24 T	18 9 37	2 45 22	12♊59	21 52	26 10	18 26	3 45	3 13	1 38	29 22	2 09	3 17	10 40	24 35	17 02	5 42	26 35
25 W	18 13 33	3 42 38	27 43	21 41	27 34	19 30	4 19	3 27	1 39	29 25	2 09	3 16	10 53	24 30	16 57	5 47	26 37
26 Th	18 17 30	4 39 54	12♋15	21 30	28 56	20 35	4 53	3 41	1 41	29 28	2 09	3 15	11 07	24 24	16 52	5 52	26 39
27 F	18 21 26	5 37 09	26 28	21 20	0♌16	21 39	5 28	3 54	1 43	29 31	2 10	3 13	11 20	24 18	16 47	5 57	26 40
28 Sa	18 25 23	6 34 24	10♌16	21 12	1 33	22 44	6 02	4 08	1 44	29 34	2 10	3 12	11 33	24 11	16 43	6 03	26 42
29 Su	18 29 19	7 31 38	23 38	21 07	2 47	23 49	6 37	4 22	1 46	29 37	2 10	3 11	11 46	24 04	16 38	6 10	26 44
30 M	18 33 16	8 28 52	6♍39	21 05	3 58	24 55	7 11	4 35	1 47	29 40	2 10	3 10	11 58	23 57	16 35	6 17	26 45

EPHEMERIS CALCULATED FOR 12 MIDNIGHT GREENWICH MEAN TIME. ALL OTHER DATA AND FACING ASPECTARIAN PAGE IN **EASTERN TIME (BOLD)** AND PACIFIC TIME (REGULAR).

JULY 2025

☽ Last Aspect			☽ Ingress			
day	ET / hr:mn / PT	asp	sign day	ET / hr:mn / PT	asp	
1	4:47 pm 1:47 pm	☍♇	♎ 1	5:16 pm 2:16 pm		
3	3:30 pm 12:30 pm	△♀	♏ 4	5:33 am 2:33 am		
6	6:04 pm 3:04 pm	✶♇	✶ 6	6:06 am 3:06 am		
7	5:29 am 2:29 am	□♄	♈ 9	4:55 am 1:55 am		
10	4:37 pm 1:37 pm	△♀	♒ 11	1:21 pm 10:21 am		
12	3:45 pm 12:45 pm	□♃	♓ 13	7:45 pm 4:45 pm		
15	1:10 pm 10:10 am	♂	♈ 15	9:32 pm		
17	8:38 pm 5:38 pm	✶♇	♉ 18	12:32 am 3:59 am 12:59 am		
19	11:43 pm		♊ 20	6:22 am 3:22 am		

☽ Last Aspect			☽ Ingress			
day	ET / hr:mn / PT	asp	sign day	ET / hr:mn / PT	asp	
20	2:43 am	✶♇	♊ 20	6:22 am 3:22 am		
21	3:52 pm 12:52 pm	□♀	♋ 22	8:26 am 5:26 am		
23	8:42 pm 5:42 pm	✶♇	♌ 24	11:28 am 8:28 am		
26	7:02 am 4:02 am	□♀	♍ 26	4:55 pm 1:55 pm		
28	8:57 pm 5:57 pm	△♀	♎ 28	10:43 pm		
29	11:59 pm 8:59 pm	△♄	♏ 31	1:25 pm 10:25 am		

☽ Phases & Eclipses			
phase		ET / hr:mn / PT	
2nd Quarter	2	3:30 pm 12:30 pm	
Full Moon	10	4:37 pm 1:37 pm	
4th Quarter	17	8:38 pm 5:38 pm	
New Moon	24	3:11 pm 12:11 pm	

Planet Ingress			
	day	ET / hr:mn / PT	
♀ □	4	11:31 am 8:31 am	
☿ ⚏	10	4:37 pm 1:37 pm	
☿ ♌	22	9:29 am 6:29 am	
♀ ♋	30	11:57 pm 8:57 pm	

Planetary Motion			
	day	ET / hr:mn / PT	
♆ ℞	4	5:34 am 2:34 am	
☿ ❋ ℞	10	9:01 pm	
♄ ℞	11	12:01 am 9:07 pm	
♆ ℞	12		
♀ ℞	13	12:07 am	
♇ ℞	17	12:45 am 9:45 pm	
♆ ℞	18	12:45 am	
♄ ℞	30	10:42 am 7:42 am	

1 TUESDAY
△ ♀ ♇ 10:43 am 7:43 am
△ ♂ ♀ 4:47 pm 1:47 pm
✶ ♃ ♄ 8:54 am 5:54 am
△ ♀ ⊙ 9:34 am 6:34 am
□ ☿ ♀ 11:27 pm

2 WEDNESDAY
△ △ 3:25 am 12:25 am
△ ♀ 6:29 am 3:29 am
△ ✶ ☽ ⊙ 10:34 am 7:34 am
✶ ☿ 3:30 pm 12:30 pm

3 THURSDAY
✶ ♀ ♇ 4:56 am 1:56 am
✶ K ✶ 5:17 am 2:17 am
△ ♇ ♄ 8:45 am 5:45 am
△ K K 9:21 am 6:21 am
△ ♀ 9:58 am 6:58 am
△ ☿ 11:46 am 8:46 am
△ ⊙ 5:06 pm 2:06 pm

4 FRIDAY
✶ ♀ 12:29 am
△ ✶ ♄ 2:20 am
✶ ⊙ 9:29 am 6:29 am

5 SATURDAY
✶ ⊙ ♄ 4:43 am 1:43 am
□ ♃ 10:47 am 7:47 am
△ ✶ 6:04 pm 3:04 pm

6 SUNDAY
△ ♄ ♇ 9:54 am 6:54 am
△ ♂ ♇ 10:26 am 7:26 am
✶ ♀ 11:37 pm

7 MONDAY
△ ✶ ♂ 12:06 am
✶ K ♄ 4:44 am 1:44 am
△ △ K 6:36 am 3:36 am
□ ♀ 5:00 pm 2:00 pm
△ ☿ ⊙ 5:29 pm 2:29 pm

8 TUESDAY
△ ✶ ♀ 2:28 am

9 WEDNESDAY
△ K K 5:05 am 2:05 am
△ □ □ 8:36 am 5:36 am
△ ♀ 9:04 am 6:04 am
△ ☿ 10:34 am 7:34 am
□ ☿ 3:54 pm 12:54 pm
✶ ♀ 5:59 pm 2:59 pm

10 THURSDAY
△ K ♇ 6:06 am 3:06 am
△ △ K 6:11 am 3:11 am
□ ♃ 4:37 pm 1:37 pm
✶ ♀ 8:53 pm 5:53 pm

11 FRIDAY
△ ✶ 1:42 am 10:42 am
△ ☿ 4:55 am 1:55 am
□ ⊙ 5:20 pm 2:20 pm

12 SATURDAY
△ ♂ ♇ 6:42 am 3:42 am
△ K 11:54 pm
✶ K 2:54 pm
☿ ⊙ 3:37 pm 12:37 pm
△ ♀ ♄ 3:45 pm 12:45 pm
✶ ♀ 4:45 pm 1:45 pm

13 SUNDAY
△ △ 3:58 am 12:58 am
△ K 8:25 am 5:25 am
□ □ 11:12 am 8:12 am
□ ✶ ♀ 11:55 am 8:55 am

14 MONDAY
△ ♀ 12:9 am
△ ♂ 6:46 am
✶ 3:3 pm 12:53 pm
△ ⊙ 10:40 pm 7:40 pm

15 TUESDAY
△ K 1:10 am
△ ♀ ⊙ 8:35 am 5:35 am
△ ♂ ♇ 9:49 am

16 WEDNESDAY
✶ ♀ 1:13 am
✶ ⊙ 3:19 am

17 THURSDAY
△ ✶ K ♀ 12:44 am
✶ ☿ ♇ 3:21 am 12:21 am
△ ✶ ⊙ 6:37 am 3:37 pm
✶ □ 8:38 pm 5:38 pm

18 FRIDAY
△ ♀ 4:45 am 1:45 am
△ K ♇ 7:13 am 4:13 am
△ □ 7:35 am 4:35 am
△ ☿ 8:38 am 5:38 am
✶ ♄ 9:37 am 6:37 am
✶ ♃ 6:57 pm 3:57 pm

19 SATURDAY
△ K 6:08 am 3:08 am
△ □ 8:00 am 5:00 am
✶ ⊙ 11:36 am 8:36 am
11:43 pm

20 SUNDAY
△ ♀ 2:43 am
✶ ☿ 7:16 am 4:16 am
△ ♀ 9:31 am 6:31 am
△ ♇ 9:53 am 6:53 am
△ ⊙ 10:52 am 7:52 am
✶ ♃ 9:56 pm 6:56 pm

21 MONDAY
△ ♀ ♇ 7:36 am 4:36 am
□ ♀ 2:23 am 11:23 am
✶ ♃ 3:52 pm 12:52 pm

22 TUESDAY
△ ♀ ♇ 8:22 am 5:22 am
△ ♂ 9:28 am 6:28 am
△ □ 11:33 am 8:33 am
△ ⊙ 12:53 pm 9:53 am
10:32 pm

23 WEDNESDAY
△ ♀ 12:56 am
△ □ 1:32 am
✶ ♀ 4:23 am 1:23 am
△ ☿ 8:47 am 5:47 am
△ ✶ 8:42 pm 5:42 pm
✶ ♂ 9:23 pm 6:23 pm

24 THURSDAY
△ ♀ 7:23 am 4:23 am
△ ♇ 12:40 pm 9:40 am
✶ ♀ 1:31 pm 10:31 am
△ ☿ 2:38 pm 11:38 am
△ ♂ 3:04 pm 12:04 pm
△ □ 3:11 pm 12:11 pm
△ ♀ 11:59 pm 8:59 pm

25 FRIDAY
☿ ♀ 1:00 pm
△ ⊙ 4:00 pm 1:00 pm
11:33 pm

26 SATURDAY
△ ♀ ♇ 2:33 am
△ □ 5:28 am 2:28 am
△ ♂ 10:58 am 7:58 am

27 SUNDAY
△ ♀ 1:07 am
△ ☿ 12:57 pm 9:57 am
△ □ 3:18 pm 12:18 pm

28 MONDAY
△ ♀ ♇ 2:43 am 11:43 am
✶ ♄ 8:57 pm 5:57 pm
✶ ♀ 11:43 pm 8:43 pm

29 TUESDAY
△ ♀ ♇ 3:21 am 12:21 am
△ ♄ 5:04 am 2:04 am
△ ♂ 5:39 am 2:35 am
✶ ⊙ 6:35 am 3:35 am
△ ☿ 3:17 pm 12:17 pm
△ ♀ 10:12 pm 7:12 pm
✶ ♀ 11:59 pm 8:59 pm

31 THURSDAY
△ ✶ K 5:11 am 2:11 am
△ △ 2:52 pm 11:52 pm
△ ♀ 3:16 pm 12:16 pm
△ ♂ 4:44 pm 1:44 pm
△ ♀ 5:26 pm 2:26 pm
✶ ♇ 6:20 pm 3:20 pm
△ ⊙ 7:03 pm 4:03 pm
✶ ♀ 7:41 pm 4:41 pm

Eastern time in bold type
Pacific time in medium type

JULY 2025

DATE	SID.TIME	SUN	MOON	NODE	MERCURY	VENUS	MARS	JUPITER	SATURN	URANUS	NEPTUNE	PLUTO	CERES	PALLAS	JUNO	VESTA	CHIRON
1 T	18 37 13	9♋26 06	19♍08	21♉04R	5♌06	26♊00	7♍46	4♋49	1♈49	29♉42	2♈10	3♒08R	12♉11	23♋49R	16♍31R	6♍24	26♈47
2 W	18 41 9	10 23 19	1♎23	21 04	6 12	27 06	8 21	5 03	1 50	29 45	2 10	3 07	12 23	23 41	16 28	6 32	26 48
3 Th	18 45 6	11 20 32	13 24	21 04	7 14	28 11	8 56	5 16	1 51	29 48	2 10	3 06	12 35	23 33	16 25	6 40	26 50
4 F	18 49 2	12 17 44	25 17	21 03	8 14	29 17	9 31	5 30	1 52	29 51	2 11	3 05	12 46	23 24	16 23	6 49	26 51
5 Sa	18 52 59	13 14 56	7♏07	21 01	9 10	0♋23	10 06	5 44	1 53	29 54	2 11R	3 03	12 58	23 15	16 21	6 58	26 53
6 Su	18 56 55	14 12 08	18 59	20 56	10 03	1 30	10 41	5 57	1 53	29 56	2 11	3 02	13 09	23 05	16 19	7 07	26 54
7 M	19 0 52	15 09 20	0♐57	20 48	10 52	2 36	11 16	6 11	1 54	29 59	2 11	3 01	13 20	22 56	16 17	7 17	26 55
8 T	19 4 48	16 06 32	13 04	20 39	11 38	3 43	11 51	6 24	1 55	0♊02	2 10	3 00	13 31	22 46	16 16	7 28	26 56
9 W	19 8 45	17 03 44	25 23	20 28	12 21	4 49	12 26	6 38	1 55	0 04	2 10	2 59	13 41	22 35	16 16	7 38	26 57
10 Th	19 12 42	18 00 55	7♑54	20 17	12 59	5 56	13 02	6 51	1 56	0 07	2 10	2 58	13 51	22 24	16 15	7 49	26 59
11 F	19 16 38	18 58 07	20 39	20 07	13 34	7 03	13 37	7 05	1 56	0 10	2 10	2 57	14 01	22 13	16 15D	8 01	27 00
12 Sa	19 20 35	19 55 19	3♒37	19 58	14 04	8 10	14 13	7 19	1 56	0 12	2 10	2 55	14 11	22 02	16 15	8 12	27 01
13 Su	19 24 31	20 52 32	16 47	19 51	14 31	9 17	14 48	7 32	1 56R	0 15	2 09	2 53	14 20	21 50	16 16	8 25	27 02
14 M	19 28 28	21 49 44	0♓09	19 47	14 52	10 25	15 24	7 45	1 56	0 17	2 09	2 51	14 30	21 38	16 16	8 37	27 02
15 T	19 32 24	22 46 57	13 41	19 46D	15 10	11 32	16 00	7 59	1 56	0 20	2 09	2 50	14 39	21 26	16 17	8 50	27 03
16 W	19 36 21	23 44 11	27 23	19 46	15 23	12 40	16 36	8 12	1 56	0 22	2 08	2 48	14 47	21 14	16 18	9 03	27 04
17 Th	19 40 17	24 41 25	11♈16	19 47	15 31	13 48	17 11	8 26	1 55	0 24	2 08	2 47	14 56	21 01	16 20	9 17	27 05
18 F	19 44 14	25 38 40	25 18	19 47R	15 34R	14 56	17 47	8 39	1 55	0 27	2 07	2 46	15 04	20 48	16 22	9 31	27 06
19 Sa	19 48 11	26 35 55	9♉29	19 46	15 33	16 04	18 23	8 52	1 54	0 29	2 07	2 44	15 12	20 35	16 24	9 45	27 06
20 Su	19 52 7	27 33 12	23 48	19 44	15 27	17 12	18 59	9 06	1 54	0 31	2 07	2 43	15 19	20 21	16 27	9 59	27 07
21 M	19 56 4	28 30 29	8♊11	19 39	15 15	18 20	19 36	9 19	1 53	0 34	2 06	2 41	15 27	20 07	16 29	10 14	27 07
22 T	20 0 0	29 27 47	22 34	19 33	14 59	19 28	20 12	9 32	1 52	0 36	2 06	2 40	15 34	19 53	16 33	10 29	27 08
23 W	20 3 57	0♌25 06	6♋53	19 25	14 39	20 37	20 48	9 46	1 51	0 38	2 05	2 39	15 40	19 39	16 36	10 45	27 08
24 Th	20 7 53	1 22 25	21 01	19 18	14 14	21 46	21 25	9 59	1 50	0 40	2 05	2 37	15 47	19 25	16 40	11 01	27 09
25 F	20 11 50	2 19 46	4♌54	19 11	13 44	22 54	22 01	10 12	1 49	0 42	2 04	2 36	15 53	19 10	16 44	11 17	27 09
26 Sa	20 15 46	3 17 06	18 28	19 05	13 11	24 03	22 38	10 25	1 48	0 44	2 04	2 34	15 59	18 56	16 48	11 33	27 09
27 Su	20 19 43	4 14 27	1♍40	19 02	12 34	25 12	23 14	10 38	1 46	0 46	2 03	2 33	16 04	18 41	16 53	11 50	27 09
28 M	20 23 40	5 11 49	14 32	19 00D	11 55	26 21	23 51	10 51	1 45	0 48	2 02	2 32	16 10	18 26	16 58	12 07	27 10
29 T	20 27 36	6 09 11	27 04	19 01	11 13	27 30	24 27	11 04	1 43	0 50	2 01	2 30	16 14	18 11	17 03	12 24	27 10
30 W	20 31 33	7 06 34	9♎19	19 02	10 29	28 39	25 04	11 17	1 42	0 52	2 01	2 29	16 19	17 55	17 08	12 42	27 10R
31 Th	20 35 29	8 03 57	21 21	19 03	9 45	29 49	25 41	11 30	1 40	0 54	2 00	2 27	16 23	17 40	17 14	12 59	27 10

EPHEMERIS CALCULATED FOR 12 MIDNIGHT GREENWICH MEAN TIME. ALL OTHER DATA AND FACING ASPECTARIAN PAGE IN **EASTERN TIME (BOLD)** AND PACIFIC TIME (REGULAR).

AUGUST 2025

☽ Last Aspect day	ET / hr:mn / PT		asp	☽ Ingress sign	day	ET / hr:mn / PT	
2	**9:07 pm**	6:07 pm	⚹♂	♐	2		11:00 pm
2	**9:07 pm**	6:07 pm	⚹♂	♐	3	**2:00 am**	
5	**11:29 am**	8:29 am	□♂	♑	5	**1:04 pm**	10:04 am
6	**1:40 pm**	10:40 am	☍♃	♒	7	**9:18 pm**	6:18 pm
9	**3:55 am**	12:55 am	☍☉	♓	9		11:50 pm
9	**3:55 am**	12:55 am	☍☉	♓	10	**2:50 am**	
10		11:55 pm	△♃	♈	12	**6:33 am**	3:33 am
11	**2:55 am**		△♃	♈	12	**6:33 am**	3:33 am
13	**6:54 pm**	3:54 pm	△☉	♉	14	**9:22 am**	6:22 am
15		10:12 pm	□☉	♊	16	**12:01 pm**	9:01 am
16	**1:12 am**		□☉	♊	16	**12:01 pm**	9:01 am
18	**7:53 am**	4:53 am	⚹☉	♋	18	**3:05 pm**	12:05 pm
20	**8:27 am**	5:27 am	☌♀	♌	20	**7:17 pm**	4:17 pm
21	**2:13 pm**	11:13 am	☌☿	♍	22		10:24 pm
21	**2:13 pm**	11:13 am	☌☿	♍	23	**1:24 am**	
25	**9:53 am**	6:53 am	⚹♀	♎	25	**10:08 am**	7:08 am
26	**10:06 pm**	7:06 pm	⚹☿	♏	27	**9:27 pm**	6:27 pm
29	**8:47 pm**	5:47 pm	□☿	♐	30	**10:04 am**	7:04 am

☽ Phases & Eclipses phase	day	ET / hr:mn / PT	
2nd Quarter	1	**8:41 am**	5:41 am
Full Moon	9	**3:55 am**	12:55 am
4th Quarter	15		10:12 pm
4th Quarter	16	**1:12 am**	
New Moon	22		11:07 pm
New Moon	23	**2:07 am**	
2nd Quarter	30		11:25 pm
2nd Quarter	31	**2:25 am**	

Planet Ingress	day	ET / hr:mn / PT	
♂ ♎	6	**7:23 pm**	4:23 pm
☉ ♍	22	**4:34 pm**	1:34 pm
♀ ♌	25	**12:27 pm**	9:27 am

Planetary Motion		day	ET / hr:mn / PT	
☿	D	11	**3:30 am**	12:30 am
⚳	℞	11	**5:36 pm**	2:36 pm

1 FRIDAY
☽□☿ **6:56 am** 3:56 am
☽□☉ **8:41 am** 5:41 am
♀□♄ **9:34 am** 6:34 am
☽△♃ **1:25 pm** 10:25 am
♀□♆ **4:49 pm** 1:49 pm
♀⚻♇ 10:46 pm

2 SATURDAY
♀⚻♇ **1:46 am**
☽⚹♂ **9:07 pm** 6:07 pm

3 SUNDAY
☽☍♅ **3:59 am** 12:59 am
☽△♄ **5:08 am** 2:08 am
☽△♆ **5:55 am** 2:55 am
☽⚹♇ **6:46 am** 3:46 am
☽⚻♀ **9:56 am** 6:56 am
☽△☿ **4:00 pm** 1:00 pm
☽△☉ 11:12 pm
☽⚻♃ 11:44 pm

4 MONDAY
☽△☉ **2:12 am**
☽⚻♃ **2:44 am**
☉⚺♃ **10:43 am** 7:43 am

5 TUESDAY
☿⚺♀ **5:09 am** 2:09 am
☽□♂ **11:29 am** 8:29 am
☽⚻♅ **3:06 pm** 12:06 pm
☽□♄ **3:54 pm** 12:54 pm
☽□♆ **4:44 pm** 1:44 pm
☽⚺♇ **5:31 pm** 2:31 pm
☽⚻☿ **11:52 pm** 8:52 pm
☽☍♀ 11:38 pm

6 WEDNESDAY
☽☍♀ **2:38 am**
☽☍♃ **1:40 pm** 10:40 am
☽⚻☉ **4:53 pm** 1:53 pm

7 THURSDAY
☽△♂ **10:35 pm** 7:35 pm
☽△♅ **11:20 pm** 8:20 pm
☽⚹♄ **11:49 pm** 8:49 pm
☽⚹♆ 9:43 pm
☽☌♇ 10:26 pm

8 FRIDAY
☽⚹♆ **12:43 am**
☽☌♇ **1:26 am**
☽☍☿ **5:52 am** 2:52 am
♂△♅ **2:45 pm** 11:45 am
☽⚻♀ **3:31 pm** 12:31 pm
☽⚻♃ **9:31 pm** 6:31 pm
♂☍♄ **10:52 pm** 7:52 pm

9 SATURDAY
☽☍☉ **3:55 am** 12:55 am
♂☍♆ **6:13 pm** 3:13 pm

10 SUNDAY
☽□♅ **4:52 am** 1:52 am
☽⚺♄ **5:05 am** 2:05 am
☽⚺♆ **6:02 am** 3:02 am
☽⚻♂ **6:37 am** 3:37 am
☽⚺♇ **6:42 am** 3:42 am
♂△♇ **8:29 am** 5:29 am
☽⚻☿ **10:18 am** 7:18 am
☽△♀ 10:12 pm
☽△♃ 11:55 pm

11 MONDAY
☽△♀ **1:12 am**
☽△♃ **2:55 am**
☽⚻☉ **12:10 pm** 9:10 am
♄⚹♅ **11:32 pm** 8:32 pm
♀☌♃ 10:30 pm

12 TUESDAY
♀☌♃ **1:30 am**
☽☌♄ **8:34 am** 5:34 am
☽⚹♅ **8:36 am** 5:36 am
☽☌♆ **9:36 am** 6:36 am
☽⚹♇ **10:14 am** 7:14 am
☽☍♂ **12:38 pm** 9:38 am
☽△☿ **1:59 pm** 10:59 am

13 WEDNESDAY
☽□♃ **6:51 am** 3:51 am
☽□♀ **9:03 am** 6:03 am
☽△☉ **6:54 pm** 3:54 pm

14 THURSDAY
☽⚺♄ **11:11 am** 8:11 am
☽⚺♅ **11:28 am** 8:28 am
☽⚺♆ **12:19 pm** 9:19 am
☽□♇ **12:57 pm** 9:57 am
☽⚻♂ **5:45 pm** 2:45 pm
☽□☿ **5:49 pm** 2:49 pm
☿⚹♂ **10:05 pm** 7:05 pm

15 FRIDAY
☽⚹♃ **10:14 am** 7:14 am
☽⚹♀ **4:16 pm** 1:16 pm
☽□☉ 10:12 pm

16 SATURDAY
☽□☉ **1:12 am**
☽⚹♄ **1:39 pm** 10:39 am
☽☌♅ **2:11 pm** 11:11 am
☽⚹♆ **2:54 pm** 11:54 am
☽△♇ **3:31 pm** 12:31 pm
☽⚹☿ **10:33 pm** 7:33 pm
☽△♂ **10:47 pm** 7:47 pm

17 SUNDAY
☽⚺♃ **1:45 pm** 10:45 am
☽⚺♀ **11:46 pm** 8:46 pm
☿⚹♂ 10:33 pm

18 MONDAY
☿⚹♂ **1:33 am**
☽⚹☉ **7:53 am** 4:53 am
☽□♄ **4:33 pm** 1:33 pm
☽⚺♅ **5:21 pm** 2:21 pm
☽□♆ **5:57 pm** 2:57 pm
☽⚻♇ **6:34 pm** 3:34 pm

19 TUESDAY
☽□♂ **4:30 am** 1:30 am
☽⚺☿ **5:00 am** 2:00 am
☽☌♃ **6:02 pm** 3:02 pm

20 WEDNESDAY
☽☌♀ **8:27 am** 5:27 am
☽⚺☉ **3:49 pm** 12:49 pm
☽△♄ **8:34 pm** 5:34 pm
☽⚹♅ **9:40 pm** 6:40 pm
☽△♆ **10:08 pm** 7:08 pm
☽☍♇ **10:47 pm** 7:47 pm

21 THURSDAY
☽⚹♂ **11:44 am** 8:44 am
☽☌☿ **2:13 pm** 11:13 am
☽⚺♃ **11:55 pm** 8:55 pm

22 FRIDAY
☽⚺♀ **7:28 pm** 4:28 pm
☽☌☉ 11:07 pm
☽⚻♄ 11:30 pm

23 SATURDAY
☽☌☉ **2:07 am**
☽⚻♄ **2:30 am**
☽□♅ **3:57 am** 12:57 am
☽⚻♆ **4:18 am** 1:18 am
☽⚻♇ **4:59 am** 1:59 am
☉⚻♄ **7:05 am** 4:05 am
☽⚺♂ **9:29 pm** 6:29 pm

24 SUNDAY
☉□♅ **3:15 am** 12:15 am
☽⚺☿ **3:35 am** 12:35 am
☉⚻♆ **6:58 am** 3:58 am
☽⚹♃ **8:14 am** 5:14 am
☉⚻♇ **4:06 pm** 1:06 pm

25 MONDAY
☽⚹♀ **9:53 am** 6:53 am
☽☍♄ **11:00 am** 8:00 am
☽△♅ **12:52 pm** 9:52 am
☽☍♆ **1:04 pm** 10:04 am
☽△♇ **1:48 pm** 10:48 am
☽⚺☉ **3:41 pm** 12:41 pm
♀△♄ **8:56 pm** 5:56 pm
☿⚺♃ **11:27 pm** 8:27 pm

26 TUESDAY
☽☌♂ **10:26 am** 7:26 am
♀⚹♅ **4:58 pm** 1:58 pm
♀△♆ **6:18 pm** 3:18 pm
☽□♃ **7:23 pm** 4:23 pm
☽⚹☿ **10:06 pm** 7:06 pm
♀☍♇ 10:54 pm

27 WEDNESDAY
♀☍♇ **1:54 am**
☽⚻♄ **10:02 pm** 7:02 pm
☽⚻♅ 9:20 pm
☽⚻♆ 9:23 pm
☽□♇ 10:10 pm

28 THURSDAY
☽⚻♅ **12:20 am**
☽⚻♆ **12:23 am**
☽□♇ **1:10 am**
☽□♀ **3:48 am** 12:48 am
☽⚹☉ **8:27 am** 5:27 am
♅⚹♆ **8:09 pm** 5:09 pm
☽⚺♂ 10:58 pm

29 FRIDAY
☽⚺♂ **1:58 am**
☽△♃ **8:38 am** 5:38 am
☽□☿ **8:47 pm** 5:47 pm

30 SATURDAY
☽△♄ **10:19 am** 7:19 am
☽△♆ **12:53 pm** 9:53 am
☽☍♅ **12:59 pm** 9:59 am
☽⚹♇ **1:42 pm** 10:42 am
☽△♀ **11:12 pm** 8:12 pm
☽□☉ 11:25 pm

31 SUNDAY
☽□☉ **2:25 am**
☽⚹♂ **5:53 pm** 2:53 pm
☽⚻♃ **9:55 pm** 6:55 pm

Eastern time in bold type
Pacific time in medium type

AUGUST 2025

DATE	SID.TIME	SUN	MOON	NODE	MERCURY	VENUS	MARS	JUPITER	SATURN	URANUS	NEPTUNE	PLUTO	CERES	PALLAS	JUNO	VESTA	CHIRON
1 F	20 39 26	9♌01 21	3♏15	19♓04R	9♌00R	0♋58	26♍18	11♋43	1♈36R	0♊57	1♈58	2♒25R	16♑27	17♒24R	17♏20	13♏17	27♈10R
2 Sa	20 43 22	9 58 45	15 07	19 04	8 16	2 07	26 55	11 56	1 36	0 57	1 58	2 25	16 31	17 09	17 26	13 36	27 10
3 Su	20 47 19	10 56 10	27 01	19 03	7 34	3 17	27 32	12 08	1 34	0 59	1 57	2 23	16 34	16 53	17 33	13 54	27 09
4 M	20 51 15	11 53 36	9♐01	19 00	6 53	4 27	28 09	12 21	1 32	1 00	1 56	2 22	16 37	16 38	17 39	14 13	27 09
5 T	20 55 12	12 51 03	21 12	18 56	6 16	5 37	28 46	12 34	1 30	1 02	1 55	2 20	16 39	16 22	17 46	14 32	27 09
6 W	20 59 9	13 48 30	3♑37	18 50	5 43	6 46	29 24	12 46	1 28	1 03	1 54	2 19	16 42	16 06	17 54	14 52	27 09
7 Th	21 3 5	14 45 58	16 18	18 45	5 14	7 56	0♎01	12 59	1 26	1 05	1 53	2 18	16 44	15 51	18 01	15 11	27 08
8 F	21 7 2	15 43 27	29 17	18 39	4 51	9 06	0 38	13 11	1 23	1 06	1 52	2 16	16 45	15 35	18 09	15 31	27 08
9 Sa	21 10 58	16 40 57	12♒34	18 35	4 33	10 17	1 16	13 24	1 21	1 08	1 51	2 15	16 46	15 19	18 17	15 51	27 08
10 Su	21 14 55	17 38 28	26 06	18 32	4 21	11 27	1 53	13 36	1 18	1 09	1 50	2 13	16 47	15 04	18 25	16 11	27 07
11 M	21 18 51	18 36 00	9♓52	18 30	4 15D	12 37	2 31	13 49	1 15	1 11	1 49	2 12	16 48R	14 48	18 34	16 32	27 06
12 T	21 22 48	19 33 33	23 49	18 30	4 17	13 48	3 08	14 01	1 12	1 12	1 48	2 11	16 48	14 33	18 42	16 52	27 06
13 W	21 26 44	20 31 07	7♈55	18 31	4 25	14 58	3 46	14 13	1 10	1 13	1 47	2 09	16 48	14 17	18 51	17 13	27 05
14 Th	21 30 41	21 28 43	22 05	18 32	4 40	16 09	4 24	14 25	1 07	1 14	1 46	2 08	16 47	14 02	19 00	17 35	27 05
15 F	21 34 38	22 26 21	6♉18	18 34R	5 03	17 19	5 02	14 37	1 04	1 15	1 45	2 07	16 46	13 46	19 10	17 56	27 04
16 Sa	21 38 34	23 24 00	20 32	18 32	5 32	18 30	5 40	14 49	1 00	1 16	1 44	2 06	16 45	13 31	19 19	18 17	27 04
17 Su	21 42 31	24 21 40	4♊43	18 34	6 09	19 41	6 18	15 01	0 57	1 18	1 42	2 04	16 43	13 16	19 29	18 39	27 02
18 M	21 46 27	25 19 22	18 51	18 30	6 53	20 52	6 56	15 13	0 54	1 19	1 41	2 03	16 41	13 01	19 39	19 01	27 01
19 T	21 50 24	26 17 06	2♋52	18 30	7 44	22 03	7 34	15 25	0 51	1 19	1 40	2 02	16 39	12 47	19 49	19 23	27 00
20 W	21 54 20	27 14 52	16 44	18 27	8 42	23 14	8 12	15 37	0 47	1 20	1 39	2 00	16 36	12 32	20 00	19 45	27 00
21 Th	21 58 17	28 12 39	0♌25	18 24	9 46	24 25	8 50	15 49	0 44	1 21	1 37	1 59	16 33	12 18	20 11	20 08	26 59
22 F	22 2 13	29 10 27	13 52	18 22	10 56	25 37	9 28	16 00	0 40	1 22	1 36	1 58	16 29	12 04	20 21	20 31	26 58
23 Sa	22 6 10	0♍08 17	27 04	18 20	12 13	26 48	10 07	16 12	0 37	1 23	1 35	1 57	16 25	11 50	20 33	20 54	26 57
24 Su	22 10 7	1 06 08	10♍00	18 19D	13 35	27 59	10 45	16 23	0 33	1 23	1 33	1 56	16 21	11 36	20 44	21 17	26 54
25 M	22 14 3	2 04 01	22 40	18 19	15 02	29 11	11 24	16 35	0 29	1 24	1 32	1 54	16 17	11 22	20 55	21 40	26 53
26 T	22 18 0	3 01 55	5♎04	18 19	16 34	0♌23	12 02	16 46	0 25	1 25	1 30	1 53	16 12	11 09	21 07	22 03	26 52
27 W	22 21 56	3 59 50	17 16	18 20	18 11	1 34	12 41	16 57	0 22	1 25	1 29	1 52	16 06	10 56	21 19	22 27	26 50
28 Th	22 25 53	4 57 47	29 17	18 22	19 51	2 46	13 19	17 09	0 18	1 26	1 28	1 51	16 01	10 43	21 31	22 51	26 49
29 F	22 29 49	5 55 45	11♏11	18 23	21 35	3 58	13 58	17 20	0 14	1 26	1 26	1 50	15 55	10 31	21 43	23 14	26 47
30 Sa	22 33 46	6 53 44	23 02	18 24	23 22	5 10	14 37	17 31	0 10	1 27	1 25	1 49	15 48	10 19	21 55	23 38	26 46
31 Su	22 37 42	7 51 45	4♐56	18 24R	25 11	6 22	15 16	17 42	0 06	1 27	1 23	1 48	15 41	10 07	22 08	24 03	26 44

EPHEMERIS CALCULATED FOR 12 MIDNIGHT GREENWICH MEAN TIME. ALL OTHER DATA AND FACING ASPECTARIAN PAGE IN **EASTERN TIME (BOLD)** AND PACIFIC TIME (REGULAR).

SEPTEMBER 2025

☽ Last Aspect / ☽ Ingress

day	ET / hr:mn / PT		asp	sign	day	ET / hr:mn / PT
1	9:45 pm 6:45 pm		☌ ☽	♑		
4	6:32 am 3:32 am		⚹ ♄	≈≈		
6	11:54 am 8:54 am		△ ♃	ℋ		
8	2:37 pm 11:37 am		□ ♀	♈		
10	4:03 pm 1:03 pm		△ ♀	♉		
12	5:38 pm 2:38 pm		△ ♄	♊		
14	8:30 pm 5:30 pm		⚹ ♄	♋		
16/17	1:20 am		△ ♃	♌		

☽ Ingress

sign	day	ET / hr:mn / PT
♑	19	8:21 am 5:21 am
≈≈	21	3:54 pm 12:54 pm
ℋ	23/24	12:02 pm 9:02 am
♈	26	1:44 pm 10:44 am
♉	29	1:44 am

☽ Ingress (second)

sign	day	ET / hr:mn / PT
♍	19	8:23 am 5:23 am
≏	21	5:41 pm 2:41 pm
♏	24	5:00 am 2:00 am
♐	26	5:37 pm 2:37 pm
♑	29	5:55 am 2:55 am
♑	29	5:55 am 2:55 am

☽ Phases & Eclipses

phase	day	ET / hr:mn / PT
Full Moon	7	2:09 pm 11:09 am
4th Quarter	14	6:33 am 3:33 am
New Moon	21	5:54 pm 2:54 pm
2nd Quarter	29	7:54 pm 4:54 pm

Planet Ingress

	day	ET / hr:mn / PT
♄ ℋ	1	4:07 am 1:07 am
♀ ♍	2	9:23 am 6:23 am
♀ ≏	13	11:10 pm 8:10 pm
☿ ≏	18	6:06 am 3:06 am
☉ ≏	19	8:39 am 5:39 am
☿ ♏	22	2:19 pm 11:19 am

Planetary Motion

	day	ET / hr:mn / PT
♄	1	9:51 pm
♇ ℞	5	12:51 am
♅ ℞	6	

---

1 MONDAY
☽ △ ♄ 7:37 pm 4:37 pm
☽ ☌ ♇ 9:39 pm 6:39 pm
☽ ⚹ ♀ 9:20 pm
☽ △ ♄ 9:35 pm
☽ ⚹ ♀ 10:09 pm

2 TUESDAY
☽ □ ♃ 12:20 am
☽ ⚹ ☿ 12:35 am
☽ ☌ ♀ 1:09 am
☿ △ ♇ 5:21 am
☽ □ ♀ 8:21 am 5:21 am
☽ △ ♅ 4:40 pm 1:40 pm
☽ ⚹ ♂ 6:23 pm 3:23 pm

3 WEDNESDAY
☽ ⚹ ☽ 1:44 am
☽ △ ♅ 10:44 pm
☽ ⚹ ♄ 7:05 am 4:05 am
☽ ⚹ ☉ 7:20 am 4:20 am
☽ △ ♂ 8:50 am 5:50 am

4 THURSDAY
☽ ☌ ♄ 6:08 am 3:08 am
☽ △ ♀ 8:52 am 5:52 am
☽ △ ♂ 9:13 am 6:13 am
☽ □ ♇ 9:40 am 6:40 am
☽ ⚹ ♂ 2:17 pm 11:17 am
☽ ☌ ♀ 10:59 pm 7:59 pm

5 FRIDAY
☽ ⚹ ♀ 5:49 am 2:49 am
☽ △ ♄ 6:16 am 3:16 am
☽ ⚹ ♂ 4:13 am 1:13 am
☽ □ ♅ 4:51 am 1:51 am

6 SATURDAY
☽ ⚹ ♇ 5:38 am 2:38 am
☽ △ ♀ 8:15 am
☽ ☌ ♄ 11:00 am
☽ □ ☿ 11:26 am
☽ △ ♃ 11:48 am

7 SUNDAY
☽ △ ♅ 3:41 am 12:41 am
☽ ⚹ ♀ 2:48 am
☽ ⚹ ☿ 8:25 am 5:25 am
☽ ☌ ♇ 10:52 am 7:52 am

8 MONDAY
☽ ⚹ ♂ 1:44 am
☽ △ ♄ 4:33 am 1:33 am
☽ □ ☿ 5:03 am 2:03 am
☽ ⚹ ♀ 5:21 am 2:21 am

9 TUESDAY
☽ ☌ ♂ 1:31 am 10:31 am
☽ ⚹ ♄ 7:35 am 4:35 am
☽ △ ☉ 9:07 pm 6:07 pm
☽ □ ♇ 10:43 pm 7:43 pm
☽ ⚹ ♀ 11:54 pm

10 WEDNESDAY
☽ ☌ ♂ 2:54 am
☽ △ ♀ 2:56 am
☽ ☌ ♄ 2:52 pm 11:56 am
☽ □ ♀ 8:27 am 5:27 am
☽ ⚹ ☿ 6:43 pm 3:43 pm
☽ △ ♂ 7:12 pm 4:12 pm

11 THURSDAY
☽ □ ♇ 10:18 am 7:18 am
☽ △ ♀ 9:29 pm
☽ ⚹ ♄ 9:39 pm
☽ △ ♅ 11:59 pm

12 FRIDAY
☽ △ ♀ 12:29 am
☽ ⚹ ♀ 2:39 am
☽ ☌ ♂ 3:10 am 12:30 am
☽ ⚹ ♄ 6:10 am 3:40 am
☽ △ ♂ 4:44 am 1:14 am
☽ □ ☉ 7:23 am 4:23 am
☽ □ ♇ 8:03 pm 5:03 pm
☽ △ ♀ 8:17 pm 5:17 pm

13 SATURDAY
☉ ☌ ♀ 6:52 pm 3:52 pm

14 SUNDAY
☽ △ ♀ 12:34 am
☽ ☌ ♂ 3:33 am
☽ ⚹ ♄ 5:17 am
☽ □ ♇ 7:10 am
☽ △ ♀ 8:41 pm

15 MONDAY
☽ □ ♄ 6:46 am
☽ ⚹ ♀ 10:13 pm
☽ △ ☿ 10:58 pm
☽ ⚹ ♂ 11:12 pm

16 TUESDAY
☽ △ ♀ 10:59 am
☽ ⚹ ♄ 11:01 am
☽ △ ♂ 11:04 pm

17 WEDNESDAY
☽ ☌ ♇ 8:18 am
☽ △ ♀ 2:53 pm
☽ ⚹ ♄ 4:53 pm
☽ ☌ ♂ 7:47 pm
☽ □ ♅ 8:52 pm
☽ △ ♀ 11:14 pm

18 THURSDAY
☽ △ ♀ 3:00 am
☽ □ ♂ 2:34 am
☽ ⚹ ☿ 2:42 pm
☽ △ ♄ 4:05 pm
☽ ☌ ♀ 1:47 pm

19 FRIDAY
☽ ☌ ☿ 7:34 am
☽ △ ♀ 6:01 am

---

20 SATURDAY
☽ △ ♀ 1:20 am
☽ □ ♂ 1:24 am
☽ △ ♄ 11:42 am
☽ ⚹ ☿ 1:59 pm

21 SUNDAY
☽ ☌ ♀ 12:34 am
☽ ⚹ ♄ 1:46 am
☽ ☌ ♂ 2:42 pm
☉ ☌ ☽ 3:54 pm
☽ △ ♇ 5:05 pm
☽ □ ♀ 11:58 pm

22 MONDAY
☽ ☌ ☉ 12:52 am
☽ △ ♀ 1:58 am

23 TUESDAY
♂ ☌ ♀ 7:01 am 4:01 am
☽ ☌ ♄ 8:53 am 5:53 am
☽ ⚹ ♇ 12:02 pm 9:02 am
☽ △ ♀ 1:10 pm 10:10 am
☽ ⚹ ♂ 10:55 pm 7:55 pm
  10:33 pm
  11:05 pm

24 WEDNESDAY
☽ ☌ ♀ 1:33 am
☽ ⚹ ♄ 2:05 am
☽ ⚹ ♂ 3:15 am 12:15 am
☽ ☌ ☿ 6:29 am 3:29 am
☽ △ ♀ 7:40 am 4:40 am
☽ ⚹ ♀ 7:52 am 4:52 am
☽ △ ♇ 7:56 am 4:56 am
☽ ☌ ♂ 8:27 am 5:27 am
☽ △ ♄ 6:18 pm 3:18 pm

25 THURSDAY
☽ ⚹ ♀ 5:15 am 2:15 am
  10:06 pm

26 FRIDAY
☽ □ ♀ 1:06 am
☽ ⚹ ♂ 1:44 am 10:44 am
☽ △ ♄ 6:58 pm 3:58 pm
☽ ⚹ ♇ 8:13 pm 5:13 pm
☽ ☌ ♀ 8:32 pm 5:32 pm
  1:34 am

27 SATURDAY
☽ △ ♀ 3:43 am 12:43 am
☽ ⚹ ♄ 2:21 am 11:21 am
  10:44 am

28 SUNDAY
☽ ⚹ ♀ 1:44 am
☽ ⚹ ♄ 2:05 am
☽ ☌ ♀ 2:00 am 11:00 am

29 MONDAY
☽ ⚹ ♀ 7:05 am 4:05 am
☽ △ ♄ 8:22 am 5:22 am
☽ ⚹ ♇ 8:43 am 5:43 am
☽ ☌ ☿ 3:55 pm 12:55 pm
☽ △ ♀ 7:54 pm 4:54 pm

30 TUESDAY
☽ ☌ ♀ 8:20 am 5:20 am
☽ △ ♀ 11:39 pm 8:39 pm
  10:40 pm

Eastern time in bold type
Pacific time in medium type

SEPTEMBER 2025

DATE	SID.TIME	SUN	MOON	NODE	MERCURY	VENUS	MARS	JUPITER	SATURN	URANUS	NEPTUNE	PLUTO	CERES	PALLAS	JUNO	VESTA	CHIRON
1 M	22 41 39	8♍49 47	16♐55	18♓24R	27♌03	7♌34	15♎55	17♋52	0♈01R	1♊27	1♈20R	1♒47R	15♈37R	9♒55R	22♏21	24♏21	26♈43R
2 T	22 45 36	9♍47 51	29♐06	18♓23	28♌56	8♌46	16♎34	18♋03	29♓57	1♊27	1♈19	1♒46	15♈27	9♒44	22♏34	24♏52	26♈41
3 W	22 49 32	10♍45 56	11♑33	18♓23	0♍17	9♌58	17♎13	18♋14	29♓53	1♊28	1♈18	1♒44	15♈19	9♒33	22♏47	25♏16	26♈39
4 Th	22 53 29	11♍44 02	23♑54	18♓22	2♍46	11♌10	17♎52	18♋24	29♓49	1♊28	1♈17	1♒43	15♈11	9♒22	23♏00	25♏41	26♈38
5 F	22 57 25	12♍42 10	7♒24	18♓21	4♍42	12♌22	18♎31	18♋35	29♓44	1♊28	1♈16	1♒42	15♈03	9♒11	23♏14	26♏06	26♈36
6 Sa	23 1 22	13♍40 19	20♒52	18♓21	6♍39	13♌35	19♎10	18♋45	29♓40	1♊28R	1♈14	1♒41	14♈54	9♒01	23♏27	26♏31	26♈34
7 Su	23 5 18	14♍38 30	4♓42	18♓20D	8♍35	14♌47	19♎50	18♋55	29♓36	1♊28	1♈12	1♒41	14♈45	8♒52	23♏41	26♏56	26♈32
8 M	23 9 15	15♍36 43	18♓51	18♓20	10♍31	16♌00	20♎29	19♋06	29♓31	1♊28	1♈11	1♒40	14♈35	8♒42	23♏55	27♏22	26♈30
9 T	23 13 11	16♍34 57	3♈15	18♓20	12♍27	17♌12	21♎08	19♋16	29♓27	1♊28	1♈09	1♒39	14♈26	8♒33	24♏09	27♏47	26♈28
10 W	23 17 8	17♍33 13	17♈48	18♓20R	14♍22	18♌25	21♎48	19♋25	29♓22	1♊27	1♈08	1♒38	14♈16	8♒24	24♏23	28♏13	26♈26
11 Th	23 21 5	18♍31 31	2♉24	18♓20	16♍17	19♌37	22♎27	19♋35	29♓18	1♊27	1♈06	1♒37	14♈06	8♒16	24♏38	28♏39	26♈24
12 F	23 25 1	19♍29 51	16♉58	18♓20	18♍11	20♌50	23♎07	19♋45	29♓13	1♊27	1♈04	1♒36	13♈55	8♒08	24♏52	29♏04	26♈22
13 Sa	23 28 58	20♍28 14	1♊25	18♓20	20♍04	22♌03	23♎47	19♋55	29♓09	1♊27	1♈03	1♒35	13♈44	8♒00	25♏07	29♏30	26♈20
14 Su	23 32 54	21♍26 38	15♊40	18♓20D	21♍56	23♌16	24♎26	20♋04	29♓04	1♊26	1♈01	1♒34	13♈33	7♒52	25♏22	29♏57	26♈18
15 M	23 36 51	22♍25 05	29♊42	18♓20	23♍47	24♌29	25♎06	20♋14	29♓00	1♊26	1♈00	1♒34	13♈22	7♒45	25♏37	0♐23	26♈16
16 T	23 40 47	23♍23 34	13♋30	18♓20	25♍37	25♌42	25♎46	20♋23	28♓55	1♊25	0♈58	1♒33	13♈11	7♒39	25♏52	0♐49	26♈14
17 W	23 44 44	24♍22 05	27♋02	18♓21	27♍27	26♌55	26♎26	20♋32	28♓50	1♊25	0♈56	1♒32	12♈59	7♒32	26♏07	1♐16	26♈12
18 Th	23 48 40	25♍20 38	10♌19	18♓21	29♍15	28♌08	27♎06	20♋41	28♓46	1♊25	0♈55	1♒31	12♈47	7♒26	26♏22	1♐42	26♈09
19 F	23 52 37	26♍19 13	23♌21	18♓22	1♎02	29♌21	27♎46	20♋50	28♓41	1♊24	0♈53	1♒31	12♈35	7♒21	26♏38	2♐09	26♈07
20 Sa	23 56 34	27♍17 50	6♍11	18♓23R	2♎48	0♍35	28♎26	20♋59	28♓36	1♊23	0♈51	1♒30	12♈22	7♒16	26♏54	2♐36	26♈05
21 Su	0 0 27	28♍16 30	18♍47	18♓23	4♎33	1♍48	29♎06	21♋08	28♓32	1♊22	0♈50	1♒29	12♈10	7♒11	27♏09	3♐03	26♈02
22 M	0 4 30	29♍15 11	1♎25	18♓22	6♎17	3♍01	29♎47	21♋17	28♓27	1♊22	0♈48	1♒29	11♈57	7♒06	27♏25	3♐30	26♈00
23 T	0 8 23	0♎13 54	13♎25	18♓22	8♎00	4♍15	0♏27	21♋25	28♓22	1♊21	0♈46	1♒28	11♈44	7♒02	27♏41	3♐57	25♈58
24 W	0 12 20	1♎12 39	25♎30	18♓18	9♎43	5♍28	1♏07	21♋33	28♓18	1♊20	0♈45	1♒28	11♈31	6♒58	27♏58	4♐24	25♈55
25 Th	0 16 16	2♎11 26	7♏27	18♓18	11♎24	6♍42	1♏48	21♋41	28♓13	1♊19	0♈43	1♒27	11♈18	6♒55	28♏14	4♐52	25♈53
26 F	0 20 13	3♎10 14	19♏20	18♓16	13♎04	7♍55	2♏28	21♋49	28♓08	1♊18	0♈41	1♒27	11♈05	6♒52	28♏30	5♐19	25♈50
27 Sa	0 24 09	4♎09 05	1♐11	18♓14	14♎43	9♍09	3♏09	21♋57	28♓04	1♊17	0♈40	1♒26	10♈51	6♒49	28♏47	5♐47	25♈48
28 Su	0 28 6	5♎07 57	13♐03	18♓12	16♎22	10♍23	3♏50	22♋05	27♓59	1♊16	0♈38	1♒26	10♈38	6♒47	29♏04	6♐14	25♈45
29 M	0 32 2	6♎06 52	25♐01	18♓10D	17♎59	11♍37	4♏30	22♋13	27♓55	1♊15	0♈36	1♒25	10♈25	6♒45	29♏20	6♐42	25♈43
30 T	0 35 59	7♎05 48	7♑09	18♓10	19♎36	12♍50	5♏11	22♋20	27♓50	1♊14	0♈35	1♒25	10♈11	6♒43	29♏37	7♐10	25♈40

EPHEMERIS CALCULATED FOR 12 MIDNIGHT GREENWICH MEAN TIME. ALL OTHER DATA AND FACING ASPECTARIAN PAGE IN **EASTERN TIME (BOLD)** AND PACIFIC TIME (REGULAR).

OCTOBER 2025

D Last Aspect / D Ingress

day	ET / hr:mn / PT	asp	sign day	ET / hr:mn / PT
1	11:33 am 8:33 am	✶ ♄	♒ 1	3:52 pm 2:52 pm
2	2:15 pm 11:15 am	△ ♀	♓ 3	10:07 pm 7:07 pm
5	8:30 pm 5:30 pm	✶ ♀	♈ 5	9:46 pm
5	8:30 pm 5:30 pm	♂ ♂	♈ 6	12:48 am
8	8:30 pm 5:30 pm	♂ ♄	♉ 8	1:12 am
8	2:24 pm 11:24 am	□ ♄	♊ 10	1:12 am
8	2:24 pm 11:24 am	△ ♀	♋ 12	2:37 am
8	8:31 pm 5:31 pm	✶ ♄	♌ 14	6:47 am
9	8:31 pm 5:31 pm	□ ♂		6:47 am
10	10:56 pm 7:56 pm	△ ♀		
13	10:56 pm 7:56 pm	△ ♄		
14	1:05 am	△ ♀		

D Ingress

sign day	ET / hr:mn / PT	
♍ 16	1:06 pm 10:06 am	
♎ 18	5:10 pm 2:10 pm	
♏ 20	8:25 pm 5:25 pm	
♐ 22	12:19 am 9:19 pm	
♑ 24	12:19 am	
♒ 26	12:53 pm 9:53 am	
♓ 28	11:55 pm 8:55 pm	
♈ 31	2:15 pm 11:15 am	

D Last Aspect

day	ET / hr:mn / PT	asp	sign day	ET / hr:mn / PT
15	11:33 am 8:33 am	✶ ♄	♒ 1	
16	1:06 pm	△ ♀		
18	5:10 pm	✶ ♀		
18	8:25 pm	♂ ♂		
20	12:48 am	♂ ♄		10:41 pm
24	12:19 am	□ ♄		11:48 pm
26	12:53 pm	△ ♀		
28	11:55 pm	✶ ♄		
31	2:15 pm	□ ♂		

D Phases & Eclipses

phase	day	ET / hr:mn / PT
Full Moon	6	11:48 pm 8:48 pm
4th Quarter	13	2:13 am 11:13 pm
New Moon	21	8:25 am 5:25 am
2nd Quarter	29	12:21 pm 9:21 am

Planet Ingress

	day	ET / hr:mn / PT
✶ ♐	1	3:55 am 12:55 am
♀ ♏	13	12:41 pm 9:41 am
☉ ♏	22	5:19 pm 2:19 pm
♀ ♏	22	5:48 am 2:48 am
♀ ♏	22	11:51 pm 8:51 pm
☉ ♏	29	7:02 am 4:02 am

Planetary Motion

	day	ET / hr:mn / PT
♀ D	4	3:17 am 12:17 am
♀ D	13	10:54 am 7:54 am

---

1 WEDNESDAY
△ ♀	2:140 am		
✶✶✶□△♄	11:33 am 8:33 am		
△ ♀	4:51 pm 1:51 pm		
△ ♀	4:59 pm 1:59 pm		
□ ♄	6:05 pm 3:05 pm		
△ ♀	6:29 pm 3:29 pm		

2 THURSDAY
△ ♀	4:29 am 1:29 am		
□ ♀	9:41 am 6:41 am		
△ ♀	10:28 am 7:28 am		

3 FRIDAY
✶ ♀	9:23 am 6:23 am		
△ ♀	11:15 am		
△ ♀	5:49 pm 2:49 pm		
□ ♀	10:56 pm 7:56 pm		

4 SATURDAY
△ ♀	12:06 am		
△ ♀	12:32 am		
□✶✶	3:36 pm 12:36 pm		
□ ♂	6:42 pm 3:42 pm		
△ ♀	8:32 pm 5:32 pm		

5 SUNDAY
✶ ♀	7:34 am 4:34 am		
□ ♀	1:15 pm 10:15 am		
△ ♀	8:30 pm 5:30 pm		
♂ ♀	11:26 pm 8:26 pm		

6 MONDAY
♂ ♀	1:28 am		
✶✶✶♂	2:35 am		
△ ♀	3:05 am		
□ ♀	4:54 am 1:54 am		
✶ ♄	6:53 am 3:53 am		
△ ♀	11:48 pm 8:48 pm		

7 TUESDAY
□ ♀	5:41 am 2:41 am		
□ ♄	10:41 am 7:41 am		
□ ♀	12:58 pm 9:58 am		
△ ♀	2:24 pm 11:24 am		
✶ ♄	8:48 pm 5:48 pm		

8 WEDNESDAY
△ ♀	1:46 am		
△ ♀	2:52 am		
□ ♀	3:24 am 12:24 am		
△ ♀	5:15 am 2:15 am		
□ ♀	7:41 am 4:41 am		
△ ♀	7:16 am 4:16 am		

9 THURSDAY
△ ♀	3:08 am 12:08 am		
△ ♀	2:39 am 11:39 pm		
△ ♀	5:12 pm 2:12 pm		
✶ ♄	8:31 pm 5:31 pm		

10 FRIDAY
✶✶ Ψ	1:33 am		
△ ♀	2:35 am		
△ ♀	10:05 am 7:05 am		
□ ♀	9:59 pm		

11 SATURDAY
♂ ♀	7:14 am 4:14 am		
△ ♀	7:17 am 4:17 am		
✶ ♀	9:40 am 6:40 am		
△ ♀	9:56 pm 6:56 pm		

12 SUNDAY
♂ ♀	3:52 am		
△ ♀	4:12 am 1:12 am		
□ ♀	6:13 pm 3:13 pm		

13 MONDAY
□ ♀	12:07 am		
♂ ♀	11:13 am 8:13 am		
✶ ♀	7:49 pm 4:49 pm		
□ ♀	10:05 pm		

14 TUESDAY
△ ♀	1:05 am		
□ ♀	8:11 am 5:11 am		
△ ♀	4:08 pm		
✶ ♀	5:10 pm		

15 WEDNESDAY
△ ♀	8:21 am 5:21 am		
□ ♀	9:14 am 6:14 am		
△ ♀	10:10 am 7:10 am		
✶ ♀	7:45 pm 4:45 pm		

16 THURSDAY
△ ♀	5:41 am 2:41 am		
✶ ♀	11:50 am 8:50 am		

17 FRIDAY
♂ ♀	1:06 am		
✶✶✶♀	2:52 am		
□ ♀	7:47 am 4:47 am		
△ ♀	3:37 pm 12:37 pm		
□ ♀	4:41 pm 1:41 pm		
△ ♀	9:35 pm 6:35 pm		

18 SATURDAY
□ ♀	1:43 am		
✶ ♀	9:10 am 6:10 am		
□ ♀	11:26 am 9:01 am		

19 SUNDAY
△ ♀	12:01 am		
□ ♀	12:43 pm		
✶ ♀	3:33 pm 12:33 pm		
△ ♀	5:10 pm 2:10 pm		

20 MONDAY
♂ ♀	2:52 am	11:44 am
△ ♀	3:24 pm	12:24 pm
		9:29 pm

21 TUESDAY
□ ♀	4:24 am 1:24 am		
✶ ♀	8:25 am 5:25 am		
□ ♀	11:44 am 8:44 am		
△ ♀	1:00 pm 10:00 am		
✶ ♀	2:29 pm 11:29 am		

22 WEDNESDAY
☉ ♏	9:25 am 6:25 am		
□ ♀	11:26 am 8:26 am		

23 THURSDAY
✶ ♀	6:55 am 3:55 am		9:11 pm
□ ♀	10:57 am 7:57 am		1:19 pm
△ ♀	1:19 pm 10:19 am		
✶ ♀	1:47 pm 10:47 am		
□ ♀	4:38 pm 1:38 pm		
		9:14 pm	

24 FRIDAY
♂ ♂	12:14 am		
✶ ♀	2:44 am		
△ ♀	3:08 am 12:08 am		
✶ ♀	9:25 am 6:25 am		
✶ ♄	11:08 am 8:08 am		

25 SATURDAY
✶✶✶♀	5:17 pm 2:17 pm		
△ ♀	5:17 pm 2:17 pm		
□ ♀	11:27 pm 8:27 pm		
		11:16 pm	

26 SUNDAY
△ ♀	2:16 am		
✶ ♀	5:01 am 2:01 am		
□ ♀	6:19 am 3:19 am		
△ ♀	12:42 pm 9:42 am		
△ ♀	1:50 pm 10:50 am		

27 MONDAY
△ ♀	3:42 pm 12:42 pm		
□ ♀	8:35 pm 5:35 pm		

28 TUESDAY
□ ♀	12:11 pm		
△ ♀	2:19 pm		
✶ ♀	1:57 pm		10:57 am

29 WEDNESDAY
✶ ♂	12:39 am		
△ ♀	2:39 am		
△ ♀	3:26 am 12:26 am		
□ ♀	12:21 pm 9:21 am		
✶ ♀	3:05 pm 12:05 pm		
△ ♀	3:36 pm 12:36 pm		

30 THURSDAY
△ ♀	3:35 pm 12:35 pm		
☉ ♀	6:06 pm 3:06 pm		
□ ♀	10:36 pm 7:36 pm		
		9:15 pm	

31 FRIDAY
□ ♀	12:15 am		
✶ ♀	2:15 am		
□ ♀	7:25 am 4:25 am		
△ ♀	8:18 am 5:18 am		
✶ ♄	10:21 am 7:21 am		
△ ♀	11:32 am 8:32 am		
△ ♀	11:42 am 8:42 am		

Eastern time in **bold type**
Pacific time in medium type

OCTOBER 2025

DATE	SID.TIME	SUN	MOON	NODE	MERCURY	VENUS	MARS	JUPITER	SATURN	URANUS	NEPTUNE	PLUTO	CERES	PALLAS	JUNO	VESTA	CHIRON
1 W	0 39 56	8≏04 45	19♏31	18♈10	21≏11	14♍04	5♏52	22♋28	27♓45R	1♊13R	0♈33R	1≈24R	9♍57R	6≏42R	29♏54	7♐38	25♈37R
2 Th	0 43 52	9 03 45	2≏13	18 12	22 46	15 18	6 33	22 35	27 41	1 11	0 31	1 24	9 44	6 41	0♐11	8 06	25 35
3 F	0 47 49	10 02 46	15 17	18 13	24 20	16 32	7 14	22 42	27 36	1 10	0 30	1 24	9 30	6 40	0 29	8 34	25 32
4 Sa	0 51 45	11 01 49	28 47	18 14	25 53	17 46	7 55	22 49	27 32	1 09	0 28	1 23	9 17	6 40D	0 46	9 02	25 30
5 Su	0 55 42	12 00 53	12♍44	18 15R	27 25	19 00	8 36	22 56	27 28	1 07	0 27	1 23	9 03	6 40	1 04	9 30	25 27
6 M	0 59 38	13 00 00	27 05	18 15	28 57	20 14	9 17	23 03	27 23	1 06	0 25	1 23	8 49	6 40	1 21	9 59	25 24
7 T	1 3 35	13 59 08	11♍47	18 14	0♏19	21 28	9 58	23 09	27 19	1 05	0 23	1 23	8 36	6 41	1 39	10 27	25 22
8 W	1 7 31	14 58 19	26 44	18 11	1 57	22 42	10 39	23 15	27 14	1 03	0 22	1 22	8 23	6 42	1 56	10 56	25 19
9 Th	1 11 28	15 57 31	11♍47	18 08	3 27	23 57	11 21	23 22	27 10	1 02	0 20	1 22	8 09	6 43	2 14	11 24	25 16
10 F	1 15 25	16 56 46	26 46	18 03	4 55	25 11	12 02	23 28	27 06	1 00	0 19	1 22	7 56	6 45	2 32	11 53	25 13
11 Sa	1 19 21	17 56 03	11♊34	18 00	6 22	26 25	12 43	23 34	27 02	0 58	0 17	1 22	7 43	6 47	2 50	12 22	25 11
12 Su	1 23 18	18 55 23	26 04	17 57	7 49	27 40	13 25	23 39	26 58	0 57	0 15	1 22	7 30	6 49	3 08	12 50	25 08
13 M	1 27 14	19 54 45	10♋12	17 55D	9 15	28 54	14 06	23 45	26 53	0 55	0 14	1 22D	7 17	6 52	3 27	13 19	25 05
14 T	1 31 11	20 54 09	23 57	17 55	10 39	0≏09	14 48	23 50	26 49	0 53	0 12	1 22	7 04	6 55	3 45	13 48	25 02
15 W	1 35 7	21 53 35	7♌19	17 55	12 03	1 23	15 30	23 56	26 45	0 52	0 11	1 22	6 52	6 58	4 03	14 17	25 00
16 Th	1 39 4	22 53 04	20 22	17 57	13 27	2 37	16 12	24 01	26 41	0 50	0 09	1 22	6 39	7 02	4 22	14 46	24 57
17 F	1 43 0	23 52 35	3♍08	17 58	14 49	3 52	16 54	24 06	26 38	0 48	0 08	1 22	6 27	7 06	4 40	15 16	24 54
18 Sa	1 46 57	24 52 08	15 38	17 59R	16 10	5 06	17 35	24 10	26 34	0 46	0 06	1 22	6 15	7 10	4 59	15 45	24 51
19 Su	1 50 54	25 51 43	27 57	17 59	17 30	6 21	18 17	24 15	26 30	0 44	0 05	1 22	6 03	7 15	5 18	16 14	24 48
20 M	1 54 50	26 51 21	10≏07	17 56	18 59	7 36	18 59	24 19	26 26	0 42	0 03	1 23	5 52	7 20	5 37	16 44	24 46
21 T	1 58 47	27 51 00	22 10	17 52	20 07	8 50	19 41	24 24	26 23	0 40	0 02	1 23	5 40	7 25	5 56	17 13	24 43
22 W	2 2 43	28 50 42	4♏08	17 46	21 23	10 05	20 23	24 28	26 19	0 38	0 01	1 23	5 29	7 30	6 15	17 42	24 40
23 Th	2 6 40	29 50 25	16 01	17 38	22 38	11 20	21 06	24 31	26 16	0 36	29♓59	1 24	5 18	7 36	6 34	18 12	24 37
24 F	2 10 36	0♏50 11	27 52	17 30	23 52	12 35	21 48	24 35	26 12	0 34	29 58	1 24	5 08	7 42	6 53	18 42	24 35
25 Sa	2 14 33	1 49 58	9♐43	17 21	25 04	13 49	22 30	24 39	26 09	0 32	29 56	1 24	4 58	7 48	7 12	19 11	24 32
26 Su	2 18 29	2 49 47	21 36	17 13	26 14	15 04	23 13	24 42	26 06	0 30	29 55	1 24	4 48	7 54	7 32	19 41	24 29
27 M	2 22 26	3 49 39	3♑33	17 07	27 22	16 19	23 55	24 45	26 02	0 28	29 54	1 24	4 38	8 01	7 51	20 11	24 26
28 T	2 26 23	4 49 31	15 39	17 03	28 28	17 34	24 38	24 48	25 59	0 26	29 52	1 25	4 29	8 08	8 10	20 41	24 24
29 W	2 30 19	5 49 26	27 58	17 03D	29 32	18 49	25 20	24 51	25 56	0 23	29 51	1 25	4 20	8 15	8 30	21 11	24 21
30 Th	2 34 16	6 49 22	10≈33	17 01	0♐33	20 04	26 03	24 53	25 53	0 21	29 50	1 25	4 11	8 23	8 49	21 41	24 18
31 F	2 38 12	7 49 19	23 30	17 02	1 31	21 19	26 45	24 56	25 51	0 19	29 49	1 26	4 03	8 31	9 09	22 11	24 16

EPHEMERIS CALCULATED FOR 12 MIDNIGHT GREENWICH MEAN TIME. ALL OTHER DATA AND FACING ASPECTARIAN PAGE IN **EASTERN TIME (BOLD)** AND PACIFIC TIME (REGULAR).

NOVEMBER 2025

D Last Aspect / D Ingress

D Last Aspect ET / hr:mn / PT		sign day		D Ingress ET / hr:mn / PT
2 **10:15 am** 7:15 am	⊼ ♀	♈	2 **10:59 am** 7:39 am	
4 **6:21 am** 3:21 am	□ ♇	♉	4 **11:45 am** 8:16 am	
6 **9:51 am** 6:51 am	△ ♄	♊	6 **10:31 pm** 7:20 am	
8 **9:32 am** 6:32 am	□ ♆	♋	8 **10:06 am** 7:06 am	
10 **12:23 pm** 9:23 am	△ ♀	♌	10 **12:34 pm** 9:34 am	
12 **6:29 pm** 3:29 pm	△ ♇	♍	12 **6:52 pm** 3:52 pm	
15 **4:08 am** 1:08 am	△ ♄	♎	15 **4:44 am** 1:44 am	
17 **6:51 am** 3:51 am	□ ♆	♏	17 **4:44 pm** 1:44 pm	
20 **4:24 am** 1:24 am	□ ♀	♐	20 **5:26 am** 2:26 am	
22 **4:48 pm** 1:48 pm	□ ♇	♑	22 **5:53 pm** 2:53 pm	

D Last Aspect ET / hr:mn / PT		asc		D Ingress sign day ET / hr:mn / PT
25 **4:10 am** 1:10 am	⚹ ♆	♒	25 **5:16 am** 2:16 am	
27 **12:53 pm** 9:53 am	□ ♀	♓	27 **2:24 pm** 11:24 am	
29 **7:05 pm** 4:05 pm	♂ ♀	♈	29 **8:07 pm** 5:07 pm	

D Phases & Eclipses

phase	day	ET / hr:mn / PT
Full Moon	5	**8:19 am** 5:19 am
4th Quarter	11	9:28 pm
4th Quarter	12	**12:28 am**
New Moon	19	10:47 pm
New Moon	20	**1:47 am**
2nd Quarter	27	10:59 pm
2nd Quarter	28	**1:59 am**

Planet Ingress

		day	ET / hr:mn / PT
♂	♐	4	**8:01 am** 5:01 am
♀	♏	6	**5:39 pm** 2:39 pm
☿	♐	9	**9:22 pm** 6:22 pm
☿	♏ R	15	**5:25 pm** 2:25 pm
☉	♐	18	**10:20 pm** 7:20 pm
♀	♐	21	**8:36 pm** 5:36 pm
☉	♐	30	**3:14 pm** 12:14 pm

Planetary Motion

		day	ET / hr:mn / PT
♄	R	9	**2:02 pm** 11:02 am
♀	D	11	**11:41 am** 8:41 am
♇	D	20	**6:57 pm** 3:57 pm
♄	D	27	**10:52 pm** 7:52 pm
♀	D	29	**12:38 pm** 9:38 am

---

1 SATURDAY

D ⚹ ♀ 10:47 pm

2 SUNDAY

D ⊼ ♀ **1:47 am**
D ⊼ ☿ 2:11 am 12:17 am
D △ ♀ **3:31 am** 1:31 am
D △ ♇ 8:17 am 5:17 am
D ⚹ ♇ **10:15 am** 7:15 am
D ⊼ ♆ 11:01 am 8:01 am
D □ ♂ **1:05 pm** 10:05 am
D △ ♄ 5:18 pm 2:18 pm
D ⊼ ♀ **6:17 pm** 3:17 pm

3 MONDAY

D ⊙ ♀ **5:11 am** 2:11 am
D ⊼ ♇ 6:57 am 3:57 am
♀ ⚹ ♂ **10:59 pm** 7:59 pm

4 TUESDAY

D ⊼ ♇ **3:25 am** 12:25 am
D △ ♀ 4:21 am 1:21 am
D □ ♇ **6:21 am** 3:21 am
D ⊼ ♇ 10:49 am 7:49 am
D ⊼ ♇ **11:25 am** 8:25 am
D □ ♀ 11:28 am 8:28 am
D △ ♀ **12:30 pm** 9:30 am
D △ ♀ 1:36 pm 10:36 am
D □ ♇ **7:47 pm** 4:47 pm

5 WEDNESDAY

D △ ♀ 5:19 am **8:19 am**
D ⚹ ♀ 11:40 am

6 THURSDAY

D ⊼ ♀ **2:40 am**
D ⊼ ♇ 3:24 am 12:24 am
D ⊼ ♀ **9:41 am** 6:41 am
D ⚹ ♆ 9:51 am 6:51 am
D ♂ ♇ **10:11 am** 7:11 am
D ⊼ ♀ 10:26 am 7:26 am
D ⚹ ♀ **11:37 am** 8:37 am
D △ ♀ 12:49 pm 9:49 am
D □ ♀ **6:31 pm** 3:31 pm
D ⚹ ♀ 8:19 pm 5:19 pm

7 FRIDAY

D □ ♇ **10:47 am** 7:47 am
D ⊼ ♀ 10:44 am 7:44 am
D ⊼ ♇ 11:13 pm
D ⊼ ♇ 11:49 pm

8 SATURDAY

D ⊼ ♇ **2:13 am**
D △ ♀ 2:49 am 6:32 am
D ⊼ ♇ **9:32 am** 7:04 am
D △ ♀ 10:04 am 9:35 am
D △ ♀ **12:35 pm** 10:52 am
D △ ♇ 1:52 pm 12:08 pm
D ⚹ ♀ **3:08 pm** 6:17 pm
D ⊼ ♀ 9:17 pm

9 SUNDAY

D △ ♇ **3:26 am**
♀ ⊼ ♀ **11:20 am** 8:20 am

10 MONDAY

D ♂ ♇ 2:09 am
D △ ♀ **4:39 am**
D ⊼ ♀ 1:54 am 8:54 am
D ⊼ ♇ **12:23 pm** 9:23 am
D ⚹ ♆ 2:16 pm 5:48 pm
D ⚹ ♀ **8:45 pm** 6:44 pm
D △ ♀ 9:44 pm 9:21 pm

11 TUESDAY

D ⊼ ♀ **12:21 am**
D △ ♀ 9:16 am 6:16 pm
 9:28 pm

12 WEDNESDAY

D ♂ ♇ **12:58 am**
D ⊼ ♀ 9:59 am 6:49 am
D ⊼ ♇ **10:14 am** 7:14 am
D ⚹ ♇ 6:05 pm 3:05 pm
D ⚹ ♇ **6:15 pm** 3:15 pm
D ⊼ ♀ 6:19 pm 3:29 pm
D ⊼ ♀ **9:30 pm** 6:50 pm

13 THURSDAY

D ⊼ ♀ **5:49 am** 2:49 am
D ⊼ ♇ 7:43 am 4:03 am
D ⚹ ♀ **10:47 am** 7:47 am

14 FRIDAY

D ♂ ♀ **2:20 pm** 11:20 am
D ⚹ ♇ 7:09 pm 4:09 pm
D ⊼ ♇ **7:30 pm** 4:30 pm

15 SATURDAY

D △ ♀ 3:50 am **12:50 am**
D ⚹ ♆ 4:08 am 1:08 am
D ⊼ ♀ **7:55 am** 4:55 am
D △ ♀ 12:40 pm 9:40 am
D ⚹ ♇ **9:16 pm** 6:16 pm

16 SUNDAY

D △ ♇ 4:14 am **1:14 am**
D ⚹ ♀ 9:08 pm

17 MONDAY

D ♂ ♀ **12:08 am**
D △ ♀ 3:56 am 12:56 am
D ⊼ ♇ **6:51 am** 3:51 am
D ⊼ ♀ 7:11 am 4:11 am
D △ ♀ **7:29 am** 4:29 am
D ⊼ ♇ 3:36 pm 12:36 pm
D △ ♀ **3:46 pm** 12:46 pm
D △ ♇ 3:56 pm 12:56 pm
D ⊼ ♀ **7:39 pm** 4:39 pm
D ⊼ ♀ 8:05 pm 5:05 pm

18 TUESDAY

D ⚹ ♀ **1:33 pm** 10:33 am
D ⊼ ♇ 11:49 pm 8:49 pm

19 WEDNESDAY

D △ ♀ 6:45 am **3:45 am**
D ⊼ ♀ 7:21 am 4:21 am
D □ ♇ **7:23 am** 4:23 am
D ⊙ ♀ 7:45 am 4:45 am
 10:47 pm
 11:15 pm

20 THURSDAY

D △ ♇ **1:47 am**
D ⊙ ♀ 2:15 am
D ⊼ ♀ **4:23 am** 1:23 am
D △ ♀ 4:24 am 1:24 am
D ⚹ ♆ **4:24 am** 1:24 am
D △ ♀ 8:52 am 5:52 am
D ⊙ ♀ **9:39 am** 6:39 am

21 FRIDAY

D ♂ ♇ **6:13 am** 3:13 am
D ⊙ ♀ 7:25 am 4:25 am
D ⊼ ♇ **8:05 am** 5:05 am
D △ ♀ 7:38 pm 4:38 pm

22 SATURDAY

D ⊼ ♀ **7:46 am** 4:46 am
D △ ♇ 8:13 am 5:13 am
D △ ♀ **8:44 am** 5:44 am
D ⊼ ♇ 1:45 pm 10:45 am
D ⊙ ♀ **4:39 pm** 1:39 pm
D △ ♀ 6:37 pm 3:37 pm
D ⚹ ♀ **7:50 pm** 4:50 pm
D ♂ ♀ 9:22 pm 6:22 pm

23 SUNDAY

D ⊙ ⚹ ♀ **2:20 pm** 11:20 am
D □ ♇ 10:14 pm 7:14 pm

24 MONDAY

D ♂ ♀ **2:24 am** 11:24 am
D △ ♇ 3:28 am 12:28 am
D △ ♀ **7:12 am** 4:12 am

25 TUESDAY

D △ ♀ **3:52 am** 12:52 am
D ⊼ ♇ 4:10 am 1:10 am
D ⚹ ♀ **8:45 am** 5:45 am
D ⊼ ♇ ⊙ ♀ **12:28 pm** 9:28 am

26 WEDNESDAY

D ♂ ♀ **11:31 am** 8:31 am
D ⊼ ♀ 12:21 pm 9:21 am
D △ ♇ **6:48 pm** 3:48 pm
D ⊼ ♆ 10:12 pm 7:12 pm

27 THURSDAY

D ⊼ ♇ **4:36 am** 1:36 am
D △ ♀ 5:23 am 2:23 am
D ⊼ ♇ **6:32 am** 3:32 am
D ⊼ ♆ 12:53 pm 9:53 am
D △ ♇ **1:19 pm** 10:19 am
D ⊼ ♀ 5:48 pm 2:48 pm
 10:59 pm

28 FRIDAY

D ♂ ♀ **1:59 am**
D □ ♀ 10:58 pm 7:58 pm

29 SATURDAY

D ⊼ ♇ **3:54 am** 12:54 am
D ♂ ♇ 10:45 am 7:45 am
D ⊼ ♀ **11:42 am** 8:42 am
D △ ♀ 6:13 pm 3:13 pm
D ⚹ ♀ **6:33 pm** 3:33 pm
D ⊼ ♀ 7:05 pm 4:05 pm

30 SUNDAY

D ☿ ♀ **9:48 pm** 6:48 pm
D △ ♇ **11:22 pm** 8:22 pm
♀ ⊼ ♀ **3:48 pm** 12:48 pm
D △ ⊙ **11:00 am** 8:00 am

Eastern time in bold type
Pacific time in medium type

NOVEMBER 2025

DATE	SID. TIME	SUN	MOON	NODE	MERCURY	VENUS	MARS	JUPITER	SATURN	URANUS	NEPTUNE	PLUTO	CERES	PALLAS	JUNO	VESTA	CHIRON
1 Sa	2 42 9	8♏49 18	6♓52	17♓03R	2♐25	22♎34	27♏28	24♋58	25♓48R	0♊17R	29♓48R	1≈27	3♏54R	8≈39	9♐29	22♐41	24♈13R
2 Su	2 46 5	9 49 19	20 43	17 03	3 16	23 49	28 11	25 00	25 45	0 14	29 46	1 27	3 47	8 47	9 49	23 11	24 10
3 M	2 50 2	10 49 21	5♈02	17 01	4 03	25 04	28 54	25 02	25 43	0 12	29 45	1 28	3 40	8 56	10 09	23 41	24 08
4 T	2 53 58	11 49 25	19 48	16 58	4 46	26 19	29 37	25 03	25 40	0 10	29 44	1 28	3 32	9 04	10 28	24 11	24 05
5 W	2 57 55	12 49 31	4♉54	16 52	5 23	27 34	0♐20	25 05	25 38	0 07	29 43	1 29	3 26	9 13	10 48	24 42	24 02
6 Th	3 1 52	13 49 39	20 12	16 44	5 54	28 49	1 03	25 06	25 35	0 05	29 42	1 30	3 20	9 23	11 08	25 12	24 00
7 F	3 5 48	14 49 48	5♊31	16 35	6 20	0♏04	1 46	25 07	25 33	0 03	29 41	1 30	3 14	9 32	11 29	25 42	23 57
8 Sa	3 9 45	15 50 00	20 39	16 26	6 38	1 19	2 29	25 08	25 31	0 00	29 40	1 31	3 08	9 42	11 49	26 13	23 55
9 Su	3 13 41	16 50 13	5♋26	16 18	6♐49R	2 34	3 12	25 08	25 29	29♉58	29 39	1 32	3 03	9 52	12 09	26 43	23 52
10 M	3 17 38	17 50 29	19 48	16 13	6 52	3 50	3 55	25 09	25 27	29 55	29 38	1 32	2 58	10 02	12 29	27 14	23 50
11 T	3 21 34	18 50 46	3♌41	16 09	6 45	5 05	4 39	25 09R	25 25	29 53	29 37	1 33	2 54	10 12	12 49	27 44	23 47
12 W	3 25 31	19 51 05	17 05	16 08D	6 29	6 20	5 22	25 09	25 23	29 51	29 36	1 34	2 50	10 23	13 10	28 15	23 45
13 Th	3 29 27	20 51 26	0♍04	16 09	6 03	7 35	6 06	25 09	25 22	29 48	29 35	1 35	2 46	10 33	13 30	28 45	23 43
14 F	3 33 24	21 51 50	12 42	16 09R	5 27	8 51	6 49	25 09	25 20	29 46	29 34	1 36	2 43	10 44	13 51	29 16	23 40
15 Sa	3 37 21	22 52 15	25 03	16 09	4 41	10 06	7 33	25 08	25 19	29 43	29 33	1 37	2 40	10 56	14 11	29 47	23 38
16 Su	3 41 17	23 52 41	7♎12	16 06	3 45	11 21	8 16	25 07	25 17	29 41	29 32	1 37	2 37	11 07	14 32	0♑17	23 35
17 M	3 45 14	24 53 10	19 12	15 54	2 41	12 36	9 00	25 06	25 16	29 38	29 32	1 38	2 35	11 18	14 52	0 48	23 33
18 T	3 49 10	25 53 41	1♏07	15 43	1 29	13 52	9 44	25 05	25 15	29 36	29 31	1 39	2 34	11 30	15 13	1 19	23 31
19 W	3 53 7	26 54 13	12 59	15 30	0 11	15 07	10 28	25 04	25 14	29 33	29 30	1 40	2 32	11 42	15 34	1 50	23 29
20 Th	3 57 3	27 54 47	24 51	15 16	28♏50	16 22	11 11	25 02	25 13	29 31	29 29	1 41	2 31	11 54	15 55	2 21	23 27
21 F	4 1 0	28 55 22	6♐43	15 09	27 29	17 38	11 55	25 00	25 12	29 28	29 29	1 42	2 31D	12 07	16 15	2 52	23 24
22 Sa	4 4 56	29 55 59	18 37	15 02	26 10	18 53	12 39	24 58	25 11	29 26	29 28	1 43	2 31	12 19	16 36	3 23	23 22
23 Su	4 8 53	0♐56 37	0♑34	14 49	24 55	20 09	13 23	24 56	25 11	29 23	29 28	1 45	2 31	12 32	16 57	3 54	23 20
24 M	4 12 50	1 57 16	12 36	14 38	23 48	21 24	14 08	24 54	25 10	29 21	29 27	1 46	2 31	12 45	17 18	4 26	23 18
25 T	4 16 46	2 57 57	24 45	14 29	22 49	22 39	14 52	24 51	25 10	29 18	29 26	1 47	2 32	12 58	17 39	4 56	23 16
26 W	4 20 43	3 58 39	7≈05	14 24	22 01	23 55	15 36	24 49	25 10	29 15	29 26	1 48	2 34	13 11	18 00	5 27	23 14
27 Th	4 24 39	4 59 22	19 38	14 21	21 24	25 10	16 20	24 46	25 09D	29 13	29 25	1 49	2 35	13 24	18 21	5 58	23 12
28 F	4 28 36	6 00 06	2♓30	14 20	20 59	26 26	17 04	24 43	25 09	29 11	29 25	1 50	2 37	13 38	18 42	6 29	23 10
29 Sa	4 32 32	7 00 51	15 43	14 20	20 45D	27 41	17 49	24 39	25 09	29 08	29 25	1 52	2 40	13 51	19 03	7 00	23 09
30 Su	4 36 29	8 01 36	29 21	14 20	20 43	28 56	18 33	24 36	25 10	29 06	29 24	1 53	2 43	14 05	19 24	7 31	23 07

EPHEMERIS CALCULATED FOR 12 MIDNIGHT GREENWICH MEAN TIME. ALL OTHER DATA AND FACING ASPECTARIAN PAGE IN **EASTERN TIME (BOLD)** AND PACIFIC TIME (REGULAR).

DECEMBER 2025

☽ Last Aspect day	ET / hr:mn / PT	asp	☽ Ingress sign day	ET / hr:mn / PT
1	**1:14 pm** 10:14 am	□ ♃	♉ 1	**10:13 pm** 7:13 pm
3	**8:50 pm** 5:50 pm	⚹ ♆	♊ 3	**9:48 pm** 6:48 pm
5	**7:55 pm** 4:55 pm	□ ♆	♋ 5	**8:54 pm** 5:54 pm
7	**8:45 pm** 5:45 pm	△ ♆	♌ 7	**9:48 pm** 6:48 pm
9	**11:56 pm** 8:56 pm	□ ♅	♍ 9	11:20 pm
9	**11:56 pm** 8:56 pm	□ ♅	♍ 10	**2:20 am**
12	**9:51 am** 6:51 am	☍ ♆	♎ 12	**11:04 am** 8:04 am
14	**10:36 pm** 7:36 pm	⚹ ♂	♏ 14	**10:51 pm** 7:51 pm
17	**10:24 am** 7:24 am	△ ♆	♐ 17	**11:38 am** 8:38 am
19	**10:41 pm** 7:41 pm	□ ♆	♑ 19	**11:53 pm** 8:53 pm
22	**9:44 am** 6:44 am	⚹ ♆	♒ 22	**10:52 am** 7:52 am
24	**4:42 pm** 1:42 pm	□ ♅	♓ 24	**8:09 pm** 5:09 pm
26	11:03 pm	☌ ♆	♈ 27	**3:02 am** 12:02 am
27	**2:03 am**	☌ ♆	♈ 27	**3:02 am** 12:02 am
28	**9:13 pm** 6:13 pm	△ ☿	♉ 29	**6:57 am** 3:57 am
31	**7:25 am** 4:25 am	⚹ ♆	♊ 31	**8:13 am** 5:13 am

☽ Phases & Eclipses phase	day	ET / hr:mn / PT
Full Moon	4	**6:14 pm** 3:14 pm
4th Quarter	11	**3:52 pm** 12:52 pm
New Moon	19	**8:43 pm** 5:43 pm
2nd Quarter	27	**2:10 pm** 11:10 am

Planet Ingress	day	ET / hr:mn / PT
☿ ♐	11	**5:40 pm** 2:40 pm
♂ ♑	14	11:34 pm
♂ ♑	15	**2:34 am**
☉ ♑	21	**10:03 am** 7:03 am
♀ ♑	24	**11:26 am** 8:26 am
⚵ ♑	29	**9:35 am** 6:35 am

Planetary Motion	day	ET / hr:mn / PT
♆ D	10	**7:21 am** 4:21 am

1 MONDAY
☽ △ ♂ **5:14 am** 2:14 am
☽ ⚻ ☿ **7:29 am** 4:29 am
☽ □ ♃ **1:14 pm** 10:14 am
☽ ⚺ ♄ **2:22 pm** 11:22 am
☽ ⚺ ♅ **8:36 pm** 5:36 pm
☽ ⚺ ♆ **9:14 pm** 6:14 pm
☽ ⚻ ♀ 10:05 pm
☽ □ ♇ 10:20 pm

2 TUESDAY
☽ ⚻ ♀ **1:05 am**
☽ □ ♇ **1:20 am**
♀ ⚹ ♇ **4:07 am** 1:07 am
☽ ⚻ ☉ **3:45 pm** 12:45 pm

3 WEDNESDAY
☽ ⚻ ♂ **7:58 am** 4:58 am
☽ ☍ ☿ **9:06 am** 6:06 am
☽ ⚹ ♃ **12:57 pm** 9:57 am
☽ ⚹ ♄ **2:15 pm** 11:15 am
☽ ☌ ♅ **8:07 pm** 5:07 pm
☽ ⚹ ♆ **8:50 pm** 5:50 pm
☽ △ ♇ 9:53 pm

4 THURSDAY
☽ △ ♇ **12:53 am**
☽ ☍ ♀ **4:49 am** 1:49 am
☽ ☍ ☉ **6:14 pm** 3:14 pm

5 FRIDAY
☽ ☍ ♂ **9:23 am** 6:23 am
☽ ⚻ ☿ **10:24 am** 7:24 am
☽ ⚺ ♃ **11:44 am** 8:44 am
☽ □ ♄ **1:19 pm** 10:19 am
☽ ⚺ ♅ **7:05 pm** 4:05 pm
☽ □ ♆ **7:55 pm** 4:55 pm
☽ ⚻ ♇ 9:07 pm

6 SATURDAY
☽ ⚻ ♇ **12:07 am**
☿ △ ♃ **8:05 am** 5:05 am
☽ ⚻ ♀ **8:22 am** 5:22 am
☽ ⚻ ☉ **9:21 pm** 6:21 pm

7 SUNDAY
♂ ⚻ ♃ **4:55 am** 1:55 am
☽ ☌ ♃ **11:51 am** 8:51 am
☿ △ ♄ **11:58 am** 8:58 am
☽ ⚻ ♂ **12:16 pm** 9:16 am
☽ △ ♄ **1:50 pm** 10:50 am
☽ △ ☿ **1:59 pm** 10:59 am
☽ ⚹ ♅ **7:44 pm** 4:44 pm
☽ △ ♆ **8:45 pm** 5:45 pm
☽ ☍ ♇ 10:18 pm

8 MONDAY
☽ ☍ ♇ **1:18 am**
☽ △ ♀ **2:56 pm** 11:56 am
♂ □ ♄ **7:16 pm** 4:16 pm

9 TUESDAY
☽ △ ☉ **4:00 am** 1:00 am
☽ ⚺ ♃ **3:14 pm** 12:14 pm
☽ ⚻ ♄ **5:47 pm** 2:47 pm
☽ △ ♂ **7:06 pm** 4:06 pm
☽ □ ☿ **10:26 pm** 7:26 pm
☽ □ ♅ **11:56 pm** 8:56 pm
☽ ⚻ ♆ 10:12 pm

10 WEDNESDAY
☽ ⚻ ♆ **1:12 am**
☽ ⚻ ♇ **6:13 am** 3:13 am
☿ ☍ ♅ **2:59 pm** 11:59 am
☽ □ ♀ 11:47 pm

11 THURSDAY
☽ □ ♀ **2:47 am**
☿ △ ♆ **5:19 am** 2:19 am
☽ □ ☉ **3:52 pm** 12:52 pm
☽ ⚹ ♃ **10:44 pm** 7:44 pm
☽ ☍ ♄ 11:00 pm

12 FRIDAY
☽ ☍ ♄ **2:00 am**
☽ □ ♂ **6:56 am** 3:56 am
☽ △ ♅ **8:20 am** 5:20 am
☽ ☍ ♆ **9:51 am** 6:51 am
☽ ⚹ ☿ **1:02 pm** 10:02 am
☽ △ ♇ **3:20 pm** 12:20 pm

13 SATURDAY
♂ ⚻ ♅ **4:44 am** 1:44 am
☿ ⚹ ♇ **11:32 am** 8:32 am
☽ ⚹ ♀ **7:54 pm** 4:54 pm

14 SUNDAY
♂ □ ♆ **6:44 am** 3:44 am
☽ ⚹ ☉ **8:20 am** 5:20 am
☽ □ ♃ **9:34 am** 6:34 am
☽ ⚻ ♄ **1:35 pm** 10:35 am
☽ ⚻ ♅ **7:49 pm** 4:49 pm
☉ ⚻ ♃ **9:30 pm** 6:30 pm
☽ ⚻ ♆ **9:36 pm** 6:36 pm
☽ ⚹ ♂ **10:36 pm** 7:36 pm

15 MONDAY
☽ □ ♇ **3:24 am** 12:24 am
☽ ⚺ ☿ **8:18 am** 5:18 am

16 TUESDAY
☽ ⚺ ♀ **3:42 pm** 12:42 pm
☽ △ ♃ **9:46 pm** 6:46 pm
☉ □ ♄ **11:34 pm** 8:34 pm
☽ △ ♄ 11:30 pm
☽ ⚺ ☉ 11:46 pm

17 WEDNESDAY
☽ △ ♄ **2:30 am**
☽ ⚺ ☉ **2:46 am**
☽ ☍ ♅ **8:25 am** 5:25 am
☽ △ ♆ **10:24 am** 7:24 am
☽ ⚺ ♂ **3:31 pm** 12:31 pm
☽ ⚹ ♇ **4:19 pm** 1:19 pm

18 THURSDAY
♂ ⚺ ♇ **4:32 am** 1:32 am
☽ ☌ ☿ **5:02 am** 2:02 am
♀ ⚻ ♃ **8:45 pm** 5:45 pm

19 FRIDAY
☽ ⚻ ♃ **9:40 am** 6:40 am
☽ ☌ ♀ **11:19 am** 8:19 am
☽ □ ♄ **3:04 pm** 12:04 pm
☉ ⚻ ♅ **6:34 pm** 3:34 pm
☽ ⚻ ♅ **8:32 pm** 5:32 pm
☽ ☌ ☉ **8:43 pm** 5:43 pm
☽ □ ♆ **10:41 pm** 7:41 pm

20 SATURDAY
☽ ⚺ ♇ **4:37 am** 1:37 am
☽ ☌ ♂ **7:42 am** 4:42 am
☉ □ ♆ **8:02 pm** 5:02 pm
♀ □ ♄ 9:09 pm
☽ ⚺ ☿ 9:54 pm

21 SUNDAY
♀ □ ♄ **12:09 am**
☽ ⚺ ☿ **12:54 am**
☽ ☍ ♃ **8:26 pm** 5:26 pm
☽ ⚹ ♄ 11:27 pm

22 MONDAY
☽ ⚹ ♄ **2:27 am**
☽ ⚺ ♀ **5:21 am** 2:21 am
☽ △ ♅ **7:26 am** 4:26 am
☽ ⚹ ♆ **9:44 am** 6:44 am
☽ ⚺ ☉ **1:05 pm** 10:05 am
☽ ☌ ♇ **3:37 pm** 12:37 pm
☽ ⚺ ♂ **10:20 pm** 7:20 pm
♀ ⚻ ♅ 10:22 pm

23 TUESDAY
♀ ⚻ ♅ **1:22 am**
☽ ⚹ ☿ **6:54 pm** 3:54 pm
☉ ⚺ ♇ **8:37 pm** 5:37 pm
♀ □ ♆ 9:31 pm

24 WEDNESDAY
♀ □ ♆ **12:31 am**
☽ ⚻ ♃ **5:40 am** 2:40 am
☽ ⚺ ♄ **12:14 pm** 9:14 am
☽ □ ♅ **4:42 pm** 1:42 pm
☽ ⚺ ♆ **7:05 pm** 4:05 pm
☽ ⚹ ♀ **9:06 pm** 6:06 pm
☽ ⚺ ♇ 9:52 pm

25 THURSDAY
☽ ⚺ ♇ **12:52 am**
☽ ⚹ ☉ **3:13 am** 12:13 am
☽ ⚹ ♂ **10:45 am** 7:45 am

26 FRIDAY
☽ □ ☿ **10:02 am** 7:02 am
♀ ⚺ ♇ **12:17 pm** 9:17 am
☽ △ ♃ **12:43 pm** 9:43 am
☽ ☌ ♄ **7:41 pm** 4:41 pm
☽ ⚹ ♅ **11:37 pm** 8:37 pm
☽ ☌ ♆ 11:03 pm

27 SATURDAY
☽ ☌ ♆ **2:03 am**
☽ ⚹ ♇ **7:37 am** 4:37 am
☿ ⚻ ♃ **8:16 am** 5:16 am
☽ □ ♀ **9:33 am** 6:33 am
☽ □ ☉ **2:10 pm** 11:10 am
☽ □ ♂ **8:05 pm** 5:05 pm

28 SUNDAY
☽ □ ♃ **4:59 pm** 1:59 pm
☽ △ ☿ **9:13 pm** 6:13 pm
☽ ⚺ ♄ 9:13 pm

29 MONDAY
☽ ⚺ ♄ **12:13 am**
☽ ⚺ ♅ **3:37 am** 12:37 am
☽ ⚺ ♆ **6:04 am** 3:04 am
☽ □ ♇ **11:24 am** 8:24 am
☽ △ ♀ **6:03 pm** 3:03 pm
☽ △ ☉ **9:22 pm** 6:22 pm
☽ △ ♂ 10:54 pm
☿ □ ♄ 11:15 pm

30 TUESDAY
☽ △ ♂ **1:54 am**
☿ □ ♄ **2:15 am**
☽ ⚹ ♃ **6:27 pm** 3:27 pm
☽ ⚹ ♄ 10:58 pm

31 WEDNESDAY
☽ ⚹ ♄ **1:58 am**
☽ ⚻ ☿ **4:34 am** 1:34 am
☽ ☌ ♅ **4:56 am** 1:56 am
☽ ⚹ ♆ **7:25 am** 4:25 am
☿ ⚻ ♅ **8:08 am** 5:08 am
☽ △ ♇ **12:35 pm** 9:35 am
☽ ⚻ ♀ **11:21 pm** 8:21 pm
☽ ⚻ ☉ 10:37 pm

Eastern time in bold type
Pacific time in medium type

DECEMBER 2025

DATE	SID.TIME	SUN	MOON	NODE	MERCURY	VENUS	MARS	JUPITER	SATURN	URANUS	NEPTUNE	PLUTO	CERES	PALLAS	JUNO	VESTA	CHIRON
1 M	4 40 26	9♐02 23	13♈27	14♓18R	20♏51	0♐12	19♐18	24♋32R	25♓10	29♉03R	29♓24R	1♒54	2♏46	14♒19	19♐46	8♑02	23♈05R
2 T	4 44 22	10 03 11	28 01	14 13	21 35	1 27	20 02	24 28	25 11	29 01	29 24	1 55	2 49	14 33	20 07	8 34	23 03
3 W	4 48 19	11 04 00	12♉59	14 05	22 10	2 43	20 47	24 24	25 11	28 58	29 23	1 57	2 53	14 47	20 28	9 05	23 02
4 Th	4 52 15	12 04 49	28 13	13 55	22 52	3 58	21 31	24 20	25 11	28 56	29 23	1 58	2 57	15 02	20 49	9 36	23 00
5 F	4 56 12	13 05 40	13♊33	13 43	23 40	5 14	22 16	24 15	25 12	28 53	29 23	1 59	3 02	15 16	21 11	10 07	22 59
6 Sa	5 0 8	14 06 32	28 48	13 32	24 33	6 29	23 00	24 11	25 13	28 51	29 23	2 00	3 07	15 31	21 32	10 39	22 57
7 Su	5 4 5	15 07 25	13♋46	13 21	25 32	7 45	23 46	24 06	25 14	28 49	29 23	2 02	3 12	15 46	21 53	11 10	22 56
8 M	5 8 1	16 08 19	28 20	13 13	26 35	9 00	24 30	24 01	25 15	28 46	29 22	2 04	3 18	16 01	22 15	11 41	22 54
9 T	5 11 58	17 09 15	12♌24	13 08	27 42	10 16	25 15	23 56	25 16	28 44	29 22	2 05	3 24	16 16	22 36	12 13	22 53
10 W	5 15 55	18 10 11	27 57	13 05	28 51	11 31	26 00	23 51	25 17	28 41	29 22D	2 07	3 30	16 31	22 57	12 44	22 52
11 Th	5 19 51	19 11 09	9♍02	13 05	0♐04	12 47	26 45	23 45	25 18	28 39	29 22	2 08	3 37	16 47	23 19	13 15	22 50
12 F	5 23 48	20 12 08	21 42	13 05	1 19	14 02	27 30	23 40	25 20	28 37	29 22	2 10	3 44	17 02	23 40	13 47	22 49
13 Sa	5 27 44	21 13 07	4♎03	13 04	2 36	15 18	28 15	23 34	25 21	28 35	29 22	2 11	3 51	17 18	24 02	14 18	22 48
14 Su	5 31 41	22 14 08	16 09	13 02	3 56	16 33	29 01	23 28	25 23	28 32	29 23	2 13	3 58	17 33	24 23	14 50	22 47
15 M	5 35 37	23 15 10	28 06	12 57	5 16	17 49	29 46	23 22	25 25	28 30	29 23	2 14	4 06	17 49	24 45	15 21	22 46
16 T	5 39 34	24 16 13	9♏57	12 49	6 38	19 04	0♑32	23 16	25 27	28 28	29 23	2 16	4 14	18 05	25 06	15 52	22 45
17 W	5 43 30	25 17 17	21 47	12 39	8 01	20 20	1 16	23 10	25 29	28 26	29 23	2 17	4 23	18 21	25 28	16 24	22 44
18 Th	5 47 27	26 18 22	3♐38	12 26	9 26	21 35	2 02	23 03	25 31	28 24	29 23	2 19	4 32	18 38	25 49	16 55	22 43
19 F	5 51 24	27 19 27	15 33	12 12	10 51	22 51	2 47	22 57	25 33	28 21	29 24	2 21	4 41	18 54	26 11	17 27	22 42
20 Sa	5 55 20	28 20 34	27 33	11 57	12 17	24 06	3 32	22 50	25 35	28 19	29 24	2 22	4 50	19 10	26 32	17 58	22 41
21 Su	5 59 17	29 21 40	9♑46	11 44	13 44	25 22	4 18	22 43	25 37	28 17	29 24	2 24	5 00	19 27	26 54	18 30	22 40
22 M	6 3 13	0♑22 48	21 51	11 33	15 11	26 37	5 04	22 36	25 40	28 15	29 25	2 26	5 10	19 44	27 16	19 02	22 40
23 T	6 7 10	1 23 55	4♒52	11 24	16 39	27 53	5 49	22 29	25 42	28 13	29 25	2 27	5 20	20 00	27 37	19 33	22 39
24 W	6 11 6	2 25 03	16 42	11 18	18 08	29 08	6 35	22 22	25 45	28 11	29 26	2 29	5 31	20 17	27 59	20 05	22 39
25 Th	6 15 3	3 26 11	29 23	11 16D	19 37	0♑24	7 20	22 15	25 48	28 09	29 26	2 31	5 41	20 34	28 20	20 36	22 38
26 F	6 18 59	4 27 19	12♓19	11 15	21 06	1 39	8 06	22 07	25 51	28 08	29 27	2 32	5 52	20 51	28 42	21 08	22 38
27 Sa	6 22 56	5 28 27	25 31	11 15R	22 36	2 55	8 52	22 00	25 54	28 06	29 27	2 34	6 04	21 08	29 04	21 39	22 37
28 Su	6 26 53	6 29 35	9♈03	11 16	24 06	4 10	9 38	21 52	25 57	28 04	29 28	2 36	6 15	21 26	29 25	22 11	22 37
29 M	6 30 49	7 30 43	22 56	11 15	25 37	5 26	10 24	21 45	26 00	28 02	29 28	2 38	6 27	21 43	29 47	22 42	22 37
30 T	6 34 46	8 31 51	7♉03	11 11	27 08	6 41	11 09	21 37	26 03	28 00	29 29	2 40	6 39	22 00	0♑08	23 14	22 37
31 W	6 38 42	9 32 59	21 50	11 06	28 40	7 57	11 55	21 29	26 07	27 59	29 30	2 41	6 52	22 18	0 30	23 46	22 36

EPHEMERIS CALCULATED FOR 12 MIDNIGHT GREENWICH MEAN TIME. ALL OTHER DATA AND FACING ASPECTARIAN PAGE IN **EASTERN TIME (BOLD)** AND PACIFIC TIME (REGULAR).

Notes

Notes

Notes